Charlie Loram has never found being indoors easy. After breaking in his boots on the fells and crags of Snowdonia, northern England and the Scottish Highlands his nomadic tendencies took him to the Himalaya. For five years he wandered the high trails as guidebook writer (author of *Trekking in Ladakh* and contributor to *Trekking in the Annapurna Region*), wilderness guide and modern-day pilgrim. Insights gained there helped create Trailblazer's British walking guide series which he worked on as author and first series editor.

At home on Dartmoor he continues his passion for walking and wilderness, guiding people to a deeper connection with nature and themselves. For his current projects see 🖳 www.wildwoodswillow.org.uk and 🖳 www.re-wild.co.uk.

Bryn Thomas was born in Zimbabwe where he grew up on a farm. His wanderlust began early with camping holidays beside the Indian Ocean in Mozambique and trips to other parts of Africa.

Since graduating from Durham University with a degree in anthropology, travel on five continents has included a Saharan journey in his home-built kit-car, a solo 2500km cycle ride through the Andes, 12 Himalayan treks and 50,000km of rail travel. His first guide, the *Trans-Siberian Handbook*, was shortlisted for the Thomas Cook Travel and Guide Book Awards. Subsequent publications have included *Trekking in the Annapurna Region*, also published by Trailblazer, and guides to India, Britain and Europe, co-authored for Lonely Planet.

In 1991 he set up Trailblazer, to produce the series of route guides for adventurous travellers that has now grown to over 40 titles.

Authors

West Highland Way

First edition: 2003; this fifth edition 2013

Publisher Trailblazer Publications
The Old Manse, Tower Rd, Hindhead, Surrey, GU26 6SU, UK
info@trailblazer-guides.com, www.trailblazer-guides.com

British Library Cataloguing in Publication Data
A catalogue record for this book is available from the British Library

ISBN 978-1-905864-50-8

Series Editor: Anna Jacomb-Hood
Editing and proof-reading: Nicky Slade and Anna Jacomb-Hood
Cartography: Nick Hill **Layout**: Bryn Thomas **Index**: Jane Thomas
Illustrations: © Nick Hill (pp75-7); Rev CA Johns (pp68-9)
Photographs: © Bryn Thomas unless otherwise indicated

The maps in this guide were prepared from out-of-Crown-copyright Ordnance Survey maps amended and updated by Trailblazer.

Acknowledgements

I'm grateful to everyone who helped with information and advice along the way, in particular to hiking companions Hilary Bradt, Susanne Härtel and Lee Miller for making what is always a wonderful walk even more enjoyable in their company. For help with research thanks to Alasdair Eckersall, Willie Grieve, Harry Wroe, Lucy Ridout and Chris Scott. Thanks also to all those readers who've written in with comments and suggestions, in particular, Jill Harrison, Mark Gilbert, Esben Jensen, Ian McTaggart, Dieuwertje Verbrugge and Marta & Wannes Sambaer.

Thanks, as always, to everyone at Trailblazer: Anna Jacomb-Hood and Nicky Slade for research, editing and proof-reading; Jane Thomas and Nick Hill for the maps and Jane Thomas for the index.

A request

The author and publisher have tried to ensure that this guide is as accurate and up to date as possible. Nevertheless, things change. If you notice any changes or omissions that should be included in the next edition of this book, please write to Trailblazer (address above) or email us at info@trailblazer-guides.com. A free copy of the next edition will be sent to persons making a significant contribution.

Warning: hill walking can be dangerous

Please read the notes on when to go (pp12-16) and outdoor safety (pp55-60). Every effort has been made by the author and publisher to ensure that the information contained herein is as accurate and up to date as possible. However, they are unable to accept responsibility for any inconvenience, loss or injury sustained by anyone as a result of the advice and information given in this guide.

Updated information will be available on: www.trailblazer-guides.com

Photos – Front cover and this page: Beinn Dorain
Overleaf: From the pass (see p169) above the Devil's Staircase it's downhill all the way to Kinlochleven

Printed on chlorine-free paper by D'Print (☎ +65-6581 3832), Singapore

West Highland WAY

GLASGOW TO FORT WILLIAM

53 large-scale maps & guides to 26 towns and villages

PLANNING – PLACES TO STAY – PLACES TO EAT

CHARLIE LORAM

FIFTH EDITION UPDATED BY

BRYN THOMAS

TRAILBLAZER PUBLICATIONS

Contents

INTRODUCTION

Contents

ABOUT THIS BOOK

This guidebook contains all the information you need. The hard work has been done for you so you can plan your trip from home without the usual pile of books, maps and guides.

When you're all packed and ready to go, there's comprehensive public transport information to get you to and from the trail and detailed maps and town plans to help you find your way along it.

The guide includes:

- All standards of accommodation with reviews of campsites, hostels, B&Bs, guesthouses and hotels
- Walking companies if you want an organised tour and baggage-carrying services if you just want your luggage carried
- Itineraries for all levels of walkers
- Answers to all your questions: when to go, degree of difficulty, what to pack, and how much the whole walking holiday will cost
- Walking times in both directions and GPS waypoints
- Cafés, pubs, tearooms, takeaways, restaurants and shops for buying supplies
- Rail, bus and taxi information for all villages and towns along the path
- Street plans of the main towns both on and off the path
- Historical, cultural and geographical background information

MINIMUM IMPACT FOR MAXIMUM INSIGHT

Nature's peace will flow into you as the sunshine flows into trees. The winds will blow their freshness into you and storms their energy, while cares will drop off like autumn leaves. **John Muir** (one of the world's earliest and most influential environmentalists, born in 1838)

Walking in wild places is about opening ourselves up to all that is 'green'. Treading lightly and with respect we give ourselves a precious chance to tap into the curative power of the natural world. Physical contact with the land makes us more in tune with it and as a result we feel all the more passionate about protecting it.

It is no surprise then that, since the time of John Muir, walkers and adventurers have been concerned about the natural environment; this book seeks to continue that tradition. There is a detailed, illustrated chapter on the wildlife and conservation of the Highlands as well as a chapter devoted to minimum impact walking with ideas on how we can broaden that ethos.

By developing a deeper ecological awareness through a better understanding of nature and by supporting rural economies, local businesses, sensitive forms of transport and low-impact methods of farming and land-use we can all do our bit for a brighter future. In the buzz-words of today there can be few activities as 'environmentally friendly' as walking.

INTRODUCTION

[Glencoe and Lochaber] had everything: peak, plateau, precipice, the thinnest of ridges, and green valley, all set between the widest of wild moors and a narrow sea-loch. **WH Murray** *Undiscovered Scotland*

WH Murray is not alone in thinking the dramatic concluding stages of the West Highland Way (Glencoe and Lochaber) are equal in beauty to anywhere in the world. The Way has become a pilgrimage for mountain lovers keen to travel simply on foot into the heart of the Scottish Highlands. A better introduction to this stunning region could not have been designed and, what is more, you don't have to wait until the end for the highlights. Right from the start the Way gives walkers a taste of the magic of Scotland's wild land and within a week you will have walked through some of the most fabulous scenery in Britain with relative ease, safety and comfort.

The Way has become a pilgrimage for mountain lovers keen to travel simply on foot into the heart of the Scottish Highlands.

Heading west from Kingshouse past Buachaille Etive Mor, the 'Great Herdsman of Etive', standing guard at the entrance to Glen Coe (see p166).
(Photo © Hilary Bradt)

There are numerous tempting hostelries to waylay you on this walk, such as the Clachan Inn (see p114), Scotland's oldest registered pub.

The Way begins kindly just 20 minutes by train from the centre of Glasgow, gently undulating through woods and farmland, easing you in to the new demands of long-distance walking. As you stroll along the length of Loch Lomond's celebrated wooded shore, lowland subtly transforms into Highlands and rugged mountain grandeur begins to dominate the scene. Ancient tracks previously used by soldiers and drovers lead you north along wide valley bottoms past historical staging posts which still water and feed today's Highland traveller.

The character of the Way becomes more serious as it climbs across the bleak, remote expanse of Rannoch Moor, skirting the entrance to Glen Coe and climbing over the Devil's Staircase, the highest point on the trail. This is true hillwalking country and the extra effort is amply repaid by breathtaking mountain views. As you approach Fort William, the end of the Way, Ben Nevis comes into view rising above the conifer forests. If you have energy left after this superb 96-mile (154km) walk, an ascent of the highest mountain in Britain makes a fitting climax.

The Victorian hunting lodge at Rowardennan is now a comfortable youth hostel (see p125).

History

The West Highland Way was the first official long-distance footpath in Scotland. The idea was conceived in the 1960s at the height of enthusiasm brought about by the opening of the Pennine Way in England.

It was a massive task to create such an ambitious right of way, requiring investigation of the best route, endless liaising between the various local authorities and the Countryside Commission for Scotland, negotiations with landowners through whose land the Way might pass and then finally, when all was agreed, the construction of the path itself. This may seem simple, yet a flagship route such as the West Highland Way required information boards, waymarks, sturdy bridges and stiles, and adequate surfacing and drainage to cope with the high numbers of walkers it would inevitably attract. As a result it took until 1980 for the Way finally to be declared open.

This striking war memorial stands beside Loch Lomond at Rowardennan (see p125).

In September 2010 the end point of the Way was moved from the roundabout on the A82 to the centre of Fort William, thereby adding one mile to the total route. A bronze sculpture of a seated weary-looking walker marks the spot.

How difficult is it?

No great level of experience is needed to walk the West Highland Way as the whole trail is on obvious, well-maintained paths with excellent waymarks where needed. The first half of the route, south of Tyndrum, is across gentle terrain generally sticking to the bottom of valleys or traversing their sides. Only on a couple of occasions does the trail rise to just over 300m (1000ft) and on the first and hardest instance, the crossing of Conic Hill, this mildly strenuous section can be avoided. On this half you are never far from help and there's plenty of shelter should the weather turn foul.

North of Tyndrum the terrain becomes a little more challenging. With fewer settlements it can even

Last views of Loch Lomond from near Ardleish as the trail rises into the Highlands.

feel quite remote. The trail crosses some high, desolate country: Rannoch Moor (445m/1460ft), the Devil's Staircase (548m/1797ft) and the Lairigmor (330m/1082ft), all of which can be exposed in bad weather. Crossing these magnificent parts gives you a true taste of Highland Scotland and you will require basic outdoor competence to do so safely (see pp55-60 for further advice).

How long do you need?

During the annual West Highland Way race the entire route is run in less than 35 hours. Admirable though this is you will probably want to take a little longer. The suggested itineraries (see pp32-3) in this book list various schedules of between six and nine days for walking from Milngavie to Fort William, showing that with a rest day you can easily complete the Way in a week to ten days. If you can afford to take longer you will have the time to climb mountains along the route, explore Glasgow, Glen Coe and Glen Nevis, or simply dawdle

With a rest day you can easily complete the Way in a week to ten days.

Below: Approaching Doune Bothy at the northern end of Loch Lomond

when the weather is kind. If this sort of wandering is more your style a fortnight should be generous enough. For walkers with less time on their hands you could conceivably catch a bus or train over the less interesting sections of the Way. For instance, missing out the rather tedious section from Inverarnan to Tyndrum, or even to Bridge of Orchy, would not upset the essential character of the walk and would shorten your time by one or even two days.

There are also some superb **day** and **weekend** walks along the best parts of the Way for those who want to sample the walk in bite-sized chunks; see p34 for these highlights.

The 18th-century Bridge of Orchy which gives its name to the tiny village (see p152). The wild campsite beside the River Orchy here is within a stone's throw of the popular bar at the hotel. (Photo © Susanne Härtel)

See pp32-3 for some suggested itineraries covering different walking speeds.

Above: Rowchoish Bothy (see p128) offers basic free shelter for the night.
Below: Looking south from the site of the old lead smelter near Tyndrum (see p145).

When to go

SEASONS

The **main walking season** in Scotland is from the Easter holiday (March/April) through to October. Balancing all the variables such as weather, number of other walkers, midges and available accommodation, the best months to walk the West Highland Way are June and September.

Spring

April is unpredictable in terms of the weather. It can be warm and sunny, though blustery days with showers are more typical and snow may often still be lying on the hills. On the plus side, the land is just waking up to spring, there won't be many other walkers about and you shouldn't encounter any midges. As far as the weather is concerned **May** can be a great time for walking in Scotland; the temperature is warm, the weather is as dry and clear as can be expected, wild flowers are out in their full glory and the midges have yet to reach an intolerable level. However, the Way is exceptionally busy at this time of year and it can be a nightmare finding accommodation if you have not booked in advance. Many B&Bs take bookings in January or earlier for people walking in May. This is not the time to go if you like walking in solitude. You'd be far better off going in **June** which has all the advantages of May without the crowds, though make sure you don't pick the weekend of the Caledonian Challenge or the day of the West Highland Way race (see p14).

Above: Blackrock Cottage, a lonely outpost on the northern fringe of Rannoch Moor (see p161). **Below**: On the trail between Kinlochleven and Glen Nevis.

Summer

The arrival of hordes of tourists in **July** and **August** along with warm, muggy weather brings out the worst in the midges. On many days you'll be wondering what all the fuss is about; that's until you encounter a still, overcast evening when you'll swear never to set foot in the Highlands again. Campers are the

❑ FESTIVALS AND ANNUAL EVENTS

The following events use part or all of the West Highland Way. They may affect your decision about when to walk. For confirmation of the dates and further information contact the West Highland Way rangers (see box p40).

Note that **Conic Hill remains open to walkers year-round** now, even during lambing. The exception is for walkers with dogs; see pp28-9 for further information.

In addition to the events below there are several festivals in Glasgow (see p83).

● **Fort William Mountain Festival** A hugely popular event held in **February** or **March** at the Nevis Centre. This week-long extravaganza began life as a mountain film festival but has grown to showcase not just films but all sorts of lectures and exhibitions. Some big names in the world of climbing have given talks in recent years, and there are films and workshops too. For further information visit: 💻 www.mountainfestival.co.uk.

● **Scottish Motorcycle Trials** Parts of the trail between Bridge of Orchy and Fort William are used for these six-day trials each year. This usually takes place over the first full week in **May**. Walkers are free to continue using the trail at this time but there's obviously some disturbance. There's also lots of competition for the accommodation, particularly in Kinlochleven where many of the competitors and spectators stay. Check 💻 www.ssdt.org for up-to-date information.

● **Caledonian Challenge** Taking place over one weekend in **June** each year, this is the largest outdoor corporate fund-raising event in Scotland. Up to 2000 walkers in teams of four cover various sections of the trail raising funds for local charities. Unless you are participating it is wise to avoid walking at the same time as the event. Since the inaugural event in 1996, over 15,000 people have successfully taken part. For further details see 💻 www.caledonianchallenge.com.

● **West Highland Way Race** This also takes place in **June** but has far fewer entrants for obvious reasons. The idea is to race from Milngavie Station to Fort William Leisure Centre, setting off at 1am and hopefully finishing before noon the next day, ie to complete the entire West Highland Way in just 35 hours. The record for men for the 95 miles (152km) was broken in 2012 by Terry Conway who completed the route in 15 hours 39 minutes and 15 seconds. Lucy Colquhoun holds the women's record, taking 17 hours 16 minutes and 20 seconds in 2007. For more information visit 💻 www.westhighlandwayrace.org.

● **Ben Race** If you are in the Ben Nevis area on the first Saturday in **September** try to watch the Ben Race when up to 500 fell-runners reach the summit and return to the glen in ludicrously short times. This spectacle began in 1895 when William Swan ran to the top and back down in 2 hours 41 minutes. Today the men's record stands at 1 hour 25 minutes 34 seconds, and the women's 1 hour 43 minutes and 25 seconds (both set in 1984, by Kenny Stuart and Pauline Haworth). For more information, visit 💻 www.bennevisrace.co.uk.

ones who should really take note of this (see pp57-8) as everyone else can escape the torture behind closed windows and doors. On some weekends it can feel as if the whole world has arrived in the Highlands; traffic is nose to tail on the roads and many hostels and B&Bs are fully booked days in advance. Surprisingly, there can also be a fair amount of rain in these months.

Climbing Ben Nevis (see p180) makes a fitting end to walking the West Highland Way.

Autumn

A slower pace of life returns when the school holidays come to an end. Early **September** is a wonderful and often neglected time for walking with fewer visitors and the midges' appetites largely sated.

Towards the end of the month and into early **October** the vivid autumn colours are at their best in the woods and on the hills but you are starting to run the risk of encountering more rain and stronger winds. The air temperature, however, is still reasonably mild.

Winter

Late **October** and **early November** can occasionally be glorious with crisp clear days, but this is also the start of winter; the days are shortening, the temperature has dropped noticeably and many seasonal B&Bs, hostels, campsites and shops have closed. You need to be pretty hardy to walk between late **November** and mid **March**. True, some days can be fantastically bright and sunny and your appreciation will be heightened by snow on the hills and few people around. You are far more likely, however, to encounter the weather the Highlands are famous for; driving rain and snow for days on end on the back of freezing northerly winds.

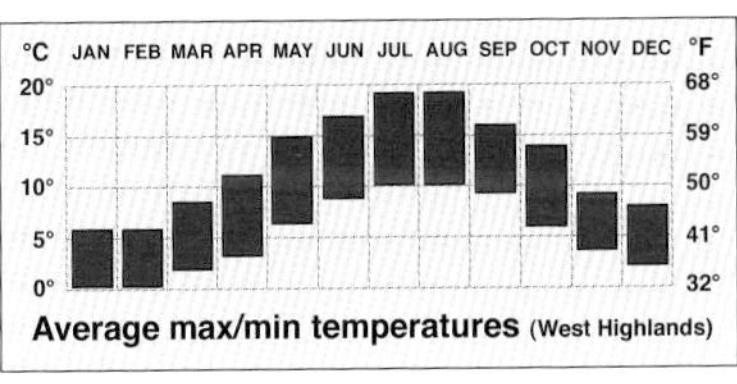

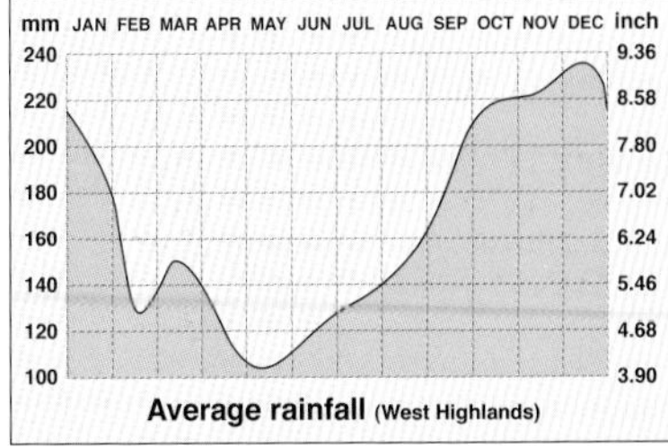

TEMPERATURE AND RAINFALL

January **temperatures** are on average 1-6°C and July temperatures are on average 10-18°C. The annual **rainfall** for the West

Highlands is about 2000mm (80 inches). As you progress north you are likely to encounter wetter weather.

The annual average for Glasgow is 1000mm, while in Glen Nevis it can be as much as 3000mm. The good news is that more than half of this precipitation falls as snow in winter.

JAN FEB MAR APR MAY JUN JUL AUG SEP OCT NOV DEC
3am
5am
7am
9am
11am
1pm
3pm
5pm
7pm
9pm
SUNRISE
SUNSET

Hours of daylight (56° North – West Highlands)

DAYLIGHT HOURS

If walking in autumn, winter and early spring, you must take account of how far you can walk in the available light. It may not be possible to cover as many miles as you would in summer. The table gives the sunrise and sunset times for each month at latitude 56° North. This runs across the southern tip of Loch Lomond so gives an accurate picture of daylight for the West Highland Way. Depending on the weather you will get a further 30-45 minutes of usable light before sunrise and after sunset.

PLANNING YOUR WALK 1

Practical information for the walker

ROUTE FINDING

The West Highland Way has been sensitively waymarked with brown wooden posts in appropriate places. Each of these is marked with the West Highland Way symbol, a white thistle within a hexagon, to confirm the line of the trail. They have an additional yellow arrow when indicating a change in direction. Used in combination with the detailed trail maps and directions in this book you have no excuse for getting lost.

Using GPS with this book

Whilst modern Wainwrights will scoff, more open-minded walkers will accept that GPS technology can be an inexpensive, well-established if non-essential, navigational aid. In no time at all a GPS receiver, given a clear view of the sky, will establish your position and altitude in a variety of formats to within a few metres.

Most of the maps throughout the book include **numbered waypoints** along the route. These correlate to the list on p195 which gives the OS grid reference and a description. You'll find more waypoints where the path is indistinct or there are several options as to which way to go. You can download the complete list for free as a GPS-readable file (that doesn't include the text descriptions) from the Trailblazer website: 💻 www.trailblazer-guides.com (click on GPS waypoints). It's also possible to buy state-of-the-art digital mapping to import into your GPS unit, assuming you've sufficient memory capacity, but it's not the most reliable way of navigating and the small screen on your pocket-sized unit will invariably fail to put places into context or give you the 'big picture'. This is also a far more expensive option than buying the traditional OS paper maps (see pp40-1) which, whilst bulkier, are always preferable.

Another way of using a GPS unit is to download a **track log** of the route from the internet. Where waypoints are single points like cairns, a track log is a continuous line like a path that appears on your

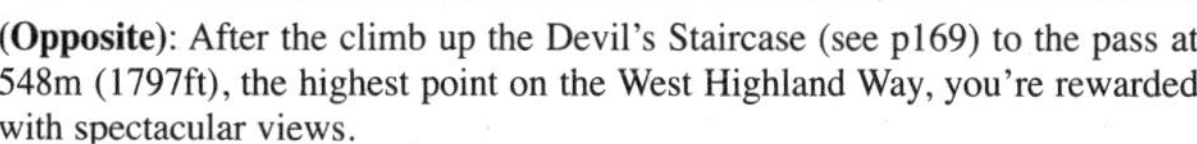
(Opposite): After the climb up the Devil's Staircase (see p169) to the pass at 548m (1797ft), the highest point on the West Highland Way, you're rewarded with spectacular views.

GPS screen; all you have to do is keep on that line. If you lose it on the screen you can zoom out until it reappears and walk towards it. While it's impressive to see the trail unfold as a track log on a calibrated map or Google Earth, many of these 'user-generated' track logs available online are imperfect because it takes an extremely trail-savvy and committed person to record a perfect track log without any gaps or confusing diversions. The fact is thousands have managed the walk without this feature.

It's worth repeating that most people who have walked the West Highland Way did so without GPS so there's no need to rush out and buy one. Your spending priorities ought to be on good waterproofs and above all footwear. However, all those thousands will also have had their frustrating moments of navigational uncertainty, and reliable technology now exists to minimise mistakes and wasted time. Correctly using this book's GPS data could get you back on track and dozing in front of the pub fireplace or tucked up in bed all the sooner.

ACCOMMODATION

Places to stay are relatively numerous and well spaced along most of the Way, allowing for some flexibility in itineraries. All bunkhouses/wigwams, hostels and B&Bs should, however, be booked ahead (see box below) if possible, especially from May to August when some get booked up weeks in advance. You can avoid a lot of this accommodation mayhem at the busy times of the year by starting your walk mid week, rather than the usual Saturday start from Milngavie. Note also that many places are closed during the winter.

Camping

There is pleasure in camping in mountains inexplicable to the unbeliever, but will at once be apparent to anyone of imagination. **WH Murray**

Even in the crowded British Isles camping can nurture a sense of freedom and simplicity which beautifully complements the act of walking. Your rucksack will of course be heavier, but carrying all the necessary equipment for sleeping out and cooking your own meals lightens the load in other ways: there's no need to book accommodation, you can make and change your plans as you go and it's by far the cheapest option (see p29). However, pitching your tent wherever you like is not allowed along the Way – see p52 for Loch Lomond restrictions. Realising

❑ Book accommodation in advance!

Always book your accommodation in advance. Not only does this ensure you have a bed for the night but it gives you an opportunity to find out more about the place, check the price and see what's included. Many B&Bs and hotels can also now be booked through a website, either their own or an agency's; however, phoning is probably best because you can check details more easily. If you have to cancel please telephone your hosts; it will save a lot of worry and possibly allow them to provide a bed for someone else.

You may also want to consider using the services of one of the walking companies listed on pp25-8 who will happily book your accommodation for you, for a small fee, saving you a considerable amount of work.

that many backpackers prefer to camp in the wild, several informal free sites with no facilities have been provided where you can pitch for one night as long as you leave no trace of being there and above all never light a fire. More information on how to camp with minimal impact is given on p52. Official sites along the Way range from those with a basic toilet and little else to luxurious establishments with shop, laundrette, restaurant and even swimming pool and sauna.

If you want to camp but not carry your tent, note that the baggage carriers listed on p25 will visit campsites.

Bothies

In terms of comfort, bothies give shelter somewhere between a tent and a bunkhouse. These unlocked huts with sleeping platform and fireplace are cared for by the Mountain Bothies Association (💻 www.mountainbothies.org.uk).

They provide very basic, free accommodation for walkers who are happy to follow the 'Bothy Code' (see box below). There are two on the eastern shore of Loch Lomond. If you are camping it can mean a welcome night without having to pitch a tent and if you intend to stay mainly in bunkhouses/hostels you must remember to bring a sleeping bag and mat for your night in a bothy.

Bunkhouses and hostels

There is a wide range of comfortable and interesting bunkhouses and hostels along the West Highland Way enabling walkers to travel on a small budget without having to carry bulky and heavy camping equipment. All have mattresses or beds to sleep on and bed linen is available, either to hire or included in the price. Many have full cooking facilities (cooker, pans, crockery and cutlery) which you can use for free and some even provide good-value cooked meals. If not, there is invariably somewhere close by for an evening meal and breakfast. It is

THE BOTHY CODE

Respect other users

- Leave the bothy clean, tidy and with dry kindling for the next visitors

Respect the bothy

- Guard against fire risk and don't cause vandalism or graffiti
- Please take out all rubbish which you don't burn
- Avoid burying rubbish: this pollutes the environment
- Please don't leave perishable food: this encourages mice and rats
- Make sure the doors and windows are properly closed when you leave

Respect the surroundings

- If there is no toilet, human waste must be buried carefully out of sight; please use the spade provided
- For health reasons never use the vicinity of the bothy as a toilet
- Keep well away from the water supply
- Conserve fuel; never cut live wood

Respect the agreement with the Estate

- Observe any restrictions on use of the bothy, eg during stag stalking or at lambing time
- Please remember bothies are available for short stays only

Respect the restriction on numbers

Because of overcrowding and lack of facilities, large groups (six or more) should not use a bothy nor camp near a bothy without first seeking permission from the owner. Bothies are not available for commercial groups.

Camping cabins at Beinglas Farm Campsite.

recommended that you take your own sleeping bag and make breakfast where possible, otherwise your trip won't be much cheaper than staying in B&Bs. You may also want to take a stove and pan to give yourself more flexibility when cooking facilities aren't available.

Simplest of all the bunkhouses are the innovative, low-impact wooden '**wigwams**' and **camping cabins**. They sleep between four and six people, are insulated and occasionally heated. The other **bunkhouses** are more like hostels with dormitory accommodation or occasionally small rooms sleeping two to four people. **Independent hostels** (💻 www.hostel-scotland.co.uk) are privately owned and are as diverse as their owners. They all have full cooking facilities, dormitory accommodation and differ from SYHA hostels in that there is no curfew and you don't need to pay more if you are not a member.

To stay at a SYHA hostel you either need to be a member of the Youth Hostel Association (Hostelling International) of your home country or you can join the **Scottish Youth Hostels Association** (Hostelling Scotland; 💻 www.syha.org.uk) at any of their hostels; it costs £10 for a year, or £2 per night for temporary membership.

Beds can be booked online through the SYHA website (see above) or by phone either by calling the central number (☎ 0845-293 7373) or the relevant hostel direct. Despite their name there is no upper age restriction for membership.

Bed and breakfast (B&B)

B&Bs are a great British institution. For anyone unfamiliar with the concept, you get a bedroom in someone's home along with an enormous cooked breakfast the following morning; in many respects it is like being a guest of the family. Staying in B&Bs is a brilliant way to walk in Scotland as you can travel with a light pack and gain a fascinating insight into the local culture. One night you may be staying in a suburban 'semi', the next on a remote hill farm.

What to expect For the long-distance walker tourist-board recommendations and star-rating systems have little meaning. At the end of a long day you will simply be glad of the closest place with hot water and a smiling face to welcome you. If they have somewhere to hang your wet and muddy clothes so much the better. It is these criteria that have been used for places mentioned in this guide, rather than whether a room has a shaver point or TV.

Bed and breakfast owners are often proud to boast that all rooms are **en suite**. This enthusiasm has led proprietors to squeeze a cramped shower and loo cubicle into the last spare corner of the bedroom. Establishments without en suite rooms are sometimes preferable as you may get sole use of a bathroom (**private facilities**) across the corridor and a hot bath is often just what you need after a hard day on the trail. In some cases you need to share the bathroom (**shared facilities**) with other guests.

Single rooms are usually poky rooms with barely enough room for the bed and certainly not enough to swing the proverbial cat. **Twin** rooms have two single beds while a **double** is supposed to have one double bed, although just to confuse things, some twins are also called doubles if the beds can be moved together. **Family** rooms sleep three or more (either with one double and one single bed, or with three single beds, or a double bed with bunk beds).

Some B&Bs provide an **evening meal** (£10-15), particularly if there is no pub or restaurant nearby, but generally you will need to have requested this in advance; check what the procedure is when you book. If an evening meal is not served, or you prefer to eat elsewhere, they may offer you a lift to a local eatery, though some places expect you to make your own arrangements anyhow.

Other services offered by many B&Bs along the Way are a **packed lunch** (£4-7) if you request one the night before, and a **pick-up/drop-off service** enabling you to stay at their establishment even if your day's walking doesn't deposit you at the front door. There's sometimes an extra charge (£3-5) for this.

Rates B&B tariffs are either quoted per room (based on two sharing) or per person per night; per person rates range from £20 for a simple room with a shared bathroom to over £40 for a very comfortable room with private bathroom, or en suite facilities, and all mod cons. Most places listed in this guide are around £25-35 per person. Be warned that if you are travelling on your own and the rate quoted is per person you are likely to be charged double in busy periods or at least a single occupancy supplement unless a single room is available. If the rate quoted is per room there may be a discount for single occupancy. Owners sometimes change their tariffs at a moment's notice in response to the number of visitors, so use the rates in this book only as a rough guide. In the low season (September to March) rates come down significantly. See also p30.

Guest houses, hotels, pubs and inns

The B&B concept has been carried through into other more upmarket establishments such as **guest houses** (and hotels). These businesses are much less personal and generally slightly more expensive but do offer more space, an evening meal and a comfortable lounge for guests.

Pubs and **inns** often turn their hand to mid-range B&B accommodation in country areas. They can be good fun if you plan to drink in the bar until closing time, though possibly a bit noisy if you want an early night.

Hotels in the true sense of the word do not attract many walkers because of their genteel surroundings and comparatively high prices; £40-80 per person, usually inclusive of breakfast. However, they can be fantastic places with great character and some walkers feel they deserve a special treat for one night of their holiday, particularly to celebrate their achievement at the end.

Holiday cottages

Self-catering cottages make sense for a group walking part of the Way and returning to the same base each night. They are normally let on a weekly basis. Cottages haven't been listed in this book; there are numerous websites dealing with holiday rentals or you could contact the local Tourist Information Centre (see p40).

FOOD AND DRINK

Breakfast and lunch

Although you may expect a bowl of Scottish porridge for your B&B **breakfast**, you're more likely to be offered a bowl of cereal or muesli followed by a full plate of bacon, eggs, black pudding and baked beans as well as toast and marmalade; ideal for setting you up for a day on the trail. If you prefer something lighter, continental breakfasts are normally available.

You will need to carry a packed **lunch** with you some days; your accommodation host may well be able to prepare one. However, there are a number of village shops and bakeries en route enabling you to buy your lunch as you pass by. There are also several cafés, pubs, hotels and teahouses on or near the trail, especially on the southern half, but not always where you need them. Use the information in the village and town facilities table (see p31) and in Part 5 to plan ahead.

Evening meals

Stumbling across a good **pub** when you're on a long walk is like manna from heaven. There are some unique and interesting ones along the West Highland Way all used to the idiosyncrasies of walkers and sometimes having a separate 'boots' or 'climbers' bar where you won't be out of place with muddy boots and a rucksack. Not only a good place to revive flagging spirits in the middle of the day or early afternoon, the local pub (or 'hotel') is often your only choice for an evening meal. Many have à la carte restaurants, but most walkers choose something from the cheaper bar menu washed down by a pint of real ale and perhaps a nip of malt whisky to bring the day to a contented close. Most menus include at least one vegetarian option.

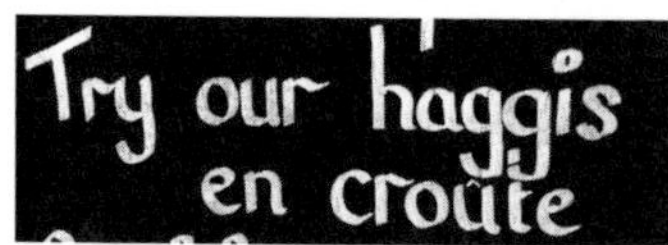

If you're looking for something different you could also try that infamous Scottish artery blocker, the deep fried Mars Bar.

In the larger villages and towns you'll have a wider choice with **take aways** serving anything as long as it's fried, and good **restaurants** dishing up culinary selections from round the world.

Buying camping supplies

There are enough shops along the Way to allow campers to buy **food** supplies frequently when cooking for yourself. All the shops are listed in Part 5. The longest you should need to carry food for is two days. Village shops are open year-round (though not always daily/all day) but those on campsites are typically only open in the main holiday season.

Getting **fuel** for camp stoves requires a little more planning. Gas canisters and methylated spirits are available in many general stores and campsite shops; Coleman Fuel is not so widely distributed. Special mention has been made in Part 5 of shops which sell fuel and the types they generally stock.

❑ Scottish food

Scotland, and most of Britain for that matter, has neglected its once fine local food culture. Sadly there is little regional differentiation on menus along the Way. As highly subsidised mass-produced food enters Britain from across the globe on the back of 'free trade', local small-scale producers are being marginalised. This is reflected in the lack of local produce in village shops and the standardisation of pub grub which bows to the economic dictates of freezer and microwave, rather than the sanity of home-grown specialities. At the end of a hard day on the trail your staple diet is more likely to be scampi and chips or lasagne, than cock-a-leekie or crappit heids. Where you do find traditional Scottish dishes all too often the 'fresh' salmon will turn out to be farmed and the 'sheep's stomach' containing the haggis, a plastic bag.

This is a shame; one of the great joys of travel is to embrace the spirit of a place and there is no better way of doing this than by sampling food that is grown and produced locally. By doing so you feed the local economy and strengthen regional identity; a direct benefit to the locality that is giving you, the traveller, so much. Now and then you will come across brave places attempting to breathe life back into rural culinary traditions and these should be actively supported. Keep an eye out for **Taste of Scotland** (🖳 www.taste-of-scotland.com) signs indicating places serving good quality, fresh Scottish produce.

Some traditional dishes include:

- **Arbroath smokies** – smoked haddock
- **Bannocks** – oatcakes baked in an oven and served with cheese
- **Bridies** – minced beef pies
- **Cock-a-leekie** – chicken and leek soup with prunes
- **Clapshot/tatties and neeps** – originating from Orkney, this is a combination of mashed potatoes, turnips, chives and butter or dripping; it usually accompanies haggis
- **Crappit heids** – lobster-stuffed haddock heads
- **Cullen skink** – smoked haddock and potato soup
- **Haggis** – minced lamb's or deer's liver and a collection of other meaty offal bits
- **Porridge** – boiled oats, often eaten for breakfast
- **Scotch broth** – a thick soup of lamb, vegetables, barley, lentils and split peas
- **Stovies** – fried potatoes and onion mixed with left-over meat and baked in an oven

Whisky, beer and water

Scotland is world famous for its alcohol production and most pubs and hotel bars have a good selection of whisky and beer. Scotch **whisky**, 'the water of life', is distilled from malted barley and other cereals and is either a blend, or a single malt made in one distillery.

A connoisseur can tell the difference between single malts distilled in different parts of the country such as the West Coast, East Coast, Lowlands, Highlands, Isle of Islay, the list goes on, and many happy evenings can be spent brushing up on this neglected skill without coming to any conclusion about which is best.

There can be little argument about which is the most appropriate whisky for walkers, however: the **Highland Way** is distilled, casked, matured, blended and bottled by the company of the same name, who took the trail as their inspiration, explaining that the stuff 'delicately captures the flavours of the Glens, Lochs and Mountains that are unique to its heritage.' Ian Macleod is another distiller associated with the Way, with the popular **Glengoyne** single malt sponsoring the West Highland Way Race – the prize for coming first being 21-year-old bottles of the stuff!

Traditional **British ale**, beer, bitter, call it what you like, is the product of small-scale regional breweries who have created a huge diversity of strengths and flavours through skill and craftsmanship. Real ale continues to ferment in the cask so can be drawn off by hand pump or a simple tap in the cask itself. It should not be confused with characterless, industrially produced beer whose fermentation is stopped by pasteurisation and therefore needs the addition of gas to give it some life and fizz. Traditionally the Highlands have not been a happy hunting ground for the real ale enthusiast. In the last few years, however, there seems to have been a resurgence in brewing and the walker in Scotland shouldn't find it hard to track down a few quality pints, with around 40 breweries now operating north of the border. Scotland has its own Traditional Beer Festival held in Edinburgh every year, during which CAMRA (the Campaign for Real Ale) hands out its Champion Beer of Scotland award: the 2012 winner was Orkney Best from Highland Brewery.

Beer from the following Scottish breweries is worth looking out for: Caledonian, Orkney, Aviemore, Inveralmond, Glenfinnan and Isle of Skye among others. The West Highland Way goes right past the door of River Leven Ales in Kinlochleven, one of Scotland's newest craft breweries.

Another particularly interesting pint to try is Fraoch Heather Ale, which is flavoured with heather flowers to give you a real taste of the country you're walking over.

Spring water, 'a noble, royal, pleasant drink' as the Highland poet Duncan Ban Macintyre would have it, is readily available for the taking along much of the West Highland Way from Rowardennan northwards, gushing in trickles and torrents off the mountainsides. In the lowland parts of the Way you can fill up your water bottle in public toilets, or alternatively ask in shops, cafés or pubs if they would mind filling it up; most people are happy to do so.

See p57 for further information on when and how to purify water.

MONEY

Plan your money needs carefully. You will have to carry a fair amount of **cash** with you on the middle part of the walk as there are no banks or cash machines between Drymen and Tyndrum, though there is a post office at Crianlarich, 20 minutes off the path, with an ATM. Small independent shops generally prefer you to pay in cash as do most B&Bs, bunkhouses and campsites but they'll often still accept a **cheque** from a British bank.

Shops that do take **credit or debit cards**, such as supermarkets, may have a cashback service so you can obtain cash but often only if you buy something at the same time. Note that some cash machines/ATMs (not those at banks) charge you for making a cash withdrawal (usually the Link machines that are sometimes found in shops and post offices; some readers using cards issued by bank abroad have had them rejected by Link machines). The table of village and town facilities on p31 indicates the whereabouts of post offices and banks. See also p39.

Getting cash from a post office

Several banks in Britain have agreements with the post office allowing customers to make cash withdrawals using their debit card with a PIN, at post offices throughout the country. This is a useful facility on the West Highland Way where there are more post offices than banks. For a full list of bank accounts accepted contact the Post Office (☎ 08457-223344, 💻 www.postoffice.co.uk/making-withdrawals-in-branch).

OTHER SERVICES

Most of the settlements through which the Way passes have little more than a **public telephone**, **general store** and a **post office**. The latter can be very useful if you have discovered you are carrying too much in your rucksack and want to send unnecessary items home to lighten your load.

Where they exist, special mention has also been made in Part 5 of other services which are of use to walkers such as **banks**, **cash machines**, **outdoor equipment shops**, **laundrettes**, **internet access**, **pharmacies/chemists**, **medical/health centres** and **tourist information centres**.

WALKING COMPANIES

For walkers wanting to make their holiday as easy and trouble free as possible there are several specialist companies offering a range of services from accommodation booking to fully guided group tours.

Accommodation booking

Arranging all the accommodation for your walk can take a considerable amount of time. For £15-28 per person someone will do all the phoning for you:

- **Easyways** (☎ 01324-714132, 💻 www.easyways.com)
- **Sherpa Van Project** (☎ 01609-883731, 💻 www.sherpavan.com)

Baggage carriers

This is one service that's well worth the money! The following companies offer a baggage-carrying service either direct to your campsite/accommodation each night or to a drop-off point in each village from about £45 per rucksack for the whole Way; all you need to carry is a small daypack with essentials in it. If you are finding the walk harder than expected you can always join one of these services at a later stage. Note that they will take camping gear and visit campsites.

Some of the taxi firms listed in this guide (see Part 5) provide a similar service within a local area if you are having problems carrying your bags.

- **AMS Scotland Ltd** (☎ 01360-312840, 💻 www.amsscotland.co.uk)
- **Sherpa Van Project** (☎ 0871-520 0124, 💻 www.sherpavan.com)
- **Travel-Lite** (☎ 0141-956 7890, 💻 www.travel-lite-uk.com)

Self-guided holidays

The following companies provide all-in customised packages which usually include detailed advice and notes on itineraries and routes, maps, accommodation booking, daily baggage transfer, and transport arrangements at the start and end of your walk. Most companies offer a range of itineraries (taking from three to ten days) and offer the walk from south to north. However, almost all are flexible and will also tailor-make holidays including from north to south.

If you don't want the whole package deal some companies can arrange accommodation-booking or baggage-carrying services on their own (see p25).

- **Absolute Escapes** (☎ 0131-240 1210, 💻 www.absoluteescapes.com), Edinburgh
- **Alpine Exploratory** (☎ 01729-823197, 💻 www.alpineexploratory.com), Settle
- **AMS-Outdoors** (☎ 08456-808246, 💻 www.ams-outdoors.com), Glasgow

❑ Information for foreign visitors

- **Currency** The British pound (£) comes in notes of £50, £20, £10 and £5, and coins of £2 and £1. The pound is divided into 100 pence (usually referred to as 'p', pronounced pee) which comes in silver coins of 50p, 20p 10p and 5p and copper coins of 2p and 1p. In Scotland you will also come across Scottish notes, including £1 and £100 notes. While English notes are accepted anywhere in Scotland, Scottish notes will sometimes be refused south of the border. Banks will happily change them, however.

  Up-to-date **rates of exchange** can be found on 💻 www.xe.com/ucc. **Travellers' cheques** can be cashed only at banks, foreign exchanges and some of the large hotels; it is probably better to use a **debit card** or bring **cash**.
- **Business hours** Most **shops** and main **post offices** are open at least from Monday to Friday 9am-5pm and Saturday 9am-12.30pm. Many choose longer hours and some open on Sundays as well. Scottish **banks** open Monday to Friday from as early as 9am to as late as 5.30pm; some also open on Saturday from 9am to 12.30pm. As a rule of thumb most are open from at least 10am to 4pm Monday to Friday. **Pubs** are generally open 11am-11pm Monday to Saturday and 12.30-3pm & 7-10.30pm on Sunday. However, opening hours are flexible so some remain open until 1am although mostly in urban rather than rural areas.
- **National (bank) holidays** Most businesses in Scotland are shut on Jan 1st and 2nd, Good Friday (Mar/Apr), the first and last Mondays in May, the first Monday in Aug, Dec 25th and 26th. Some businesses also close on St Andrew's Day, Nov 30th.
- **School holidays** School holidays in Scotland are generally: a one-/two-week break mid October, two weeks around Christmas and the New Year, up to a week mid February, 2-3 weeks around Easter, and from late June/early July to mid August.
- **EHICs and travel insurance** The European Health Insurance Card (EHIC) entitles cardholders to any necessary medical treatment under the UK's National Health Service while on a temporary visit here; treatment is only given on production of the card so bring it with you. However, the EHIC is not a substitute for proper medical cover on your travel insurance, eg for getting you home should that be necessary.

  Also consider cover for loss and theft of personal belongings, especially if you are camping or staying in hostels, as there may be times when you have to leave your luggage unattended.
- **Emergency services** For police, ambulance, fire and mountain rescue dial ☎ 999, (or the EU standard number ☎ 112).

- **Bespoke Highland Tours** (☎ 01997-421474, 🖳 www.highland-tours.co.uk), Inverness
- **C-N-Do Scotland** (☎ 01786-445703, 🖳 www.cndoscotland.com), Stirling
- **Contours Walking Holidays** (☎ 01629-821900, 🖳 www.contours.co.uk), Derbyshire
- **Celtic Trails** (☎ 01291-689774, 🖳 www.celtic-trails.com), Chepstow
- **Discovery Travel** (☎ 01904-632226, 🖳 www.discoverytravel.co.uk), York
- **Easyways** (☎ 01324-714132, 🖳 www.easyways.com), Stirlingshire
- **Explore Britain** (☎ 01740-650900, 🖳 www.explorebritain.com), Durham
- **Frontier Holidays** (☎ 0141-956 1569, 🖳 www.westhighlandwayinfo.com, Milngavie
- **Gemini Walks** (☎ 01324-410260, 🖳 www.geminiwalks.com), Stirlingshire
- **Let's Go Walking** (☎ 01837-880075, 🖳 www.letsgowalking.com), Devon

• **Smoking** Smoking in public places is banned; this includes pubs and restaurants, as well as B&Bs, hostels and hotels. These latter have the right to designate one or more bedrooms where the occupants can smoke, but the ban is in force in all enclosed areas open to the public – even if they are in a private home such as a B&B. Should you be foolhardy enough to light up in a no-smoking area, which includes pretty well any indoor public place, you could be fined £50 or more, but it's the owners of the premises who suffer most if they fail to stop you, with a potential fine of £2500.

• **Time** During the winter, the whole of Britain is on Greenwich Mean Time (GMT). The clocks move one hour forward on the last Sunday in March, remaining on British Summer Time (BST) until the last Sunday in October.

• **Telephone** The international access code for Britain is +44, followed by the area code minus the first 0, and then the number you require. To call a number with the same area code as the phone you are calling from you can omit the code unless calling from a mobile phone. If calling from a landline it is cheaper to phone at weekends and after 6pm and before 8am on weekdays.

If you have brought your mobile phone you may want to buy a British Pay-as-you-go SIM card. These can be bought from any mobile phone retailer and shouldn't cost more than a couple of pounds. Then all you need to do is buy some credit – and your calls within Britain will be considerably cheaper than using your existing SIM card from your home country.

• **Weights and measures** The European Commission is no longer attempting to ban the pint or the mile: so, in Britain, milk can be sold in pints (1 pint = 568ml), as can beer in pubs, though most other liquid including petrol (gasoline) and diesel is sold in litres. Distances on road and path signs will also continue to be given in miles (1 mile = 1.6km) rather than kilometres, and yards (1yd = 0.9m) rather than metres. The population remains split between those who still use inches (1 inch = 2.5cm), feet (1ft = 0.3m) and yards and those who are happy with millimetres, centimetres and metres; you'll often be told that 'it's only a hundred yards or so' to somewhere, rather than a hundred metres or so.

Most food is sold in metric weights (g and kg) but the imperial weights of pounds (lb: 1lb = 453g) and ounces (oz: 1oz = 28g) are often displayed too. The weather – a frequent topic of conversation – is also an issue: while most forecasts predict temperatures in centigrade (C), many people continue to think in terms of fahrenheit (F; see temperature chart on p15 for conversions).

• **Macs Adventure** (☎ 0141-530 8886, 💻 www.macsadventure.com), Glasgow
• **Make Tracks Walking Holidays** (☎ 0131-229 6844, 💻 www.maketracks.net), Edinburgh
• **Mickledore Travel** (☎ 017687-72335, 💻 www.mickledore.co.uk), Keswick
• **North-West Frontiers** (☎ 01997-421474, 💻 www.nwfrontiers.com), Scotland
• **NorthWest Walks** (☎ 01257-424889 , 💻 www.northwestwalks.co.uk), Wigan
• **Sherpa Expeditions** (☎ 020-8545 9030, 💻 www.sherpa-walking-holidays.co.uk), London
• **Transcotland** (☎ 01887-820848, 💻 www.transcotland.com), Perthshire
• **Walkabout Scotland** (☎ 0845-686 1344, 💻 www.walkaboutscotland.com), Edinburgh
• **Walkers Ways** (☎ 01838-400 338, 💻 www.walkersways.co.uk), Perthshire
• **Wilderness Scotland** (☎ 01479-420020, 💻 www.wildernessscotland.com), Aviemore

Group/guided walking tours

Fully guided tours are ideal for individuals wanting to travel with others and for groups of friends wanting to be guided. Packages usually include meals, accommodation, transport arrangements, mini-bus backup, baggage transfer, as well as a qualified guide. Companies' specialities differ with varying size of groups, standards of accommodation, age range of clients, distances walked and professionalism of guides; it's worth checking out several before making a booking.

• **Alpine Exploratory** (☎ 01729-823197, 💻 www.alpineexploratory.com) offers a 7 stage trek in a small group
• **C-N-Do Scotland** (☎ 01786-445703, 💻 www.cndoscotland.com) has an 8-day small group trip
• **Easyways** (☎ 01324-714132, 💻 www.easyways.com) has a budget guided walk with accommodation based in bunkhouses and a hotel/B&B-based walk
• **HF Holidays** (☎ 0845-470 7558, 💻 www.hfholidays.co.uk) runs a 10-day full-board package with the last four nights at their own country house hotel, Altshellach
• **NorthWest Walks** (☎ 01257-424889, 💻 www.northwestwalks.co.uk) offers a 9-day holiday, south to north
• **Ramblers** (☎ 01707-386800, 💻 www.ramblerscountrywide.co.uk) has a 10-day walk, south to north
• **Scot-Trek** (☎ 0141-334 9232, 💻 www.scot-trek.co.uk) covers the Way in sections
• **Sherpa Expeditions** (020-8545 9030, 💻 www.sherpa-walking-holidays.co.uk) has a 7-night/8-day guided walking trip
• **Walkabout Scotland** (☎ 0845-686 1344, 💻 www.walkaboutscotland.com), Edinburgh; fully bespoke, each trip is arranged with the clients, south to north

WALKING WITH DOGS (see also pp198-9)

You can take your dog with you along all of the West Highland Way for most of the year. The old restrictions around Conic Hill, Inversnaid to Crianlarich and

Tyndrum to Bridge of Orchy no longer apply, provided that your dog is kept under proper control. The only exception to this is on the eastern side of Conic Hill where there are two enclosed lambing fields, which are closed for the last three weeks in April and the first three weeks in May. (Though in practice they are usually closed for less than this time, it pays to plan your trip as if they are closed to dogs for all of this time, as precisely when the trail in this section is closed to dogs is announced only in March.) If you do come with your dog at this time, you will be sent on a diversion via Milton of Buchanan which doesn't add any time or distance to your walk.

Though the path is now open to dogs for most of the year, owners are still expected to keep their dogs under close control on a short lead in areas of farmland, in public places, and in moorland, forests and grasslands during the breeding bird season that runs from April to July. You should also make sure that your dog does not damage the path and that you always clear up after your dog when it defecates on the walk, and remove all faeces. A number of guest houses and B&Bs accept dogs, though in many cases this is by arrangement; look for the symbol in the accommodation information in Parts 4 & 5. See also pp198-9.

You can find out the latest information about walking with your dog by visiting www.outdooraccess-scotland.com.

MOUNTAIN BIKING

The West Highland Way is designed and maintained as a walking route. There are a few sections which would be ideal for mountain biking, particularly some parts of the old military and drove roads in the north. However, they are interspersed with lengthy, unrideable parts making it impractical and unfulfilling to plan a ride of anything longer than a couple of hours or so along the trail. Tackling longer sections of the Way is really not an option.

The number of people walking also detracts from the Way's suitability as an off-road route. You'll be constantly slowing down to pass walkers and be unable to ride as hard as you might like. Rather than stir up antagonism, why not use the mountain bike's potential to really get off the beaten track. Being able to cover large distances quickly opens up tracks that are impractical to walk. Take a look at Ralph Storer's excellent *Exploring Scottish Hill Tracks* for some of the incredible routes that abound.

Details of bike-hire companies along the Way are given in Part 5 if you want to explore further afield. The owners will be able to suggest good routes.

Budgeting

If you're **camping**, most sites charge around £5-8 per person so you can get by on as little as £12 per person per day using the cheapest sites and the free 'wild' sites/bothies as often as possible. This assumes you would be cooking all your own food from staple ingredients rather than eating convenience food. Most people find that the best-laid plans to survive on the bare minimum fall flat after a couple of hard days' walking or in bad weather. Assuming the odd end-of-day drink and the occasional pub meal or takeaway, a budget of £16-22 is more realistic.

A **hostel/bunkhouse** bed invariably costs from £10 to £20 per person. Every SYHA hostel has a self-catering kitchen (but not all independent hostels/ bunkhouses) and the larger ones offer breakfast (£4.50-6), packed lunches (£5.50) and evening meals (£7/9.95/11.95 for 1/2/3 courses). Allowing £30-35 per day will enable you to have the occasional meal out and enjoy sampling a few of the local brews. If you don't want to carry a stove, cook in a hostel's kitchen or are planning on eating out most nights add another £10 per day.

If you're staying in **B&Bs**, you won't be cooking for yourself. Bearing in mind that B&B prices vary enormously, £45-60 per person per day is a rough guide based on spending about £25 on a packed lunch, evening pub meal and a couple of drinks. If staying in a **guesthouse** or **hotel** expect to spend £50-70 per day. If you are travelling alone you must also expect to pay a single occupancy supplement. See also p21.

Don't forget to set some money aside, perhaps £100-150, for the inevitable extras: postcards, bus/train fares, taxis, cream teas, whisky and beer, using a baggage-carrying service, or any changes of plan.

Itineraries

Walkers are individuals. Some like to cover large distances as quickly as possible, others are happy to stroll along stopping whenever the fancy takes them. You may want to walk the West Highland Way all in one go, tackle it over a series of weekends or use the trail for linear day walks; the choice is yours. To accommodate these differences this guidebook has not been divided into rigid daily stages which often leads to a fixed mindset of how you should walk. Instead, it's been designed to make it easy for you to plan your own perfect itinerary.

The **overview map** and **stage maps** (see end of the book) and **table of village and town facilities** (opposite) summarise the essential information.

Alternatively, to make it even easier, have a look at the **suggested itineraries** (see p32) and simply choose your preferred type of accommodation and speed of walking.

There are also suggestions on p34 for those who want to experience the best of the trail over a day or a weekend. The **public transport map and table** on pp44-8 may also be useful at this stage.

Having made a rough plan, turn to **Part 5**, where you will find summaries of the route; full descriptions of accommodation, places to eat and other services in each village and town; as well as detailed trail maps.

VILLAGE AND TOWN FACILITIES

PLACE*	DISTANCE* MILES/KM	BANK (ATM)	POST OFFICE	TOURIST INFO*	EATING PLACE*	FOOD SHOP*	CAMP-SITE*	BUNK/ HOSTEL*	B&B*
(Glasgow)		✔✔✔	✔✔✔	TIC	✔✔✔	✔✔✔		YHA/H	✔✔✔
Milngavie	WHW start	✔	✔	VC	✔✔✔	✔✔	✔		✔✔✔
(Blanefield)					✔✔	✔			
Strathblane					✔				✔
Dumgoyne	7/11		✔		✔				
(Killearn)		✔	✔		✔✔✔	✔			✔
Gartness	3/5				✔		✔		
Easter Drumquhassle	1/1.5						✔	B	
Drymen	1/1.5	✔	✔		✔✔✔	✔			✔✔✔
Milton of Buchanan	(4/6)								✔
Balmaha	7/11 (1.5/2.5)			NPC	✔	✔	✔	B	✔✔✔
Cashel	3/5						✔✔		✔✔
Rowardennan	4/6				✔			YHA/B	✔✔
								(Rowchoish bothy)	
Inversnaid	7/11				✔✔		✔	B	✔
								(Doune bothy)	
(Ardlui)					✔	✔	✔	B	✔
Inverarnan	6.5/10				✔✔	(✔)	✔	B	✔✔✔
Crianlarich	6.5/10	ATM	✔		✔✔✔	✔		YHA	✔✔✔
Strathfillan	3.5/6					(✔)	✔	B	✔✔✔
Tyndrum	2.5/4	ATM	✔	TIC	✔✔✔	✔	✔	B/H	✔✔✔
Bridge of Orchy	7/11		✔		✔		(✔)	B	✔
Inveroran	3/5				✔		(✔)		✔
Kingshouse	10/16				✔		(✔)		✔
(Glencoe)		ATM	✔	VC	✔✔	✔	✔	YHA/H/B	✔✔✔
Kinlochleven	8.5/14	ATM	✔		✔✔✔	✔	✔	B/H	✔✔✔
Glen Nevis	12.5/20			VC	✔✔✔	(✔)	✔	YHA/H/B	✔
Fort William	2/3	✔✔	✔	TIC	✔✔✔	✔✔✔		B/H	✔✔✔

*NOTES

PLACE Places in brackets (eg Blanefield) are a short walk off the route. Glencoe, however, is nine miles off the West Highland Way.

DISTANCE Distances given are between places directly on the West Highland Way. Gartness, for example, is 10 miles/16km from Milngavie. Distances in brackets are for the alternative route via Milton of Buchanan

TOURIST INFO TIC = Tourist information centre; VC = visitor centre; NPC = national park centre

EATING PLACE ✔ = one place, ✔✔ = two, ✔✔✔ = three or more; (✔) = seasonal

FOOD SHOP (✔) = seasonal **CAMPSITE** (✔) = wild camping

BUNK/HOSTEL YHA = Youth hostel, H = independent hostel, B = bunkhouse/cabins

B&B ✔ = one place, ✔✔ = two, ✔✔✔ = three or more

❑ **Walking from Glasgow to Milngavie**

Highly recommended is to add an extra (short) day to your itinerary and walk from the centre of Glasgow to Milngavie and the official start of the West Highland Way. Far from trudging along pavements beside busy streets, as you might imagine a walk out of a city might entail, you follow two rivers, the Kelvin and the Allander, through parks and then beside fields. Two official footpaths, the **Kelvin Walkway** and the **Allander Walkway**, follow the rivers and if you stay overnight near Kelvingrove Park, you can join the route right there. From Kelvingrove Park to Milngavie is approximately 10 miles (16km) and this easy day's walk is a great way to start; see pp94-8.

WHICH DIRECTION?

Most walkers find the lure of the Highlands, and Ben Nevis in particular, more appealing than the suburbs of Glasgow so walk the Way south to north. This traditional northern direction of travel has been followed in the layout of this book. There are other practical reasons for heading north rather than south; the prevailing wind and rain (south-westerly) is behind you, as is the sun, and the gentler walking is at the start giving you time to warm up before tackling the steeper climbs of the last few days.

That said, there is no reason why you shouldn't walk in the other direction, especially if just tackling a part of the Way. The maps in Part 5 give timings for both directions and, as route-finding instructions are on the maps rather than in blocks of text, it is straightforward using this guide back to front.

SUGGESTED ITINERARIES

These itineraries (below and opposite) are suggestions only; adapt them to your needs. They have been divided into different accommodation types and each

STAYING IN B&Bs

	Relaxed pace		Medium pace		Fast pace	
Night	Place	Approx Distance miles/km	Place	Approx Distance miles/km	Place	Approx Distance miles/km
0	Milngavie		Milngavie		Milngavie	
1	Drymen	12/19.5	Drymen	12/19	Balmaha	19/30.5
2	Cashel	10.5/17	Cashel	10.5/17	Inversnaid	14/22.5
3	Inversnaid	10.5/17	Inverarnan	17/27	Tyndrum	19/30.5
4	Crianlarich	13/21	Tyndrum	12.5/20	Kingshouse	20/32
5	Bridge of Orchy*	12/19.5	Kingshouse	20/32	Kinlochleven	8.5/13.5
6	Kingshouse	13/21	Kinlochleven	8.5/13.5	Fort William	15/24
7	Kinlochleven	8.5/13.5	Fort William	15/24		
8	Fort William	15/24				

* B&B at Bridge of Orchy is expensive but one of the two bunkhouses has twin rooms.

table has different itineraries to encompass different walking paces. **Don't forget to add your travelling time before and after the walk**.

HILLWALKING SIDE TRIPS

The majesty of the Highlands can only be fully grasped by climbing out of the valleys and onto the summits. The West Highland Way passes below many of the best-loved mountains in Scotland presenting the well-equipped walker with

CAMPING

Night	Relaxed pace Place	Approx Distance miles/km	Medium pace Place	Approx Distance miles/km	Fast pace Place	Approx Distance miles/km
0	Milngavie		Milngavie		Milngavie	
1	Gartness	10/16	Gartness	10/16	Gartness	10/16
2	Loch Lomond	11/18	Sallochy	14.5/23.5	Sallochy	14.5/23.5
3	Rowchoish Bothy	8.5/13.5	Inverarnan	15/24	Inverarnan	15/24
4	Inverarnan	13.5/22	Strathfillan	9/14.5	Bridge of Orchy	19.5/31.5
5	Strathfillan	9/14.5	Bridge of Orchy	10/16	Kingshouse	13/21
6	Bridge of Orchy	10/16	Kingshouse	13/21	Kinlochleven	8.5/13.5
7	Kingshouse	13/21	Kinlochleven	8.5/13.5	Glen Nevis	12.5/20
8	Kinlochleven	8.5/13.5	Glen Nevis	12.5/20		
9	Glen Nevis	12.5/20				

Note that the extra weight of camping equipment is likely to add a day onto your trip compared with staying in hostels or B&Bs. See p52: Loch Lomond camping restrictions.

STAYING IN BUNKHOUSES & HOSTELS

Night	Relaxed pace Place	Approx Distance miles/km	Medium pace Place	Approx Distance miles/km	Fast pace Place	Approx Distance miles/km
0	Milngavie		Milngavie		Milngavie	
1	E Drumquhassle	10/16	E Drumquhassle	10/16	Balmaha	19/30.5
2	Rowardennan	16/26	Rowardennan	16/26	Rowardennan	7/11.5
3	Inverarnan	13.5/22	Inverarnan	13.5/22	Inverarnan	13.5/22
4	Tyndrum	12.5/20	Bridge of Orchy	19.5/31.5	Bridge of Orchy	19.5/31.5
5	Bridge of Orchy	7/11.5	Glencoe*	13/21	Kinlochleven	21.5/34.5
6	Glencoe*	13/21	Kinlochleven	8.5/13.5	Fort William**	15/24
7	Kinlochleven	8.5/13.5	Fort William**	15/24		
8	Fort William**	15/24				

* Glencoe is 9 miles (14.5km) off the Way. The above itineraries assume you will catch a bus or hitchhike from Kingshouse to Glencoe and back again.

** or Glen Nevis – 12.5miles (20km) from Kinlochleven.

PLANNING YOUR WALK

a wonderful opportunity for a few days' hillwalking. There are detailed route descriptions in Part 5 for climbing the two most popular peaks, Ben Lomond and Ben Nevis, and planning information for a few other convenient peaks above Bridge of Orchy, between Inveroran and Kingshouse, and in Glen Coe.

Popular routes to the top of over 40 Munros (see box opposite) leave either from or near the West Highland Way so there's ample scope for peak bagging if you are bitten by that bug. See some of the walking guidebooks, including Trailblazer's *Scottish Highlands – The Hillwalking Guide*, on p42 for more information.

Although not particularly high when compared with other mountains round the world, the Scottish mountains can be dangerous for the unprepared at any time of year. Read 'Mountain Safety' on p56, and also 'Access' on pp53-5 to make sure your planned walk doesn't interfere with other users of the hills.

❑ DAY AND WEEKEND WALKS

There's nothing quite like walking a whole long-distance footpath from beginning to end but some people just don't have the time. The following highlights offer outstanding walking and scenery coupled with good public transport (see pp44-7) at the start and finish. If you are fit and experienced and like the idea of a challenge, each of the weekend walks can be walked in a long day.

Day walks

- **Milngavie to Killearn** An easy 9-mile (14.5km) walk straight out of the city into beautiful countryside with buses from Killearn to get you back; see pp103-11.
- **Drymen to Balmaha via Conic Hill** A spectacular 7-mile (11.5km) walk climbing to the top of Conic Hill with wonderful views over Loch Lomond; see pp116-21.
- **Rowardennan to Inversnaid** A 7-mile (11.5km) walk along the pretty eastern shore of Loch Lomond and taking a boat back (see p132 and pp125-6); see pp128-33.
- **Rowardennan to Inverarnan** An extension of the above suggestion taking in the wildest stretch of Loch Lomond, 13½ miles (22km); see pp128-39.
- **Bridge of Orchy to Kingshouse** A beautiful and challenging 13-mile (21km) walk across Rannoch Moor, see pp155-62.
- **Kingshouse to Kinlochleven** A wonderful 8½-mile (13.5km) mountain walk up the Devil's Staircase packed with stunning views – Glen Coe, the Mamores, Ben Nevis, Blackwater Reservoir and Loch Leven; see pp166-76.

Weekend walks

- **Balmaha to Inverarnan** A lovely 20½-mile (33km) walk along the eastern shore of Loch Lomond staying overnight at Rowardennan, Rowchoish Bothy or Inversnaid; see pp121-39. If you want to add a few extra miles either start at Drymen or climb Ben Lomond en route.
- **Inverarnan south to Rowardennan** A wild walk along Loch Lomond (13½ miles, 22km) on day one, with a fitting finish **climbing Ben Lomond**, Scotland's most southerly Munro, the next day; see from p134 back to p125.
- **Bridge of Orchy to Kinlochleven** 21½ miles (34.5km) combining two of the most spectacular day walks above; see pp155-76.
- **Kingshouse to Fort William** A strenuous 23-mile (37km) mountain walk through the heart of the Highlands finishing at the foot of Ben Nevis, Britain's highest mountain. If you have an extra day you could climb 'the Ben' as well; see pp166-86.

❑ **Munros**

In 1891 Sir Hugh Munro, soldier, diplomat and founder member of the Scottish Mountaineering Club (SMC), published a list of all Scottish mountains over the magical height of 3000ft (or the rather clumsy metric equivalent of 914m). He had been aware that many peaks had gone unrecognised and his new tables came up with 538 'tops' over 3000ft, 283 of which, because of certain distinguishing features, merited the status of 'separate mountains'. Unwittingly he had given birth to the mountaineering equivalent of train-spotting; ticking off as many 'Munros' as possible by climbing to their summit. The craze caught on quickly. By 1901 Reverend Robertson was the first to climb them all and since then nearly 5000 hill walkers have followed his lead.

'Munro-bagging' has encouraged many walkers to explore some of the finest country in Scotland, luring them away from the popular honey-pot areas to reach a specific hill. Yet when it becomes an obsession, as it frequently does, there is a danger that other equally wonderful areas of wild land are ignored and the true esoteric reasons for walking are lost. Much to the dismay of purists the goalposts occasionally shift as the tables are revised following the latest surveying data. The number of Munros currently stands at 282. Interestingly Sir Hugh never completed his own round, failing repeatedly to climb the Inaccessible Pinnacle on Skye before he died at the age of 63.

What to take

How much you take with you is a very personal decision which takes experience to get right. For those new to long-distance walking the suggestions below will help you strike a sensible balance between comfort, safety and minimal weight.

KEEP YOUR LUGGAGE LIGHT

In these days of huge material wealth it can be a liberating experience to travel **as light as possible** to learn how few possessions we really need to be safe and comfortable. It is all too easy to take things along 'just in case' and these little items can soon mount up. If you are in any doubt about anything on your packing list, be ruthless and leave it at home.

To liberate themselves entirely from their luggage, many people now make use of **baggage-carrying companies** (see p25).

HOW TO CARRY IT

The size of your **rucksack** depends on how you plan to walk. If you are camping along the Way you will need a pack large enough to hold a tent, sleeping bag, cooking equipment and food; 65 to 75 litres' capacity should be ample. This should have a stiffened back system and either be fully adjustable, or exactly the right size for your back. If you carry the main part of the load high and close to your body with a large proportion of the weight carried on your hips (not on your shoulders) by means of the padded hip belt you should be able to walk in comfort for days on end. Play around with different ways of packing your gear and adjusting all those straps until you get it just right. It's also handy to have a **bum/waist bag** or a very light **day pack** in which you can carry your camera, guidebook and other essentials when you go off sightseeing or for a day walk.

If you are staying in bunkhouses you may want to carry a sleeping bag (see p39) and possibly a small stove and pan, though strictly speaking neither of these is essential (see p19); a 40- to 60-litre pack should be fine. If you are indulging in the luxury of B&Bs you should be able to get all you need into a 30- to 40-litre pack.

Pack similar things in different-coloured **stuff sacks** so they are easier to pull out of the dark recesses of your pack. Put these inside **waterproof rucksack liners**, or tough plastic sacks, that can be slipped inside your pack to protect everything from the inevitable rain. It's also worth taking a **waterproof rucksack cover**; most rucksacks these days have them 'built in' to the sack, but you can also buy them separately for less than a tenner.

Of course, if you decide to use one of the baggage-carrying services you can pack most of your things in a **suitcase** and simply carry a small day-pack with the essentials you need for the day's walking.

FOOTWEAR

Boots

Your boots are the **single most important item** that can affect the enjoyment of your walk. In summer you could get by with a light pair of trail shoes if you're carrying only a small pack, although they don't give much support for your ankles and you'll get wet, cold feet if there is any rain. Some of the terrain is rough so a good pair of walking boots would be a safer option. They must fit well and be properly broken in. A week's walk is not the time to try out a new pair of boots. Refer to p57 for some blister-avoidance strategies.

If you plan to climb any of the mountains along the Way good boots are essential. For winter hillwalking side-trips your boots must be able to take crampons.

Socks

The traditional wearing of a thin liner sock under a thicker wool sock is no longer necessary if you choose a high-quality sock specially designed for walking. A high proportion of natural fibres makes them much more comfortable. Three pairs are ample. Some people, however, still prefer to use thin liner socks (silk being best) as these are much easier to wash than thick socks, so you can change them more regularly than thick socks.

Extra footwear

Some walkers like to have a second pair of shoes to wear when they are not on the trail. Trainers, sport sandals or flip flops are all suitable as long as they are light.

❑ **Cheaper alternatives**
Modern synthetic outdoor clothing is light and quick-drying but doesn't come cheap. If you are new to walking and feel the expense of equipping yourself properly is prohibitive of course you can get by with 'normal' cotton clothing under a good waterproof layer, especially in summer. However, if this is the case, you must carry a complete spare set of clothes that is always kept dry. If this means pulling on the damp clothes you wore the day before, do so.

CLOTHES

Scotland's wet and cold weather is notorious; even in summer you should come prepared for wintry conditions. It can also be spectacularly glorious so clothes to cope with these wide variations are needed. Experienced walkers pick their clothes according to the versatile layering system: a base layer to transport sweat from your skin; a mid-layer or two to keep you warm; and an outer layer or 'shell' to protect you from any wind, rain or snow. (See also box above).

Base layer

Cotton absorbs sweat, trapping it next to the skin which will chill you rapidly when you stop exercising. A thin lightweight **thermal top** made from synthetic material is better as it draws moisture away keeping you dry. It will be cool if worn on its own in hot weather and warm when worn under other clothes in cooler conditions. A spare would be sensible. You may also like to bring a **shirt** for wearing in the evening.

Mid-layers

From May to September a woollen jumper or mid-weight polyester **fleece** will suffice. For the rest of the year you will need an extra layer to keep you warm. Both wool and fleece, unlike cotton, stay reasonably warm when wet.

Outer layer

A **waterproof jacket** is essential year-round and will be much more comfortable (but also more expensive) if it's also 'breathable' to prevent the build-up of condensation on the inside. This layer can also be worn to keep the wind off.

Leg wear

Whatever you wear on your legs it should be light, quick-drying and not restricting. Many British walkers find polyester tracksuit bottoms comfortable. Poly-cotton or microfibre trousers are excellent. Denim jeans should never be worn; if they get wet they become heavy and cold, and bind to your legs.

A pair of **shorts** is nice to have on sunny days. Thermal **longjohns** or thick tights are cosy if you're camping and necessary for winter walking.

Waterproof trousers are necessary most of the year but in summer could be left behind if your main pair of trousers is reasonably windproof and quick-drying. **Gaiters** are not needed unless you come across a lot of snow in winter.

Underwear

Three changes of what you normally wear is fine. Women may find a **sports bra** more comfortable because pack straps can cause bra straps to dig into your shoulders.

Other clothes

A **warm hat** and **gloves** should be carried at all times of the year. Take two pairs of gloves in winter. In summer you should carry a **sun hat** and possibly a **swimsuit** if you enjoy swimming in cold lochs and rivers. There are also a few swimming pools along the route which can be good at the end of a hot day. A small **towel** will be needed if you are not staying in B&Bs.

If camping in summer a **head net** to protect you from the midges can be invaluable. These can be bought at various places along the Way.

TOILETRIES

Only take the minimum: a small bar of **soap** in a plastic container (unless staying in B&Bs) which can also be used instead of shaving cream and for washing clothes; a tiny tube of **toothpaste** and a **toothbrush**; and one roll of **loo paper** in a plastic bag. If you are planning to defecate outdoors you will also need a lightweight **trowel** for burying the evidence (see p51 for further tips). In addition a **razor**; **tampons/sanitary towels**; **deodorant**; a high-factor **sun screen** (these latter two are available as wipes, saving on space and weight); and a good **insect repellent** for the midges (see pp58-9) should cover all your needs.

FIRST-AID KIT

You need only a small kit to cover common problems and emergencies; pack it in a waterproof container.

A basic kit will contain **Ibuprofen** or **paracetamol** for treating mild to moderate pain and fever; **plasters/Band Aids** for minor cuts; '**moleskin**', '**Compeed**', or '**Second Skin**' for blisters; a **bandage** for holding dressings, splints, or limbs in place and for supporting a sprained ankle, an **elastic knee support** (tubigrip) for a weak knee, a small selection of different-sized **sterile dressings** for wounds; **porous adhesive tape**; **antiseptic wipes**; **antiseptic cream**; **safety pins**; **tweezers**; **scissors**.

GENERAL ITEMS

Essential

Anyone walking in the mountains should carry a 'Silva' type **compass** and know how to use it; the modern equivalent, a GPS (see pp17-18), can be just as useful though again you need to know how to use it properly and to make sure you have enough spare batteries for your walk. An emergency **whistle** for summoning assistance (see p60) is also very useful, as are the following: a **water bottle** or **pouch** holding at least one litre; a **torch** (flashlight) with spare bulb and batteries in case you end up walking after dark; **emergency food** which your body can quickly convert into energy (see p56); a **penknife**; a **watch** with an alarm; and several degradable **plastic bags** for packing out any rubbish you accumulate.

If you're not carrying a sleeping bag or tent you should also carry an emergency plastic **bivvy bag**.

Useful

Many would list a **camera** as essential but it can be liberating to travel without one once in a while; a **notebook** can be a more accurate way of recording your impressions; a **book** to pass the time on train and bus journeys or for the evenings; a pair of **sunglasses** in summer or when there's snow on the ground; **binoculars** for observing wildlife; a **walking stick** or pole to take the shock off your knees; and a **vacuum flask** for carrying hot drinks.

Many walkers carry **mobile phones** (don't forget to bring the charger) but it is important to remember that the network may not provide full coverage of the area through which you are walking owing to the terrain. Take the mobile by all means but don't rely on it.

SLEEPING BAG

Unless you are staying in B&Bs all the way you will find a sleeping bag useful. Bunkhouses and hostels always have some bedding but you'll keep your costs down if you don't have to hire it. A three-season bag will cope with most eventualities although many walkers will be able to make do with one rated for one or two seasons; it's a personal choice.

CAMPING GEAR

If you're camping you will need a decent **tent** (or bivvy bag if you enjoy travelling light) able to withstand wet and windy weather with netting on the entrance to keep the midges at bay; a **sleeping mat** (also invaluable for anyone planning to stay in a bothy); a **stove** and **fuel** (there is special mention in Part 5 of which shops stock which fuel; bottles of meths and the various gas cylinders are readily available, Coleman fuel is sometimes harder to find); a **pan** with a lid that can double as a frying pan/plate is fine for two people; a **pan handle**; a **mug**; a **spoon**; and a wire/plastic **scrubber** for washing up (there's no need for washing-up liquid and, anyway, it should never be used in streams, lochs or rivers). **Incense sticks** to burn in your tent have been recommended as a midge repellent.

MONEY

There are few banks on the West Highland Way so most of your money will need to be carried as **cash**, especially if you do not have an account with a bank that has an agreement with the Post Office (see p25). A **debit card** is the easiest way to draw money either from banks or cash machines and that or a **credit card** can often be used to pay in larger shops, restaurants and hotels. A **cheque book** is still useful for walkers for paying at B&Bs that do not accept cards.

MAPS

The hand-drawn maps in this book cover the trail at a scale of 1:20,000, which is a better scale than any other map currently available, and we've also included plenty of detail and information so you should not need any other map if you're walking just the Way.

If you want to climb any of the mountains along the route, however, you must also take a map from Ordnance Survey (☎ 08456-050505, 🖳 www.ordnancesurvey.co.uk) or Harvey (☎ 01786-841202, 🖳 www.harveymaps.co.uk) so that you can navigate accurately with a compass. The best-buy map of the Way is published by Harvey (£11.95) with the trail arranged in strips at a scale of 1:40,000. Its coverage either side of the trail is limited though it extends to Ben Lomond, Ben Dorain and Ben Nevis.

The Ordnance Survey Explorer maps (orange cover) at a scale of 1:25,000 (£7.99) are excellent but you need seven maps (Nos 342, 348, 347, 364, 377, 384

❑ SOURCES OF FURTHER INFORMATION

Trail information

• **West Highland Way website** The latest information on the trail can be found on the West Highland Way's dedicated website: 🖳 www.west-highland-way.co.uk.

• **Rangers** West Highland Way rangers can provide knowledgeable advice and information about all aspects of the trail: **Southern section – Milngavie to Tyndrum** (☎ 01389-722100, 🖳 info@west-highland-way.co.uk), Loch Lomond and Trossachs National Park Centre, Balmaha (see p120); **Northern section – Tyndrum to Fort William** (☎ 01397-705922, 🖳 westhighlandway@highland.gov.uk), West Highland Way (North) Ranger, Glen Nevis Visitor Centre (see p174).

• 🖳 **www.tyndrumbytheway.com** The website for Tyndrum By The Way Hostel and Campsite (see p146) contains lots of practical information for West Highland Way walkers.

Tourist information

• **Tourist information centres (TICs)** Many towns in Britain have a TIC which provides all manner of locally specific information for visitors and an accommodation-booking service (for which there is usually a charge). There are TICs along the Way in **Glasgow** (see p82), **Tyndrum** (see p146), and **Fort William** (see p187). In addition there is a national park centre at Balmaha (see p120) and visitor centres at **Milngavie** (see pp102-3), **Glencoe** (see p162) and **Glen Nevis** (see p174).

Tourist boards For general information on the whole of Scotland contact the **Scottish Tourist Board** (🖳 www.visitscotland.com). Each region of Scotland has its own tourist board which can provide general information on its locality and a glossy brochure/accommodation guide; they also each have a useful website and an accommodation-booking service. However, for accommodation along the Way their listings are not as comprehensive as this guidebook's since they include only paying members.

• **Greater Glasgow and Clyde Valley Tourist Board** (🖳 www.seeglasgow.com) covers the route between Glasgow and Milngavie.

• **Argyll, the Isles, Loch Lomond, Stirling and Trossachs Tourist Board** (🖳 www.visitscottishheartlands.com) covers Milngavie to Rannoch Moor.

• **The Highlands of Scotland Tourist Board** (🖳 www.visithighlands.com) covers the Way from Glencoe to Fort William.

and 392) to cover the whole trail. Alternatively there are the Landranger maps (pink cover), Nos 64, 56, 50 and 41 at a scale of 1:50,000 (£6.99). Other possible maps for use on hillwalking side trips are listed in the relevant route descriptions.

Enthusiastic map buyers can reduce the often considerable expense of purchasing them: members of **Ramblers** (see box below) can borrow up to 10 maps for a period of six weeks at 50p per map (£1 for laminated maps) from their library; members of the **Backpackers Club** (see box below) can purchase maps at a significant discount through their map service.

Digital maps

Ordnance Survey have recently started producing digital/'memory maps' for PCs and GPS systems. As well as the regular 1:25,000 maps they also include a 1:250,000 road map, full aerial photography of the route and a search-and-display index to over 250,000 places! They're great fun but at £48.94 for the CD, they're not cheap.

Organisations for walkers

- **Backpackers Club** (🖳 www.backpackersclub.co.uk) A club aimed at people who are involved or interested in lightweight camping whether through walking, cycling, cross-country skiing or canoeing.

  They produce a quarterly magazine, provide members with a comprehensive information service (including a library) on all aspects of backpacking, organise weekend trips and also publish a farm-pitch directory. Membership costs £12 per year (£15 for a family); under 18s and over 65s £7.
- **British Mountaineering Council** (🖳 www.thebmc.co.uk) Promotes the interests of British hillwalkers, climbers and mountaineers. Among the many benefits of membership are an excellent information service, a quarterly magazine and travel insurance designed for mountain sports. Annual membership is £29.95, family membership £51, concessions (unemployed, students, U18s) £17.35.
- **The Long Distance Walkers' Association** (LDWA; 🖳 www.ldwa.org.uk) An association of people with the common interest of long-distance walking. Membership includes a journal, *Strider*, three times per year giving details of challenge events and local group walks as well as articles on the subject. Information on over 730 paths is presented in *The UK Trailwalkers' Handbook*, published by Cicerone LDWA, which members can buy for £13.95 (RRP £18.95).

  Membership is £13 a year (family membership £19.50) and is for the calendar year though anyone joining after 1st October will be given membership for the following calendar year.
- **Mountaineering Council of Scotland** (MCS; 🖳 www.mcofs.org.uk) The MCS is the main representative body for mountaineers and hillwalkers in Scotland. Among the many benefits of membership is a very useful information service. Membership is £28.55, £17.10 for unemployed, OAPs and students, or £47.75 families.
- **Ramblers** (formerly Ramblers' Association; 🖳 www.ramblers.org.uk) Looks after the interests of walkers throughout Britain. They publish a quarterly *Walk* magazine (£3.60 to non-members). Their website also has information about walking in Scotland (🖳 www.ramblers.org.uk/scotland).

  Annual membership is £31, £19.50 concessions, £41 for two people living at the same address.

RECOMMENDED READING

General guidebooks

There are several good guidebooks for exploring away from the trail. Footprint, Lonely Planet and Rough Guides all produce a *Scotland* guide for the whole country and Rough Guides also publish *Scottish Highlands and Islands* for travelling in the remoter parts of west Scotland. Footprint publish a similar title; *Scotland Highlands and Islands Handbook*.

Walking guidebooks

Scottish Highlands – The Hillwalking Guide by Jim Manthorpe (Trailblazer) has detailed route descriptions and maps for the ascents of some of Scotland's best-known, and some less well-known, mountains.

Ralph Storer's *100 Best Routes on Scottish Mountains* (Warner Books) is an excellent book to get you into the mountains with information on many of the peaks along the Way; it's light enough to carry in your rucksack.

The Pathfinder guides to *Loch Lomond and the Trossachs* and *Fort William and Glen Coe* are useful area guidebooks with a selection of low- and high-level day walks, each illustrated with OS map excerpts. *Ben Nevis and Glen Coe* by Chris Townsend (Collins Ramblers' Guide) is a similar book with a comprehensive selection of day routes illustrated with Harvey maps. Lonely Planet's *Walking in Scotland* is a useful overall planning guide.

If the West Highland Way has fired your enthusiasm for walking long-distance trails check out the other titles in this Trailblazer series: see p208.

Flora and fauna field guides

Scottish Birds by Valerie Thom and *Scottish Wild Flowers* by Michael Scott (both Collins) are ideal pocket-sized field guides to take with you. The RSPB also publish their own *Handbook of Scottish Birds*, by Holden and Housden.

Getting to and from the West Highland Way

Travelling to the start of the West Highland Way by public transport makes sense. There's no need to worry about the safety of your temporarily abandoned vehicle while walking, there are no logistical headaches about how to return to your car after the walk and it's obviously one of the biggest steps you can take towards minimising your ecological footprint. Quite apart from that, you'll simply feel your holiday has begun the moment you step out of your front door, rather than having to wait until you've slammed the car door behind you.

NATIONAL TRANSPORT

Glasgow, only 20 minutes from the official start of the West Highland Way at Milngavie, is easily reached by rail, road or air from the rest of Britain. For information on getting from Glasgow to Milngavie see p82.

By rail

Glasgow is on the West Coast rail line (currently operated by Virgin Trains, see below) and is served by frequent trains from the rest of Britain making it easy to get to the start of the West Highland Way letting the train take the strain. Fort William is on the stunning West Highland Line from where you can either go north to Mallaig or south to Glasgow.

Timetable and fare information can be obtained from **National Rail Enquiries** (☎ 08457-484950; 24hrs; 💻 www.nationalrail.co.uk) or the relevant train companies, particularly **Virgin Trains** (☎ 0871-977 4222, 💻 www.virgintrains.co.uk) and **Scotrail** (see box p45). Tickets can be bought direct from Virgin Trains, or from websites such as 💻 www.thetrainline.com and 💻 www.qjump.co.uk. However, there may be additional charges such as a booking fee, or for using a debit/credit card.

If you plan to take a bus when you arrive consider getting a plusbus (💻 www.plusbus.info) ticket and if you want to book a taxi Traintaxi's website (💻 www.traintaxi.co.uk) gives details of the companies operating at railway stations.

Of particular use if you're travelling from the south of England is the comfortable overnight (Sunday to Friday only) **sleeper service from London**

❑ Getting to Britain

- **By air** There are plenty of cheap flights from around the world to London's airports: Heathrow, Gatwick, Luton, London City and Stansted; these are all about 5½ hours by train from Glasgow. However, Glasgow Airport (💻 www.glasgowairport.com), right at the start of the Way, Prestwick (💻 www.glasgowprestwick.com), near Glasgow, and Edinburgh (💻 www.edinburghairport.com), only one hour by train from Glasgow, have a limited number of international flights from North America and Europe and would be far more convenient.

  For details about airlines that fly to Glasgow and Edinburgh, and destinations served, visit the respective airport's website.

- **From Europe by train** Eurostar (💻 www.eurostar.com) operates a high-speed passenger service via the Channel Tunnel between Paris/Brussels and London. The Eurostar terminal in London is at St Pancras International station which has connections to the London Underground and to all other main railway stations in London.

  For more information about rail services from Europe contact your national rail service provider, or Railteam (💻 www.railteam.eu).

- **From Europe by coach** Eurolines (💻 www.eurolines.com) have a huge network of long-distance bus services connecting over 500 cities in Europe to London (Victoria Coach Station). See the website for contact details for your home country.

- **From Europe by ferry (with or without a car)** There are numerous ferries plying routes between the major North Sea ports, as well as across the Irish Sea and the English Channel. A useful website for information about the routes and the ferry operators is 💻 www.directferries.com.

- **From Europe by car** Eurotunnel (💻 www.eurotunnel.com) operates the shuttle train service for vehicles via the Channel Tunnel between Calais and Folkestone taking one hour between the motorway in France and the motorway in Britain.

(Euston) to either Fort William or Glasgow (Central) with accommodation either in single or twin cabins, or seats. The Fort William Caledonian sleeper service stops en route at Arrochar & Tarbet, Ardlui (on request only), Crianlarich, Upper Tyndrum and Bridge of Orchy so is very convenient for West Highland Way walkers. However, if you want to go to Glasgow it is best to take the direct service. For further details contact Scotrail (☎ 08457-550033, 🖳 www.scotrail.co.uk).

Tickets can be bought about 12 weeks in advance. Buy a ticket as early as possible. Only a limited number of tickets are sold at discounted prices. It helps to be as flexible as possible and don't forget that most of these tickets carry some restrictions, so check what they are before you buy your ticket. Travel in peak hours and on a Friday may be more expensive than at other times.

❑ PUBLIC TRANSPORT SERVICES

Notes: The details below were correct at the time of writing but services and operators change so it is essential to check before travelling.

Many of the services listed operate year-round; however, they may operate less frequently in the winter months (generally November to March/April).

Services operate with the same frequency in the opposite direction.

Bus services

First Group (🖳 www.firstgroup.com)

• First Scotland East (South East and Central Scotland)

C8/8 Glasgow to Balfron via Milngavie, Carbeth & Drymen, Mon-Sat 3-5/day
C10/10/10A Glasgow to Balfron via Milngavie, Strathblane & Killearn, Mon-Fri 20/day, Sat 15/day, Sun 7/day plus 2/day to Aberfoyle – most services connect with C12/12 (see below) from Balfron
C11 Balfron to Stirling via Aberfoyle, Mon-Fri 3/day, Sat 4/day
C12/12 Balfron to Stirling, Mon-Sat 11/day, Sun 2/day
C13 Balfron to Balloch via Killearn & Drymen, Mon-Sat 4/day plus 1/day to Drymen

• First Glasgow (Greater Glasgow)

1/1A Glasgow to Balloch via Alexandria (different stops en route), Mon-Sat 3-4/hr, Sun 1-2/hr

McGill's (☎ 0800-051 5651, 🖳 www.mcgillsbuses.co.uk)

204X Glasgow to Balloch, Mon-Sat 3-5/hr
305 Alexandria to Luss via Balloch 9/day
306 Alexandria to Helensburgh, Mon-Sat 3-5/day, Sun 1/day
309 Alexandria to Balmaha via Balloch & Drymen, 9-10/day

Scottish Citylink (☎ 08705-505050, 🖳 www.citylink.co.uk)

913 Edinburgh to Fort William via Stirling, Callander, Crianlarich, Tyndrum, Bridge of Orchy & Glencoe 1-3/day (late May to early Oct)
914 Glasgow to Fort William via Luss, Inverbeg, Tarbet, Sloy (power station), Ardlui, Inverarnan, Crianlarich, Tyndrum, Bridge of Orchy & Glencoe, 4/day (1/day winter)
915 route as above and continues to Portree, 2/day (1/day winter)
916 route as above and continues to Uig, 2/day
918 Fort William to Oban, Mon-Sat 2/day (operated by West Coast Motors)

By coach

Travel by coach is usually cheaper than by rail but does take longer. Advance bookings carry discounts so be sure to book at least a week ahead. If you don't mind an uncomfortable night there are overnight services on some routes.

National Express (☎ 08717-818178; 💻 www.nationalexpress.com) is the principal coach (long-distance bus) operator in Britain. The NX544 goes to Glasgow (1/day) via Manchester. The NX588 (1/day overnight) service stops in Glasgow en route between London and Inverness; the NX590 (1/day) & NX592 (1/day overnight via Heathrow Airport) stop there en route to Aberdeen. Note that tickets booked over the phone are now subject to a £2 charge. Another company to consider is **Megabus** (💻 www.megabus.com) which has several services a day between London and Glasgow via Manchester (from £13 one way).

919 Fort William to Inverness, Mon-Sat 4-6/day, Sun 2/day (see also Stagecoach Highlands No 19 below)
926 Glasgow to Campbeltown via Luss, Inverbeg & Tarbet, 4/day
973 Dundee/Perth to Oban via Crianlarich & Tyndrum, 3/day (late May to early Oct)
976 Glasgow to Oban via Luss, Inverbeg & Tarbet, 2-3/day

Stagecoach in the Highlands
(☎ 01463-233371, 💻 www.stagecoachbus.com)
19 Fort William to Inverness, Mon-Sat 4/day (see also Citylink No 919 above)
41 Glen Nevis Lower Falls to Roy Bridge via SYHA Glen Nevis and Fort William, summer daily 5/day, winter Roy Bridge to Fort William via Nevis Range Visitor Centre, Mon-Sat 4-5/day (1/day to/from SYHA Glen Nevis), Sun Fort William to Nevis Range Visitor Centre, 2/day
44 Kinlochleven to Fort William via Glencoe Junction, Mon-Sat 13-14/day, Sun 3/day

Shiel Buses (☎ 01967-431272, 💻 www.shielbuses.co.uk)
500 Fort William to Mallaig, Mon-Fri 3/day, summer Sat 1/day

Train services

Scotrail (☎ 0845-601 5929, 💻 www.scotrail.co.uk)

- Glasgow Queen St to Milngavie via Partick & Hyndland, Mon-Sat 2/hr
- Glasgow Central to Milngavie via Partick & Hyndland, daily 2/hr
- Glasgow Queen St to Balloch via Partick, Hyndland & Alexandria, daily 2/hr
- *Glasgow Queen St to Oban via Helensburgh Upper, Arrochar and Tarbet, Ardlui, Crianlarich & Lower Tyndrum, 4/day
- *Glasgow Queen St to Mallaig, stops as above to Crianlarich and then via Upper Tyndrum, Bridge of Orchy, Rannoch, Roy Bridge & Ft William, 2-4/day
- Glasgow Queen St to Stirling, daily 2-3/hr

*Note: all services start in Edinburgh.

Water bus/ferry services

Cruise Loch Lomond (☎ 01301-702356, 💻 www.cruiselochlomond.co.uk/ferries; services operate end Mar to end Oct)
Luss to Balmaha, 4/day via Inchcailloch 3/day
Luss to Rowardennan, 1/day
Tarbet to Inversnaid, 3/day; Tarbet to Rowardennan, 3/day
Inveruglas to Tarbet via Inversnaid, 1/day

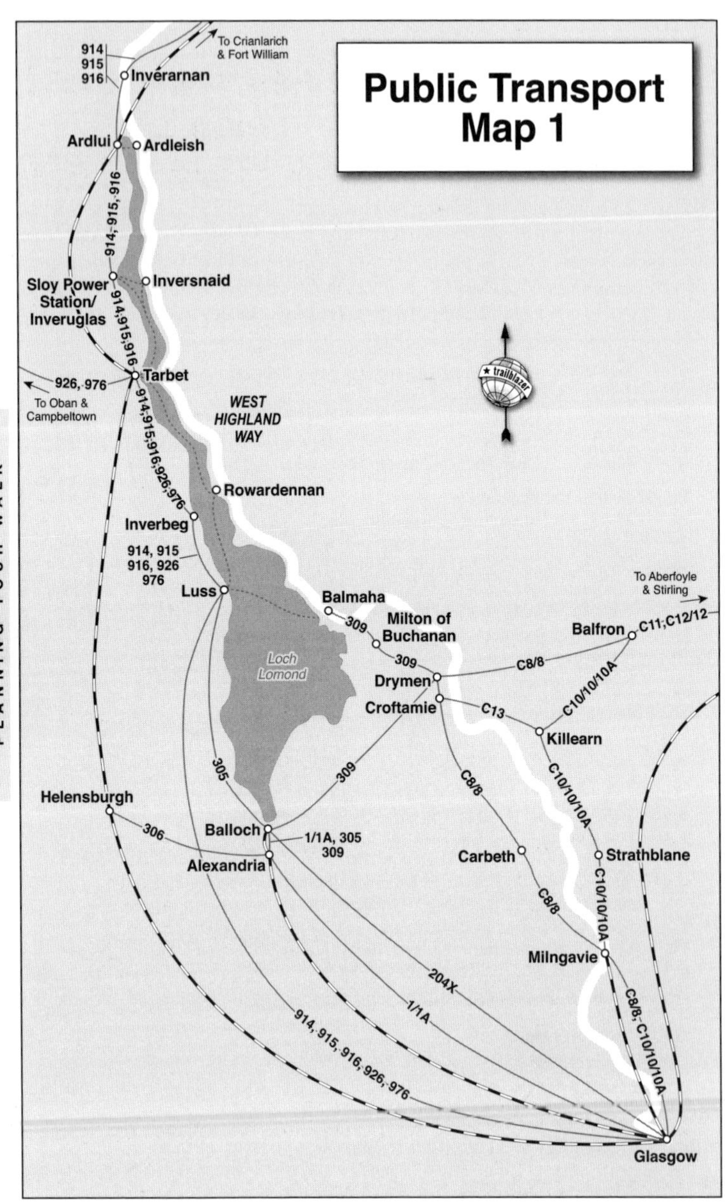

PLANNING YOUR WALK

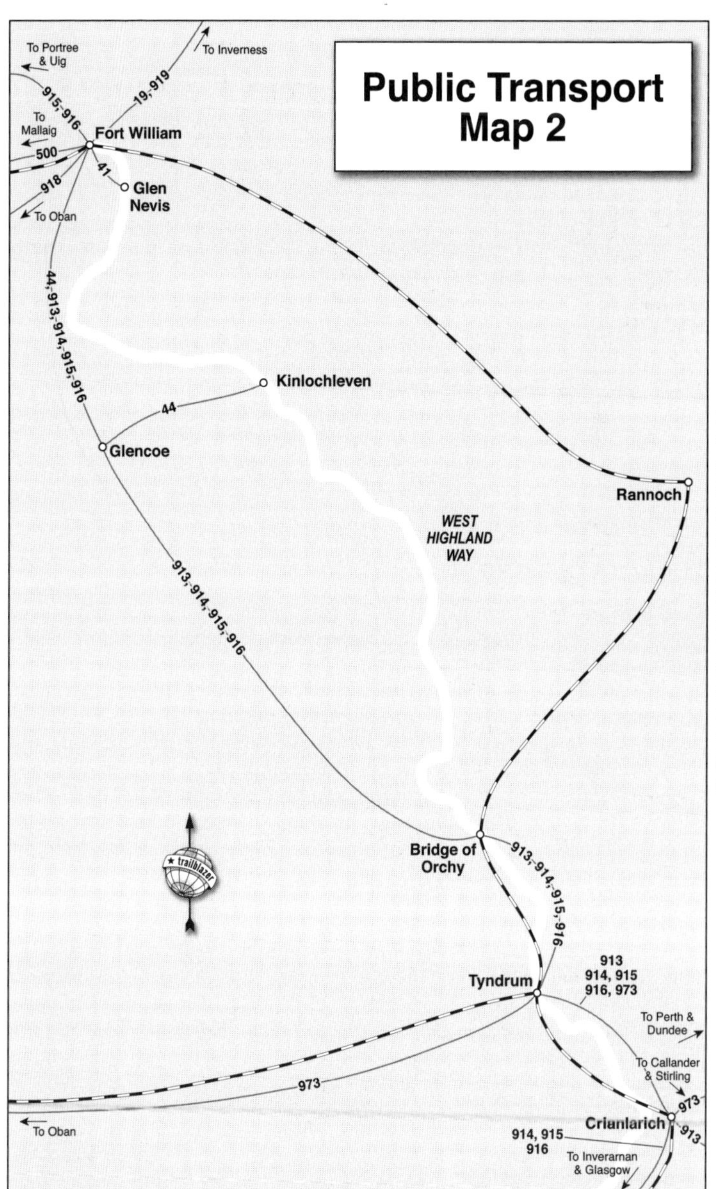
Public Transport
Map 2
To Portree
& Uig
915, 916
To Inverness
19, 919
To
Mallaig
500
Fort William
918
To Oban
41
Glen
Nevis
44, 913, 914, 915, 916
Kinlochleven
44
Glencoe
Rannoch
WEST
HIGHLAND
WAY
913, 914, 915, 916
Bridge of
Orchy
913, 914, 915, 916
trailblazer
Tyndrum
913
914, 915
916, 973
To Perth &
Dundee
To Callander
& Stirling
973
973
To Oban
Crianlarich
973
914, 915
916
To Inverarnan
& Glasgow

For coach travel within Scotland the main operator is **Scottish Citylink** (☎ 0871-266 3333; 💻 www.citylink.co.uk).

By car

Milngavie is simple to get to by car using the motorway network via Glasgow. There is free parking outside Milngavie station with CCTV in operation, or you can leave your car on the road outside the police station. Please let them know if you decide to do this and give them your registration number and an emergency contact number.

Some B&Bs will let you park outside for the duration of your walk. This is the best option if leaving your car in Fort William.

By air

With many bargain tickets to **Glasgow Airport** (see box p43) available from the rest of Britain and short flight times this can seem an alluring way to cover large distances. Bear in mind, however, the time and expense of travelling to and from the airports and the extra time you need to allow for check-in. Glasgow Airport is nine miles west of the city; **Prestwick Airport** (see box p43), used by some budget airlines, is 29 miles to the west.

Air travel is by far the least environmentally sound option (see 💻 www.chooseclimate.org for the true costs of flying).

LOCAL TRANSPORT

Getting to and from most parts of the West Highland Way is relatively simple thanks to a comprehensive public transport network including trains, coaches and bus services.

The **public transport maps** (pp46-7) give an overview of routes which are of particular use to walkers. The **public transport table** on pp44-5 gives the approximate frequency of services in both directions, the relevant stops, and who you should contact for detailed timetable information. If the enquiry lines for bus information prove unsatisfactory telephone **traveline** (☎ 0871-200 2233, 💻 www.travelinescotland.com) which has public transport information for the whole of the UK.

Timetables can also be picked up from tourist information centres and Glasgow's Buchanan St bus station.

Because of its proximity to Glasgow the southern section of the Way is well served by buses and trains. As you progress north the most useful services are trains, which run on the West Highland line parallel to the trail until Bridge of Orchy, and Scottish Citylink coaches along the A82, also never far from the Way. Ferries in summer can get you to the less accessible eastern shore of Loch Lomond. The frequency of public transport services in the area opens up the potential for linear walks from an hour to several days without the worry of where to park the car and how to get back to it.

MINIMUM IMPACT & OUTDOOR SAFETY

2

Minimum impact walking

Walk as if you are kissing the Earth with your feet **Thich Nhat Hanh**

Scotland's large and sparsely populated countryside is the closest you can get to true wilderness anywhere in Britain. Visitors have come in large numbers for over a century to sample the healing balm that comes from walking in these less touched places and as the world gets increasingly faster, more polluted and urbanised there is an even greater need for wild country where you can go for re-creation in the true sense of the word.

Inevitably this too brings its problems. As more and more people enjoy the freedom of the hills so the land comes under increasing pressure and the potential for conflict with other land-users is heightened. Everyone has a right to this natural heritage but with it comes a responsibility to care for it too.

By following some simple guidelines while walking the West Highland Way you can have a positive impact, not just on your own well-being but also on local communities and the environment, thereby becoming part of the solution.

ECONOMIC IMPACT

Support local businesses

Rural businesses and communities in Britain have been hit hard in recent years by a seemingly endless series of crises. The countryside through which the West Highland Way passes is no exception and there is a lot that the walker can do to help. Playing your part today involves much more than simply closing the gate and not dropping litter; there is something else you can do – **buy local** – and with it comes huge social, environmental and psychological benefits.

Look and ask for local produce to buy and eat. Not only does this cut down on the amount of pollution and congestion that the transportation of food creates, so-called 'food miles', but also ensures you are supporting local farmers and producers. It's a fact of life that money spent at local level – perhaps in a market, or at the greengrocer, or in an independent pub – has a far greater impact for good on that community than the equivalent spent in a branch of a

Support local traders!

national chain store or restaurant. If you can find local food which is also organic so much the better.

While no-one would advocate that walkers should boycott the larger supermarkets, which after all do provide local employment, it's worth remembering that businesses in rural communities rely heavily on visitors for their very existence. If we want to keep these shops and post offices, we need to use them.

ENVIRONMENTAL IMPACT

By choosing a walking holiday you have already made a positive step towards minimising your impact on the wider environment. By following these suggestions you can also tread lightly along the West Highland Way.

Use public transport whenever possible

Traffic congestion in the Highlands during peak holiday times is becoming more and more of a nightmare. Conversely public transport to and along the West Highland Way is excellent and the more people who use it the better the services will become. This not only benefits visitors but also local people and the environment.

Never leave litter

Leaving litter shows a total disrespect for the natural world and others coming after you. As well as being unsightly litter kills wildlife, pollutes the environment and can be dangerous to farm animals.

Please carry a degradable bag so you can dispose of your rubbish in a bin in the next village. It would be very helpful if you could pick up litter left by other people too.

• **Is it OK if it's biodegradable?** Not really. Apple cores, banana skins, orange peel and the like are unsightly, encourage flies and wasps and ruin a picnic spot for others. Using the excuse that they are natural and biodegradable just doesn't cut any ice. When was the last time you saw a banana tree in Scotland?

• **The lasting impact of litter** A piece of orange peel left on the ground takes six months to decompose; silver foil 18 months; a plastic bag 10 years; clothes 15 years; and an aluminium drinks can 85 years.

Erosion

• **Stay on the main trail** The effect of your footsteps may seem minuscule but when they are multiplied by several thousand walkers each year they become rather more significant. Avoid taking shortcuts, widening the trail or creating more than one path; your boots will be followed by many others.

• Consider walking out of season Maximum disturbance by walkers coincides with the time of year when nature wants to do most of its growth and repair. In high-use areas, like that along much of the Way, the trail never recovers. Walking at less busy times eases this pressure while also generating year-round income for the local economy. Not only that, but it may make the walk a more relaxing experience for you as there are fewer people on the path and there's less competition for accommodation.

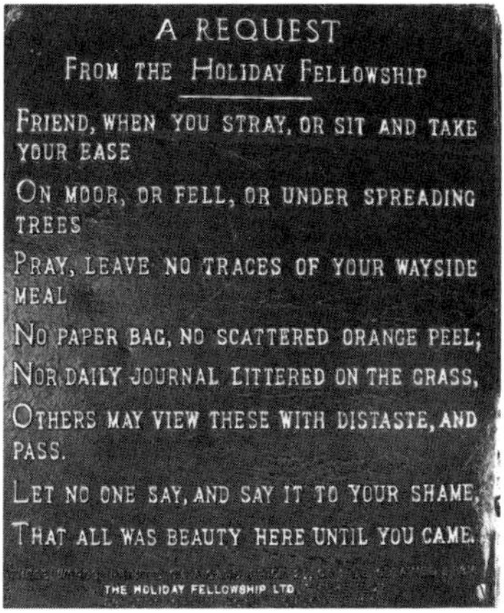

The Holiday Fellowship who supplied this plaque with its gentle reminder to its holidaymakers to take their litter home is still going strong, its name abbreviated to HF Holidays. Dating from the 1930s, the plaque is set in the wall of the Rowardennan Hotel, right beside the Way.

Respect all wildlife

Care for all wildlife you come across on the Way; it has just as much of a right to be there as you. Tempting as it may be to pick wild flowers leave them so the next people who pass can enjoy them too. Don't break branches off or damage trees in any way.

If you come across wildlife keep your distance and don't watch for too long. Your presence can cause considerable stress particularly if the adults are with young or in winter when the weather is harsh and food scarce. Young animals are rarely abandoned. If you come across deer calves or young birds keep away so that their mother can return.

The code of the outdoor loo

'Going' in the outdoors is a lost art worth reclaiming, for your sake and everyone else's. As more and more people discover the joys of the outdoors this is becoming an important issue. In some parts of the world where visitor pressure is higher than in Britain walkers and climbers are required to pack out their excrement. This could one day be necessary here. Human excrement is not only offensive to our senses but, more importantly, can infect water sources.

• Where to go Wherever possible **use a toilet**. Public toilets are marked on the trail maps in this guide and you will also find facilities in pubs, cafés and campsites. The West Highland Way is not a wilderness area and the thousands of walkers using it each year mean you need to be as sensitive as possible.

If you do have to go outdoors choose a site at least **30 metres away from running water** and 200 metres away from high-use areas such as huts and bothies. Carry a small trowel and **dig a hole** about 15cm (6") deep to bury your excrement in. It decomposes quicker when in contact with the top layer of soil or leaf mould. Use a stick to stir loose soil into your deposit as well as this speeds up decomposition even more. Do not squash it under rocks as this slows down the composting process. If you have to use rocks to hide it make sure they are not in contact with your faeces.

Make sure you do not dig any holes on ground that is, or could be, of historic or archaeological interest.

● **Toilet paper and tampons** Toilet paper takes a long time to decompose whether buried or not. It is easily dug up by animals and can then blow into water sources or onto the trail. The best method for dealing with it is to **pack it out**. Put the used paper inside a paper bag which you place inside a (degradable) plastic bag (or two). Then simply empty the contents of the paper bag at the next toilet you come across and throw the bag away. You should also pack out **tampons** and **sanitary towels** in a similar way; they take years to decompose and may be dug up and scattered about by animals.

Wild camping

Along the West Highland Way there are a number of informal sites where you are allowed to camp wild. There is deep, lasting pleasure to be gained from living outdoors close to nature but all too often people ruin that enjoyment for those who come after them. Camping without any facilities provides a valuable lesson in simple, sustainable living where the results of all your actions, from going to the loo to washing your plates in a stream, can be seen. Follow these suggestions for minimising your impact and encourage others to do likewise.

Note that wild camping is no longer allowed along the eastern shore of Loch Lomond within the national park between 01 March and 31 October. Signs show the extent of the No Camping zone. See 🖳 www.lochlomond-trossachs.org.

● **Be discreet** Camp alone or in small groups, spend only one night in each place and pitch your tent late and move off early.

● **Never light a fire** The deep burn caused by camp fires, no matter how small, seriously damages the turf and can take years to recover. Cook on a camp stove instead. Be aware that accidental fire is a great fear for farmers and foresters; take matches and cigarette butts out with you to dispose of safely.

● **Don't use soap or detergent** There is no need to use soap; even biodegradable soaps and detergents pollute streams and lochs. You won't be away from a shower for more than a couple of days. Wash up without detergent; use a plastic or metal scourer, or failing that, a handful of fine pebbles from the stream or some bracken or grass.

● **Leave no trace** Enjoy the skill of moving on without leaving any sign of having been there: no moved boulders, ripped up vegetation or dug drainage ditches. Make a final check of your campsite before heading off; pick up any litter that you or anyone else has left, so leaving it in at least as good a state as you found it, if not better.

ACCESS

The West Highland Way, as a designated 'Long Distance Footpath', is a right of way with open access to the public. Access laws in Scotland were for many years very different from those in England and Wales largely due to an uneasy tradition of 'freedom to roam' going back many centuries. This freedom to roam was, until recently, little more than a moral right rather than a legal one. This changed with the Land Reform (Scotland) Act 2003 that established statutory rights of access to land and inland water for outdoor recreation which came into effect in February 2005. The law now states that there is a right of access to land that is considered, among other designations, moorland and mountain.

Walkers need to be aware of the wider access situation, especially if planning to leave the Way to explore some of the remoter country around it. In the past there has been some conflict between the interests of large sporting estates and walkers. The new access legislation relies on an attitude of co-operation between landowners and those wishing to use the land for peaceful recreation. Hillwalkers therefore have a responsibility to be considerate to those using the land for other purposes such as farming, forestry and field sports. This means following the Scottish Outdoor Access Code (see box p54) and respecting the lambing and deer-stalking seasons (see p55).

For more information see **Scottish Rights of Way Society** (www.scotways.com), a charity that works to develop and protect public rights of way.

❑ The sheep-farmer's year

May – lambing
June – young rams (*tups*) are clipped and dosed against parasites; sheep are gathered to mark lambs; clipping of year-old lambs (*hogs*) and ewes with no lambs
July – ewes with lambs clipped
August – lambs gathered and sold
October – sheep gathered for marking, counting, dosing and dipping against ticks; ewes older than six years are sold; hogs are taken to winter pastures on the east coast
November – tups put out with ewes (three tups per hundred ewes)
January – tups gathered and those older than four or five years sold
February – sheep gathered for dosing
March – sheep dipped; lambing begins
April – hogs return from winter pastures to be dipped and dosed.

Other points to consider on the West Highland Way

- All along the Way there are stiles and kissing gates through boundaries. If you have to climb over a gate which you can't open, always do so at the hinged end.
- Walkers should take special care on country roads. Cars travel dangerously fast on narrow winding lanes. To be safe, walk facing the oncoming traffic and carry a torch or wear highly visible clothing when it's getting dark. Conversely, if you are driving go carefully on country roads and park your car with consideration for others' needs; never block a gateway.

❑ THE SCOTTISH OUTDOOR ACCESS CODE

Scotland has its own 'Countryside code' for those looking to enjoy the outdoors. The full code runs to 67 pages, a copy of which can be found on their website 💻 www.outdooraccess-scotland.com. However, they also publish a brief summary of the code, the main points of which are listed below.

Take personal responsibility for your own actions
You can do this by:
- Caring for your own safety by recognising that the outdoors is a working environment and by taking account of natural hazards;
- Taking special care if you are responsible for children as a parent, teacher or guide to ensure that they enjoy the outdoors responsibly and safely.

Respect people's privacy and peace of mind
- Use a path or track, if there is one, when you are close to a house or garden;
- If there is no path or track, keep a sensible distance from houses and avoid ground that overlooks them from close by;
- Take care not to act in ways which might annoy or alarm people living in a house; and at night, take extra care by keeping away from buildings where people might not be expecting to see anyone and by following paths and tracks.

Help land managers and others to work safely and effectively
You can do this by:
- Following any precautions taken or reasonable recommendations made by the land manager, such as to avoid an area or route when hazardous operations, such as tree felling and crop spraying, are underway;
- Checking to see what alternatives there are, such as neighbouring land, before entering a field of animals;
- Never feeding farm animals;
- Avoiding causing damage to crops by using paths or tracks, by going round the margins of the field, by going on any unsown ground or by considering alternative routes on neighbouring ground; and by leaving all gates as you find them;
- Not hindering a land management operation, by keeping a safe distance and following any reasonable advice from the land manager.

Care for your environment
You can do this by:
- Not intentionally or recklessly disturbing or destroying plants, birds and other animals, or geological features;
- Following any voluntary agreements between land managers and recreation bodies;
- Not damaging or disturbing cultural heritage sites;
- Not causing any pollution and by taking all your litter away with you.

Keep your dog under proper control
- Never let it worry or attack livestock;
- Never take it into a field where there are calves or lambs;
- Keep it on a short lead or under close control in fields with farm animals;
- If cattle react aggressively and move towards you, keep calm, let the dog go and take the shortest, safest route out of the field;
- Keep it on a short lead or under close control during the bird breeding season (usually April to July) in areas such as moorland, forests, grassland and loch shores;
- Pick up and remove any faeces if your dog defecates in a public open place.

● Make no unnecessary noise. Enjoy the peace and solitude of the outdoors by staying in small groups and acting unobtrusively. Avoid noisy and disruptive behaviour which might annoy residents and other visitors and frighten farm animals and wildlife.

Lambing

This takes place from mid March to mid May and is a critical economic time for the hard-pressed hill farmers. Please do not interfere with livestock farming in any way. If a ewe or lamb seems to be in distress contact the nearest farmer. See also pp28-9.

Dogs should be kept off land where sheep are grazing throughout this season so that the pregnant ewes are not disturbed.

Deer-stalking

Large areas of the Highlands have been actively managed for deer shooting, or stalking as it is known, since the 19th century when it became fashionable for the aristocracy and the newly rich industrialists to partake in all forms of field sports. Little has changed today except that the wealthy now come from all over the world and contribute £30 million to the Highland economy every year providing much-needed income for many estates.

Stalking is partly responsible for the deer population spiralling out of control, doubling in number since the early 1960s, which has ironically enabled stalkers to play a more legitimate role in culling the deer. As red deer have no natural predators other than man this is a necessary activity. In addition, no matter what one's ethical stance on the sport may be, while our laws and methods of land ownership remain as they are, alternative means for estates to generate an income, such as conifer plantations, ski developments and the like, would be far worse for both walkers and the environment. Deer stalking is also an important conservation measure; it maintains a healthier herd of deer and aids vegetation recovery and habitat improvement.

Access restrictions during the deer-culling seasons should therefore be respected when walking on land owned by sporting estates and you should try to cause the minimum of disturbance. Stags are culled between July 1st and October 20th, hinds are culled between October 21st and February 15th. Details of access restrictions are usually posted on signs in the vicinity of stalking activities and on the internet at 💻 www.snh.org.uk/hillphones.

Outdoor safety

The West Highland Way is not a particularly difficult or dangerous walk and with common sense, some planning and basic preparation most hazards and hassles can easily be avoided. The information given here is just as valid for walkers out on a day walk as for those walking the entire Way.

AVOIDANCE OF HAZARDS

Always make sure you have suitable **clothes** (see pp37-8) to keep you warm and dry, whatever the conditions, and a spare change of inner clothes. A **compass**, **whistle**, **torch** and **first-aid kit** should also be carried. Take plenty of **food** and **water** (see opposite) with you for the day. You will eat far more walking than you do normally so make sure you have enough, as well as some high-energy snacks, such as chocolate, dried fruit or biscuits, in the bottom of your pack for an emergency. Stay alert and know exactly where you are throughout the day. The easiest way to do this is to **regularly check your position** on the map. If visibility suddenly decreases with mist and cloud, or there is an accident, you will be able to make a sensible decision about what action to take based on your location.

Walking alone

If you are walking alone you must appreciate and be prepared for the increased risk. It is always a good idea to leave word with somebody about where you are going; you can always ring ahead to your accommodation and let them know you are walking alone and what time you expect to arrive. Don't forget to contact whoever you have left word with to let them know you've arrived safely. Carrying a mobile phone can be useful though you cannot rely on getting good reception.

Mountain safety

If you plan to climb any of the mountains along the West Highland Way there are further precautions you need to take. You must always take a **map** and **compass** with you on the Scottish mountains and be able to navigate accurately with them as paths are rare and visibility often poor. In addition to the emergency equipment, food and clothes you would normally carry, you may also want to take a **survival bag**. In summer the temperature on the summits of Scottish mountains can be as much as 12°C lower than in the valley so take an extra warm layer and always pack a **hat** and **gloves**. Gales carrying sleet, hail and snow can blow in with little warning at any time of the year; be prepared.

In **winter** you should not venture onto the hills unless you are a competent mountaineer. The typical Arctic conditions require crampons, ice axe and specialist clothing as well as knowledge of snow conditions, avalanche and cornices.

Mountain guides

If you feel your skills need polishing there are a number of experienced mountain guides and instructors in the region who run courses (and also provide accommodation): **Snowgoose Mountain Centre** (☎ 01397-772467, 💻 www.highland-mountain-guides.co.uk) and **Alan Kimber** (☎ 01397-700451, 💻 www.westcoast-mountainguides.co.uk).

WEATHER FORECASTS

The weather in Scotland can change with incredible speed. At any time of the year you must be prepared for the worst. Most hotels, some B&Bs and TICs will have pinned up somewhere a summary of the **weather forecast**.

Alternatively you can get a forecast through Mountain Weather Information Service 💻 www.mwis.org.uk/wh.php, Winterhighland 💻 www.winterhighland.info) or reports that also take in the whole country: 💻 www.bbc.co.uk/weather, or 💻 www.metoffice.gov.uk.

WATER

You need to drink lots of water while walking; 2-4 litres a day depending on the weather. If you're feeling drained, lethargic or just out of sorts it may well be that you haven't drunk enough. Thirst is not a reliable indicator of how much you should drink. The frequency and colour of your urine is better and the maxim, 'a happy mountaineer always pees clear' is worth following.

Tap water is safe to drink unless a sign specifies otherwise. In upland areas above habitation and away from intensively farmed land walkers have traditionally drunk straight from the stream and many continue to do so with no problems. It must be said, however, that there is a very small but steadily increasing risk of catching giardia from doing this. Just a few years ago this disease was only a threat to travellers in the developing world. As more people travel some are returning to the UK with the disease. If one of these individuals defecates too close to a stream or loch that water source can become infected and the disease transmitted to others who drink from it. If you want to minimise the risk either purify the water using a filter or iodine tablets, or collect water only from a tap.

Far more dangerous to health is drinking from natural water sources in the lowlands. The water may have run off roads, housing or agricultural fields picking up heavy metals, pesticides and other chemical contaminants that we humans liberally use. Such water should not be drunk; find a tap instead.

BLISTERS

You will prevent blisters by wearing worn-in, comfortable boots and looking after your feet; air them at lunchtime, keep them clean and change your socks regularly. If you feel any 'hot spots' on your feet while you are walking, stop immediately and apply a few strips of zinc oxide tape and leave it on until it is pain free or the tape starts to come off.

If you have left it too late and a blister has developed you should surround it with 'moleskin' or any other 'blister kit' to protect it from abrasion. Popping it can lead to infection. If the skin is broken keep the area clean with antiseptic and cover it with a non-adhesive dressing material held in place with tape.

BITES

For the summer-time walker these few bugs are more irritating than dangerous.

Midges

The Gaelic name for this annoying blood-sucker is *meanbh-chuileag* – tiny fly. When you see its diminutive size it's inconceivable to think that it can cause such misery, but it never works alone. The culprits are the pregnant females who critically need a regular supply of fresh blood to develop their eggs. On finding a victim she sends out a chemical invitation to other hungry females and you are soon enveloped in a black gyrating cloud. A single bite would pass unnoticed, but concurrent bites are itchy and occasionally mildly painful.

The key to dealing with this wee beasty is understanding its habits. The main biting season is from June to August, so planning a holiday outside this time obviously makes sense. For many though, this is not an option. It's worth knowing that the midge is also extremely sensitive to light and only comes out when the sun's radiation is below a certain intensity; dawn, dusk, long summer twilight hours and dull overcast days are its favourite hunting times. The message for campers is get into your tent early, get up late and don't camp in conifer forests which can often be dark enough to trigger a feeding frenzy.

The other factor on your side is wind. It only needs a gentle breeze of 5½ mph to keep the midge grounded. Try to camp on raised ground which will catch any hint of a breeze or, if you're walking on a still overcast day, keep moving. The apparent wind created is often enough to keep them away. Insect repellents vary in effectiveness with different brands working for different people. The simplest methods are often the best: long-sleeved shirts, trousers and midge-proof headnets are all worth wearing, preferably in a light colour which the midges find less attractive. Weirdly, Avon Skin So Soft, a moisturising body lotion, has proved to be the most effective repellent against midges and is even now sold in many camping shops along the way.

When all is lost and there is nothing you can do to keep them away, try to seek solace from the final words of George Hendry's fascinating little book, *Midges in Scotland*, '… the Scottish Highlands remain one of the most under-populated landscapes with a timelessness difficult to find anywhere at the start of the twenty-first century … If, as seems likely, the biting midge is a significant factor in limiting our grossest capacities for unsustainable exploitation then this diminutive guardian of the Highlands deserves our lasting respect.'

Ticks

Ticks are small, wingless creatures with eight legs which painlessly bury their heads under your skin to feed on your blood. After a couple of days' feasting they will have grown to about 10mm and drop off. There is a very small risk that they can infect you with **Lyme Disease**. Because of this you should check your body thoroughly after a walk through long grass, heather or bracken; the tick's favoured habitat.

If you find a tick remove it promptly. Use fine point tweezers and grasp the tick where its head pierces your skin; do not squeeze its body. Tug gently and repeatedly until the tick lets go and falls off. Be patient, this will take time. Keep the area clean with disinfectant and over the next month watch for any flu-like symptoms, a spreading rash or lasting irritation at the site of the bite which could indicate Lyme Disease. If any of these symptoms appear see a doctor and let them know you suspect Lyme Disease. It is treatable with antibiotics but the sooner you catch it the easier this will be.

Prevention is always better than cure so wear boots, socks and trousers when walking through or sitting on long grass, heather and bracken.

For further information look up 💻 www.lymediseaseaction.org.uk.

Horseflies and mosquitoes

In July and August **horseflies**, or *clegs*, can be a nuisance on warm bright days. Their bite is painful and may stay inflamed for a few days.

There are several species of **mosquito** in Scotland which tend to bite at night leaving an itchy, painful mark. Insect repellents such as Jungle Formula or Autan may help deter horse flies and mosquitoes but they do not offer a permanent solution. You can take other preventative measures such as wearing a midge net over your head (available from outdoor shops and local village shops throughout the Highlands) and wearing light-coloured clothing: most insects are attracted to dark colours. If you are bitten, rest assured that Scottish mosquitoes and horse flies carry no nasty viruses or diseases. The worst that will happen is that the bite will become itchy and swollen for a day or two. To soothe the affected area, cover it with an antihistamine gel.

Adders

The adder is the only venomous snake present in the British Isles. It is very rare to be bitten by one and deaths are even rarer, although children and pets are more vulnerable. In the unlikely event of a bite you should stay calm and try to move as little as possible to prevent the venom circulating quickly. Send a companion to call for help.

Prevention is better than cure. If you see an adder, give it a wide berth and move on. It will only attack if you provoke it. Adders are active on warm, sunny days, so look out for them in open, grassy areas. See also p74.

HYPOTHERMIA

Also known as exposure, this occurs when the body can't generate enough heat to maintain its normal temperature, usually as a result of being wet, cold, unprotected from the wind, tired and hungry. It is easily avoided by wearing suitable clothing, carrying and eating enough food and drink, being aware of the weather conditions and checking the morale of your companions.

Early signs to watch for are feeling cold and tired with involuntary shivering. Find some shelter as soon as possible and warm the victim up with a hot drink and some chocolate or other high-energy food. If possible give them another warm layer of clothing and allow them to rest until feeling better.

If allowed to worsen, strange behaviour, slurring of speech and poor coordination will become apparent and the victim can quickly progress into unconsciousness, followed by coma and death. Quickly get the victim out of wind and rain improvising a shelter if necessary. Rapid restoration of bodily warmth is essential and best achieved by bare-skin contact: someone should get into the same sleeping bag as the patient, both having stripped to their underwear, with any spare clothing under or over them to build up heat. Send urgently for help.

HYPERTHERMIA

Hyperthermia occurs when the body generates too much heat, eg heat exhaustion and heatstroke. Not ailments that you would normally associate with the Highlands of Scotland, these are serious problems nonetheless.

Symptoms of **heat exhaustion** include thirst, fatigue, giddiness, a rapid pulse, raised body temperature, low urine output and, if not treated, delirium and finally a coma. The best cure is to drink plenty of water.

Heatstroke is more serious. A high body temperature and an absence of sweating are early indications, followed by symptoms similar to hypothermia (see above) such as a lack of coordination, convulsions and coma. Death will follow if treatment is not given instantly. Sponge the victim down, wrap them in wet towels, fan them and get help immediately.

DEALING WITH AN ACCIDENT

- Use basic first aid to treat any injuries to the best of your ability.
- Work out exactly where you are.
- Try to attract the attention of anybody else who may be in the area. The **emergency signal** is six blasts on a whistle, or six flashes with a torch.
- If possible leave someone with the casualty while others go for help. If there is nobody else, you have a dilemma. If you decide to get help leave all spare clothing and food with the casualty.
- Telephone ☎ **999** and ask for the police. They will alert the volunteer mountain rescue team.
- Report the exact position of the casualty and their condition.

THE ENVIRONMENT AND NATURE

3

Introduction

Nature is our medicine. **Henry D Thoreau**

The West Highland Way encompasses the Lowlands and Highlands, passing from wooded glen to high mountain and all manner of habitats in between. This abundance of countryside (97% of Scotland has not been built on) with few people living in it (about eight people per square kilometre in the Highlands) has resulted in a rich variety of wildlife. For the walker interested in the natural environment it is a feast for the senses.

It would take a book several times the size of this to list the thousands of species which you could come across on your walk. A brief description of the more common animals and plants you may encounter as well as some of the more special species for which Scotland is well known is given on pp65-77. If you want to know more refer to the field guides listed on p42.

Conservation issues are also explored on the premise that to really learn about a place you need to know more than the names of all the plants and animals in it. It is just as important to understand the interactions going on between them and man's relationship with this ecological balance.

Conserving Scotland's nature

[Since 1945] the normal landscape dynamics of human adaptation and natural alteration had been replaced by simple destruction. The commonest cause was destruction by modern agriculture; the second, destruction by modern forestry. **Oliver Rackham** *The Illustrated History of the Countryside*

The statistics of how the Scottish land has been treated over the last 70 years do not make comfortable reading. Half of the hedgerows which existed at the end of the Second World War have been pulled up; a quarter of the broadleaved woods have disappeared; a third of heather moorland has been destroyed; half the lowland peat mires have been lost. These are all important habitats for a diverse range of wildlife species. When they are replaced by monocultural conifer

plantations or sheep grassland the rich web of plant and animal life also disappears leaving behind a poor substitute for nature's bounty. The stark results of this destruction are highlighted by the decline in Scotland's farmland birds over the last 35 years. The numbers of skylark, bullfinch and linnet for example have diminished by almost two-thirds, while partridge numbers are down by three-quarters. Species of all kinds have suffered similar fates as habitats continue to be destroyed.

Nature conservation arose tentatively in the middle of the nineteenth century out of concern for wild birds which were being slaughtered to provide feathers for the fashion industry. As commercial exploitation of land has increased over the intervening century so too has the conservation movement. It now has a wide sphere of influence throughout the world and its ethos is upheld by international legislation, government agencies and voluntary organisations.

SCOTTISH NATURAL HERITAGE (SNH)

This is the main government body concerned with the preservation of wildlife and landscape in Scotland. They manage the 65 **National Nature Reserves** (NNRs), of which Loch Lomond is a prime example, to conserve some of the best examples of Scotland's varied habitats. Along with the land owned and managed by voluntary conservation groups there are some 55 local nature reserves across Scotland creating refuges for many endangered species.

However, about 94% of Scottish land is in the hands of foresters and farmers who generally put economic returns above concern for habitat and wildlife. SNH has the difficult job of protecting this land from the grossest forms of damage using a complex array of land designations and statutory mechanisms, all shortened to mind-boggling acronyms.

One of the most important designations and one that covers 12.9% of Scotland is **Site of Special Scientific Interest** (SSSI; there were 1456 at the time of writing). These range in size from those of just a few acres protecting natural treasures such as wild-flower meadows, important nesting sites or a notable geological feature, to vast swathes of upland, moorland and wetland. Owners and occupiers of 'triple S Is' as they are often known, have to abide by strict guidelines and must notify SNH of any proposed actions which would affect the land.

There are 40 areas in Scotland designated as a **National Scenic Area** (NSA). This has provided some recognition for outstanding landscapes such as

❑ Statutory bodies

- **Scottish Natural Heritage** (🖳 www.snh.org.uk) Government body for the conservation and enhancement of Scotland's natural heritage.
- **Forestry Commission** (🖳 www.forestry.gov.uk) Government department for establishing and managing forests for a variety of uses.
- **Association of National Park Authorities** (🖳 www.nationalparks.gov.uk); **Loch Lomond and The Trossachs National Park Authority** (🖳 www.lochlomond-trossachs.org) and **Cairngorms National Park Authority** (🖳 www.cairngorms.co.uk).

❑ **The value of tourism**

In the past land was valued only for the produce or resources which could be taken from it; today a figure can be put on the economic value of the Scottish scenery itself. Tourism generates over £4 billion every year for the Scottish economy and the number one reason given for visiting is 'the scenery'. In a world which increasingly values nothing unless it can be given a monetary figure it is good to know that even the humble walker is playing a part in protecting the landscape by simply being there.

Ben Nevis and Glen Coe, through which the West Highland Way passes. Along with these designations Scotland finally has two **national parks** (see box p67) to call its own in the shape of Loch Lomond and the Trossachs, and the Cairngorms.

These are all encouraging steps but on their own will never provide complete protection. New developments such as roads and housing still get pushed through in so-called protected areas under the guise of being in the public interest and some landowners ignore the designations, and suffer the rather insignificant penalties when it is in their interest to do so. There is still a long way to go before all our land is treated as something more than just an economic resource to be exploited.

CAMPAIGNING AND CONSERVATION ORGANISATIONS

These voluntary organisations started the conservation movement back in the mid-1800s and they are still at the forefront of developments. Independent of government but reliant on public support, they can concentrate their resources either on acquiring land which can then be managed purely for conservation purposes, or on influencing political decision-makers by lobbying and campaigning.

Managers and owners of land include: the **Royal Society for the Protection of Birds** (RSPB, 💻 www.rspb.org.uk/scotland), which manages 150 nature reserves, 44 of which are in Scotland, and is the largest voluntary conservation body in Europe with over a million members; and the **National Trust for Scotland** (💻 www.nts.org.uk) which, with about 300,000 members, is Scotland's largest conservation charity. It protects, through ownership, both countryside and historic buildings.

Lesser known but equally important groups include: the **John Muir Trust** (💻 www.jmt.org) which is dedicated to safeguarding and conserving wild places (the trust owns and manages about 50,000 acres (20,000 hectares) in Skye, Knoydart, Sutherland, Perthshire and Lochaber, including Ben Nevis); **Trees for Life** (💻 www.treesforlife.org.uk), a group committed to the regeneration of the Caledonian Forest (see p70) in the Highlands; **Woodland Trust** (💻 www.woodland-trust.org.uk); **Scottish Wildlife Trust** (💻 www.scottishwildlifetrust.org.uk) which covers all aspects of conservation across Scotland through a network of local groups; and the Scottish branch of **Butterfly Conservation** (💻 www.butterfly-conservation.org/scotland).

Lobbying groups, such as the **Association for the Protection of Rural Scotland** (💻 www.ruralscotland.btck.co.uk) also play a vital role in environmental protection by raising public awareness and occasionally co-operate with government agencies such as SNH when policy needs to be formulated. A huge increase in membership over the last 20 years and a general understanding that environmental issues can't be left to government 'experts' is creating a new and powerful lobbying group; an informed electorate.

BEYOND CONSERVATION

... we are not safe in assuming that we can preserve wildness by making wilderness preserves. Those of us who see that wildness and wilderness need to be preserved are going to have to understand the dependence of these things upon our domestic economy and our domestic behaviour. **Wendell Berry** *Standing on Earth*

The ideas embodied in nature conservation have served us well over the last century. Without the multitude of designations which protect wildlife and landscape there is no doubt that the countryside of Scotland would be far more impoverished than it is today. However, in some respects the creation of nature reserves and other protected areas is an admission that we are not looking after the rest of our environment properly.

If we can't keep the soil, air and water free from contamination or prevent man's activities from affecting the world's climate nature reserves will have little lasting value. Similarly, if decisions made by national government, the European Union (EU) or the World Trade Organisation (WTO) continue to fragment communities and force farmers, foresters and fishermen to adopt unsustainable practices, those who are best placed to protect the land and wildlife end up destroying it. Those who care about Scotland's wildlife and countryside now need to step beyond the narrow focus of conservation. We need to find ways to reconnect with the natural world and relearn how to live in balance with it. This not only demands action on a personal level, for which walking in the wild is surely an ideal tutor, but also a wholesale rethink of the basic assumptions underlying the political and economic policies that created our critical situation in the first place. Wendell Berry in *Standing on Earth* puts it more bluntly:

The wildernesses we are trying to preserve are standing squarely in the way of our present economy, and the wildernesses cannot survive if our economy does not change.

(Opposite) Top: You'll pass numerous isolated patches of Caledonian pine (see p69), such as this one in Glen Falloch. **Bottom left**: Feral goat (see p72), Loch Lomond. (Photo © Lee Miller). **Middle right**: Ptarmigan (see p77) high on the slopes of Ben Nevis. **Bottom right**: One of Britain's more unusual species of flora, the carnivorous sundew plant (see p166). (Photo © Henry Stedman). Another carnivorous plant you may see on the northern section of the walk is the butterwort (photo opposite p65).

Common Dog Violet
Viola riviniana

Honeysuckle
Lonicera periclymemum

Dog Rose
Rosa canina

Self-heal
Prunella vulgaris

Germander Speedwell
Veronica chamaedrys

Herb-Robert
Geranium robertianum

Lousewort
Pedicularis sylvatica

Rowan (tree)
Sorbus aucuparia

Yellow Rattle
Rhinanthus minor

Common Knapweed
Centaurea nigra

Ramsons (Wild Garlic)
Allium ursinum

British Bluebell
Hyacinthoides non-scripta

Marsh Marigold
Caltha palustris

Meadow Buttercup
Ranunculis acris

Gorse
Ulex europaeus

Tormentil
Potentilla erecta

Birdsfoot-trefoil
Lotus corniculatus

Ox-eye Daisy
Leucanthemum vulgare

St John's Wort
Hypericum perforatum

Primrose
Primula vulgaris

Cowslip
Primula veris

Common Ragwort
Senecio jacobaea

Hemp-nettle
Galeopsis speciosa

Cotton Grass
Eriophorum angustifolium

Common Butterwort
Pinguicula vulgaris

Early Purple Orchid
Orchis mascula

Spear Thistle
Cirsium vulgare

Bell Heather
Erica cinerea

Heather (Ling)
Calluna vulgaris

Wood Sorrel
Oxalis acetosella

Rosebay Willowherb
Epilobium angustifolium

Common Vetch
Vicia sativa

Common Fumitory
Fumaria officinalis

Meadow Cranesbill
Geranium pratense

Water Avens
Geum rivale

Red Campion
Silene dioica

Flora and fauna

FLOWERS

Hedgerows

On the southern part of the Way the hedgerows and wood margins along the trail provide the best displays of wild flowers. In early summer look out for the pink flowers of **red campion** (*Silene dioica*), **wood cranesbill** (*Geranium sylvaticum*) and the more fragile **herb robert** (*Geranium robertianum*) along with the bright yellow displays of **creeping** and **meadow buttercup** (*Ranunculus repens* and *R. acris*). In summer **broad-leaved willowherb** (*Epilobium montanum*) and **foxgloves** (*Digitalis purpurea*) make an appearance in hedges and woods while **rosebay willowherb** (*Chamerion angustifolium*) often colonises the sides of footpaths and waste ground.

The tall white-flowering heads of members of the carrot family, such as **sweet cicely** (*Myrrhis odorata*), **cow parsley** (*Anthriscus sylvestris*) and **hogweed** (*Heracleum sphondylium*), are another familiar sight along verges. In the autumn the hedgerows produce their edible harvest of delicious blackberries which can be eaten straight from the thorny **bramble** (*Rubus fruticosus*) and rose-hips of the **dog rose** (*Rosa canina*), best made into a syrup which provides 20 times the vitamin C of oranges.

Grassland

There is much overlap between the hedge/woodland-edge habitat and that of pastures and meadows. You will come across **common birdsfoot-trefoil** (*Lotus corniculatus*), **germander speedwell** (*Veronica chamaedrys*), **tufted** and **bush vetch** (*Vicia cracca* and *V. sepium*) and **meadow vetchling** (*Lathyrus pratensis*) in both.

Often the only species you will see in heavily grazed pastures are the most resilient. The emblem of Scotland, the thistle, is one of these. The three most common species are **creeping thistle**, **spear thistle** and **marsh thistle** (*Cirsium arvense*, *C. vulgare* and *C. palustre*). Among them you may find **common ragwort** (*Senecio jacobaea*), **yarrow** (*Achillea millefolium*), **sheep's** and **common sorrel** (*Rumex acetosella* and *R. acetosa*), and **white** and **red clover** (*Trifolium repens* and *T. pratense*).

Other widespread grassland species include **Scottish bluebell** (*Campanula rotundifolia*), known as harebell in England, delicate yellow **tormentil** (*Potentilla erecta*) which will often spread up onto the lower slopes of mountains along with **devil's-bit scabious** (*Succisa pratensis*). Also keep an eye out for orchids such as the **fragrant orchid** (*Gymnadenia conopsea*) and **early purple orchid** (*Orchis mascula*).

Woodland

Springtime is when the lowland woods are at their best. In birch and oak woods during May and June the floor will be dotted with **primroses** (*Primula vulgaris*),

wood anemones (*Anemone nemorosa*), **dog's mercury** (*Mercurialis perennis*), **lesser celandine** (*Ranunculus ficaria*), **wood sorrel** (*Oxalis acetosella*), **wild hyacinth** (*Hyacinthoides non-scripta*, called bluebell in England), **common** and **small cow-wheat** (*Melapyrum pratense* and *M. sylvaticum*) and **common dog-violets** (*Viola riviniana*).

Moorland

To a fool who cries 'Nothing but heather!' where in September another
Sitting there and resting and gazing around
Sees not only the heather but blaeberries
With bright green leaves and leaves already turned scarlet,
Hiding ripe blue berries; and amongst the sage-green leaves
Of the bog-myrtle the golden flowers of tormentil shining;
And on the small bare places, where the little Blackface sheep
Found grazing, milkworts blue as summer skies;
And down in neglected peat-hags, not worked
Within living memory, sphagnum moss in pastel shades
Of yellow, green and pink; sundew and butterwort
Waiting with wide-open sticky leaves for their tiny winged prey;
And nodding harebells vying in their colour
With the blue butterflies that poise themselves delicately upon them,
And stunted rowan with harsh dry leaves of glorious colour.
'Nothing but heather!' – How marvellously descriptive! And incomplete!

Hugh MacDiarmid *Lucky Poet*

Common **heather** (*Calluna vulgaris*), or ling, is the flower most often associated with the Scottish moors bursting into purple blooms at the end of summer. Its natural habitat is the native pine woods but the regular burning of the moors as part of their management for grouse shooting keeps it regenerating on open ground. **Bell heather** (*Erica cinerea*) has larger flowers and is usually found on dry peaty soils and **cross-leaved heath** (*Erica tetralix*) prefers wetter boggier ground. Other members of the heather family include **blaeberry** (*Vaccinium myrtilis*, called bilberry in England), **bog bilberry** (*V. uliginosum*) and **cow-berry** (*V. vitis-idaea*) which all have edible berries.

In boggy areas such as Rannoch Moor look for **bog myrtle** (*Myrica gale*), **common** and **harestail cottongrass** (*Eriophorum angustifolium* and *E.*

❑ Heather

Heather is an incredibly versatile plant which is put to many uses. It provides fodder for livestock, fuel for fires, an orange dye and material for bedding, thatching roofs, basketwork and brooms. It is still used in place of hops to flavour beer and the flower heads can be brewed to make a good tea. It is said that Robert Burns used to drink such a 'moorland tea' made from heather tops and the dried leaves of blackberry, speedwell, bilberry, thyme and wild strawberry.

Bees are also responsible for heather honey, widely acclaimed the world over. In high summer the heather moorlands are in bloom and the bees will collect pollen exclusively from this source. The result is a much sought-after dark amber honey full of flavour.

❑ Scotland's first national park

Thousands of tired, nerve-shaken, over-civilized people are beginning to find out that going to the mountains is going home; that wildness is a necessity; and that mountain parks and reservations are useful not only as fountains of timber and irrigating rivers, but as fountains of life. **John Muir** *Our National Parks*

Right up to the end of the 20th century Scotland was one of only a handful of countries yet to embrace the concept of national parks. This despite the Scotsman John Muir instigating the first national parks in North America over 100 years ago and England and Wales bowing to pressure from walkers by granting ten national parks in the 1950s. Objectors included both landowners and local planning authorities who view the national park system as unnecessary bureaucracy heaped on top of an already mountainous pile of landscape and wildlife designations. When such places are still threatened, however, it can only be right to grant these outstandingly beautiful areas the highest level of landscape protection available.

Loch Lomond and the Trossachs, through which the West Highland Way passes, was the first national park, opened in 2002 and followed by the **Cairngorms** in 2003. As a result resources are being made available to manage the parks in an integrated way for conservation, quiet recreation and sustainable economic activities.

Many people would like to see the designation extended over a wider area. Surely if Loch Lomond is worthy on the grounds of landscape quality most of the Highlands and Islands of Scotland should also qualify? Perhaps one day this vision of such an extensive national park will become a reality.

vaginatum) and the incredible carnivorous **round-leaved sundew** (*Drosera rotundifolia*) which traps and digests small insects. On drier heaths you can't miss the prickly **whin** (*Ulex europaeus*) bushes, called gorse in England, with their yellow flowers and the similar but spineless bushes of **broom** (*Cytisus scoparius*).

Mountain

If you explore some of the mountains along the way you may come across alpine plants, in particular **starry**, **purple**, **yellow** and **mossy saxifrage** (*Saxifraga stellaris*, *S. oppositifolia*, *S. aizoides* and *S. hypnoides*) whose dramatic name means 'rock-breaker'. Other flowers to look out for are **alpine lady's-mantle** (*Alchemilla alpina*), **trailing azalea** (*Loiseleuria procumbens*) and **northern bedstraw** (*Galium boreale*).

TREES

In the past 500 years we have destroyed over 99 per cent of our equivalent of the rainforests. **David Minns** *The Nature of Scotland*

The woods of Caledon

When the Romans arrived in Scotland almost 2000 years ago they named it Caledonia or 'wooded heights'. By the time Samuel Johnson and James Boswell toured the country in 1773 it was possible to remark, 'A tree might be a show in Scotland as a horse in Venice'. The tree cover which so amazed the

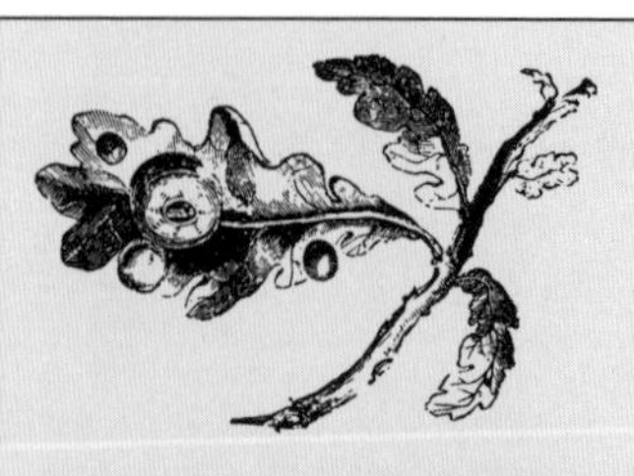

❑ **Oak leaves showing galls**
Oak trees support more kinds of insects than any other tree in Britain and some affect the oak in unusual ways. The eggs of gall-flies cause growths known as galls on the leaves. Each of these contains a single insect. Other kinds of gall-flies lay eggs in stalks or flowers, leading to flower galls, growths the size of currants.

Romans consisted of oak in the lowlands with Scots, or Caledonian, pine in the Highlands. This is still Scotland's natural pattern of woodland and it has existed for 7000 years, since the end of the last Ice Age. However, today less than 1% of the original woods remain.

Before the Romans tree cover had already been much reduced by Neolithic peoples. As the population expanded over the following centuries so the forests continued to shrink as land was converted to agriculture. In more recent times large areas of timber were felled for industry and warfare. However, from the 18th century onwards it was the more subtle processes of sheep grazing and the management of land for field sports that ensured that once the trees were gone they would never return. Overgrazing the land with sheep and deer (which eat young trees) and the burning of heather to maintain the grouse moors have meant that new trees never get established.

Hazel (with flowers)

Indigenous trees on the Way

There are some glorious examples of **oak woodland** on the southern half of the Way, in particular along Loch Lomond. The two native species of oak, the common or pedunculate (*Quercus robur*) and the sessile (*Q. petraea*), grow here along with many hybrids. These woods can't strictly be described as natural as most were planted in the early 19th century but they provide a wonderful home for a wide range of species and offer beautiful walking. Some of the islands in the Loch support semi-natural oak woods with a more random planting pattern, wider age range of trees and consequently more natural diversity. The oak woods are far more diverse than their single species name

Ash (with seeds)

No doubt as **Chalara ash dieback disease** spreads north over the next few years it will also kill many of the ash trees in Scotland. In Denmark, where the disease appears to have originated, up to 90% of the trees have been infected.

would suggest. **Elm** (*Ulmus glabra*), **hazel** (*Corylus avellana*) and **ash** (*Fraxinus excelsior*; see illustration below) intermingle with the oaks on good soil while pioneer species such as **rowan** (*Sorbus aucuparia*), **silver birch** (*Betula pendula*) and **downy birch** (*B. pubescens*) and the much-rarer **aspen** (*Populus tremula*) congregate on poorer soils along with **holly** (*Ilex aquifolium*). Pioneer species play the vital role in a forest ecosystem of improving the soil. In a natural system unaffected by man they would gradually be succeeded by longer-lived species such as oak and Scots pine. Being hardy, brave lone rowans and birches are often to be seen growing in inaccessible ravines or high up on crags where they are safe from sheep and deer. In wet marshy areas and along rivers and streams you will find **alder** (*Alnus glutinosa*).

Birch (with flowers)

Alder (with flowers)

Sadly there is little left of the once-majestic **Caledonian pine** (*Pinus sylvestris*) forests which would have covered so much of Scotland in the distant past. Walkers on the Way will pass numerous isolated patches of these beautiful old trees but nothing that could be described as a forest. Some of the oldest Scots pines in Scotland are over 500 years old, they can grow up to 120ft (36m) high and can have a girth of 12ft (3.6m). They are easily identified by their reddish brown upper trunk and pairs of blue-green needles about 2 inches (5cm) long.

The so-called pinewoods also support **juniper** (*Juniperus communis*), **birch** (*Betula pendula* and *B. pubescens*) and **willow** (*Salix spp.*).

Juniper (with berries)

Conifer plantations

On the face of it the 20th century was a boom time for trees in Scotland. Tree cover leapt from a disastrous 4% at the start of the century to 14% by the end (although still rather poor when compared with other European countries such as France with 27% and Germany with 30%). What these figures disguise is that over 90% of this planting was in conifer plantations; certainly no substitute for oak and Scots pine, and in terms of land use and ecology, about as far removed from the native forests as it is possible to get while still growing trees.

The mass planting of the uplands with conifers was fuelled by the need for a strategic reserve of timber after two world wars. The low quality land in the hills supported marginal sheep farming and was of little value to agriculture. Why not utilise it for growing timber? The Forestry Commission, a government agency funded by the tax payer, needed a tree which grew fast with little management and at low cost. The **Sitka spruce** (*Picea sitchensis*), a native of North America, fitted the bill. Industrial methods of cultivation totally inapplicable to remote parts of the British uplands could be used and soon gangs of contract workers were ploughing up the land behind caterpillar tractors.

The 2000 square miles (3000 sq km) made into forest by the Forestry Commission was substantially added to during the 1970s and '80s when tax arrangements allowed many wealthy private investors to use forestry as a way

❑ Ecological restoration

The Forestry Commission has learnt a few lessons from the past and now has a wider remit to balance timber production alongside environmental and social concerns. Where mature conifers are felled the area is replanted with a wider range of species. This will in time produce more varied habitats for wildlife, be more sympathetic to the landscape and encourage the use of forests for recreation. Good examples of these new-look plantations are the Forest Enterprise managed forests in **Glen Nevis** at the northern end of the trail.

While these new plantations are a slight improvement on what went before they do little to regenerate Scotland's damaged ecosystems. Far more encouraging is the rising interest in a new field of scientific research; that of ecological restoration. If we are to improve the life-carrying capacity of the earth large parts of land which have been severely degraded by man must be restored to their former vitality and diversity. Walkers will see work already underway along the eastern shore of **Loch Lomond** to regenerate the indigenous woodlands. Cashel Forest (see box p122) was just one of over 80 projects throughout the country under the umbrella of the Millennium Forest for Scotland funded largely by the lottery helping to curb the decline of native woodland which at present covers only 1% of Scotland's land area.

In the north of Scotland another ambitious project is being co-ordinated by Trees for Life; their vision is to restore the **Caledonian pine forest** to a 600-square-mile area west of Inverness, between Glen Carron and Glen Moriston. Since 1989 Trees for Life staff and volunteers, with assistance from Forest Enterprise and the National Trust for Scotland, have planted over half a million Scots pine trees in this area. If you would like to get involved with this commendable scheme see p63 for their contact details.

This really is ground-breaking work. Unlike most other projects which have some utilitarian purpose, this is being conducted purely for the sake of restoring the wild forest as a home for wildlife and to perform its true ecological function for the Earth. Although several groups are working to restore the Scots pine forests this is the only one to do so over such a large area. Ultimately restoring such large ecosystems as the Caledonian Forest is the only way to start to reverse man's impact on the planet.

to shelter their earnings. These short-sighted policies produced the eye-sores accurately described as 'blanket forestry'; same-age trees planted close together in neat regimented rows enclosed by miles of straight-running deer-proof fencing. By the time you reach Fort William you will be familiar with these as parts of the Way follow forest rides through such plantations.

The visual impact is almost inconsequential when compared to their **ecological impact**. Thousands of acres of species-rich moorland have been ploughed up and replaced by a monoculture of conifers. With it go birds such as the merlin and golden plover. Once mature the plantations cannot support much wildlife as the close canopy allows little light to penetrate to the forest floor. Nothing else can grow and as a consequence few animals venture into this sterile environment.

As with all monocultures pests easily build up and have to be controlled with chemicals. The deep ploughing and use of heavy machinery damages soil structure and also leads to a higher incidence of flash-floods as drainage patterns are altered. It has also been found that acid rain gets trapped in the trees and is released into the streams during a downpour killing young fish and invertebrates. What's more, the end product from this environmentally damaging land-use is a low-grade timber used mainly for paper, a hideous waste of a valuable raw material. Perversely and misleadingly this is often advertised as 'paper from sustainable forestry'.

Thankfully, now that we have entered the 21st century, even big business is beginning to recognise the importance of conservation and environmentally friendly practices. While there are still many stands of tightly packed sitka spruce across Scotland, the Forestry Commission does now have an active conservation programme (see box opposite) through which they plant native species and leave clear areas, particularly around streams and rivers, to encourage wildlife.

MAMMALS

The animal most frequently associated with the Scottish Highlands is the **red deer** (*Cervus elaphus*), justifiably referred to as 'the monarch of the glen'. This is Britain's largest land mammal and one that most walkers will have a good chance of seeing. They can be found either in their preferred habitat of natural woodland, like that along Loch Lomond, or out on the open hills, a harsh environment to which the red deer has had to adapt since the demise of deciduous woods. Although traditionally a forest dweller you will rarely see deer in the sterile environment of mature conifer plantations. In summer they often move onto windy high ground to avoid midges while in winter they come down into the valley bottoms to find better food.

Male deer (stags) grow beautiful antlers every year. They are discarded in April or May and will be fully regrown by July or August ready for the rut in late September. At this time of year you may hear stags roaring at each other across the glens, the beginning of the competition for mating rights with a harem of hinds (females). If a stag is out-roared he will usually back down and concede his harem to the challenger. Occasionally the competition will move on to the next stage where the stags lock antlers in a battle of strength until one of them submits. Calves are usually born the following June. If they survive their first precarious year, despite the dangers of bad weather and predators such as foxes and golden eagles, they can expect to live for up to 15 years.

Population estimates vary between 300,000 and 750,000; even if the lower figure is the correct one this still represents the highest it's ever been and is felt by many to be jeopardising the ecology of the Highlands. In particular, such high numbers prevent the natural regeneration of many important trees and flowers. This imbalance was caused by man through the eradication of their natural predators, the wolf (the last wolf was killed in 1743), lynx and brown bear, and by maintaining high deer numbers for stalking on sporting estates (see p55). Today's marksmen are trying harder to emulate natural predators by weeding out the old, weak and young and by culling more hinds (as opposed to the traditional target of large healthy stags for trophies) in an attempt to redress the balance.

The red deer is most likely to be confused with the non-native **fallow deer** (*Cervus dama*), which is smaller, much less common and distinguished by prominent white spots on its reddish brown coat. The males have impressive spade-like antlers. Fallow deer are found mainly in deciduous woodland. **Roe deer** (*Capreolus capreolus*) are an even smaller native species, again mainly to be seen in woodland and they can sometimes be identified by their loud bark made when running away.

Other common and familiar mammals include **foxes** (*Vulpes vulpes*), **badgers** (*Meles meles*), **mountain hares** (*Lepus timidus*), **stoats** (*Mustela erminea*), and their smaller relation, the **weasel** (*Mustela nivalis*), **hedgehogs** (*Erinaceus europaeus*), **voles**, **mice** and **shrews**. More unusual are the **feral goats** (*Capra hircus*) living in the caves and woods north of Rowardennan on the eastern shore of Loch Lomond. These are descendants of goats which escaped and became feral during the Highland clearances (see 'Sheep' opposite) in the 18th and 19th centuries.

The Highlands, being relatively unpopulated, are a vital refuge for some key British species which elsewhere have either disappeared altogether or are nearing extinction. The woods and forests, for example, are the last stronghold of Britain's only native squirrel, the **red squirrel** (*Sciurus vulgaris*). Their numbers have fluctuated dramatically over the years, disappearing almost entirely by the mid 1700s due to the clearing of ancient pine forests and epidemics of disease, and then establishing themselves once again in the new conifer plantations. Here this delightful creature exists in moderate numbers and has so far avoided the recent catastrophic decline experienced in much of England. The introduction of the American **grey squirrel** (*Sciurus carolinensis*) at the end of the 19th century is blamed for this demise south of the border and it is only by keeping this species out of Scotland's red squirrel habitats that a similar fate can be avoided. It is one of those conservation paradoxes that the commendable attempts to increase the amount of deciduous woodland in the Highlands may also be aiding the spread of the grey squirrel. Coniferous forests are now having to be managed specifically for red squirrels in order to keep this alien invader out.

❑ Sheep

Sheep have played an important role in shaping the Highlands. Medieval peasant farmers kept them in small numbers alongside goats and black cattle as part of a mixed, semi-communal system of farming. In summer some of the villagers moved the livestock from the low-lying villages up to the higher *shielings* to make the most of the new hill grass. In autumn they returned to harvest the oats in the glen, an annual cycle that existed for centuries.

Things began to change dramatically in the 18th century with the increased commercialisation of farming. New methods of sheep husbandry were developing in the Scottish Borders and prices for wool and mutton were increasing because of the swelling urban population. Lowland shepherds looked to the Highlands for grazing their **Cheviot** and **Blackface** sheep and Highland landlords, eager to make a profit, were happy to rent out the shielings. The peasant farmers were 'encouraged' to move by increased rents and occasionally by force and were given poor land on the coast, called *crofts*, as compensation. When crofting failed to give the expected returns from fishing, seaweed harvesting and marginal farming, thousands of Highlanders emigrated to the cities and to the New World, thus completing the so-called Clearances of the Highlands.

Little has changed today. The Highlands are still sparsely populated and Blackface sheep are the predominant stock on the high moorland. By their selective grazing they have created the vegetation synonymous with the area, encouraging the growth of bracken and coarse grasses and preventing the regeneration of trees. Sheep farming along with tourism is how most people now make a living in the Highland countryside.

The **pine marten** (*Martes martes*) is another rare woodland species which has disappeared from England and Wales but is making a comeback in Scotland. In the 19th and early 20th centuries it suffered relentless persecution from gamekeepers which along with habitat loss and the demise of its favourite food, the red squirrel, took it to the brink of extinction. With more enlightened management on sporting estates and the increased spread of woodland this protected species is now able to re-colonise some of its former territory, such as the wooded banks of Loch Lomond. However, you would be very lucky indeed to catch a glimpse of this elusive creature.

An equally shy and similarly persecuted animal is the **wildcat** (*Felis silvestris*), which is similar in appearance to its domestic cousin. It became extinct from southern England as far back as the 16th century and nearly disappeared altogether from Britain in the early 1900s. Reduced harassment from gamekeepers and increased forestry have allowed it to re-colonise much of Scotland north of the central industrial belt.

The **otter** (*Lutra lutra*), that great symbol of clean water and a healthy environment, is also now thriving in the Western Highlands after a sudden decline in the 1950s and '60s which was caused by a combination of water pollution (in particular by organochlorine pesticides), loss of well-vegetated river banks and hunting by otter hounds. In the Highlands they inhabit river banks and sea lochs as fish are their primary food.

Highland cattle

These domesticated wild-looking shaggy beasts fit perfectly into the dramatic scenery of the Highlands and are uniquely native to Scotland. They are descended from the wild ox, which was living in Scotland before humans, and from the Celtic Shorthorn which was brought to Britain about 5000 years ago. As a result they are well suited to the harsh environment and meagre grazing of the hills. The wealth of the Highlands was based on these cattle until the 17th century. At that time they would have been predominantly black in colour; today the toffee-coloured coat is preferred. You can tell the difference between cows and bulls by the horns: cows' horns are upturned while bulls' turn downwards.

REPTILES

The **adder** (*Vipera berus*) is the only common snake in Scotland and, of the three species which exist in Britain, the only poisonous one. They pose very little risk to walkers and will not bite unless provoked, doing their best to hide. Their venom is designed to kill small mammals such as mice, voles and shrews so deaths in humans are very rare, but a bite can be extremely unpleasant and occasionally dangerous particularly to children and the elderly. You are most likely to encounter them in spring when they come out of hibernation and during the summer when pregnant females warm themselves in the sun. They are easily identified by the striking zigzag pattern on their back. Should you be lucky enough to encounter one of these beautiful creatures enjoy it and leave it undisturbed. See also p59.

BUTTERFLIES

With around 33% of the land but only 10% of the human population, Scotland is ideal country for Britain's butterfly and moth population. A lepidopterist could spend many a happy hour here finding and identifying such seldom-seen species as the **pearl-bordered fritillary**, which is threatened by habitat loss elsewhere in the UK. Other species prevalent in the highlands include the **large heath butterfly**, **mountain ringlet** and **mountain burnet**.

Despite the wide range of species, Scotland's butterflies are still under pressure from habitat loss and the intensive use of farmland. Thankfully, bodies such as **Butterfly Conservation Scotland** (🖳 www.butterfly-conservation.org/scotland) work to preserve habitats for butterflies, moths and other species. To find out more about their work, visit their website where you can also learn how to help with their conservation efforts: they often run surveys on certain species, asking for reports of sightings.

BIRDS

Streams, rivers and lochs

Along lochs and wooded rivers look out for the striking **goosander** (*Mergus merganser*), a sawbill duck which hunts for fish, and the well-known **mallard** (*Anas platyrhynchos*), the ancestor of the farmyard duck. If you are walking in autumn you may catch the evocative sight of **white-fronted** (*Anser albifrons*) and **grey-lag** (*Anser anser*) **geese** flying in from Greenland to over-winter on Loch Lomond. The white-fronted goose is distinguished by the white on the front of its head at the base of the bill. They return north again at the start of spring.

The **grey wagtail** (*Motacilla cinerea*) and the **dipper** (*Cinclus cinclus*) are two delightful birds which can be seen year-round bobbing up and down on boulders along loch shores or in the middle of fast-flowing streams. With its blue-grey head and back and bright-yellow underparts the grey wagtail is the most striking of all the wagtails. The dipper is unmistakable with its dinner-jacket plumage (black back and white bib) and can perform the amazing feat of walking underwater along the bed of streams. They are joined in summer by **common sandpipers** (*Tringa hypoleucos*), a tame long-legged, long-billed wader easily identified by its wagtail-like dipping action.

Woodland

The familiar woodland residents of chaffinches, robins, tits, songthrushes, blackbirds and tawny owls are joined by spring and summer visitors. Tropically bright **redstarts** (*Phoenicurus phoenicurus*), relatives of the robin, spend much time on the ground looking for food, often motionless before suddenly pouncing on insects or worms; acrobatic **pied flycatchers** (*Ficedula hypoleuca*) dart after insects in mid air; rather nondescript brown **tree pipits** (*Anthus trivialis*) perform song flights while darting from one high perch to another; yellow and green **wood warblers** (*Phylloscopus sibilatrix*) restlessly flit around in the woodland canopy along with tiny **willow warblers** (*Phylloscopus trochilus*), those miracles of bird migration who travel 2000 miles at a never faltering speed of 25mph to spend the winter in central Africa.

In hilly woodland these species may be joined by the increasingly rare **black grouse** (*Lyrurus tetrix*). The male blackcock is unmistakable with his blue-black plumage but the female could be confused with the red grouse, though they rarely share the same habitat.

In **pine forests** you will find seed-eating finches such as **siskins** (*Serinus serinus*), **red crossbills** (*Loxia curvirostra*) and **Scottish crossbills** (*Loxia scotica*). The latter is very special indeed as it is found nowhere else but Scotland, the only bird with this distinction. This canary-like bird uses its powerful crossover bill to prise open the tough cones of the Scots pine to extract the seed, its principal food. With few remnants of Caledonian pinewood left in Scotland this unique bird is considered a threatened species with a population of only 1500 birds.

Black Grouse
L: 580mm/23"

The **capercaillie** (*Tetrao urogallus*), the largest game-bird in Britain, is another casualty of scant pinewood habitat. This turkey-like member of the grouse family has suffered a significant decline over the last 30 years from about 40,000 birds down to about 5000. This is not the first time this species has come under attack. In the 18th century the bird was hunted to extinction and those seen in Scotland today originate from Swedish capercaillie used to reintroduce the species in 1837. The capercaillie is regarded as an accurate indicator species, its low numbers alerting us to the decline of mature, varied forests. Some forward-thinking people are well aware of this bleak situation and are already working to restore Scotland's beautiful pinewoods (see box p70). This should bring a brighter future not only for these birds but also for the whole ecology of the Highlands.

Open hillside and moorland

Golden plovers (*Pluvialis apricaria*), **meadow pipits** (*Anthus pratensis*) and **stonechats** (*Saxicola torquata*) are joined in summer by **whinchats** (*Saxicola rubetra*) and **wheatears** (*Oenanthe oenanthe*) out on the open hills. In autumn huge flocks of **redwings** (*Turdus iliacus*) and **fieldfares** (*Turdus pilaris*) fly over from Scandinavia to feed on ripe berries.

STONECHAT
L: 135MM/5.25"

Walkers on heather moorland often put up a covey of **red grouse** (*Lagopus lagopus*) which will speed downwind gliding and whirring just above the ground. This plump copper-coloured bird is highly valued for its sporting potential and is probably best known for its association with the 'Glorious Twelfth', the start of the grouse-shooting season in August, one of those over-hyped British rituals. There is no doubt, however, that if it weren't for grouse shooting we wouldn't have the magnificent upland moors we have today. They would almost certainly have been given over to the green deserts of conifer forests and sheep-grazing.

Birds of prey likely to be seen on moorland include **kestrels** (*Falco tinnunculus*), a small falcon often seen hovering in search of beetles or mice, the much less common **merlin** (*Falco columbarius*), the smallest falcon, which swoops low over the moors twisting and banking as it flies after meadow pipits, and **buzzards** (*Buteo buteo*) which fly in slow wide circles looking for small mammals. Although a large bird, the buzzard is significantly smaller than a golden eagle and can be distinguished by its drawn-out mewing cry.

High mountain

The **golden eagle** (*Aquila chrysaetos*), Britain's largest and most majestic bird of prey, is synonymous with Scotland's mountains and touches the essence of

GOLDEN EAGLE
L: 910MM/36"

wilderness. All 442 breeding pairs of golden eagle live in Scotland. Spiralling upwards on the thermals this huge bird with its seven-foot (2m) wingspan and long open primary feathers couldn't be confused with any other. It feeds mainly on grouse, ptarmigan and mountain hares but won't turn down dead sheep and other carrion.

GOLDEN EAGLE (SILHOUETTE)

As thrilling a sight as the golden eagle is the **peregrine falcon** (*Falco peregrinus*) in flight. This king of the air can reach speeds of 50mph (80km/h) in level flight with swift shallow beats of its long pointed wings interspersed by long glides. But it shows off its true talents when diving after pigeon or grouse, its principal prey, sometimes reaching an incredible 180mph (290km/h). In the 1950s the population of peregrines dropped suddenly and disastrously. During this crisis Scotland held the only healthy population of peregrines in the world. The species was probably saved by the RSPB's and British Trust for Ornithology's painstaking research which linked the decline to the use of pesticides, in particular dieldrin and DDT. These chemicals were being used by farmers to treat their grain which was then ingested by seed-eating birds who in turn were eaten by peregrines. The revival of the species is one of the great success stories of modern conservation.

Above 2000ft (600m) you are likely to see fearless **ptarmigan** (*Lagopus mutus*), a cousin of the red grouse, scurrying across the ground in front of you. In winter its grey speckled plumage turns to pure white except for a black tail. **Snow buntings** (*Plectrophenax nivalis*), looking like pale sparrows, occasionally nest in the high mountains but most arrive in the winter migration from the Arctic.

RAVEN
L: 650MM/25"

Also haunting these heights are jet black **ravens** (*Corvus corax*), a massive crow with a powerful beak which soars at great speed across the sky occasionally rolling onto its back with half-folded wings as if to prove its mastery of flight.

4

Glasgow

City guide

Everyone walking the West Highland Way really should take a few days at the beginning or end of their walk to spend some time in this the best of all Scottish cities, once known as the 'Second City of the Empire'. The recession has hit the city hard but in summer 2014 the city hosts the Commonwealth Games, giving it a welcome boost in investment and employment.

Glasgow's a fascinating and lively place, populated by some of the friendliest people in the country. Here you'll find some of the top museums and art galleries in Britain including the inspiring new **Riverside Museum**, designed by Zaha Hadid; the fabulous **Burrell Collection**; numerous shrines to the world-famous architect and designer, **Charles Rennie Mackintosh**; interesting museums such as **The Tenement House**, an early 20th-century time capsule, and the award-winning **St Mungo's Museum of Religious Life & Art**; the gothic **Glasgow Cathedral**; top-class **restaurants**, vibrant **nightlife** and a lively **arts scene**.

En route to or from the West Highland Way you'll be coming through the city anyway but ideally you should plan your holiday so that you have time both to spend a few days here and to do the half-day walk from Glasgow to Milngavie, rather than simply take the train (or a bus) to the start of the West Highland Way.

ORIENTATION

The centre of the city is on the north side of the River Clyde, with the M8 motorway sweeping across the north and through the west. The two main railway stations and bus station are in the centre. The two main accommodation areas we've given details about are just north of the main shopping street, Sauchiehall, and west of the M8 in the Kelvingrove area. The main commercial area is Merchant City and around George Square. Milngavie (see p100) and the start of the West Highland Way are 10 miles north-west of the centre.

ARRIVAL AND DEPARTURE

Glasgow airport (🖳 www.glasgowairport.com) is nine miles west of the city. First's Glasgow Shuttle bus service (🖳 www.first group.com/ukbus/glasgow) No 500 leaves (24 hours a day; 2-6/hr;

❑ A brief history of Glasgow

Glasgow dates back to the founding of the first cathedral and shrine to St Mungo in about 1125. The cathedral was constructed on the spot where Mungo was said to have built a wooden church in the 6th century.

Glasgow grew first as a place of pilgrimage to St Mungo but by the 18th century it had become a major centre for international commerce, handling much of the tobacco trade between Europe and America. This trade helped to finance the growth of local industries including textiles, shipbuilding, ironworks and coal-mining. In the mid-19th century there were 140 cotton mills in the Glasgow area and the shipyards accounted for more than 80% of all vessels built in Britain. The city's heyday came in the second half of the 19th century when many of the grand Victorian buildings you can see today were constructed. By the mid-20th century these industries were in decline and there was widespread unemployment.

In the ensuing decades Glasgow coped remarkably well with the loss of its heavy industries, many jobs having been created in service industries. Parts of the city and suburbs, however, are still depressed and not helped by the current recession. Tourism is now an important revenue earner; Glasgow is one of the most-visited cities in Britain.

approx 25 mins; £6/8.50 sgl/rtn within 28 days) from Stance 1 outside the main terminal building for the city centre and railway and bus stations. A taxi costs around £22 depending on the time of day.

Note that some budget airlines use **Prestwick airport** (💻 www.glasgowprestwick.com), 29 miles to the west of the city. There are trains from here to Central station (2-3/hr; 50 mins; approx £7.40/9.60 sgl/rtn) as well as a bus service (Stagecoach's X77; £5.20/9.90 sgl/rtn; or the X99/X100 for early morning/late evening services; £10 sgl; approx 50 mins) to **Buchanan St bus station**, two blocks north of Queen St station, which is the terminus for both local and national bus and coach services.

There are two main railway stations: **Central station** for Milngavie, south Scotland and the rest of Britain, and **Queen St station** also for Milngavie and for north and east Scotland. A shuttle bus (No 398; 3-6/hr) links the two, continuing to the bus station; if you have a connecting rail ticket there's no charge to use it. It only takes about 15 minutes to walk, though.

GETTING AROUND – AND TO MILNGAVIE

For information on public transport in and around Glasgow visit one of Strathclyde Public Transport's (SPT) travel centres at Buchanan bus station, Glasgow airport, or either St Enoch or Hillhead subway stations. Alternatively look at SPT's website (💻 www.spt.co.uk) or contact Traveline Scotland (☎ 0871-200 2233, national rate call, 💻 www.travelinescotland.com).

Subway

The Glasgow Subway (💻 www.spt.co.uk/subway) operates a circular route around the city. A single/return ticket costs £1.40/2.60 and a **10-journey ticket** costs £12; a **Discovery ticket** (£3.80) gives unlimited travel on the system for a day but you can't use it before 9am Monday to Friday.

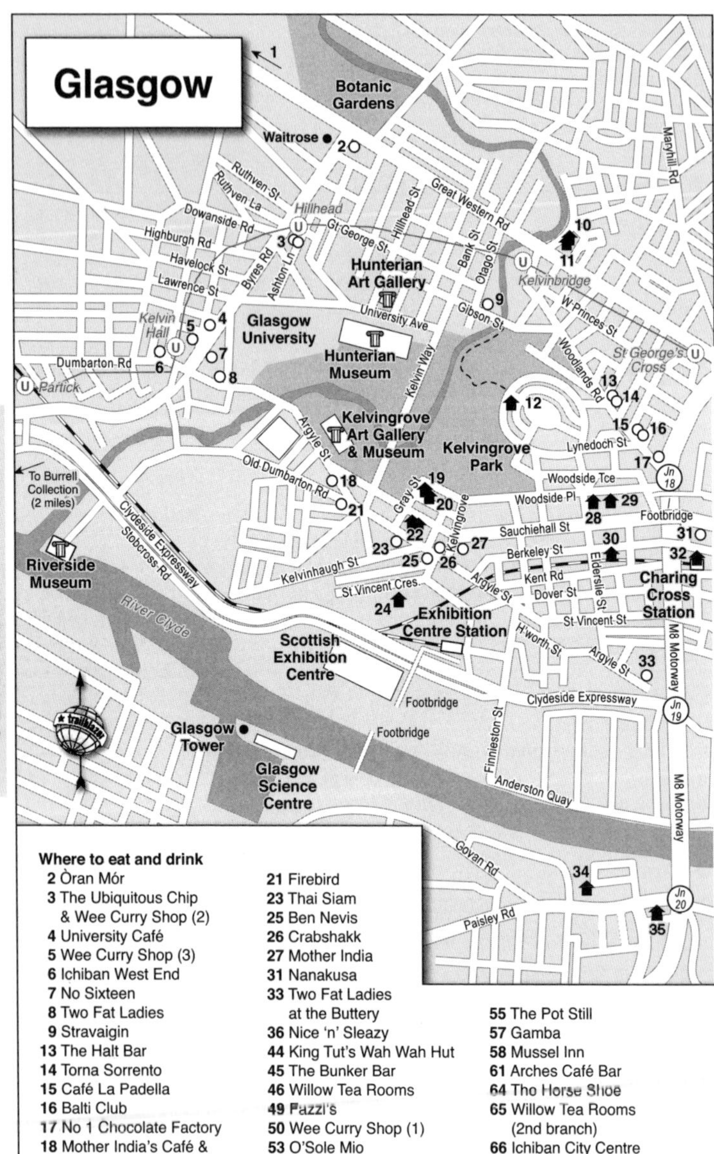
Glasgow
1
Botanic Gardens
Waitrose
2
Ruthven St
Ruthven La
Hillhead
Dowanside Rd
Highburgh Rd
Havelock St
Lawrence St
Byres Rd
Ashton Ln
Gt George St
Hillhead St
Great Western Rd
Bank St
Otago St
10
11
Kelvinbridge
3
Hunterian Art Gallery
University Ave
Gibson St
9
W Princes St
Kelvin Hall
4
5
Glasgow University
Hunterian Museum
Kelvin Way
Woodlands Rd
St George's Cross
Dumbarton Rd
6
7
8
Partick
13
14
12
Argyle St
Kelvingrove Art Gallery & Museum
Kelvingrove Park
15
16
Lynedoch St
17
Jn 18
To Burrell Collection (2 miles)
Old Dumbarton Rd
18
19
Woodside Tce
21
Gray St
20
Kelvingrove
Woodside Pl
28
29
Footbridge
22
Sauchiehall St
30
31
Clydeside Expressway
Stobcross Rd
23
27
Berkeley St
32
Riverside Museum
Kelvinhaugh St
25
26
Kent Rd
Elderslie St
Charing Cross Station
St Vincent Cres
Argyle St
Dover St
River Clyde
24
Exhibition Centre Station
St Vincent St
Scottish Exhibition Centre
H'worth St
Argyle St
33
M8 Motorway
Footbridge
Clydeside Expressway
Jn 19
Glasgow Tower
Footbridge
Finnieston St
trailblazer
Glasgow Science Centre
Anderston Quay
M8 Motorway
Govan Rd
34
Paisley Rd
Jn 20
35
Where to eat and drink
2 Òran Mór
3 The Ubiquitous Chip & Wee Curry Shop (2)
4 University Café
5 Wee Curry Shop (3)
6 Ichiban West End
7 No Sixteen
8 Two Fat Ladies
9 Stravaigin
13 The Halt Bar
14 Torna Sorrento
15 Café La Padella
16 Balti Club
17 No 1 Chocolate Factory
18 Mother India's Café & Dining In with Mother India
21 Firebird
23 Thai Siam
25 Ben Nevis
26 Crabshakk
27 Mother India
31 Nanakusa
33 Two Fat Ladies at the Buttery
36 Nice 'n' Sleazy
44 King Tut's Wah Wah Hut
45 The Bunker Bar
46 Willow Tea Rooms
49 Fazzi's
50 Wee Curry Shop (1)
53 O'Sole Mio
54 Café Wander
55 The Pot Still
57 Gamba
58 Mussel Inn
61 Arches Café Bar
64 The Horse Shoe
65 Willow Tea Rooms (2nd branch)
66 Ichiban City Centre
68 Cossachok

Where to stay

1 To Hotel du Vin One Devonshire Gardens (¾ mile off map)
10 Albion Hotel
11 Amadeus Guest House
12 Glasgow Youth Hostel
19 Alamo Guest House
20 Beersbridge Lodge
22 Argyll Guest House & Smiths Hotel
24 The Flower House
28 Acorn Hotel
29 15 Glasgow
30 Blue Sky Hostel
32 Premier Inn Charing Cross
34 Ibis Budget Glasgow
35 Travelodge Paisley Road
37 McLays
38 Margaret Macdonald House
39 Willow Hotel
40 Rennie Mackintosh Art School Hotel
41 Old School House
42 Ibis Glasgow City Centre
43 Malmaison
47 Travelodge Glasgow Central
48 easyHotel Glasgow
51 citizenM
52 Premier Inn Buchanan Galleries
59 Hotel Indigo Glasgow
60 Premier Inn Argyle Street
62 Rennie Mackintosh Station Hotel
67 Euro Hostel
69 Premier Inn George Square
70 Campus Village

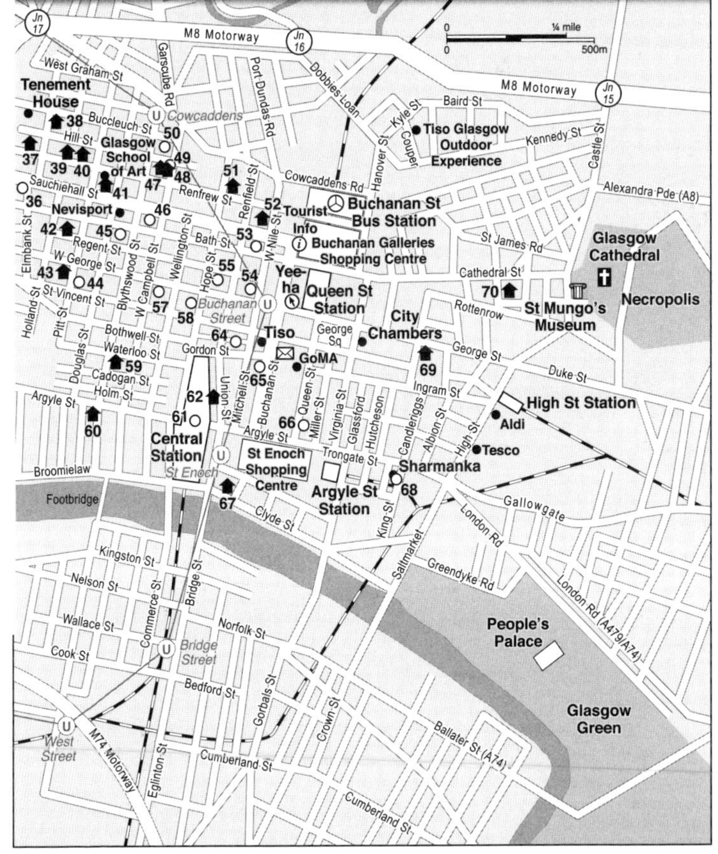

Bus

There's a good bus service around the city; tickets for short/long journeys cost £1.15/1.85. Pay the driver as you board. First Glasgow's **All Day ticket** allows a day's travel on all its buses for £4.50; coverage includes the journey to Milngavie.

Taxi

If you're in a small group it may be worth taking a taxi (☎ 0141-429 7070, 💻 glasgowtaxis.co.uk. From Central station it should cost £8-9 to the Youth Hostel and £16-18 to Milngavie.

To and from Milngavie

The quickest way to Milngavie is by **train**. Direct services **from Central station** (£3.10; 24-30 mins) leave twice an hour between about 7am and 11.30pm/midnight, Monday to Saturday, and on Sunday between about 9am and 11pm. You can also take a train **from Queen St** station (note that the trains depart from the platforms that are below ground level) but this may require a change; connections are good, though, with a wait of only a few minutes.

First Group (Greater Glasgow) **bus** No 119 (Mon-Sat 1-3/hr, Sun 1/hr) operates between Buchanan St bus station and Milngavie (Craigton Rd). The journey takes roughly 40 minutes with the first bus leaving around 7am (Mon-Sat) and around 9am (Sun). The last bus leaves between 11pm and midnight (daily). You can also jump on First South East and Central Scotland's C10/10/10A service or the infrequent C8/8: the first service leaves Glasgow at around 7am (Mon-Fri), 9am (Sat) or 11am (Sun). Both services go to Milngavie Station. See also pp44-8 for further details.

SERVICES

Tourist information

Glasgow tourist information centre (☎ 0141-204 4400, 💻 www.seeglasgow.com; Mon-Sat 9am-6pm, Sun Sep to July noon-4pm, July & Aug 9am-5pm), has moved from George Square to 170 Buchanan St. It has information on all parts of Scotland as well as the city. There's a giftshop and an accommodation-booking service (£4 fee; 10% deposit required but this is then deducted from the final bill.)

Post office

The main, or at least most central, post office (Mon-Sat 9am-5.30pm) is on Vincent St, two blocks west of George Sq. In addition to the usual services there is a **bureau de change** here.

Internet access

Many restaurants and coffee shops have free wi-fi now, as do hotels. If you need an internet café, **Yeeha** (☎ 0141-332 6543, 💻 www.yeeha-internet-cafe.co.uk, 48 West George St; Mon-Fri 9.30am-7pm, Sat 10am-6pm, Sun noon-6pm; £1.25/15 mins, £2.50/1hr; cash only) is near the bus station on Buchanan St.

Left luggage
Left-luggage facilities are available at both of Glasgow's mainline railway stations and at Buchanan St bus station. This can be really useful if you've time to kill in Glasgow but aren't staying overnight. The charge is around £5-7 per day.

Outdoor equipment shops
There are several outdoor equipment shops for any last-minute purchases you need to make before setting off into the wilds. The most exciting is **Tiso Glasgow Outdoor Experience** (☎ 0141-559 5450; Mon, Tue, Fri, Sat 9am-6pm; Wed 9.30am-6pm; Thur 9am-7pm; Sun 10am-5pm) north-east of Buchanan St bus station on Couper St, just off Kyle St. This is a mountain-sports superstore like no other complete with 40ft climbing wall, a 20ft dry-tooling wall, a good ***café*** and a 300ft simulated mountain footpath! In the city centre **Tiso** have a more conventional store on Buchanan St. **Nevisport** is on Sauchiehall St.

FESTIVALS & EVENTS

The main festivals include: **Glasgow Film Festival** (🖳 www.glasgowfilm.org/festival), in mid February; **Glasgow Music Festival** (🖳 www.glasgowmusicfestival.org), which opens on the first Saturday in March; a **comedy festival** (🖳 www.glasgowcomedyfestival.com) in the same month; the Notting-Hill-Festival-like **West End Festival** (🖳 www.westendfestival.co.uk) in June; and a **jazz festival** (🖳 www.jazzfest.co.uk), usually in late June.

Accommodation may be a little hard to come by during these periods so make sure you book well in advance – or avoid these weekends altogether. Note that the **Commonwealth Games** (🖳 www.glasgow2014.com) will be held here in 2014 (late July/early August) when accommodation will be at a premium.

WHERE TO STAY

Budget accommodation
Glasgow has an excellent choice of budget accommodation. For 18-35 year olds only, ***Blue Sky Hostel*** (☎ 0141-221 1710, 🖳 www.blueskyhostel.com, 65 Berkeley St; 48 beds plus 20 beds in their annex; WI-FI) is a well-located self-catering backpackers' hostel. It's a scruffy but friendly place with an average of 6-8 beds in a dorm (£11.50-25pp). They also have a double/twin room and a twin/triple room (£25-30 per room for up to two sharing, £32-45 for three) and a triple/quad (£30-48). Rates include free internet access and the hostel also has a Jacuzzi. It's a popular place so you need to book well in advance. They claim there are 50 pubs within a five-minute walk of the hostel.

If you're only in Glasgow overnight the soulless ***Euro Hostel*** (☎ 0141-222 2828, 🖳 www.euro-hostels.co.uk, 318 Clyde St; 364 beds; all en suite; WI-FI), in a high-rise building overlooking the River Clyde, is very convenient for the rail and bus stations. Their dorms are modern and they have single rooms (£20-60), twin rooms (£12-24pp) and up to 14-bed dorms (£10-20pp); the rate includes a continental breakfast. Discounts (10%) are available for students with an ISIC card or bookings made through Facebook.

If you're visiting in the summer another place worth trying close to the city centre is ***Margaret Macdonald House*** (☎ 0141-331 1261, 💻 www.gsa.ac.uk/visit-gsa/vacation-accommodation/; 89 Buccleuch St). For most of the year this houses students from Glasgow School of Art (GSA) but from July to mid September rooms are let to visitors on a self-catering basis. All rooms are single and cost from £19 if you share a bathroom with one other person, or from £25pp for an en suite room. They also own ***Old School House*** (same contacts as above), a more traditional building, on Renfrew St and still within the GSA campus with singles, twins and doubles, all en suite, with rates starting at £25pp.

High up on Park Terrace overlooking the leafy expanse of Kelvingrove Park is the spacious and traditional ***Glasgow Youth Hostel*** (☎ 0141-332 3004, 💻 www.syha.org.uk/hostels-in-scotland/lowlands/glasgow.aspx, 8 Park Terrace; 141 beds, one single, seven 2-bed and 4-bed, eleven 6-bed, three 8-bed, all en suite; WI-FI on the ground floor; £14-32pp). The hostel is licensed and meals are available. It also has internet access (£1 for an hour). If you're staying here consider taking the train to Partick station (on the line to Milngavie) since it is marginally closer to the Youth Hostel than Central station. Also, if you're planning to walk the whole way from Glasgow to Fort William, the route to Milngavie described on pp95-8 begins from Kelvingrove Park – right outside your door if you're staying here.

GLASGOW CITY GUIDE

Budget chain hotels

The quality of cheaper guesthouses and B&Bs can be very variable making the budget hotel chains a reliable option if you book online far enough in advance to get one of their special deals.

From £29 for a room ***Premier Inn*** (central reservations ☎ 0871-527 9222, 💻 www.premierinn.com) is particularly recommended for their comfortable beds and good rooms. They have four central hotels: ***Charing Cross*** (10 Elmbank Gardens), ***George Square*** (187 George St), ***Argyle Street*** (377 Argyle St) and ***Buchanan Galleries*** (St Andrew House, 141 West Nile St). A full cooked breakfast costs £8.25 (£5.25 for a light breakfast).

Another chain offering reliable cheap accommodation is Ibis. Again, to get good prices you must book online well in advance. ***Ibis Glasgow City Centre*** (☎ 0141-619 9000, 💻 www.ibis.com; 220 West Regent St; 141D or T; WI-FI free in lobby/restaurant; 🐕 £10) has rooms from £29; breakfast is £7.95. South of the river and with rooms from £22, ***Ibis Budget Hotel Glasgow*** (☎ 0141-429 8013, 💻 www.ibis.com, 2a Springfield Quay; 165D, T or F; WI-FI free in lobby/café; 🐕 £3) is clean and functional with a range of rooms some including doubles with a bunk bed. Continental buffet breakfast is £4.25.

Less good but sometimes offering even more attractive online deals (£19 for a room), ***Travelodge*** (💻 www.travelodge.co.uk – reserve online rather than phoning the expensive numbers below) has two hotels in Glasgow. ***Travelodge Glasgow Central*** (☎ 0871-984 6141, 5 Hill St; 95D or F; ♥; WI-FI free in bar/café, £5/hr in rooms; 🐕 £20) is the better located but you should check that the long-term building works nearby have finished; ***Travelodge Glasgow Paisley Road*** (☎ 0871-984 6142, 251 Paisley Rd; 75D or F; ♥; WI-FI £5/hr;

> ❑ **Prices and room types**
> The number and type of rooms are given after the address of each entry: S = single room, T = twin room (two beds), D = double room (one double bed), F = family room (sleeps at least three people). Rates quoted are either per person (pp) or per room. Rooms have bathrooms attached (en suite) unless shared facilities are mentioned.
> The text also indicates whether the premises have **wi-fi** (WI-FI); if a **bath** is available (🛁) in at least one room; and whether **dogs** (🐕) are welcome.

🐕 £20) is just south of the river, half a mile from Central railway station. A buffet breakfast at either branch is £7.95pp.

Another budget chain operator offering well-located accommodation is easyHotel. Their ***easyHotel Glasgow*** (online reservations only: 💻 www.easyhotel.com, 1 Hill St; 83D/35T; WI-FI £3/hr) has functional rooms from £25. As with easyJet, it's those extras that add up – a TV is £5, WI-FI costs from £3 and if you check out after 10am they may bill you for another night.

B&Bs and mid-range hotels

Worth listing for its size and range of rooms, ***McLays*** (☎ 0141-332 4796, 💻 www.mclays.com, 260-76 Renfrew St; 21S/61D, T or F; some share facilities; 🛁; WI-FI in public areas; £24-32.50pp, sgl £21-42, £60-120 for a family room) is a large, rambling place that's very well located. It could do with a tidy but it's fine and reasonably priced.

On the same street is the more upmarket ***Rennie Mackintosh Art School Hotel*** (☎ 0141-333 9992, 💻 www.renniemackintoshartschoolhotel.co.uk, 218-20 Renfrew St; 11S/9T/3D/1F; WI-FI; £34-44pp, sgl £34-50, family room £100) which uses the obvious Glasgow theme but the effect is pleasing. There's another branch near Central station: ***Rennie Mackintosh Station Hotel*** (☎ 0141-221 0050, 💻 www.renniemackintoshstationhotel.co.uk, 59 Union St; 14S/12T/ 12D/ 3F; 🛁; WI-FI in lounge and bar; £30-45pp, sgl £49-70, family room £75-109).

Amadeus Guest House (☎ 0141-339 8257, 💻 www.amadeusguesthouse.co.uk, 411 North Woodside Rd; 3S/2D/4T or F; two singles share facilities; 🛁; WI-FI; 26-29pp, sgl £30-40, family room £70-88) is a popular place to stay and justifiably so, not just for the experience of breakfast with Mozart!

Nearby is ***Albion Hotel*** (☎ 0141-339 8620, 💻 www.glasgowhotelsandapartments.co.uk/albion, 405 North Woodside Rd; 6S/11D, T or F; WI-FI; £31-41pp, sgl £46-56, family room £78-98).

Willow Hotel (☎ 0141-332 2332, 💻 www.willowhotelglasgow.com, 228 Renfrew St; 11S/3T/8D/17F; WI-FI; £22.50-30pp, sgl £30-35, family room £75) is cheap and well located but nothing special. ***Smiths Hotel*** (☎ 0141-339 6363, 💻 www.smiths-hotel.com, 963 Sauchiehall St; 15S/8T/8D/11F; some share facilities; WI-FI; £20-26pp, sgl £21-36, family room £48-69) is similarly basic. It's near Kelvingrove Park so is convenient if you're walking from Glasgow to Milngavie. Nearby, you could try ***Argyll Guest House*** (☎ 0141-357 5155, 💻 www.argyllguesthouseglasgow.co.uk, 970 Sauchiehall St; 3S/17D, T or F; 🛁;

WI-FI; £30pp, sgl £40-45) or ***Beersbridge Lodge Guesthouse*** (☎ 0141-338 6666, 🖳 www.beersbridgelodge.hostel.com, 50 Bentinck St; 2T/5D/2F; WI-FI; £12-22.50pp, sgl occ £20-30, family room £60), which serves a continental breakfast.

Alamo Guest House (☎ 0141-339 2395, 🖳 www.alamoguesthouse.com, 46 Gray St; 1S/1T/1D or T/6D/2T or F; some share facilities; ☕; WI-FI; £35-59pp, sgl £49, sgl occ £99, family room £99-155) also has a suite (£125-149) with a 42" LCD TV. Note that in the peak season there is a minimum two-night stay policy. In the same area is ***Acorn Hotel*** (☎ 0141-332 6556, 🖳 www.acorn-hotel.com, 140 Elderslie St; 5S/2T/11D; WI-FI; £30-42.50pp, sgl £45-65) which has a computer that guests can use.

From mid June to mid September the **University of Strathclyde** (☎ 0141-553 4148, 🖳 www.rescat.strath.ac.uk/accommodation.html, 50 Richmond St) has B&B accommodation in many of their halls of residence buildings such as ***Campus Village (John Anderson Campus)***, on Cathedral St, a 5- to 10-minute walk from Buchanan St bus station. It has over 500 single rooms costing £27.60/39.60pp for a standard/en suite (with breakfast £32.70/42).

The Flower House (☎ 0141-204 2846, 🖳 www.scotland2000.com/flower house, 33 St Vincent Crescent; 1S/1T/2D; ☕; WI-FI; £30pp, sgl £40-45) is also recommended, not least for the stunning floral displays around the main entrance.

GLASGOW CITY GUIDE

Upmarket & boutique hotels

15 Glasgow (☎ 0141-332 1263, 🖳 15glasgow.com, 15 Woodside Place; 5D; ☕; WI-FI; £99-180) is a luxurious boutique B&B with super king-sized beds and monsoon showers, close to Kelvingrove Park. At the weekends there is a two-night stay policy.

Hotel Indigo Glasgow (☎ 0871-423 4942, www.ichotelsgroup.com/hotelindigo, 75 Waterloo St; 94D or T; ☕; WI-FI; from £93) is a clever conversion of the beautiful old power station, perfectly located in the centre of the city. They have a wide range of packages and the hotel is part of the Intercontinental chain.

citizenM (online booking only: 🖳 www.citizenm.com, 60 Renfrew St; 198D; WI-FI; £70-140) claims to be the trendiest hotel in Glasgow and probably is. The rooms have large comfortable beds, mood lighting and free movies on demand.

Stylish ***Malmaison*** (☎ 0141-572 1000, 🖳 www.malmaison-glasgow.com, 278 West George St; 10T/62D; ☕; WI-FI; 🐕 £10; about £85pp, sgl occ full room rate) is housed in a former Episcopal church. At times they have special offers so it is worth checking with them.

Five-star ***Hotel du Vin One Devonshire Gardens*** (☎ 0141-339 2001, 🖳 www.hotelduvin.com/locations/glasgow/; 8D or T/32D/9D or F; ☕, WI-FI; 🐕 £10; £75-255pp, sgl occ from £109), on Gt Western Rd, occupies five townhouses.

WHERE TO EAT AND DRINK

There's no shortage of places to eat in Glasgow, everything from the usual chain restaurants to more exciting culinary ventures.

Scottish

You'll find haggis, tatties and neeps on almost every menu but modern Scottish cuisine goes far beyond that.

No Sixteen (☎ 0141-339 2544, 💻 number16.co.uk, 16 Byres Rd; Mon-Sat noon-2.30pm & 5.30-10pm, Sun 1-3pm & 5.30-9.30pm) is a small restaurant with a large reputation. They offer a 2-/3-course lunch menu (£11.95/14.95; Mon-Sat noon-2.30pm, Sun 1-3pm) and a pre-theatre menu (£13.95/16.95, Mon-Thur 5.30-7pm, Fri 5.30-6.30pm) featuring dishes such as Vietnamese fish broth with rice noodles, mussels and whiting.

Stravaigin (☎ 0141-334 2665, 💻 www.stravaigin.com, 28 Gibson St; café-bar food served Mon-Fri 9am-1am, Sat & Sun from 11am, restaurant daily 5-11pm, also Sat noon-5pm, Sun 12.30-4pm) produces top-notch fare that's probably best described as Scottish fusion food and the T-shirts and signs proclaim 'Think global, eat local'. Best value is their lunch menu (£11.95/14.95 two/three courses; Mon-Fri noon-5pm, Sat 11am-5pm); there's also a pre/post theatre menu (£13.95/15.95 two/three courses; 5-6.30pm & 10-11pm). You could have anything from a full Scottish breakfast to Nasi Goreng at their popular Sunday Brunch (from 11am), washed down with a Bloody Mary, of course!

The Ubiquitous Chip (☎ 0141-334 5007, 💻 www.ubiquitouschip.co.uk, 12 Ashton Lane; daily 11am-1am, food served Mon-Sat noon-2.30pm & 5.30-11pm, Sat & Sun 12.30-3pm & 5-11pm) is just off Byres Rd and is a Glasgow institution, open for more than 40 years. There is a bar menu, a brasserie menu and a restaurant menu. How does grilled haunch of Carsphairn roe deer, chocolate crumb, 'hot pot' potatoes, caraway and rosemary salsa sound? Main dishes cost £24 to £35 but there are set lunches from £15.95.

Fish

Crabshakk (☎ 0141-334 6127, 💻 www.crabshakk.com, 1114 Argyll St; Tue-Sat 11am to midnight, Sun noon to midnight) is tiny but excellent and you'll need to book. Shellfish chowder is £7.50, fish & chips is £9.95, crab claws are £12.50, oysters are £10.95 for half a dozen and half a lobster costs £24. Highly recommended and there's a great pub (Ben Nevis) opposite for a drink beforehand.

Mussel Inn (☎ 0141-572 1405, 💻 www.mussel-inn.com, 157 Hope St; Mon-Thur noon-2.30pm & 5-10pm, Fri-Sat noon-10pm, Sun 5-10pm) does tasty kilo pots of mussels (from £10.30) with crusty bread to soak up the juices. There's also shellfish pasta for £15.25 and queen scallops (12 for £15.50).

For a celebratory dinner it would be hard to beat ***Two Fat Ladies at the Buttery*** (☎ 0141-221 8188, 💻 twofatladiesrestaurant.com, 652 Argyle St; Mon-Sat noon-3pm & 5.30-10.30pm, Sun noon-9pm), though you might not think it from the location near the M8. Two/three courses cost £14.50/15.50 at lunch and pre/post theatre; a main dish in the evening is around £20. The original branch, ***Two Fat Ladies West End*** (☎ 0141-339 1944, 🖳 twofatladiesrestaurant.com, 88 Dumbarton Rd; Mon-Sat noon-3pm & 5.30-10.30pm, Sun 1-9pm) is less grand and cheaper but still recommended.

Gamba (☎ 0141-572 0899, 🖳 www.gamba.co.uk; 225 West George St; Mon-Sat noon-2.15pm & 5-10pm, Sun 5-9pm) is another top-class fish restaurant. Main dishes cost from £16.50 (eg roast sea bream) to £26 (lobster thermidor). They also set menus such as a three course lunch and dinner for £25.

World cuisines

Balti Club (☎ 0141-332 5495, 🖳 www.balticlub.co.uk, 66 Woodlands Rd; Mon-Wed 4.30pm to midnight, Thur-Sun 4.30pm-4am) is a take-away that does everything from balti (£7.25) to burgers (from £2.50) and has been running for years.

The best pizza in Glasgow is said to be at ***Firebird*** (☎ 0141-334 0594, 🖳 www.firebirdglasgow.com; 1321 Argyle St; daily noon-10.30pm), a large popular bistro with a mixed menu including soup and sandwich combos (£9) for lunch and wood-fired pizza from £9.

Torna Sorrento (☎ 0141-332 2288, 148 Woodlands Rd; Tue-Sat noon-2.30pm & 5.30-9.30pm, Sun 5.30-9.30pm) is run by a truly Italian family serving up good unpretentious traditional dishes; pasta dishes cost £7.50-12. More contemporary in style is ***Fazzi's*** (☎ 0141-332 5815, 🖳 www.fazzi-restaurant.co.uk, 65 Cambridge St; Mon-Sat 9am-9pm, Sun 11am to late), with pizza from £7.45 and pasta from £6.70. There's also ***O' Sole Mio*** (☎ 0141-331 1397, 🖳 www.osolemio-glasgow.com; 32-4 Bath St; daily 11am-10.30pm), which has a wood-fired pizza oven; pizzas cost from £7.50 and pasta from £8.25.

Café La Padella (☎ 0141-332 6104, 124 Woodlands Rd; Mon-Thur 9am-9pm, Fri & Sat to 10pm, Sun to 8pm) is an organic Turkish restaurant with tasty dishes such as stuffed aubergines (£5.50) and spicy meatballs (£6.50).

Ichiban Sushi & Noodle Café (🖳 ichiban.co.uk) has two branches. ***Ichiban West End*** (☎ 0141-334 9222) is at 184 Dumbarton Rd and ***Ichiban City Centre*** (☎ 0141-204 4200) is in the heart of the city at 50 Queen St. Both are open the same hours (Mon-Thur noon-10pm, Fri & Sat noon-11pm, Sun 1-10pm) and offer excellent-value dishes for £8-9. There's a range of noodles (soba, udon or ramen) as well as tempura and sushi. There is a lunch menu (£4.95 or £7.50) and service is swift.

For a greater range of Japanese cuisine, visit the well-reviewed ***Nanakusa*** (☎ 0141-332 6303, 🖳 www.nanakusa.co.uk, 441 Sauchiehall St; Mon-Thur noon-2.30pm & 5-11pm, Fri & Sat noon-midnight, Sun 5-11pm), a Japanese grill restaurant that serves sushi, sashimi, noodles and yakitori. There's a set lunch for £5.95 and bento boxes from £10.90 to £14.90.

There's excellent borscht at ***Cossachok*** (☎ 0141-553 0733, 🖳 www.cossachok.com; 10 King St; Tue-Sat 11am-11pm, Sun 4-11pm), the Russian café-gallery near Sharmanka (see p92), and you can follow this with blinis, an Uzbek lamb pilaf or beef Stroganoff. Main dishes are around £8.95 and there's a tempting range of vodkas.

For good Thai food, ***Thai Siam*** (☎ 0141-229 1191, 🖳 www.thaisiamglasgow.com, 1191 Argyle St; Mon-Sat noon-2.30pm & 5-10.30pm; Sun 5-10.30pm) is popular; try the monkfish curry (£16.90).

There are numerous Indian restaurants. ***Mother India*** (☎ 0141-221 1663, 🖳 www.motherindiaglasgow.co.uk, 28 Westminster Tce; Mon-Thur 5.30-10.30pm, Fri & Sat noon-11pm, Sun noon-10pm) is probably the best. It's a large place with a variety of dining options and good vegetarian choices. Main dishes range from vegetable karahi at £7.50 to slow-cooked roast leg of lamb with almond sauce, rice and breads (£28 for two people). In the same family is ***Mother India's Café*** (☎ 0141-339 9145, 🖳 www.motherindiaglasgow.co.uk, 1355 Argyle St; Mon-Thur noon-10.30pm, Fri & Sat noon-11pm, Sun noon-10pm) which is based on a clever concept – it's an Indian tapas bar. You order four to five dishes (£3.95-5.95 each) for every two people in your party and share them. You can't book but service is rapid and the food excellent. The empire is spreading and next door is ***Dining in with Mother India*** (☎ 0141-334 3815, 1347 Argyle St open similar hours), a restaurant and deli.

Highly-recommended is the ***Wee Curry Shop*** (☎ 0141-353 0777, 🖳 www.weecurryshopglasgow.co.uk, 7 Buccleuch St; Mon-Sat noon-2.30pm, Mon-Thur 5.30-10pm, Fri & Sat to 10.30pm, Sun 5.30-10.30pm), three blocks north of Sauchiehall St. Because it's so small you should certainly book ahead. Main dishes cost £5.90-11.85. There's a second branch at 29 Ashton Lane (☎ 0141-357 5280; Mon-Tue noon-2.30pm & 5-11pm, Wed-Sat noon-11pm, Sun 1-10.30pm), opposite The Ubiquitous Chip, and a third at 41 Byres Rd (☎ 0141-339 1339; Tue-Thur noon-2.30pm & 5.30-10pm, Fri & Sat noon-2pm & 5-10.30pm, Sun 5.30-10.30pm).

Cafés

University Café (☎ 0141-339 5217, 87 Byres Rd; Mon-Thur & Sun 9am-10pm, Fri & Sat to 10.30pm), like the Ubiquitous Chip, is a Glasgow institution and has been running since 1918. It's very popular and serves incredibly cheap traditional café fare such as burgers, from £2.15, and has an adjoining chip shop. Don't miss the wonderful ice-cream made by the Italian family who run the café. Cones from £1.30.

In the heart of the action ***Café Wander*** (☎ 0141-353 3968, 🖳 www.cafewander.com; Mon-Fri 7.30am-5pm, Sat 9am-5pm), on West George St, is a basement café serving an imaginative variety of dishes from delicious smoothies (from £2.55) to scrumptious porridge with apple and cinnamon (£3.30).

No 1 Chocolate Factory (☎ 0141-353 6017, 🖳 www.1chocolatefactory.com, 63 St Georges Rd; daily 8am-8pm) is a combined café, chocolate shop and 'children's entertainment centre'. The wee bairns can get messy in a securely-segregated chocolate workshop while the parents tuck into a cup of almost solid chocolate (£3) and a salad or panini.

Arches Café Bar (☎ 0141-565 1035, 🖳 www.thearches.co.uk; 253 Argyle St; Mon-Sat 11am to late, Sun noon to late, food served till 8.45pm) is more of a bistro than a café, but it serves imaginative dishes, such as smoked haddock risotto, that are excellent value (£6.50 at lunchtime); evening mains are slightly pricier but still good value (£8.95-14.95). It's located by the south entrance to Central station.

Tearooms

The Mackintosh connection means that a visit to a tearoom seems an integral part of a visit to Glasgow. In 1878 Kate Cranston opened the first of what was to become a little chain of city tearooms. She employed local artists and architects such as George Walton and Charles Rennie Mackintosh to design some of them. Most famous is the ***Willow Tea Rooms*** (☎ 0141-332 0521, 🖳 www.willowtearooms.co.uk, 217 Sauchiehall St; Mon-Sat 9am-4.30pm, Sun 11am-4.15pm); though closed in 1928 it has been faithfully recreated and reopened – complete with those uncomfortable high-backed Mackintosh chairs. It's a popular place; queues can be long. In addition to teas (afternoon tea £12.75) they do delicious all-day breakfasts such as scrambled egg and smoked salmon (£6.95). There's **another branch** with the same menu, opening hours and décor at 97 Buchanan St (☎ 0141-204 5242).

Bars, pubs and pub food

Kelvinside parish church has undergone an astonishing transformation into a very popular entertainment venue known as ***Òran Mór*** (☎ 0141-357 6200, 🖳 www.oran-mor.co.uk, top of Byres Rd/Great Western Rd; daily 9am to at least 2am) with a range of bars, restaurants, music and theatre venues.

A more traditional drinking place is ***The Pot Still*** (🖳 www.thepotstill.co.uk, 154 Hope St; Mon-Sat 11am-midnight, Sun 6pm-midnight), which boasts several hundred single malts. ***The Halt Bar*** (☎ 0141-353 6450, 160 Woodlands Rd; Mon-Thur 11am-11pm, Fri-Sat 11am-midnight, Sun 12.30pm-midnight) is another traditional pub. There's live music on Tuesdays. Near Central Station, ***The Horse Shoe*** (🖳 www.horseshoebar.co.uk) is famous as the place to go for a pie and a pint at lunchtime.

Opposite Crabshakk at 1147 Argyle St, ***Ben Nevis*** (🖳 thebennevis.co.uk), is a very pleasant place for a wee dram.

While there are fewer traditional pubs around than there once were, there's no shortage of stylish bars, particularly along Hope St, Bath St, Sauchiehall St and Byres Rd. ***The Bunker Bar*** (🖳 www.thebunkerbar.com; Mon-Wed noon-1am, Thur to 2am, Fri & Sat to 3am, Sun 12.30pm-1am; food noon-9pm, from 12.30pm on Sunday), on Bath St, gets raucous by night but by day it's a good spot for lunch with soup for £4, chilli con carne for £7.50 and burgers from £7.95.

Nice 'n' Sleazy (🖳 www.nicensleazy.com, 421 Sauchiehall St; daily 12.30pm-3am) has an excellent juke box, good-value food (burgers and fries from £4.95), which is served daily 12.30-9pm, and is the place to plug into Glasgow's alternative music scene.

There's also a good selection of bar food (Mon-Sat noon-8pm, show day Sun 5-8pm) at long-running ***King Tut's Wah Wah Hut*** (☎ 0141-221 5279, 🖳 www.kingtuts.co.uk, 272a St Vincent St; Mon-Sat noon-midnight, Sun 6pm-midnight); it is still a great place for live rock music.

WHAT TO SEE AND DO

Glasgow Cathedral

(🖳 www.glasgowcathedral.org.uk; Apr-Sep Mon-Sat 9.30am-5.30pm, Sun 1-5pm, Oct-Mar Mon-Sat 9.30am-4.30pm, Sun 1-4.30pm; services Sun 11am & 4pm; no admission charge but a donation is requested) This is the only medieval cathedral on the Scottish mainland to have survived the Reformation and it's an excellent example of the Gothic style. Much of the current building dates from the 13th century; the original cathedral was built in about 1125 as a shrine to Mungo, the 6th-century priest who later became the city's patron saint. His remains still lie here; in the Middle Ages they were the focus of thousands of pilgrims each year.

When money became available in the 1990s for renovations the bishop sensibly spent it not on sandblasting the smoke-stained exterior but on a new central heating system. The immense blackened mass of the cathedral with the grand memorials of the **Necropolis** rising up on the hill behind only add to the wonderful Gothic effect. The best view of this is from the top floor of nearby St Mungo's Museum.

St Mungo's Museum of Religious Life & Art

(🖳 www.glasgowlife.org.uk, click on museums, 2 Castle St; Tue-Thur & Sat 10am-5pm, Fri & Sun 11am-5pm; admission free) Right opposite the cathedral and another attraction you should not miss, this museum was opened in the early 1990s. In addition to the galleries devoted to Religious Life and Religious Art (covering the world's main religions), there is one outlining the history of religion in Scotland, as well as a Zen garden.

Riverside Museum

(🖳 www.glasgowlife.org.uk; Clydeside Expressway; Tue-Thur & Sat 10am-5pm, Fri & Sun 11am-5pm; admission free) This wonderful modern building was designed by Zaha Hadid and opened in 2011. The fact that it is a museum of transport should not put you off if cars and trains aren't your thing, as the exhibits are cleverly displayed and the building itself is spectacular. Zaha Hadid is the architect who designed the Aquatics Centre for the 2012 Olympics. Glasgow has a long and distinguished history of building ships and trains and a rather less distinguished history of building cars (the Albion and the Hillman Imp, for example).

People's Palace

(🖳 www.glasgowlife.org.uk; Glasgow Green; Tue-Thur & Sat 10am-5pm, Fri & Sun 11am-5pm; admission free) Set in the park known as Glasgow Green this museum tells the story of Glasgow and its impact on the world as the 'Second City of the Empire'. It's attached to the Winter Gardens (daily 10am-5pm), a vast Victorian glasshouse filled with tropical plants and a convenient tea garden.

Sharmanka

(☎ 0141-552 7080, 💻 www.sharmanka.com, Trongate 103; short show Wed-Sun 3pm, £5; full show Thur & Sun 7pm, £8) This unforgettable performance of Russian mechanical carved figures is, quite simply, unique. It was created by Eduard Bersudsky and Tatyana Jakovskaya who moved to Glasgow from St Petersburg in 1996. The themes are very Russian: 'the human spirit struggling against the relentless circles of life and death' and there are literary influences such as Bulgakov's *The Master and Margarita*. A magical 45 (or 70) minutes of jingly-jangly Russian madness.

Since they sometimes close to go on tour it is always worth checking their website or contacting them in advance to check details.

Mackintoshiana

The Art Nouveau designs of Charles Rennie Mackintosh are almost a cliché but he is Scotland's most famous architect and designer and many of the buildings he designed are in Glasgow – and well worth seeing. Born in 1868 he studied at Glasgow School of Art and later won a competition to design its new building.

Glasgow School of Art (💻 www.gsa.ac.uk, 167 Renfrew St; shop daily mid Jun to mid Sep 9.30am-6.30pm, rest of year daily 10/10.30am-5pm, tours mid June to mid Sep 10am-5pm 10/day, rest of year 11am, 1pm & 3pm; building tours £8.75/7 adult/concessions) is regarded as his greatest achievement. Since places on the tour of the building are limited booking in advance is recommended, especially in the summer; for further information and to check details call the shop (☎ 0141-353 4526); it is also possible to book online (💻 www.gsa.ac.uk/tours). In the summer they offer guided walking tours: one tour covers Mackintosh and his contemporaries; and the other post industrial, ie more recent art and architecture. Tours last 2¾ hours and cost £24.50/concessions £19.50. Phone for details.

In the **Hunterian Art Gallery** (💻 www.gla.ac.uk/hunterian; Tue-Sat 10am-5pm, Sun 11am-4pm; admission free, charge for special exhibitions) you can see an extensive collection of Mackintosh's work as well as reconstructed rooms from Mackintosh's own house (tours lasting 30 mins operate up to 4pm). Follow your visit to the art gallery with sustenance at one of the branches of the **Willow Tea Rooms** (see p90), which were reconstructed using Mackintosh designs.

The Tenement House

(☎ 0844-493 2197, 💻 www.nts.org.uk/Property/59, 145 Buccleuch St; Mar-Oct daily 1-5pm, last entry 4.30pm, £6.50, free to National Trust members) Don't miss this little time capsule which is just a short walk north of Sauchiehall St. Tenements were four- or five-storey buildings arranged around a square that provided a communal space for the flats, some only a room or two, within the buildings. This is how many Glaswegians lived in the first half of the 20th century. What is fascinating about this rather more upmarket flat that comprised several rooms and even a bathroom, is that the last owner, Agnes Toward, changed little in all the time she was here, from 1911 to 1965. There are still gas lights, snug bed closets by the fireplace and Izal-medicated lavatory paper in the loo.

Burrell Collection

(💻 www.glasgowlife.org.uk, click on museums; Pollok Country Park; Mon-Thur & Sat 10am-5pm, from 11am Fri & Sun; admission free) Set in a park this is one of Britain's top art galleries. It's notable partly because it's a very personal collection: about 8000 objects assembled by Sir William Burrell (1861-1958), the Glasgow shipping magnate; and partly for the way these items are displayed: in a modern, purpose-built gallery that allows the light and views of the surrounding park to stream in.

The Burrell Collection is a ten-minute walk into the park; you can reach the park by train (from Central station to Pollokshaws West). It's also on First's bus routes Nos 35, 45 and 57 from the city centre; services stop on Pollokshaws Rd opposite the main entrance to the park.

Other things to see

Gallery of Modern Art (GoMA) (☎ 0141-287 3050, 💻 www.glasgowlife.org.uk/museums; Mon-Wed 10am-5pm, from 11am Fri & Sun, until 8pm on Thurs; admission free), housed in a beautiful former library, is well worth a visit with pieces from Turner nominees and changing exhibitions.

Kelvingrove Art Gallery & Museum (💻 www.glasgowlife.org.uk/museums; Mon-Thur & Sat 10am-5pm, from 11am Fri & Sun; admission free) is the most popular free tourist attraction in the country, bringing in over a million people a year. The art gallery is strong on 19th- and 20th-century works, particularly those by Scottish artists. One of the benefits of the gallery's recent massive restoration was that it can now display about 8000 items. However, there are about 200,000 historical objects in the building.

Glasgow Science Centre (☎ 0141-420 5000, 💻 www.glasgowsciencecentre.org; Apr-Oct daily 10am-5pm, Nov-Mar Wed-Fri 10am-3pm, Sat & Sun 10am-5pm; £9.95/7.95 adult/concessions) has a Science Mall with interactive displays and an IMAX cinema. Beside it is the 127m, rotating **Glasgow Tower**, the tallest free-standing structure in Scotland; on a clear day there are superb views over the city and up towards Loch Lomond and the route of the West Highland Way. However, at the time of research it was closed for maintenance and renovation and it was not certain when it would reopen. Contact the Science Centre for the latest information.

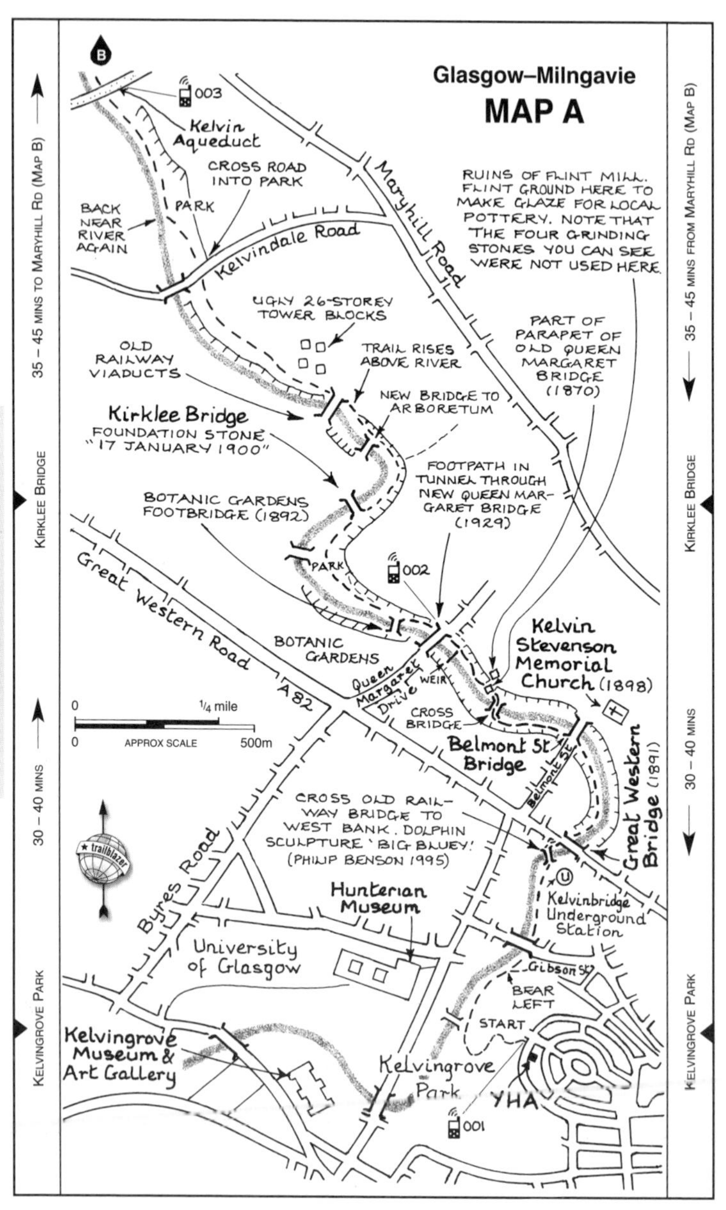

GLASGOW TO MILNGAVIE

Walking from Glasgow to Milngavie

Walking from Glasgow to Milngavie is highly recommended for two reasons. First, being only 10 miles (16km) in length and easy walking on the flat – it takes **3¼-4hrs** (walking time only; see box p99) – it's a good way to warm up for the longer days ahead. Second, it's a great walk in its own right: not tramping along busy streets as you might expect but following the River Kelvin through parks before emerging into fields beyond the city. Two miles before Milngavie the Kelvin is joined by another river, Allander Water, which you follow to reach the official start of the West Highland Way. The route is well signposted following two official footpaths, the Kelvin Walkway and the Allander Walkway.

There's nowhere right on the route to get food and drink so it's best to **take water and lunch with you**. On the Kelvingrove Park to Maryhill section, however, since you are walking through the city you could leave the trail and climb up to one of the many bridges you pass beneath to get back into the city but this would rather detract from the serenity of the walk. Alternatively, a short distance off the Maryhill to Milngavie section, two miles from Milngavie, the ***Tickled Trout*** pub (Map C, p97; ☎ 01360-621968, 🖳 www.vintageinn.co.uk/thetickledtroutbearsden) is open Monday to Saturday 11am-11pm (food served noon-10pm) and Sunday 12.30-9.30pm (food served throughout).

ROUTE OVERVIEW

The best place to start is in Kelvingrove Park: the Kelvin Walkway runs right through it. Some of the places to stay in Glasgow are within walking distance of the park; alternatively take the subway to Kelvinbridge station.

Kelvingrove Park to Maryhill [Map A, Map B, p96]

This section is just under 3½ miles (5.5km, 1¼-1½hrs) and an easy walk all along the River Kelvin as it winds through the city. For most of the time, however, you won't be aware of the fact that you're in an urban landscape as the city is often high above the river and you're insulated from it by thick tree cover.

In **Kelvingrove Park**, follow the path along the east bank of the river and you'll go under a bridge (Gibson St) as you leave the park. You then reach the site of the former Kelvinbridge Railway Station with the current **Kelvinbridge underground station** nearby. The route now crosses to the west bank of the river for the next half-mile and a very peaceful wooded stretch of walking beside the slow-flowing river with the bustling city 50ft above you. It then returns to the east bank and the ruins of a **flint mill**.

After a further two miles of walking along the river you leave it along a side road (Dalsholm Rd, Map B) to emerge onto Maryhill Rd and the suburbs of

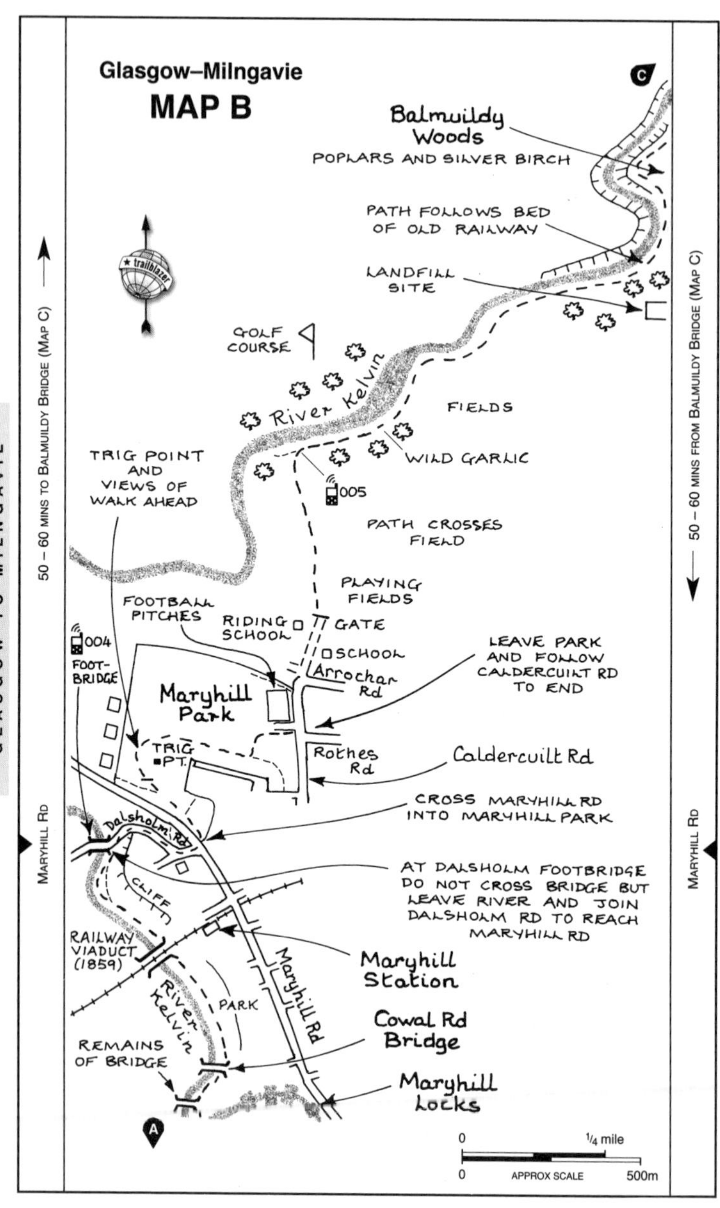
Glasgow–Milngavie
MAP B
Balmuildy Woods
POPLARS AND SILVER BIRCH
PATH FOLLOWS BED OF OLD RAILWAY
LANDFILL SITE
GOLF COURSE
River Kelvin
FIELDS
WILD GARLIC
005
PATH CROSSES FIELD
PLAYING FIELDS
TRIG POINT AND VIEWS OF WALK AHEAD
FOOTBALL PITCHES
RIDING SCHOOL
GATE
SCHOOL
004
FOOT-BRIDGE
Arrochar Rd
LEAVE PARK AND FOLLOW CALDERCUILT RD TO END
Maryhill Park
TRIG PT.
Rothes Rd
Caldercuilt Rd
CROSS MARYHILL RD INTO MARYHILL PARK
Dalsholm Rd
CLIFF
AT DALSHOLM FOOTBRIDGE DO NOT CROSS BRIDGE BUT LEAVE RIVER AND JOIN DALSHOLM RD TO REACH MARYHILL RD
RAILWAY VIADUCT (1859)
Maryhill Station
River Kelvin
PARK
Maryhill Rd
Cowal Rd Bridge
REMAINS OF BRIDGE
Maryhill Locks
0 1/4 mile
0 APPROX SCALE 500m
50 – 60 MINS TO BALMUILDY BRIDGE (MAP C)
50 – 60 MINS FROM BALMUILDY BRIDGE (MAP C)
MARYHILL RD
MARYHILL RD

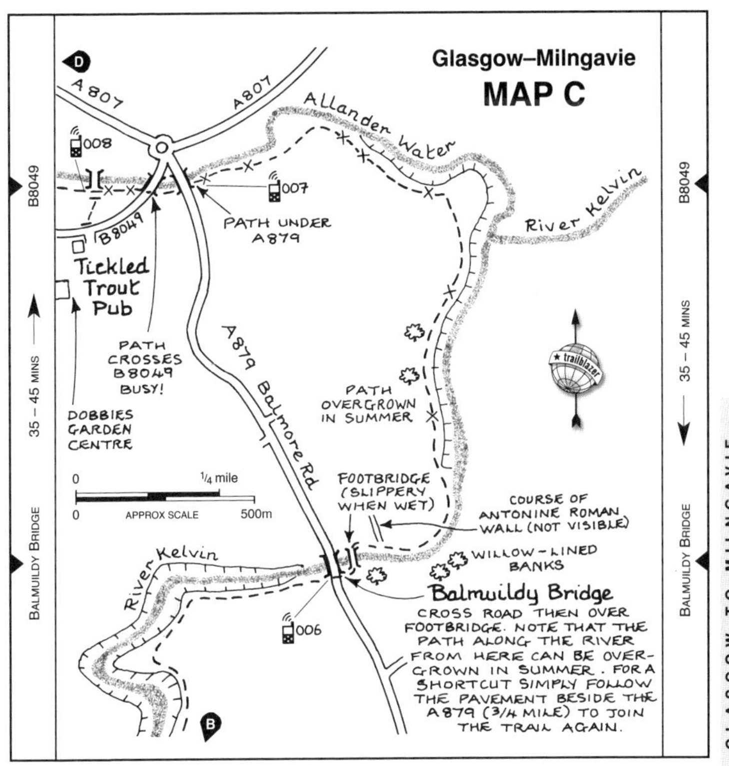

Glasgow. **Maryhill Station** is to the right but you continue ahead, crossing Maryhill Rd and entering Maryhill Park.

Maryhill to Milngavie [Map B; Map C; Map D, p98]

This is the countryside section of the walk. It's just over 6½ miles long (10.5km, 2-2½hrs) and also easy walking.

From Maryhill Park there are views of the walk ahead and the last views of Glasgow. Leaving the park and passing through a field you rejoin the path along the River Kelvin. After 1½ miles following the river you reach Balmuildy Bridge and the A879 (Map C). Depending on the time of year, the riverside trail can be fairly overgrown. If this was the case between Maryhill and Balmuildy Bridge you can be sure that the next section will be even more overgrown. If it's also raining you may want to keep your boots and legs dry and take the short-cut along the A879 (20-25 mins) to join Allander Water, which you follow almost all the way into Milngavie.

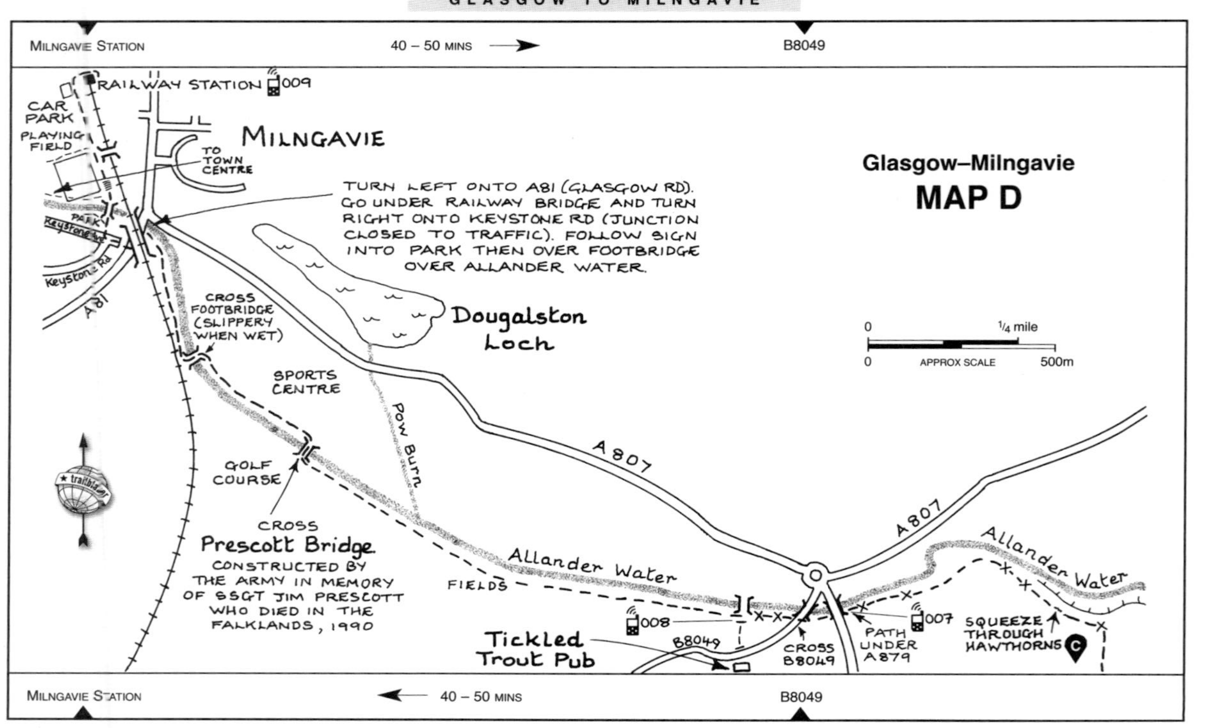
GLASGOW TO MILNGAVIE
MILNGAVIE STATION
40 – 50 MINS
B8049
RAILWAY STATION
009
CAR PARK
PLAYING FIELD
MILNGAVIE
TO TOWN CENTRE
PARK
Keystone Rd
Keystone Rd
A81
TURN LEFT ONTO A81 (GLASGOW RD). GO UNDER RAILWAY BRIDGE AND TURN RIGHT ONTO KEYSTONE RD (JUNCTION CLOSED TO TRAFFIC). FOLLOW SIGN INTO PARK THEN OVER FOOTBRIDGE OVER ALLANDER WATER.
Glasgow–Milngavie
MAP D
0 1/4 mile
0 APPROX SCALE 500m
Dougalston Loch
CROSS FOOTBRIDGE (SLIPPERY WHEN WET)
SPORTS CENTRE
Pow Burn
A807
GOLF COURSE
CROSS
Prescott Bridge
CONSTRUCTED BY THE ARMY IN MEMORY OF SSGT JIM PRESCOTT WHO DIED IN THE FALKLANDS, 1990
Allander Water
FIELDS
A807
Allander Water
008
B8049
Tickled Trout Pub
CROSS B8049
PATH UNDER A879
007
SQUEEZE THROUGH HAWTHORNS
C
MILNGAVIE STATION
40 – 50 MINS
B8049

ROUTE GUIDE & MAPS 5

Using this guide

The trail guide and maps have not been divided into rigid daily stages since people walk at different speeds and have different interests. The **route summaries** describe the trail between significant places and are written as if walking the Way from south to north.

To enable you to plan your own itinerary, **practical information** is presented clearly on the trail maps. This includes walking times for both directions, waypoints (see pp195-7 for full list), all places to stay, camp and eat, as well as shops where you can buy supplies. Further service **details** are given in the text under the entry for each place.

For **map profiles** see the colour pages at the end of the book. For a condensed overview of this information see 'Itineraries' pp30-5 and the village and town facilities table on p31.

TRAIL MAPS

Scale and walking times [see map key, p192]

The trail maps are to a scale of 1:20,000 (1cm = 200m; 3 1/8 inches = one mile). Walking times are given along the side of each map and the arrow shows the direction to which the time refers. The black triangles indicate the points between which the times have been taken. **See box below on walking times**.

The time-bars are a tool and are not there to judge your walking ability; there are so many variables that affect walking speed, from the weather conditions to how many beers you drank the previous evening. After the first hour or two of walking you will be able to see how your speed relates to the timings on the maps.

Up or down?

Other than when on a track or bridleway the trail is shown as a dotted line. An arrow across the trail indicates the slope; two arrows

> **❑ Important note – walking times**
> Unless otherwise specified, **all times in this book refer only to the time spent walking**. You will need to add 20-30% to allow for rests, photography, checking the map, drinking water etc, not to mention time simply to stop and stare. When planning the day's hike count on 5-7 hours' actual walking.

show that it is steep. Note that the arrow points towards the higher part of the trail. If, for example, you are walking from A (at 80m) to B (at 200m) and the trail between the two is short and steep it would be shown thus: A— — — >> — — – B. Reversed arrow heads indicate a downward gradient.

GPS waypoints

The numbered GPS waypoints refer to the list on pp195-7.

Accommodation

Apart from in large towns where some selection of places has been necessary, everywhere to stay that is within easy reach of the trail is marked. Details of each place are given in the accompanying text.

The number of rooms of each type is given at the beginning of each entry, ie: S=Single, T=Twin room, D=Double room, F=Family room (sleeps at least three people). The rates are also given; some establishments quote rates *per person* (pp) per night (with a supplement for single occupancy) and others *per room* based on two people sharing (in this case there may be a discount for single occupancy). Rates are for the summer high season.

Unless otherwise specified, rooms have bathrooms attached and most of these have only a shower. In the text ◆ signifies that at least one room has a bathroom with a **bath**, or access to a bath, for those who prefer a relaxed soak at the end of the day. The text also mentions whether the premises have **wi-fi** (WI-FI) and whether **dogs** (🐕) are welcome and the charge, if there is one.

Other features

Features are marked on the map when pertinent to navigation. In order to avoid cluttering the maps and making them unusable not all features have been marked each time they occur.

Milngavie to Fort William

See pp94-8 for the route guide and maps covering the walking route from **Glasgow to Milngavie**.

MILNGAVIE

The West Highland Way officially begins in Milngavie (pronounced 'mullguy'). This middle-class commuter suburb on the northern edge of Glasgow has few attractions to entice the walker to spend much time here but it's a nice-enough place to stay if you arrive too late to begin your walk.

The small pedestrian centre has plenty of shops and if you've got time to spare **Lillie Art Gallery** (☎ 0141-578 8847; Tue-Sat 10am-1pm & 2-5pm, admission free) is worth visiting to see one of Scotland's best collections of home-grown 20th-century art.

Services

Walking from the station to the start of the West Highland Way you pass through the main shopping precinct.

Milngavie Information Point & Frontier Holidays (☎ 0141-956 1569; mid Mar to mid Oct, Mon-Fri 8am-5pm, Sat-Sun 8am-noon; winter Mon-Fri 9am-5pm),

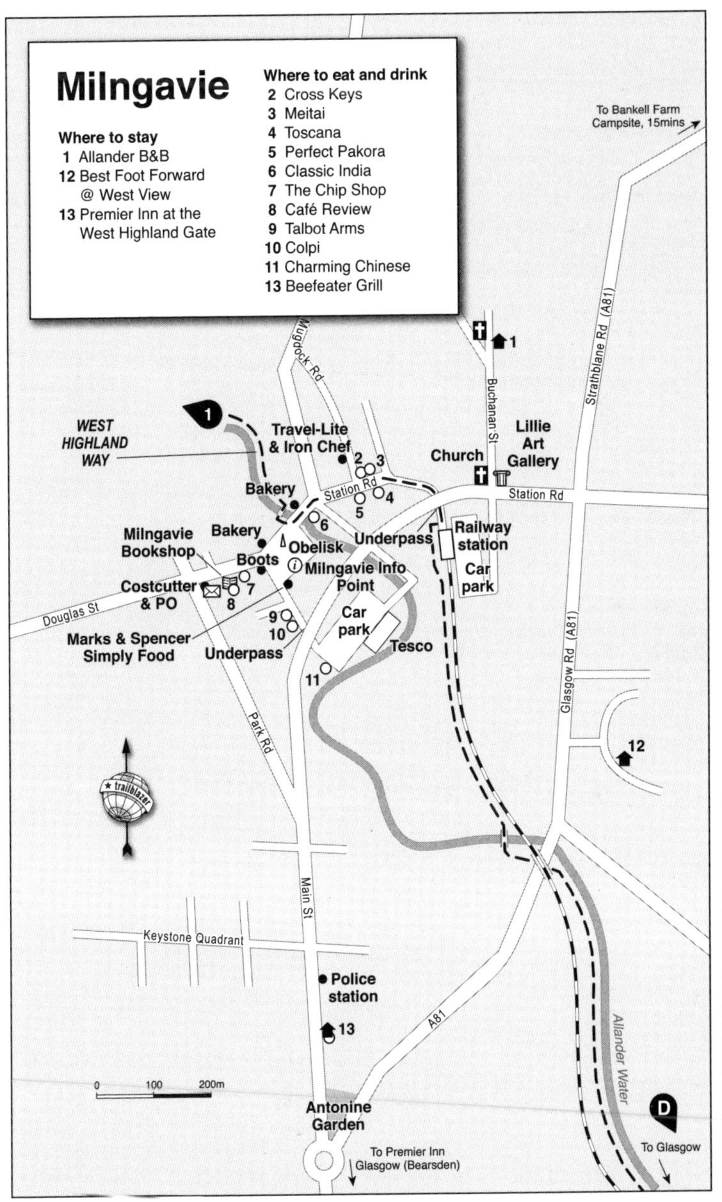
Milngavie
Where to stay
1 Allander B&B
12 Best Foot Forward @ West View
13 Premier Inn at the West Highland Gate
Where to eat and drink
2 Cross Keys
3 Meitai
4 Toscana
5 Perfect Pakora
6 Classic India
7 The Chip Shop
8 Café Review
9 Talbot Arms
10 Colpi
11 Charming Chinese
13 Beefeater Grill
To Bankell Farm Campsite, 15mins
Mugdock Rd
Buchanan St
Strathblane Rd (A81)
WEST HIGHLAND WAY
Travel-Lite & Iron Chef
Church
Lillie Art Gallery
Station Rd
Bakery
Milngavie Bookshop
Obelisk
Underpass
Railway station
Boots
Milngavie Info Point
Car park
Costcutter & PO
Douglas St
Marks & Spencer Simply Food
Underpass
Tesco
Glasgow Rd (A81)
Park Rd
Main St
Keystone Quadrant
Police station
A81
Allander Water
0 100 200m
Antonine Garden
To Premier Inn Glasgow (Bearsden)
To Glasgow

in the square, offers information on the West Highland Way. You can buy books and a West Highland Way log book (£5) which requires stamps along the route and eventually earns you a certificate. Frontier Holidays operates from here offering self-guided holidays on the Way (see p27).

The Iron Chef/Travel-Lite (☎ 0141-956 4597; Mon-Sat 9am-5pm) is a great place for all those bits and pieces you left behind, such as midge repellent, batteries, stoves and fuel for your stove and other outdoor gear plus up-to-the-minute trail information from the West Highland Way enthusiast and proprietor, Gilbert McVean. He also runs Travel-Lite **baggage-carrying service** (see p25) from here so you could arrange to use it if you found the walk from the station too taxing!

Milngavie Bookshop (☎ 0141-956 4752, 🖳 www.milngaviebookshop.co.uk; Mon-Sat 9am-5pm, Sun 12-4pm), at 37 Douglas St, has an interesting stock of books both of local interest and more general subjects. There's an excellent café here (see Café Review opposite).

Stock up with cash while you have the chance; the four **banks** here have cash machines: there are branches of Bank of Scotland and Lloyds TSB on Station Rd, and Clydesdale and Royal Bank of Scotland have branches on Douglas St. There's also a **post office** (Mon-Fri 8.30am-5.30pm, Sat 9am-3.30pm) inside Costcutter, a couple of **bakers** either side of the bridge with plenty of pies and pasties to set you up for the day's walk, a Boots **chemist** (on the main square) and three **supermarkets**: Marks & Spencer Simply Food (Mon-Fri 8.30am-8pm, Sat 8.30am-7pm, Sun 10am-6pm) on the main square, and Tesco (Mon-Sat 6am-midnight, Sun 8am-10pm) the other side of Woodburn Way.

Transport

[See also pp44-8] Scotrail's **train** service between Milngavie Station and Glasgow takes about 30 minutes and operates twice an hour.

First South East and Central Scotland's C10/10/10A service, or the less frequent C8, run to Glasgow. In the other direction the C8 goes to Drymen and the C10/10/10A to Strathblane and Killearn.

Two local **taxi** firms are Ambassador Taxis (☎ 0141-956 2956; 🖳 ambassador_taxis@btconnect.com) who have an office at 29 Douglas St, just off the main square, and Station Taxis (☎ 0141-563 4555).

Where to stay

The **campsite** at ***Bankell Farm*** (☎ 0141-956 1733, 🖳 www.bankellfarm.co.uk; £6pp, open all year) is handy for campers arriving late in the day as the next site is near Drymen, often too far to walk before dark. The farm is a 30- to 40-minute walk from Milngavie station along Strathblane Rd (the A81). It's the second turning on the right after Esporta Health Club; there's a small sign. They allow car parking for walkers for £2 per night.

Long-running and welcoming, ***Best Foot Forward @ West View*** (☎ 0141-956 3046, 🖳 www.bestfootforward.eu.com; 1 Dougalston Gardens South; 1D/2D or T/3F; ☕; WI-FI; 🐕 £5; £30pp, sgl occ £45-60) is a comfortable place that specialises in providing accommodation for West Highland Way walkers. The family rooms sleep up to four people and one has a bath.

Allander B&B (☎ 0141-956 5258, 🖳 allanderbandb-milngavie.co.uk; 2T; WI-FI; small 🐕; £30pp, sgl occ £40-45), at 28 Buchanan St, is small but comfortable with good breakfasts.

There are two **Premier Inns** (🖳 www.premierinn.com) here and if you book well in advance you can get a room (most accommodate up to two adults and two children aged 15 or under) for as little as £19. However, rates vary daily and depend on demand so, unless you book very early, expect to pay around £60 for a room. ***Premier Inn at the West Highland Gate*** (☎ 0141-956 7835; 2D/59F; ☕; WI-FI) is at 103 Main St, and ***Premier Inn Glasgow (Bearsden)*** (☎ 0141-931 9100; 4D/57F; ☕; WI-FI) at 279 Milngavie Rd. At both, a continental/cooked breakfast is an extra £5.25/£8.25pp; WI-FI is free for the first 30 minutes and then £3 for 24 hours. The first hotel has a ***Beefeater Grill*** (Mon-Sat 11am-midnight, Sun 12.30pm-11pm) attached.

Where to eat and drink

The number of places where you can eat is surprising for such a small town. For something quick and cheap to take away head for Douglas St and ***The Chip Shop***. A couple of doors up is ***Café Review*** (Mon-Sat 9am-4.30pm) in the back of the bookshop with its tea garden. It's a nice place to come for lunch. If an ice cream is all you're after you can't do better than Scots-Italian ***Colpi***, (near Talbot Arms) who've been serving them since 1928.

The ***Talbot Arms*** (☎ 0141-955 0981) is a traditional pub and a great place to start the evening. Other than crisps and nuts, though, they don't do food. The ***Cross Keys*** was being refurbished at the time of writing but should now be open as a bistro-style restaurant and pub.

On station Rd, ***Toscana*** (☎ 0141-956 4020; Mon-Sat 9.30am-4.30pm, Thur-Sat 6-9.30pm) has pizza from £7.25 and pasta from £7.95. It's popular so you may need to book. Nearby, ***Meitai*** (☎ 0141-956 5413; Mon-Thur noon-2pm & 5-10.30pm, Fri-Sat noon-2pm & 5-11pm, Sun 5-10.30pm) serves good value Thai, Chinese and Japanese food. A takeaway lunch is £3.99. Opposite, Indian food for takeaway is also available from ***Perfect Pakora*** (☎ 0141-955 1888; Mon-Sat 9.30am-6pm), an Indian delicatessen.

Classic India (☎ 0141-956 6360; Sun-Thur 5pm-midnight, Fri-Sat 5pm-1am) aims to 'spoil and pamper' you with an excellent range of Indian dishes including all-you-can-eat buffets starting at £9.95 (£12.95 on Fri & Sat) served 5-10pm. Turn left immediately before crossing the bridge over Allander Water and you'll find the restaurant hidden away in a car park.

The ***Charming Chinese Restaurant*** (☎ 0141-956 2255; daily noon-4pm & 4.30-10.30pm), in a sensitively converted mill by the Tesco car park, is a fairly stylish restaurant with a typically extensive menu of oriental dishes, with a two-course lunch for £6, and a three-course evening meal for £9.90 if dining between 4.30 and 7pm (not Saturdays).

MILNGAVIE TO DRYMEN — MAPS 1-8

This beginning stage is **12 miles (19km)** and takes **3¾-5hrs** to walk (walking time only). It neatly splits into three distinctly different sections.

The walk starts officially at the obelisk (see Map 1). The first 6 miles (10km, 1¾-2¼hrs) provide easy and interesting walking along gentle paths through amenity parks and woodland leading you quickly out of the suburbs into genuine countryside. You pass **Craigallian Loch** (Map 2) with its surprise views of the rugged Campsie Fells and then, after crossing the B821, you arrive on an indistinct ridge overlooking Blane Valley. From here there are distant views to the Highlands tantalising you with the splendour of the hills that are to come. A superb descent across open grassland drained by tiny streams takes you round the

❑ Mugdock Country Park

A short detour can be made to see the remains of the fortified **Mugdock Castle** dating back to the 14th century and the much newer **Craigend Castle** built as a residence in 1815, now also in ruins. Follow the fingerpost signs in Mugdock Wood (Map 1). These will also lead you to the **Visitor Centre** (☎ 0141-956 6100, 🖳 www.mugdock-country-park.org.uk; daily Apr-Oct 9am-9pm, Nov-Mar to 6pm). The park itself is open all the time but the car park (free) at the visitor centre is open the same hours as the visitor centre. ***Stables Tearoom*** is open daily 10am-5pm and the ***Garden House Restaurant*** daily 9am-5.30pm (to 5pm in winter); there are also two gift shops, a garden centre, and an art and craft gallery. There is no admission charge.

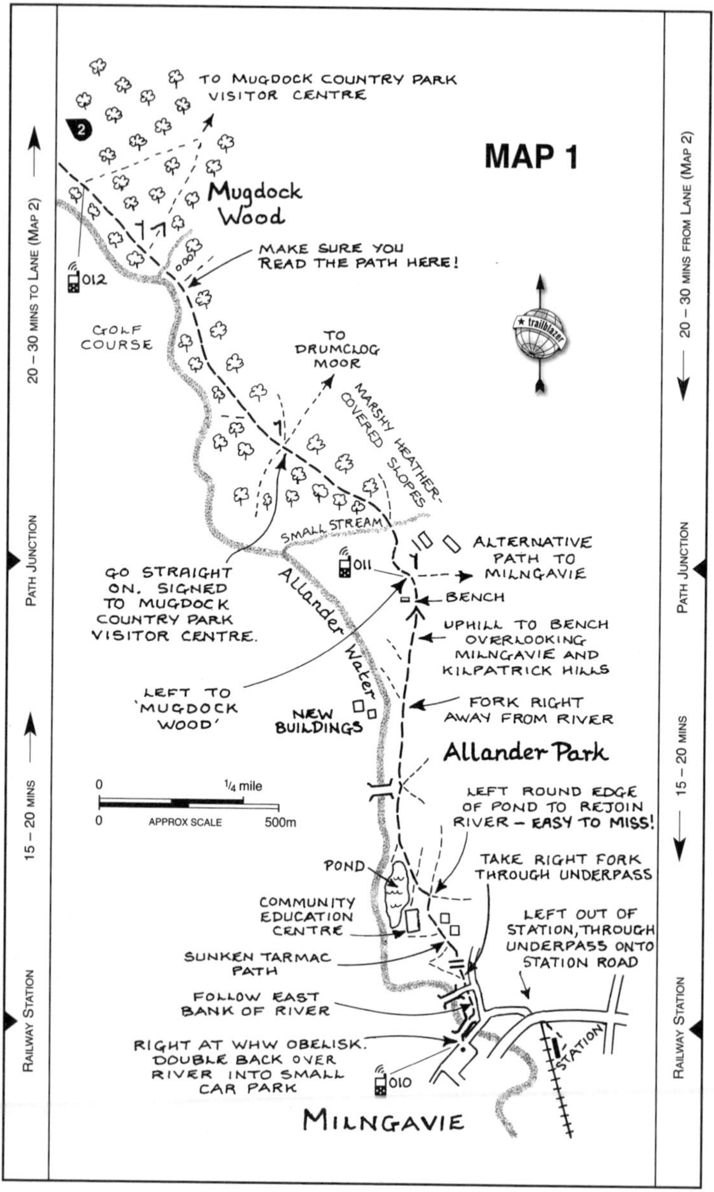
MAP 1
TO MUGDOCK COUNTRY PARK VISITOR CENTRE
2
Mugdock Wood
MAKE SURE YOU READ THE PATH HERE!
012
GOLF COURSE
TO DRUMCLOG MOOR
MARSHY HEATHER-COVERED SLOPES
SMALL STREAM
ALTERNATIVE PATH TO MILNGAVIE
011
BENCH
GO STRAIGHT ON. SIGNED TO MUGDOCK COUNTRY PARK VISITOR CENTRE.
Allander Water
UPHILL TO BENCH OVERLOOKING MILNGAVIE AND KILPATRICK HILLS
LEFT TO 'MUGDOCK WOOD'
NEW BUILDINGS
FORK RIGHT AWAY FROM RIVER
Allander Park
0 1/4 mile
0 APPROX SCALE 500m
LEFT ROUND EDGE OF POND TO REJOIN RIVER – EASY TO MISS!
POND
TAKE RIGHT FORK THROUGH UNDERPASS
COMMUNITY EDUCATION CENTRE
LEFT OUT OF STATION, THROUGH UNDERPASS ONTO STATION ROAD
SUNKEN TARMAC PATH
FOLLOW EAST BANK OF RIVER
RIGHT AT WHW OBELISK. DOUBLE BACK OVER RIVER INTO SMALL CAR PARK
STATION
010
MILNGAVIE
20 – 30 MINS TO LANE (MAP 2)
PATH JUNCTION
15 – 20 MINS
RAILWAY STATION
20 – 30 MINS FROM LANE (MAP 2)
PATH JUNCTION
15 – 20 MINS
RAILWAY STATION

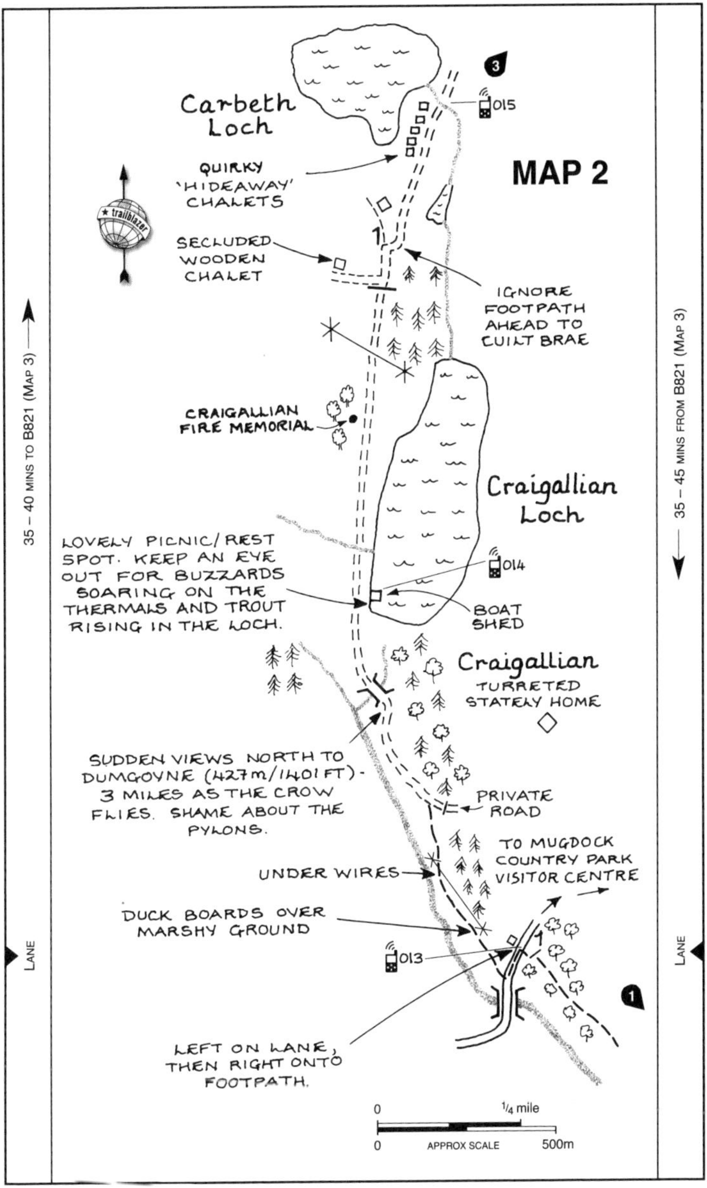

MAP 2

Carbeth Loch

QUIRKY 'HIDEAWAY' CHALETS

015

SECLUDED WOODEN CHALET

IGNORE FOOTPATH AHEAD TO CUILT BRAE

CRAIGALLIAN FIRE MEMORIAL

Craigallian Loch

LOVELY PICNIC/REST SPOT. KEEP AN EYE OUT FOR BUZZARDS SOARING ON THE THERMALS AND TROUT RISING IN THE LOCH.

014

BOAT SHED

Craigallian TURRETED STATELY HOME

SUDDEN VIEWS NORTH TO DUMGOYNE (427m/1401FT) - 3 MILES AS THE CROW FLIES. SHAME ABOUT THE PYLONS.

PRIVATE ROAD

TO MUGDOCK COUNTRY PARK VISITOR CENTRE

UNDER WIRES

DUCK BOARDS OVER MARSHY GROUND

013

LEFT ON LANE, THEN RIGHT ONTO FOOTPATH.

0 ¼ mile

0 APPROX SCALE 500m

35 – 40 MINS TO B821 (MAP 3)

35 – 45 MINS FROM B821 (MAP 3)

LANE

LANE

pretty wooded knoll of **Dumgoyach** to the valley bottom. Here the Way follows the bed of a disused railway (see box p108) for 4 miles (6km, 1½-2hrs). Straight and level it is easy, if unglamorous, walking through gentle farmland, though the constant background hum from the traffic on the A81 can be intrusive.

Only yards from the trail is **Glengoyne Distillery** (☎ 01360-550254, 🖳 www.glengoyne.com). It would be a shame to pass without a quick visit and a revitalising wee dram. There are several tours: the cheapest costs £7.50, which allows you to sample their 12-year-old Highland single malt whisky, or £10 if you would like to follow the tour with a shot of their 18-year-old one. Tours (Mar-Nov daily 10am-4pm, Dec-Feb daily 10am-3pm) start on the hour.

The Way joins a quiet hedge-lined minor road at the pretty sandstone hamlet of **Gartness** (Map 6) and follows it for two miles (3km, ½-¾hr) to the outskirts of **Drymen**, a large and bustling village where many choose to spend the night.

BLANEFIELD — Map 3

West Highland Way walkers rarely detour to this small village as it lies just over a mile (20-25 mins) east of the trail. However, with the excellent Pestle & Mortar Delicatessen (open all week) and a couple of other places serving **food** it may be worth a brief visit but for somewhere to stay you need to go to Strathblane (see below). ***Pestle and Mortar Delicatessen*** (☎ 01360-771110; Mon-Fri 9.15am-7pm, Sat 9.15am-6pm, Sun 10am-5pm) has filled rolls from £2.20; their **coffee shop**, which closes half an hour earlier than the deli, has ciabatta rolls for £4.75 and salads from £6.25. There is also ***Chillies Tandoori Takeaway*** (☎ 01360-770727; open summer daily 4-11pm, winter Tue-Sun 4-10pm) and ***Blane Valley Inn*** (☎ 01360-770303) which serves breakfasts daily from 9am to noon, and a wide variety of bar meals Sunday to Thursday noon-8pm, Friday and Saturday to 9pm.

STRATHBLANE — off Map 3

A further 10 minutes' walk east along the A81 takes you to the smart ***Kirkhouse Inn*** (☎ 01360-771771, 🖳 www.kirkhouseinn.com; 4T/11D; ▼; WI-FI; £29.50-37.50pp, sgl occ £65). **Food** is available either in the reasonably priced lounge bar (daily 10am-9pm) or in the à la carte restaurant (daily noon-9pm).

First's C10/10/10A **bus** service (for details see pp44-8) stops here.

❑ Craigallian Fire memorial site

The West Highland Way passes right beside a new memorial (see **Map 2, p105**) to an important time in social history. It marks a site that became famous in the 1920s and '30s as an informal meeting place for a range of passers-by that included travellers, climbers and walkers as well as the unemployed escaping the Great Depression in Glasgow and the Clyde. People would stop to sit round the fire that was often started here, drink tea, tell stories and discuss the wider issues of the world. In a time before the internet, coming together with like-minded people was the only way, particularly for poorer people, to share ideas. A few of the so-called fire-sitters would go on to fight in the Spanish Civil War and others – less romantically but more importantly for walkers such as us – to campaign for greater access to the countryside. For more information see 🖳 www.craigallianfire.org.uk.

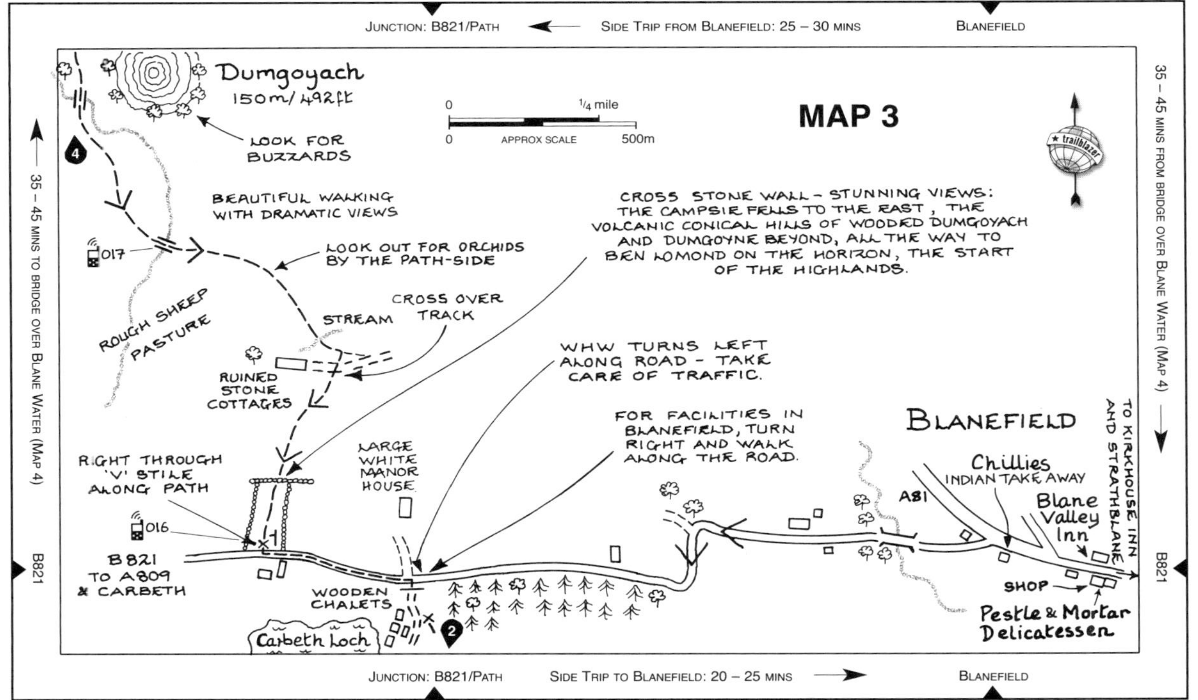
Junction: B821/Path
Side Trip from Blanefield: 25 – 30 mins
Blanefield
35 – 45 mins from bridge over Blane Water (Map 4)
35 – 45 mins to bridge over Blane Water (Map 4)
B821
B821
Junction: B821/Path
Side Trip to Blanefield: 20 – 25 mins
Blanefield
Dumgoyach
150m/492ft
0
1/4 mile
0
APPROX SCALE
500m
MAP 3
trailblazer
4
LOOK FOR BUZZARDS
BEAUTIFUL WALKING WITH DRAMATIC VIEWS
017
LOOK OUT FOR ORCHIDS BY THE PATH-SIDE
CROSS STONE WALL - STUNNING VIEWS: THE CAMPSIE FELLS TO THE EAST, THE VOLCANIC CONICAL HILLS OF WOODED DUMGOYACH AND DUMGOYNE BEYOND, ALL THE WAY TO BEN LOMOND ON THE HORIZON, THE START OF THE HIGHLANDS.
ROUGH SHEEP PASTURE
STREAM
CROSS OVER TRACK
RUINED STONE COTTAGES
WHW TURNS LEFT ALONG ROAD - TAKE CARE OF TRAFFIC.
FOR FACILITIES IN BLANEFIELD, TURN RIGHT AND WALK ALONG THE ROAD.
BLANEFIELD
TO KIRKHOUSE INN AND STRATHBLANE
RIGHT THROUGH 'V' STILE ALONG PATH
LARGE WHITE MANOR HOUSE
016
B821 TO A809 & CARBETH
WOODEN CHALETS
Carbeth Loch
2
A81
Chillies INDIAN TAKE AWAY
Blane Valley Inn
SHOP
Pestle & Mortar Delicatessen

DUMGOYNE Map 4

A pub (Beech Tree Inn), **telephone box**, **post office** (Mon, Tue, Thur & Fri 9am-12.30pm & 1.30-5.30pm, Wed & Sat mornings only), Glengoyne Distillery, and a handful of houses comprise the extent of this small hamlet.

The trail goes past the back door of ***Beech Tree Inn*** (☎ 01360-550297, 💻 www.thebeechtreeinn.co.uk; **food** served Apr-Sep daily 10.30am-9pm, Oct-Mar Wed-Mon noon-9pm, to 4pm Mon & Wed; **breakfast hut** open May-Sep, Sat-Mon 9-11am). This is the only place on the trail between Milngavie and Gartness where you can get a bite to eat and is about 2½-3 hours from the start so, if you are making good time, this comfortable pub can be a good stopping place for lunch. The large and varied menu includes hoagies (wholemeal rolls) from £4.65, soup and a filled roll for £5.95 to more exotic fare such as kangaroo sausages (£9.95), camel steak (£17.95) or that old Scottish favourite you hardly ever see on menus nowadays, the deep fried Mars Bar (£4.75). They also have a special garden set aside that picnicking walkers can use as long as they buy at least a drink at the bar.

❑ Blane Valley Railway

Between Dumgoyach Farm (Map 4) and Gartness (Map 6) the Way runs along the route of the former Blane Valley Railway which, between 1882 and 1951, carried passengers from Aberfoyle to Glasgow. The old Dumgoyne Station was by the Beech Tree Inn (see above). The route is now not only used by the West Highland Way but also by a pipeline hidden in the raised embankment carrying water from Loch Lomond to homes and businesses in Central Scotland.

KILLEARN Map 5, p111

Killearn is not actually on the West Highland Way; it lies a good 20 minutes' walk east. It is not worth a special detour on its own but some walkers may find its services useful. It's an attractive village overlooking the Campsie Fells and Loch Lomond and is built around the original 18th-century cottages of a planned village. It was here that George Buchanan, a leading historian, scholar and tutor to Mary Queen of Scots and King James VI, was born in 1506. An impressive 31m (103ft) obelisk stands behind Killearn Kirk in memory of him.

Services

Both Spar (daily 7am-10pm) and Co-op (Mon-Sat 8am-10pm, Sun 9am-9pm) have **mini-supermarkets** in the village. There's also a **post office** (Mon, Tue, Thur, Fri 9am-1pm & 2-5.30pm, Wed & Sat 9am-12.30pm), **health centre** (☎ 01360-550339; Mon-Fri 8.30am-6pm) and a branch of **Bank of Scotland** with a cash machine (24hrs). There is also a cash machine in the Co-op.

Transport

[See pp44-8] First's C12/12 (to Stirling via Balfron) **bus** service and the C10/10/10A (to Glasgow and Strathblane via Milngavie) call here regularly throughout the day so it is a convenient place to start or finish a day walk along the West Highland Way.

Where to stay and eat

The only accommodation is at the upmarket ***Black Bull Hotel*** (☎ 01360-550215, 💻 www.blackbullhotel.com, 2 The Square; 10D/1F; ♥; WI-FI; 🐕 £10; £30pp, sgl occ £39.95-49.95). The **food** (served daily noon-9pm) here is reputedly excellent; expect to pay around £10.95 for a main course in the restaurant, bistro or bar. The menu is the same wherever you eat.

Cheaper food is available at the ***Town and Country Coffee Shop*** (daily 10am-5pm) where you can enjoy homemade soup, sandwiches, pastries and cakes.

A little further along the road is ***The Old Mill*** (☎ 01360-550068, 💻 www.old-mill-killearn.co.uk; food served daily noon-9pm), a delightful old place with exposed

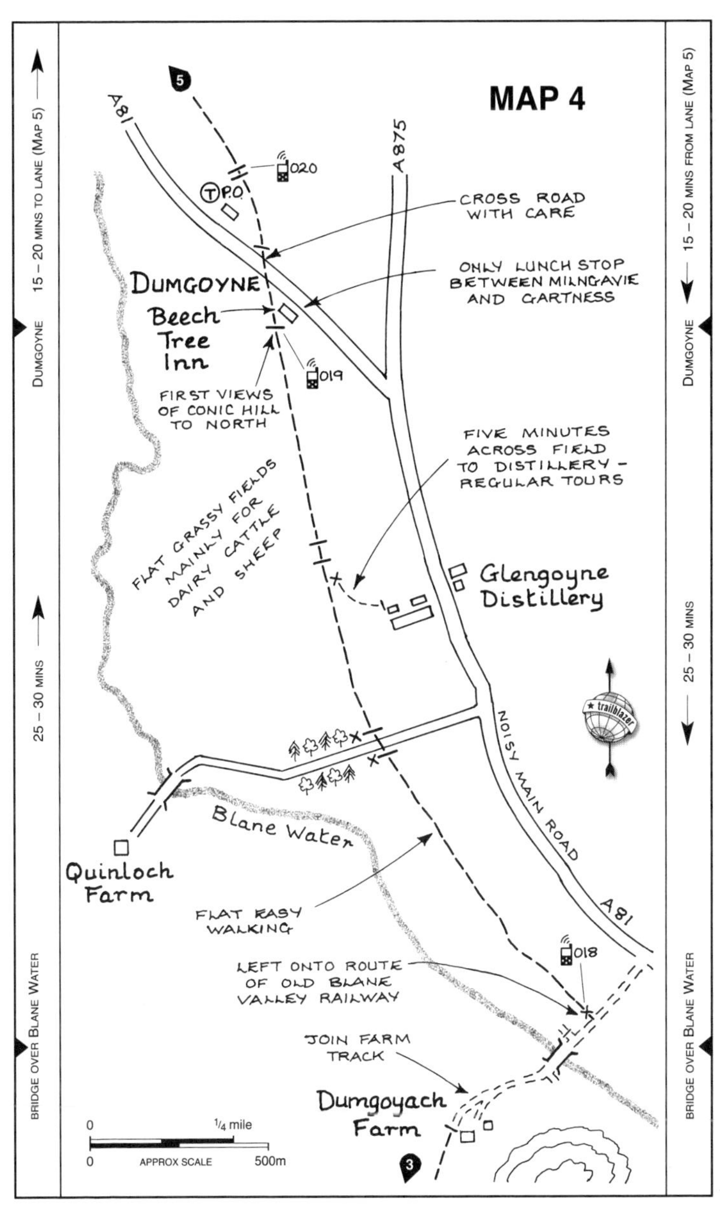
MAP 4
15 – 20 MINS TO LANE (MAP 5)
DUMGOYNE
25 – 30 MINS
BRIDGE OVER BLANE WATER
15 – 20 MINS FROM LANE (MAP 5)
DUMGOYNE
25 – 30 MINS
BRIDGE OVER BLANE WATER
5
A81
A875
020
P.O
CROSS ROAD WITH CARE
ONLY LUNCH STOP BETWEEN MILNGAVIE AND GARTNESS
DUMGOYNE
Beech Tree Inn
019
FIRST VIEWS OF CONIC HILL TO NORTH
FIVE MINUTES ACROSS FIELD TO DISTILLERY - REGULAR TOURS
FLAT GRASSY FIELDS MAINLY FOR DAIRY CATTLE AND SHEEP
Glengoyne Distillery
trailblazer
NOISY MAIN ROAD
Blane Water
Quinloch Farm
FLAT EASY WALKING
A81
018
LEFT ONTO ROUTE OF OLD BLANE VALLEY RAILWAY
JOIN FARM TRACK
Dumgoyach Farm
0
1/4 mile
0
APPROX SCALE
500m
3

ceiling beams and open fires which serves light lunch items for about £5.90, as well as a wide variety of main courses including a steakburger for £9.50; up to 6pm two courses are £9.95, after 6pm £13.95.

GARTNESS Map 6, p112

Wishingwell Farmhouse Coffee Shop (☎ 01360-551038, 🖳 www.wishingwellfarmhouse.co.uk; Tue-Sat 10am-5pm) is right by the trail before you cross over the bridges into Gartness. The menu offers a large selection of local produce including Loch Fyne smoked salmon, Hardiesmill beef, Rannoch venison and Orkney herring. Packed lunches are £5.95. There's also a good backpackers' **campsite** here costing £5 per person. It's basic but has a hot shower and a picnic area under the old railway bridge which is very welcome when it's raining.

CROFTAMIE off Map 7, p113

Croftburn (☎ 01360-660796, 🖳 www.croftburn.co.uk; 2T/1D, all with private facilities; Mar-Oct; ▾; WI-FI) offers B&B from £30pp, £37 single occupancy.

You can easily walk to Croftamie along the Sustrans cycle path which leaves the Way just after Gartness by the bridge over the river. However, the owners offer free transfers from Drymen; a charge is made for transfers from Rowardennan or Milngavie. They also offer packed lunches (£5.50), if requested in advance.

EASTER DRUMQUHASSLE Map 7, p113

Half a mile further on and only 1½ miles (25 mins) short of Drymen is ***Drymen Camping*** (☎ 01360-660597, 🖳 www.drymencamping.co.uk; Apr-Oct), next door to Easter Drumquhassle Farm. They charge £5pp which includes the cost of a shower and there is a barn to shelter in if the weather turns against you. There's also a washing machine and dryer (£2 each). Alternatively, groups (or individuals) can hire an entire **wigwam** (see p20) sleeping up to four people (£30 per night; shower included), or an entire **kocoon** (£25 per night sleeping up to two people). The latter is a lined wooden structure with memory foam benches on either side. Sleeping bags are not included in the rate but can be hired (£2.50). Breakfast (£5pp) may be available in the farmhouse – email for more details.

DRYMEN Map 8, p115

Pronounced 'drimmen', this is a large attractive village arranged round a neat green. It's a popular first night halt for many walkers on the West Highland Way, even though the trail actually bypasses the village to the east. There is plenty of accommodation both on the outskirts and within the village, several places to eat, a few handy shops and a library.

Services

The **library** (Mon, Fri 9.30am-1pm & 2-5pm; Tue, Thur 9am-1pm & 2-7pm; Sat 9am-1pm; closed Wed), where there is free **internet** access, is open throughout the year. There's a village **store** (Mon-Fri 7.30am-5.30pm, Sat 7.30am-5pm, Sun 8am-1.30pm) with the local **post office** (Mon-Fri 9am-12.30pm & 1.30-5.30pm, Sat 9am-1pm) inside and a branch of **Royal Bank of Scotland** with a cash machine. Make sure you have enough cash to get to Tyndrum where the next ATM on the West Highland Way is located.

If you're camping stock up on food in the Spar **supermarket** (Mon-Sat 6.30am-10pm, Sun 8am-10pm) as you won't have such a good selection again until Crianlarich. You may also like to consider paying a visit to the **butcher** (Tue-Sat

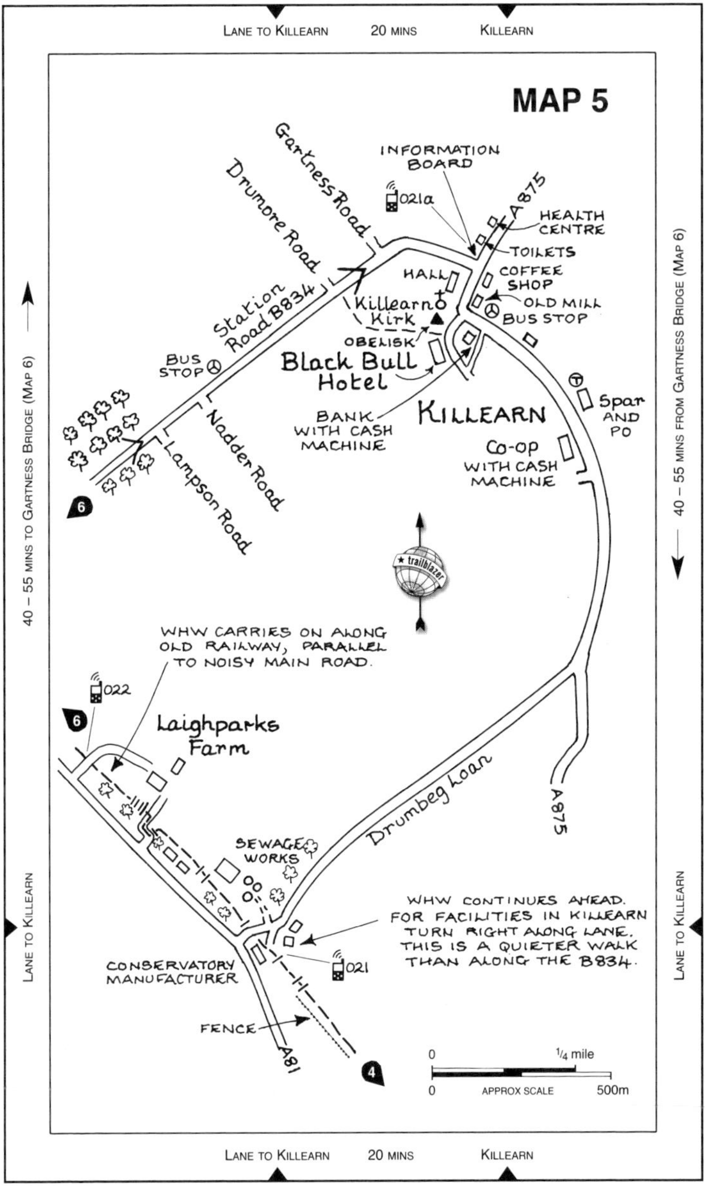

LANE TO KILLEARN 20 MINS KILLEARN

MAP 5

Gartness Road
Drumore Road
INFORMATION BOARD
021a
A875
HEALTH CENTRE
TOILETS
COFFEE SHOP
HALL
Killearn Kirk
OLD MILL
BUS STOP
Station Road B834
OBELISK
BUS STOP
Black Bull Hotel
Spar AND PO
BANK WITH CASH MACHINE
KILLEARN
Nadder Road
Lampson Road
Co-op WITH CASH MACHINE
6
40 – 55 MINS TO GARTNESS BRIDGE (MAP 6)
40 – 55 MINS FROM GARTNESS BRIDGE (MAP 6)
WHW CARRIES ON ALONG OLD RAILWAY, PARALLEL TO NOISY MAIN ROAD.
022
6
Laighparks Farm
Drumbeg Loan
A875
SEWAGE WORKS
WHW CONTINUES AHEAD. FOR FACILITIES IN KILLEARN TURN RIGHT ALONG LANE. THIS IS A QUIETER WALK THAN ALONG THE B834.
CONSERVATORY MANUFACTURER
021
FENCE
A81
4
0 1/4 mile
0 APPROX SCALE 500m
LANE TO KILLEARN
LANE TO KILLEARN

LANE TO KILLEARN 20 MINS KILLEARN

8.30am-12.30pm & 1.30-5.30pm), on the south side of the Green, where they make fantastic steak pies in three sizes, perfect for next day's lunch. Other services in the village include a **health centre** (☎ 01360-660203; Mon-Fri 8.30am-noon & 1-6pm).

The **Haven Spa** (☎ 01360-660999; 💻 www.the-haven.biz) is at the Buchanan Arms Hotel. There are various treatments on offer, eg 4-7pm, Thur-Fri the Twilight Spa costs £50pp.

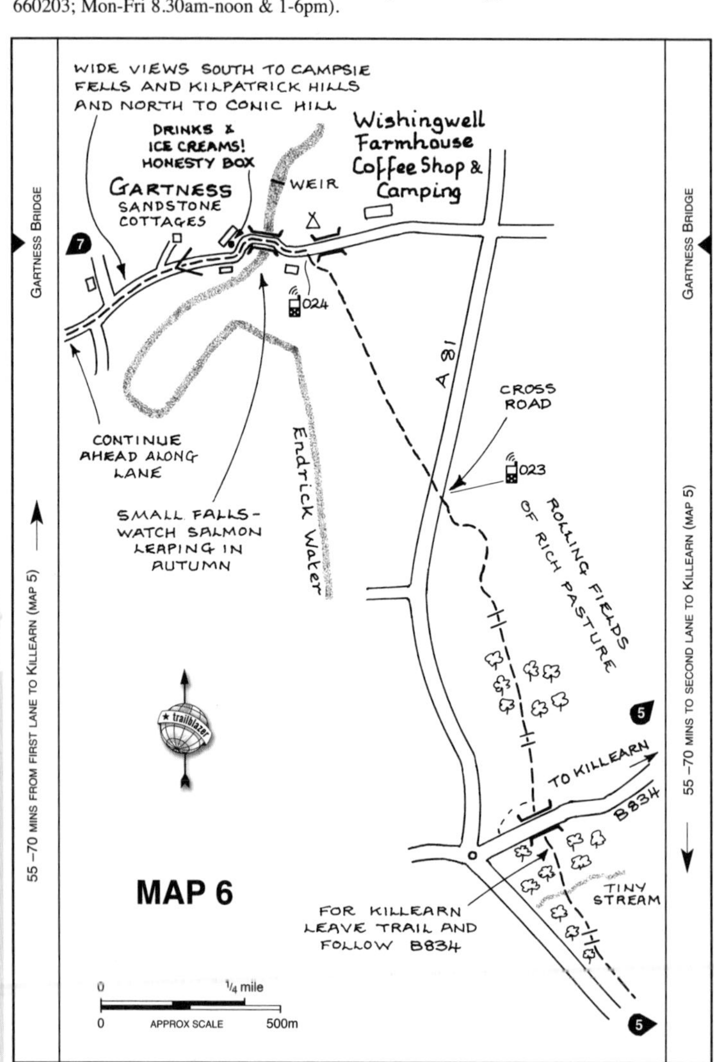

Transport

[See pp44-8] Drymen is well served by **buses** (First's C8/8, 10, 11A, 13 & McColls No 309).

For a cab call **Drymen Taxis** (☎ 01360-660077).

Where to stay

Most backpackers **camp** at Drymen Camping (see p110).

As you enter Drymen ***The Hawthorns*** (☎ 01360-661222, 🖳 www.hawthorns-drymen.com; 1S/1D/1D or T/3D, T or F; ☛;

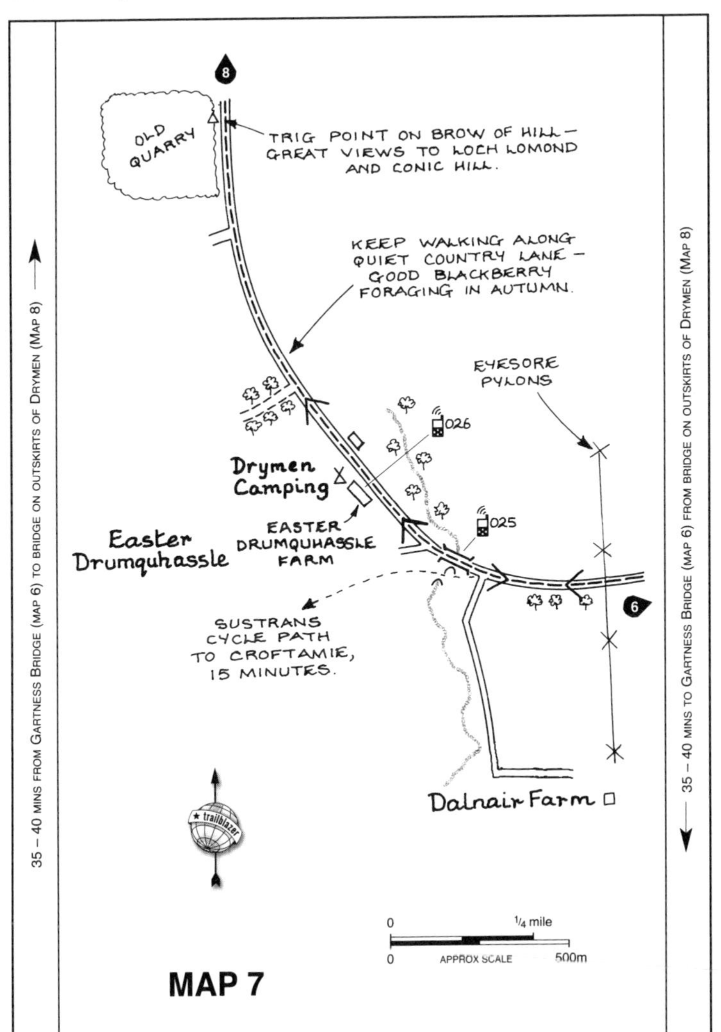

WI-FI; £25-40pp, sgl £40-50, sgl occ £45-55; the family rooms cost £70-140 per room) is the first B&B you come to. A packed lunch costs £6 and they have a drying room. It's a good place to stay.

Winnock Hotel (☎ 01360-660245, 🖳 www.winnockhotel.com; 6S/19T/29D/19F; ●; WI-FI; £69pp, sgl £99) is on the Square. Rates include breakfast. It's worth phoning to see if they have any special deals.

The owners of ***Hillview*** (☎ 01360-661000, 🖳 hill view@drymensquare.com; 2T/2D/1F; WI-FI; 🐕 £5; 35pp, sgl occ £40) operate the taxi company (see p113) and will pick guests up at Rowardennan and drive them back the next day if it is not possible to get accommodation there. A packed lunch costs £7.

Next door is the old ***Clachan Inn*** (☎ 01360-660824, 🖳 www.clachaninndrymen.co.uk; 2S/1T/1D, shared bathroom; ●; WI-FI; £30pp, sgl occ £35), on The Square. Note that as the rooms are above the bar it might be noisy at the weekend though after the first day on the trail you'll probably sleep through anything!

Ashbank B&B (☎ 01360-660049, 🖳 www.ashbank-drymen.co.uk; 2D or T/1D /T or F; WI-FI; £35pp, sgl occ £50) is at 1 Balmaha Rd. A packed lunch costs £5 and one room has a wet room which a previous resident, Eric Liddell (the athlete whose story is told in *Chariots of Fire*), certainly would not recognise.

Braeside B&B (☎ 01360-660989, www.braeside-drymen.co.uk; 2D/2T; ●; WI-FI; £30-40pp, sgl occ £45-50) opened in 2012. It's a very comfortable place run by friendly, enthusiastic owners. There's also a self-contained barn (2T) with a small kitchen. Packed lunches are available.

There are several places along Stirling Rd. Long-running and welcoming, ***Lander B&B*** (☎ 01360-660273, 🖳 www.bandb.labbs.com; 1T/1T or F; shared facilities; WI-FI; £29pp, sgl occ from £35) is at No 17. Packed lunches are available. ***Elmbank*** (☎ 01360-661016, 🖳 www.elmbank-drymen.com; 2T/3D/1D, T or F; some rooms share facilities; £28-35pp, sgl occ from £30), at 10 Stirling Rd, is a large house converted into B&B accommodation. They also have a couple of apartments which may be available on a nightly basis if they aren't booked for the week.

East of Drymen is the welcoming ***Glenalva*** (☎ 01360-660491, 🖳 www.glenalva-drymen.co.uk; 2D/T or F; WI-FI; £32-35pp, sgl occ £64-70; Mar-Nov), famed for its excellent breakfasts and a good place to stay as it's right on the Way.

Bramblewood B&B (☎ 01360-660450, 🖳 www.bramblewood.uk.com; 2D or T/1D, T or F; ●; WI-FI; £32.50-35pp; sgl occ £50; additional person in family room £20) is a lodge-style building set in an attractive wooded spot on the north-west edge of Drymen on the road to Balmaha. A packed lunch costs £5.

The Buchanan Arms Hotel & Spa (☎ 01360-660588, 🖳 www.buchananarms.co.uk; 9S/30T/9D/2F; ●; WI-FI; 🐕 £15; £30-75pp, sgl from £55) is part of the Best Western chain. It's a stylish hotel that is nevertheless friendly and relaxed and which offers very good value indeed particularly if booked well in advance. The spa is an added attraction.

If you hit Drymen in peak season and find everywhere is booked it's worth trying a few B&Bs further away. A mile south-west in the grounds of **Buchanan Castle** is ***Green Shadows*** (☎ 01360-660289, 🖳 www.visitdrymen.co.uk; 1S/1D/1D, T or F; WI-FI), which charges from £38pp, sgl £45, sgl occ £60. They offer a pick-up service (after 4pm and if booked in advance) saving you a long walk – they will also take you back to Drymen for an evening meal and back in the morning.

Where to eat and drink

In the village there's ***Clachan Inn*** (see Where to stay) which claims to be Scotland's oldest registered pub, established in 1734. It's a popular place to drink and eat (food is served Mon-Sat noon-4pm & 6-10pm, Sun 12.30-4pm & 5-10pm, in the winter months food may be served to 9pm) with something on the menu to suit most tastes from sausage, beans and chips to a variety of steaks with a range of sauces. They also have a good vegetarian selection.

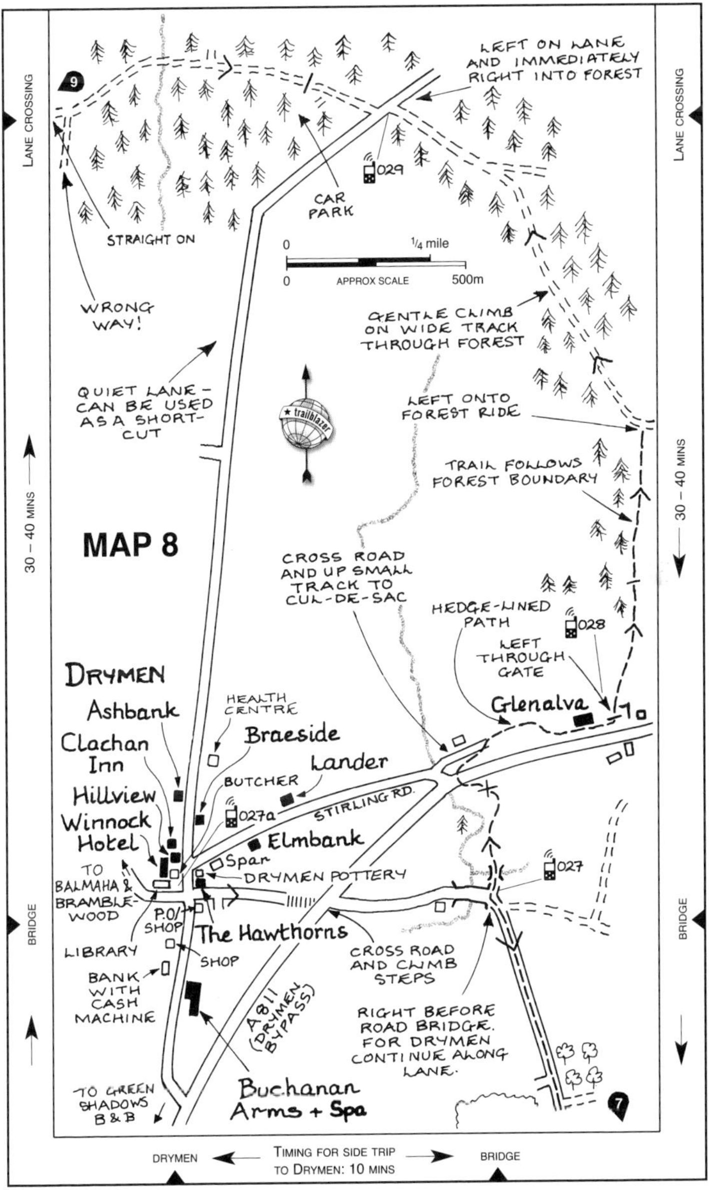

LEFT ON LANE AND IMMEDIATELY RIGHT INTO FOREST
9
LANE CROSSING
LANE CROSSING
029
CAR PARK
STRAIGHT ON
0 1/4 mile
0 APPROX SCALE 500m
WRONG WAY!
GENTLE CLIMB ON WIDE TRACK THROUGH FOREST
QUIET LANE - CAN BE USED AS A SHORT-CUT
trailblazer
LEFT ONTO FOREST RIDE
TRAIL FOLLOWS FOREST BOUNDARY
30 – 40 MINS
30 – 40 MINS
MAP 8
CROSS ROAD AND UP SMALL TRACK TO CUL-DE-SAC
HEDGE-LINED PATH
028
LEFT THROUGH GATE
DRYMEN
Ashbank
HEALTH CENTRE
Glenalva
Clachan Inn
Braeside
Lander
BUTCHER
Hillview
027a
STIRLING RD.
Winnock Hotel
Elmbank
Spar
TO BALMAHA & BRAMBLEWOOD
DRYMEN POTTERY
027
BRIDGE
BRIDGE
P.O/ SHOP
The Hawthorns
LIBRARY
SHOP
CROSS ROAD AND CLIMB STEPS
BANK WITH CASH MACHINE
A811 (DRYMEN BYPASS)
RIGHT BEFORE ROAD BRIDGE. FOR DRYMEN CONTINUE ALONG LANE.
TO GREEN SHADOWS B & B
Buchanan Arms + Spa
7
DRYMEN
TIMING FOR SIDE TRIP TO DRYMEN: 10 MINS
BRIDGE

At the **pub/café** ***Drymen Pottery Public House and Café*** (☎ 01360-660458) you can eat upstairs in the bar (daily 5-9pm, to 8pm in winter), or downstairs in the conservatory café by the pottery (Sep-Mar Mon-Sat 8.30am-5.30pm, Apr-Aug until 9.30pm, Sun from 10am). Meals include haggis baked potatoes for £7.25, Highland beef pie & chips (£10.25) and 6"/9"/12" pizzas from £5.95/7.95/9.95. The bar upstairs is open Mon-Thur 5pm-midnight and Fri-Sat 11am-1am, Sun 12.30pm-midnight. ***Winnock Hotel*** (see Where to stay) has bar meals (daily noon-9.30pm) including traditional favourites such as cullen skink and a roll for £5.95 or a steak baguette and chips for £8.95. In the restaurant (daily 6.30-9.30pm) it's £19.50 for three courses.

The ***Buchanan Arms*** (see Where to stay; daily noon-5pm & 6-9pm) has a fine restaurant offering an à la carte menu with main courses for around £13.95 though steaks are more expensive. The bar serves light meals (daily 11am-9pm) including sandwiches from £4.25 and a roast on Sunday (£9.95).

DRYMEN TO BALMAHA — MAPS 8-11

This is a wonderful **seven-mile (11km)** section to the edge of the Highlands. Wide tracks climb gently through **Garadhban Forest** (Map 9), a large mature conifer plantation, to a clearing where the trail divides (1-1¼hrs). The **easier route** descends to **Milton of Buchanan** and follows the pavement beside the B837 road for almost 2 miles (3km) to Balmaha (45-60 mins).

The tiring yet spectacular **high route** (1½-2hrs) winds through more forest and then out onto open moorland before ascending to just below the top of **Conic Hill** (Map 10; 361m/1184ft), see box below.

A short climb to one of the multiple summits gives an incredible vantage point over Loch Lomond and the surrounding countryside. The steep descent takes you swiftly down to the honey-pot hamlet of **Balmaha** on the loch shore; a hive of boating activity in summer.

❑ One foot in the Highlands and one in the Lowlands

Conic Hill (Map 10, p118) lies on the Highland Boundary Fault, a massive geological fracture separating the Lowlands from the Highlands. Standing on top of the hill you can see the line of islands across Loch Lomond clearly marking the direction of the fault zone which runs right across the width of Scotland from Kintyre to Stonehaven, just south of Aberdeen.

MILTON OF BUCHANAN — Map 9

Milton is a tiny hamlet on the quicker alternative route to Balmaha. Even if you wanted to take the high route to Conic Hill it takes only 15 to 20 minutes to walk down to ***Mar Achlais*** (☎ 01360-870300, 🖳 www.marachlais.com; 1D/1D, T or F; ♥; WI-FI; 🐕; £30pp, sgl occ £40); they will provide an evening meal if booked in advance.

❑ Important note – walking times

Unless otherwise specified, **all times in this book refer only to the time spent walking**. You will need to add 20-30% to allow for rests, photography, checking the map, drinking water etc, not to mention time simply to stop and stare. When planning the day's hike count on 5-7 hours' actual walking.

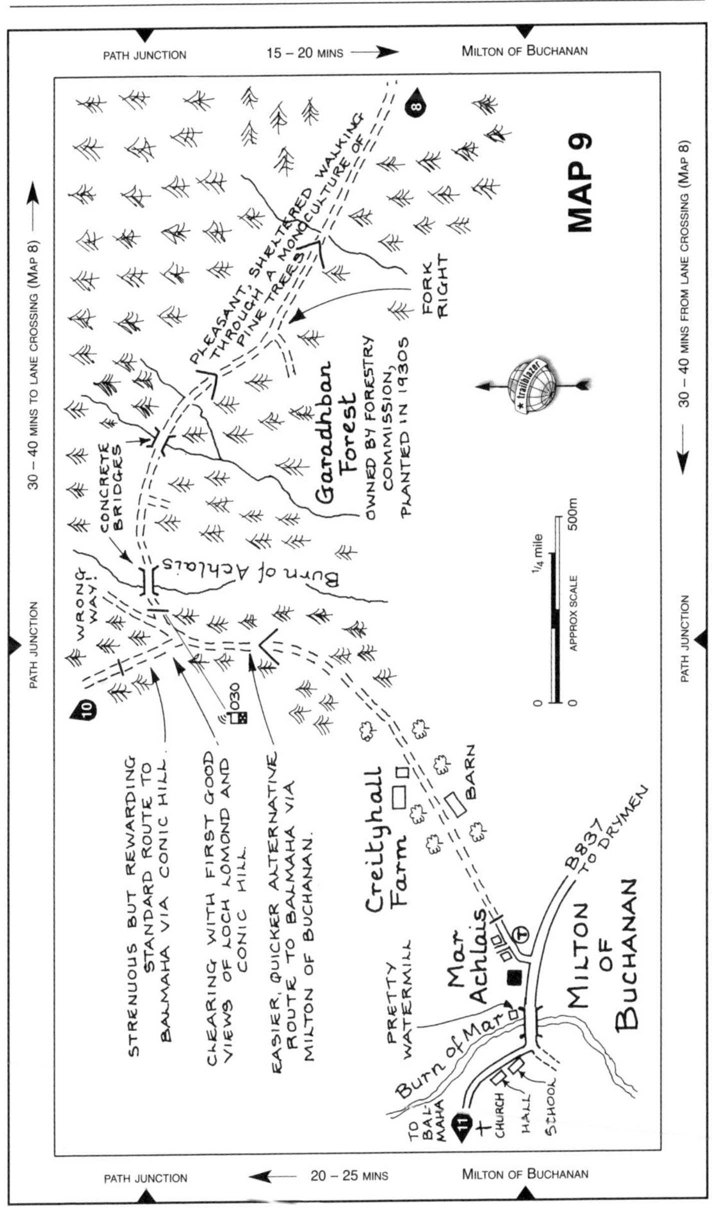
PATH JUNCTION
15 – 20 MINS →
MILTON OF BUCHANAN
30 – 40 MINS TO LANE CROSSING (MAP 8) →
PATH JUNCTION
← 30 – 40 MINS FROM LANE CROSSING (MAP 8)
PATH JUNCTION
PATH JUNCTION
← 20 – 25 MINS
MILTON OF BUCHANAN
MAP 9
8
PLEASANT, SHELTERED WALKING THROUGH A MONOCULTURE OF PINE TREES
FORK RIGHT
Garadhban Forest
OWNED BY FORESTRY COMMISSION, PLANTED IN 1930S
CONCRETE BRIDGES
Burn of Achlais
WRONG WAY!
10
030
STRENUOUS BUT REWARDING STANDARD ROUTE TO BALMAHA VIA CONIC HILL.
CLEARING WITH FIRST GOOD VIEWS OF LOCH LOMOND AND CONIC HILL.
EASIER, QUICKER ALTERNATIVE ROUTE TO BALMAHA VIA MILTON OF BUCHANAN.
Creityhall Farm
BARN
B837 TO DRYMEN
MILTON OF BUCHANAN
Mar Achlais
PRETTY WATERMILL
Burn of Mar
TO BALMAHA
11
CHURCH
HALL
SCHOOL
trailblazer
0
APPROX SCALE
1/4 mile
0
500m

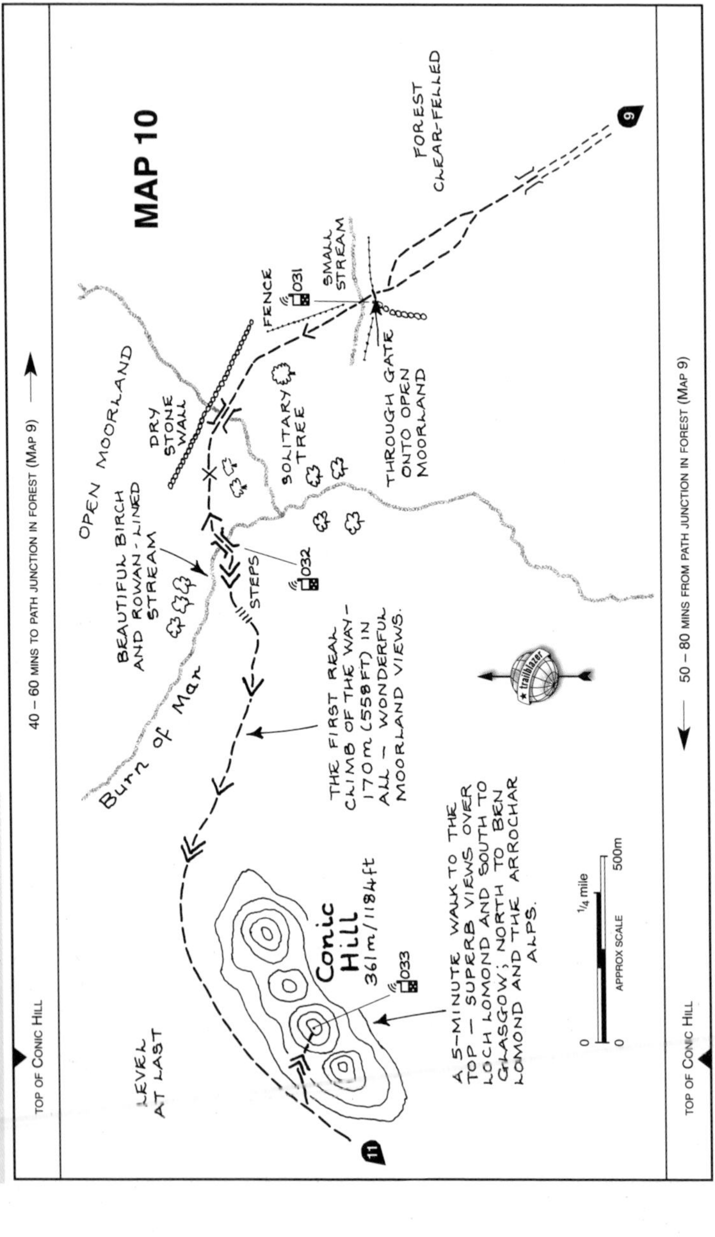

MAP 10

TOP OF CONIC HILL

40 – 60 MINS TO PATH JUNCTION IN FOREST (MAP 9) →

← 50 – 80 MINS FROM PATH JUNCTION IN FOREST (MAP 9)

TOP OF CONIC HILL

FOREST CLEAR-FELLED

SMALL STREAM

FENCE

031

THROUGH GATE ONTO OPEN MOORLAND

OPEN MOORLAND

DRY STONE WALL

SOLITARY TREE

BEAUTIFUL BIRCH AND ROWAN-LINED STREAM

032

STEPS

Burn of Mar

THE FIRST REAL CLIMB OF THE WAY – 170m (558FT) IN ALL – WONDERFUL MOORLAND VIEWS.

Conic Hill 361m/1184ft

033

A 5-MINUTE WALK TO THE TOP – SUPERB VIEWS OVER LOCH LOMOND AND SOUTH TO GLASGOW; NORTH TO BEN LOMOND AND THE ARROCHAR ALPS.

LEVEL AT LAST

0 ¼ mile

0 500m

APPROX SCALE

trailblazer

9

11

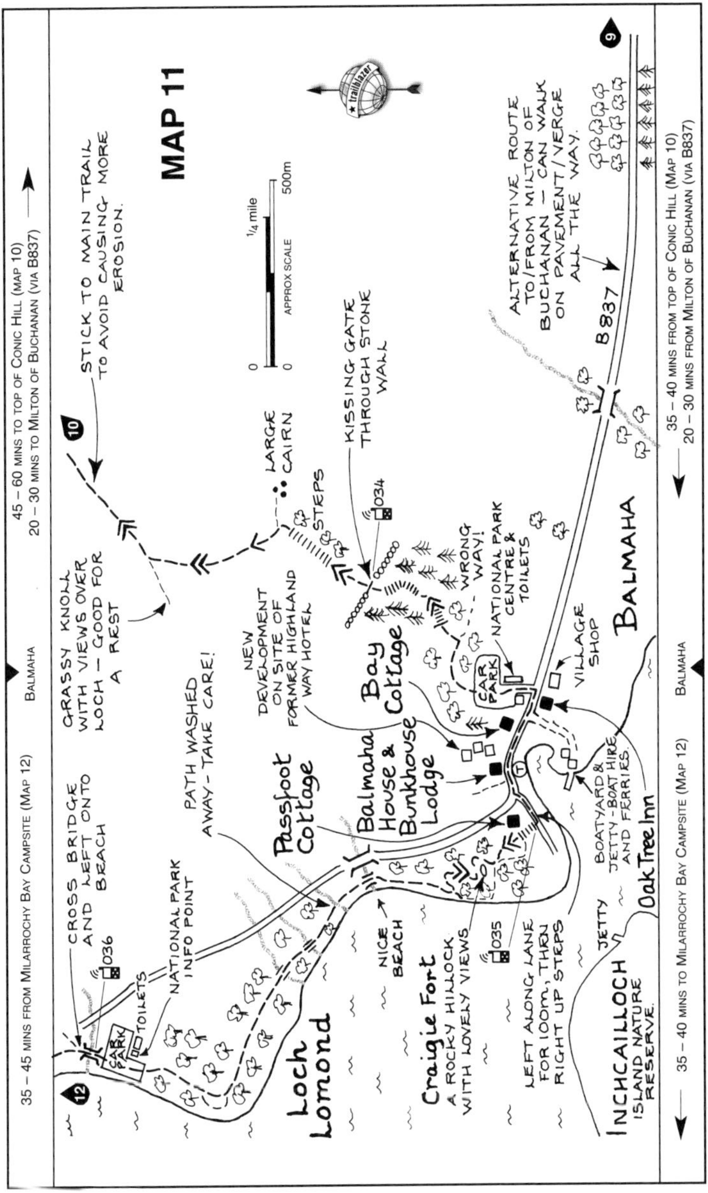

35 – 45 MINS FROM MILARROCHY BAY CAMPSITE (MAP 12)

BALMAHA

45 – 60 MINS TO TOP OF CONIC HILL (MAP 10)
20 – 30 MINS TO MILTON OF BUCHANAN (VIA B837)

MAP 11

12

CROSS BRIDGE AND LEFT ONTO BEACH

036

CAR PARK

TOILETS

NATIONAL PARK INFO POINT

GRASSY KNOLL WITH VIEWS OVER LOCH – GOOD FOR A REST

10

STICK TO MAIN TRAIL TO AVOID CAUSING MORE EROSION.

PATH WASHED AWAY - TAKE CARE!

NEW DEVELOPMENT ON SITE OF FORMER HIGHLAND WAY HOTEL

LARGE CAIRN

0 ¼ mile
0 APPROX SCALE 500m

Loch Lomond

Passfoot Cottage

STEPS

KISSING GATE THROUGH STONE WALL

034

NICE BEACH

Balmaha House & Bunkhouse Lodge

Bay Cottage

Craigie Fort
A ROCKY HILLOCK WITH LOVELY VIEWS

WRONG WAY!

035

CAR PARK

NATIONAL PARK CENTRE & TOILETS

LEFT ALONG LANE FOR 100m, THEN RIGHT UP STEPS

ALTERNATIVE ROUTE TO/FROM MILTON OF BUCHANAN – CAN WALK ON PAVEMENT/VERGE ALL THE WAY.

VILLAGE SHOP

JETTY

BOATYARD & JETTY - BOAT HIRE AND FERRIES.

B837

9

INCHCAILLOCH
ISLAND NATURE RESERVE.

Oak Tree Inn

BALMAHA

35 – 40 MINS TO MILARROCHY BAY CAMPSITE (MAP 12)

BALMAHA

35 – 40 MINS FROM TOP OF CONIC HILL (MAP 10)
20 – 30 MINS FROM MILTON OF BUCHANAN (VIA B837)

BALMAHA

Map 11, p119

This small village at the foot of Conic Hill is situated round an idyllic bay providing a sheltered anchorage for pleasure boats.

It's also a convenient departure point for **cruises** round the string of islands stretching across Loch Lomond to the western shore. At the **boatyard** MacFarlane & Son (☎ 01360-870214, 💻 www.balmahaboatyard.co.uk) run trips throughout the year at 2pm, 3pm, 4pm and 4.30pm (£7 for an hour, £4 for a half-hour cruise). Rowing (Clinker-style) boats can be hired for £10 an hour (£20 with an outboard motor). They also operate a service to North Pier on Inchcailloch for £5.

Sadly, what once must have been a pretty hamlet has been spoiled by modern tourist development. On a summer weekend the car park, bigger than the village itself, can swell to capacity as hordes drive to Loch Lomond's 'secluded' eastern shore to enjoy the 'freedom' of the countryside. This popularity does of course mean there is plenty of accommodation for the walker.

Services

The **National Park Visitor Centre** (☎ 01389-722100; Apr-Sep daily 9.30am-4.30pm and into Oct Mon-Fri; weekends only in winter) in the car park provides information on the area including an interesting exhibition on the geology of the area. There's free WI-FI here; the loos cost 20p.

The **Village Shop** (daily 9am-8pm in the summer) is well stocked and has a selection of emergency items for walkers – snacks, socks, plasters, maps.

McGill's No 309 **bus** calls here (for details see pp44-8).

Where to stay and eat

Between May and September and by prior arrangement **camping** (☎ 01389-722600; see also box below) is allowed at a designated site at Port Bawn on the island of Inchcailloch. This simple site has a composting toilet for human waste only and can be reached by catching the small ferry operated by MacFarlane & Son (see opposite).

As you walk out of the car park into Balmaha, directly opposite is the walker-friendly ***Oak Tree Inn*** (☎ 01360-870357, 💻 www.oak-tree-inn.co.uk; 2S/11T/14D/3F; 🐕; WI-FI (intermittently); £37.50-50pp, sgl £60, sgl occ £75, family room £120-150 per room) constructed from local timber and slate. There are also two **bunkhouse** rooms which sleep four and cost £30pp for two or more (sgl occ £50); the rate includes breakfast. There are no cooking facilities in the bunkhouse. Note that some of the rooms are in separate buildings a short walk away. The Inn offers a wide range of **food** (daily noon-9pm) including deli subs for £7.25, pizzas from £9.45 and excellent cullen skink £5.95. This is the only place to eat at in the village but they also do food to takeaway.

For something more homely one of the best places is ***Passfoot Cottage*** (☎ 01360-870324, 💻 www.passfoot.com; 1D/1T; WI-FI; £37.50pp, sgl occ £55; Apr-Sep), a sweet

❑ Loch Lomond National Nature Reserve

Just offshore from Balmaha is the beautiful wooded island of **Inchcailloch** (Map 11, p119) which, along with four small neighbouring islands and the mouth of the Endrick Water just south of Balmaha, forms Loch Lomond National Nature Reserve. Inchcailloch can be visited by boat (see above) any time of the year and there is a nature trail explaining the natural and human history of the island. The woods are arguably at their most beautiful in spring when the bluebells and primroses are in flower. Inchcailloch, which translates as Island of Nuns, has long been associated with Christianity and specifically St Kentigema, a missionary from Ireland who settled here in the 8th century. A church was built on the island in the 12th century; the remains of it can be seen on the nature trail walk. The associated burial ground was used up until 1947.

traditional cottage overlooking the bay and away from the tourist hubbub.

Other places to consider are ***Bay Cottage*** (☎ 01360-870346, 🖳 www.baycottagebalmaha.co.uk; 3D, T or F; WI-FI; 🐕 £5; £38pp, sgl occ £42-57; Mar-Oct) where the rate includes use of the hot tub on the deck outside and afternoon tea with scones; a packed lunch costs £6 and the owner will do a load of washing for £5. One room is in the main house, one in an annex and another, the studio, is right next to the hot tub.

Balmaha House (☎ 01360-870218; 🖳 www.balmahahouse.co.uk; 1S/2D; WI-FI; £35pp, £30pp without breakfast, sgl occ £50) had a change of ownership in 2012. They're open all year and also operate ***Balmaha Bunkhouse Lodge*** (1D/1T/4-bed and 6-bed room; 🐕 £5; WI-FI; £20pp, sgl occ of double or twin £30), a smart purpose-built bunkhouse with an open-plan kitchen offering accommodation in four rooms. The rate includes a toast/cereal breakfast; a packed lunch costs £4.50. The lodge is situated both right on the Way and on the lakeshore and canoes/kayaks are available for hire. There is also a **self-catering chalet** (£60 for two people plus £10 per additional person; 🐕 £5) with a double bed and a sofa (double) bed.

BALMAHA TO ROWARDENNAN — MAPS 11-15

This is the first **seven miles (11km, 2½-3¼hrs)** of interesting walking along the 'bonnie banks' of **Loch Lomond** (see box p126). There are no major climbs though the well-maintained path does rise and fall many times as it meanders through beautiful re-established native woodland punctuated by rocky coves and tiny beaches. For short sections it is forced to join the road which runs parallel to the Way as far as Rowardennan. In summer this can be busy with holidaymakers driving between the various caravan sites, car parks and beauty spots.

Rowardennan is the starting point for the long but rewarding climb to the top of **Ben Lomond** (see pp126-8) which stands above this tiny scattered settlement.

CASHEL Map 12 p122 & Map 13 p123

Milarrochy Bay Campsite (☎ 01360-870236, 🖳 www.campingandcaravanningclub.co.uk; late Mar to late Oct; £4.30-6.90 for Camping and Caravanning Club members, £5.95-8.80 for walkers who are not members) is a large family-orientated **campsite** for caravans and tents on the water's edge. One unit is set aside for backpackers to use for stove cooking; there are also showers, toilets and lockers which can be used to dry clothes. It has a small **shop** (daily 9-11am & 4-6pm; high season 9am-5pm) selling staples such as milk, bread, cheese, biscuits and sweets.

Cashel Caravan and Campsite (☎ 0845-130 8224, 🖳 www.campinginthefor est.co.uk/scotland/cashel-campsite; £8.05-10.85pp; late Mar to end Oct) is just under a mile further on and is beautifully located by the loch. Facilities include a **laundry** and a well-stocked **shop** (daily 9am-noon & 4-6pm; high season 8.30am-6pm) which not only has a good selection of food but also midge repellent, maps and all fuels for camping stoves. Be warned: stocks may run out towards the end of the season.

Anchorage Cottage (☎ 01360-870394, 🖳 www.anchoragecottage.co.uk; early Apr to Sep; 1T/1D or T; WI-FI; £45pp, sgl occ £90) is a very comfortable house overlooking the loch. They don't do evening meals but if you have booked in advance they will pick you up from Rowardennan Hotel any time between 4.30pm and 9pm; so walk on, have an evening meal and then call them. A packed lunch costs £6.50.

The Shepherd's House (☎ 01360-870105, 🖳 theshepherdshouse.co.uk; Feb-Nov), provides accommodation in a self-

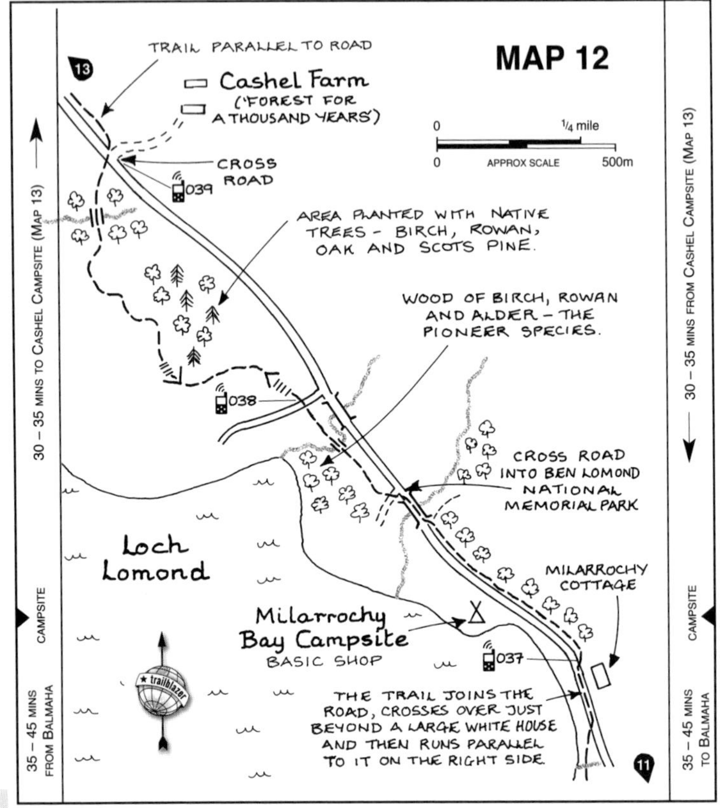

❑ Cashel – the forest for a thousand years

The restoration of native woodland is very much in vogue on the shores of Loch Lomond. The project taking place at Cashel Farm (☎ 01360-870450, 💻 www.cashel.org.uk), see Map 12, is one of the most ambitious aiming to re-create a native woodland (oak, birch, aspen, alder, hazel, juniper, holly and Scots pine) over 3000 acres of land. Local community involvement and public access is an important objective and will hopefully show the way ahead for sound woodland management which benefits everyone. You can contribute by sponsoring a tree; see the website for details. They have a small, unmanned, visitor centre (Easter-Oct, Tue-Sun 10am-4pm) with an interpretation board and toilets. You can also enjoy one of their three **woodland trails**, each of which showcases the variety of native woodland that exists in the Highlands. A walk around these regenerating woodlands highlights the importance of reforestation projects such as this in righting some of the damage done to our environment. See also box p70.

contained apartment (The Shepherd's Rooms; 1D; WI-FI; £40pp, sgl occ £60-80) or in a cosy little hut (The Shepherd's Hut; 1D; WI-FI; 🐕 £10; £35pp, sgl occ £50-70). Both places are equipped with a digital radio and iPod dock. A packed lunch costs £5. If arranged in advance they offer walkers a free lift from the Rowardennan Hotel at around 7.30pm and a lift back there the next morning.

Sallochy Campsite (💻 www.forestry.gov.uk/forestry/INFD-8HVHUY; £5pp; 01 Apr to 31 Oct) must be booked online in advance. There are 20 pitches, composting toilets and a water tap. A warden is on site 8.30am-noon and 4.30-8pm.

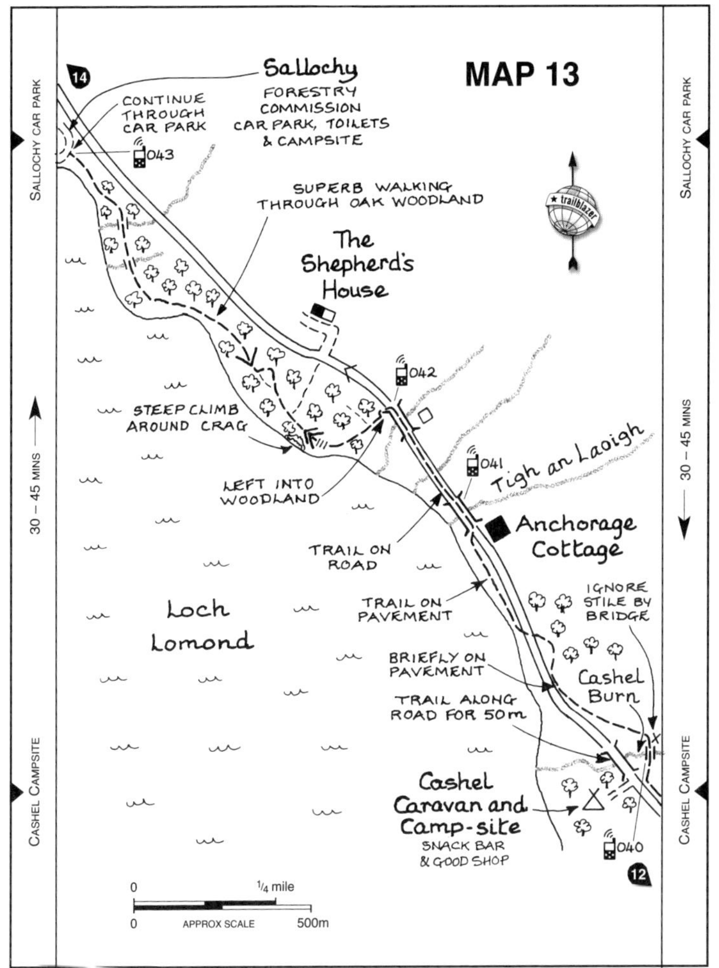

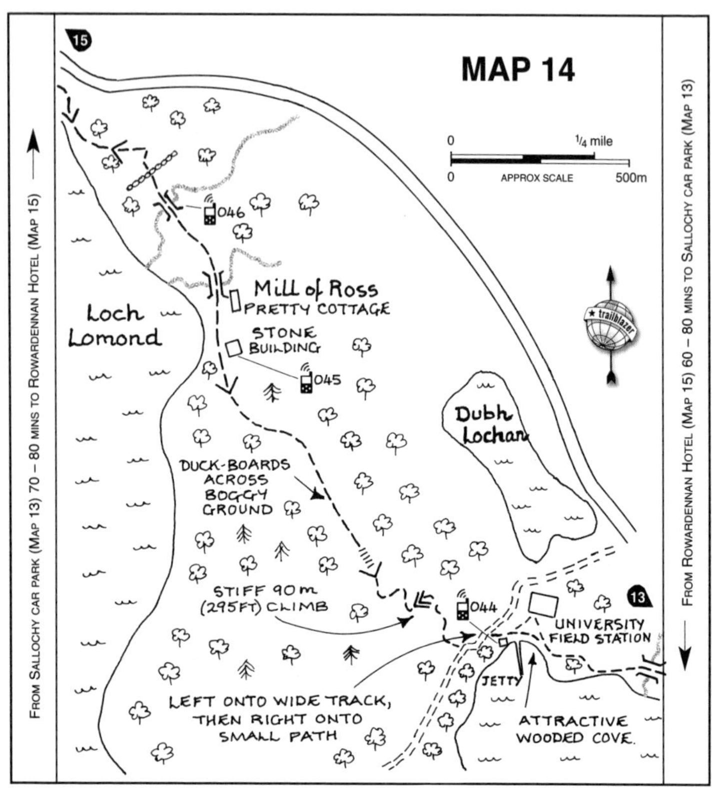

❑ Loch Lomond

Loch Lomond is the **largest area of fresh water** in Britain; 23 miles (37km) long, up to 5 miles (8km) wide and 190m (623ft) deep at it deepest point near Rowchoish bothy. It was gouged out by a glacier about 10,000 years ago and at its northern end displays a typical fjord-like landscape with steep mountain walls on each side of the narrow ribbon of water. Its southern end is dotted with most of the 38 islands which have been lived on at one time or another. The loch provides up to 450 million litres of water a day to people in Central Scotland which incredibly lowers the water level by only 6mm.

The **wildlife** of the area is incredibly rich. Naturalists have found a quarter of Britain's flowers, 200 species of birds and 19 species of fish, more than in any other loch. It is renowned for giant pike which grow to huge weights in the depths and you will often see anglers trolling for them behind small motor boats. Two of the more unusual species present are powan (*Coregonus lavaretus*), a type of freshwater herring, and lamprey (*Petromyson marinus*), an eel-like parasite which can grow to almost a metre in length. It latches on to other fish with its sharp teeth and sucker mouth producing a saliva which liquifies the victim's muscles, often killing it in the process.

ROWARDENNAN Map 15

This tiny settlement provides accommodation for campers and hostellers as well as those with a healthy budget but nothing in between.

The first place you come to is ***Rowardennan Hotel*** (☎ 01360-870273, 💻 www.rowardennanhotel.co.uk; 4D/12D or T/2F; ☕; WI-FI; 🐕 £10; £45-55pp, sgl occ £66-85, £120-144 for a family room sleeping up to four people). Most walkers only pop in for a restorative pint and perhaps some 'haggis from the Highlands' from the Rob Roy or Clansmen bars. They have a garden by the loch, the perfect place for a stop. **Food** is served daily from 11am to 9pm, Sat to 9.30pm.

Five minutes further on is a beautiful Victorian hunting lodge, now ***Rowardennan Lodge Youth Hostel*** (☎ 01360-870259, 💻 www.syha.org.uk; 62 beds; two 2-bed, three 3-bed, three 4-bed, five 6-bed, one 7-bed; £16-18pp, 2-/3-bed room from £42/60, some rooms are en suite; mid Mar to mid Oct); the reception is closed between 10am and 3pm. It is licensed and meals are provided but there is also a very basic food **shop** at the reception. There's a washing machine (£2) and drying room.

Just beyond the hostel the old ranger centre has been converted into ***Ardess Lodge Bunkhouse*** (☎ 0844-493 2108, 💻 www.nts.org.uk/Holidays /Specialist-properties/ Base-Camps/; 10 beds in two rooms; £19pp or £70 for 6 or fewer people) with a great living room and wood-burning stove.

For details of **Cruise Loch Lomond**'s ferry service

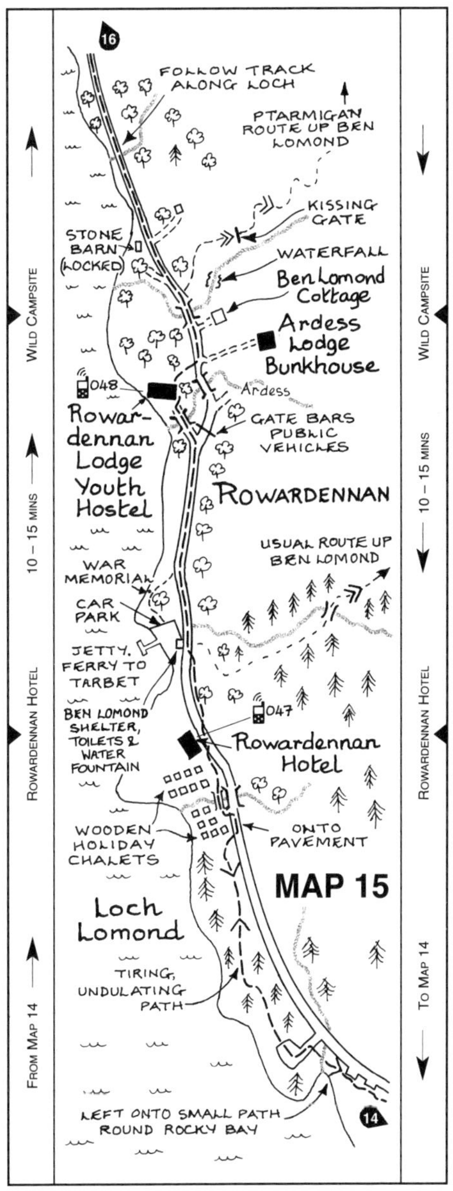

between Tarbet and Rowardennan see p45; the journey (45 mins). The fare is £8/12 single/return; bikes (£1 each way) are welcome and dogs are free. Call in advance to be sure of a place. See the public transport map and table on pp44-8 for onward connections from Tarbet (Scottish Citylink bus Nos 914, 915, 916, 926 & 976).

If you're planning to climb Ben Lomond (see below) it's worth popping into the Ben Lomond Shelter in the car park en route; this is a beautiful and innovative building built out of straw bales and rendered in lime; sensitive, low-impact building materials that fit with the ecological remit of the national park. It has displays on the local history and wildlife and there is a drinking-water tap and public toilets.

❑ '...the bonnie bonnie banks of Loch Lomond' – but for how much longer?
This world-famous line was written by a condemned Jacobite prisoner who lamented that he would never see his true love again on the shore of the loch. Popularised by William Wordsworth, Gerard Manley Hopkins and Walter Scott, Loch Lomond (see box p124) is still regarded as one of the most beautiful places in Scotland and by walking the West Highland Way you get to journey along its entire length.

In recent years camping by the eastern shore of the loch became hugely popular, thanks it would seem, to the Scottish Outdoor Access Code which allows greater freedom for wild camping. Whilst wild camping is a worthwhile way of enjoying the outdoors it is only acceptable if done so responsibly. Sadly, Loch Lomond seems particularly vulnerable to hugely irresponsible campers, some of whom arrive with the sole purpose of partying on the beaches, leaving beer cans and other rubbish scattered in the sand after they have gone. As a result **new camping restrictions now apply – see p52**.

The leisure industry is also having a big impact on the area: oil pollution, sewage and noise from boats is interfering with wildlife and other recreational users such as bathers and fishermen. The thousands of walkers and picnickers who flock to the shores in summer leave behind an incredible amount of litter and their cars choke the roads for miles around. Nearby forestry and farming have also had an effect by polluting the water with fertiliser nutrients and an increasing amount of silt which is washed into the loch when the drainage of the hillsides is modified.

With such high intensity usage and so many conflicting interests it was the obvious choice for the first National Park in Scotland (see box p67). It is hoped that increased funding and an integrated management strategy will help conserve the beauty of this popular area but it also requires campers and the leisure industry to play their part.

Side trip – Ascent of Ben Lomond

Ben Lomond, Scotland's most southerly Munro (see box p35), is the first real mountain you pass on the Way and is a great excuse for taking a day out from your progress north. At 974m (3195ft) the summit is an excellent vantage point from which to view Loch Lomond and a large portion of the West Highland Way.

Route options There are two principal ways to the top. The **most straightforward** but least exciting is to follow the popular well-maintained path beginning opposite the Ben Lomond Shelter at the Rowardennan car park which ascends through forest onto the broad southerly ridge of the mountain and follows this to the summit. To return do the route in reverse.

The **interesting alternative** ascends via the subsidiary summit of Ptarmigan before climbing the steep north-west ridge to the top and then descends along the normal route. This route is described below. The whole trip

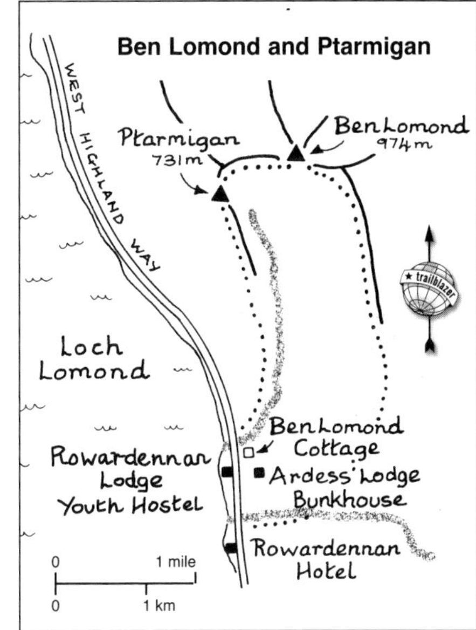

takes 4½-5½ hours allowing for short stops along the way.

Safety Steep corries on the north and north-east flanks of Ben Lomond mean that you should take particular care when nearing the summit, especially if visibility is poor or when there is snow and ice on the ground. No matter how good the weather is, you must know how to navigate well with map and compass and be properly equipped (see p56), conditions can change quickly and with little warning. You'll need one of the following maps: OS Landranger sheet 56 (1:50,000) or OS Explorer 364 (1:25,000).

The Ptarmigan Route (See also Map 15) The Ptarmigan Route leaves the West Highland Way just after **Ben Lomond Cottage**. Watch for the small trail on the right immediately after crossing the concrete bridge. It's opposite the free camping area. Take this small trail through the woods passing a **waterfall** on the right and then under the wide branches of an old oak tree. Climb the bracken-covered hillside, go through a **kissing gate** and on up steepening ground keeping a deer-fence on your right; ignore any ladder-stiles over it.

After 15-20 minutes the deer-fence and regenerated woodland veer off to your right; continue along the well-worn trail underneath some small crags with a conifer plantation far below to the left. As you round a small bend the knobbly summit of Ptarmigan appears and the path can be seen zigzagging up to it. In 10-15 minutes go through another kissing gate and continue on the trail along the west side of Ptarmigan's south-reaching ridge.

In five minutes you cross a small burn (fill up with water), then gradually climb onto the south ridge to the zigzags which lead steeply up to **Ptarmigan** (731m/2398ft); 20 minutes. It's then gentle walking round and over rocky hummocks past some small lochans up to the highest hummock marked with a cairn (751m/2463ft); 15 minutes. Descend to the peat-covered **Bealach Buidhe**, crossed on some large stepping stones, and begin the ascent of Ben Lomond's north-west ridge on a good path. Though steep, the path is easy to follow and you'll reach the **summit** in 20-25 minutes. Allowing for short stops you should get to the summit in 2½ to 3 hours from the start.

The wide, easily angled **tourist route** makes a pleasant and quick descent and you can appreciate that it would be a sluggish, uninspiring way up. Fifty minutes to one hour after leaving the summit you pass through a **kissing gate**, descend steeply momentarily, before levelling across the cattle-grazed hillside.

Fifteen minutes later cross the small bridge over the **Ardess Burn** into the coniferous forest. Five minutes further on you descend a rocky step (slippery in the wet) and then continue down some well-made stone steps, over a small bridge, weaving through heather, bracken and birch. You emerge from the forest opposite the Ben Lomond Shelter 15 minutes later.

ROWARDENNAN TO INVERSNAID — MAPS 15-19

A lovely wooded walk along the shore of Loch Lomond for **7 miles (11km, 2¼-3½hrs)**, away from both traffic and tourists.

Within a short distance there is a choice of routes. The easier **high route** stays on the undulating forestry track passing several waterfalls and yielding occasional surprise views through the trees. A harder **alternative route** drops down to the loch on a small path which forges a tortuous route clinging as close to the shore as it dares. Many short, steep climbs, fallen trees and rocky sections make the going slow and arduous. The rewards for this are being immersed in glorious oak woods with wonderful lochside views.

The two routes rejoin just beyond ***Rowchoish Bothy*** (see Map 17), a simple shelter with sleeping platform and fire. The Way continues on a well-made path along the shore through further stretches of old oak woodland. If you take the **high route** you will reach **Inversnaid Hotel** in **2¼ to 3 hours**. Via the **low route** it will take **2½ to 3½ hours**.

> *What would the world be, once bereft*
> *Of wet and wildness? Let them be left,*
> *O let them be left, wildness and wet;*
> *Long live the weeds and the wilderness yet.*
> **Gerard Manley Hopkins** *Inversnaid*

❑ Ben Lomond National Memorial Park

This park runs along 8 miles (13km) of the loch's eastern shore, from Milarrochy to Rowardennan, right up to the summit of Ben Lomond. It was officially opened in 1997 as a reminder of those who have fought for their country and it is held in trust for the public in perpetuity.

The park is jointly managed and owned by the National Trust for Scotland and Forestry Commission Scotland and is an excellent example of how the priorities of these organisations are changing for the better. Until a few years ago this land was covered in uniform conifer plantation the purpose of which was purely economic. Now the conifers are being grubbed up and the woodland is slowly being brought back to the native birch and oak which have traditionally covered the banks of Loch Lomond. In the process the number of plants, animals and insects that these woods can support will increase; just compare ground beneath a conifer plantation with the floor of a native woodland. The project will span over 40 years. Pioneer species such as rowan, birch and alder must first get established to naturally prepare the ground for the oak which will then follow. Deer can quickly destroy the young saplings so a high fence has had to be erected until the trees can fend for themselves.

Guided walks and other events are organised by the rangers (☎ 0844-493 2217; 🖳 www.nts.org.uk) at Rowardennan throughout the year.

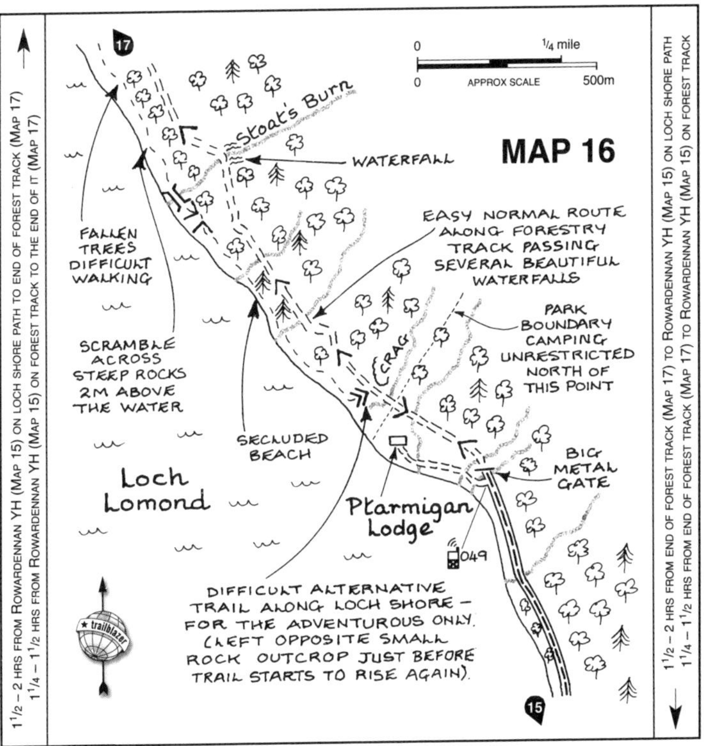

INVERSNAID **Map 19, p133**

Inversnaid Bunkhouse (☎ 01877-386249, 💻 www.inversnaid.com; Apr-Sep), housed in what was once a church (some of the stained-glass windows are still in situ), is a remote and cosy place which offers a range of accommodation. A free pick-up service from the Way is available, which is useful, considering its location 800m uphill from the Way (just follow the road up from the hotel). A bed in the **bunkhouse** (27 beds; two 2-bed/two 3-bed/two 4-bed and one 5-bed room) costs £17-21pp. They also have a **log cabin** (2D; shared facilities; 🐕; £54 per cabin). The rate for **campers** is £7pp including use of the facilities. Note, however, that they do not have a self-catering kitchen, though the ***Top Bunk Bistro***, a licensed restaurant serves food (Apr-Sep daily 8-9.30am, noon-4pm & 6-9pm). A buffet breakfast costs £4.50 and an evening meal from £8.50; it is recommended that non residents book for evening meals. They also offer free **internet access** and WI-FI, a wide range of evening entertainment, a hot tub (£2.50 per session), and a laundry service (wash and dry £3.50 per load). Packed breakfasts (£4.50) and lunches (£5.50) are also available. Group accommodation only between November and March.

Inversnaid Hotel (☎ 01877-386223, 💻 www.lochsandglens.com; 10S/103D, T or F; ☕; WI-FI in public areas; £35pp, sgl £70) is a welcome relief for many walkers as it's the only place on the Way between Rowardennan and Inverarnan that provides food and drink. The walkers' entrance is around the back and it's appreciated if you

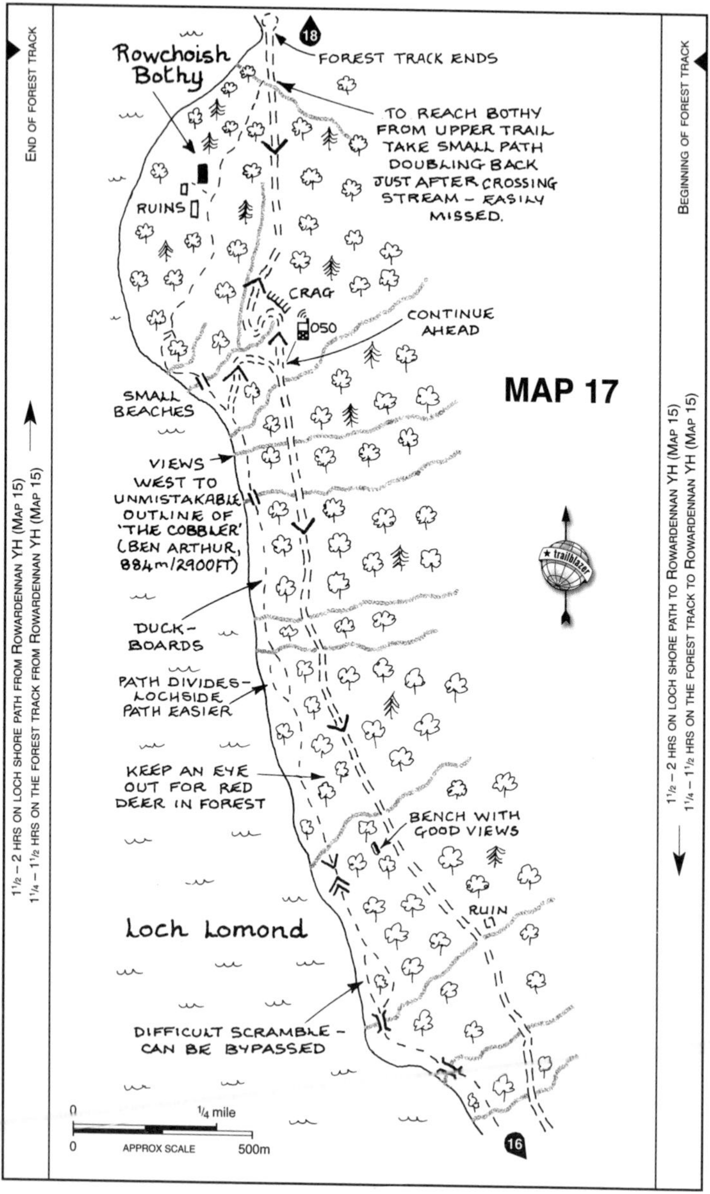

END OF FOREST TRACK

BEGINNING OF FOREST TRACK

Rowchoish Bothy

FOREST TRACK ENDS

TO REACH BOTHY FROM UPPER TRAIL TAKE SMALL PATH DOUBLING BACK JUST AFTER CROSSING STREAM – EASILY MISSED.

RUINS

CRAG

050

CONTINUE AHEAD

SMALL BEACHES

MAP 17

VIEWS WEST TO UNMISTAKABLE OUTLINE OF 'THE COBBLER' (BEN ARTHUR, 884m/2900FT)

DUCK-BOARDS

PATH DIVIDES – LOCHSIDE PATH EASIER

KEEP AN EYE OUT FOR RED DEER IN FOREST

BENCH WITH GOOD VIEWS

RUIN

Loch Lomond

DIFFICULT SCRAMBLE – CAN BE BYPASSED

0 ¼ mile

0 APPROX SCALE 500m

18

16

trailblazer

1½ – 2 HRS ON LOCH SHORE PATH FROM ROWARDENNAN YH (MAP 15)
1¼ – 1½ HRS ON THE FOREST TRACK FROM ROWARDENNAN YH (MAP 15)

1½ – 2 HRS ON LOCH SHORE PATH TO ROWARDENNAN YH (MAP 15)
1¼ – 1½ HRS ON THE FOREST TRACK TO ROWARDENNAN YH (MAP 15)

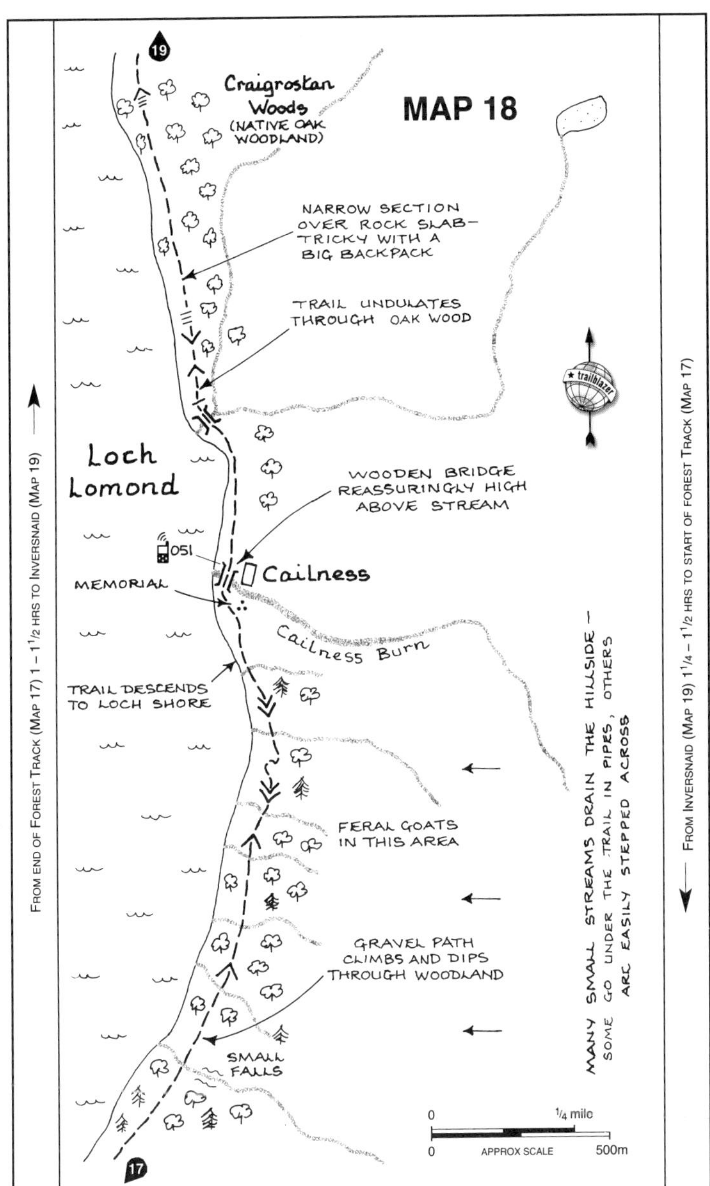
MAP 18
Craigrostan Woods
(NATIVE OAK WOODLAND)
NARROW SECTION OVER ROCK SLAB – TRICKY WITH A BIG BACKPACK
TRAIL UNDULATES THROUGH OAK WOOD
Loch Lomond
WOODEN BRIDGE REASSURINGLY HIGH ABOVE STREAM
051
Cailness
MEMORIAL
Cailness Burn
TRAIL DESCENDS TO LOCH SHORE
FERAL GOATS IN THIS AREA
GRAVEL PATH CLIMBS AND DIPS THROUGH WOODLAND
SMALL FALLS
MANY SMALL STREAMS DRAIN THE HILLSIDE – SOME GO UNDER THE TRAIL IN PIPES, OTHERS ARE EASILY STEPPED ACROSS
FROM END OF FOREST TRACK (MAP 17) 1 – 1½ HRS TO INVERSNAID (MAP 19)
FROM INVERSNAID (MAP 19) 1¼ – 1½ HRS TO START OF FOREST TRACK (MAP 17)
0 ¼ mile
0 APPROX SCALE 500m
19
17
trailblazer

remove wet and muddy clothes before going in. The bar (Easter-Oct daily noon-9pm) serves good-value **food**: take-away meals, such as burgers & chips (£5) are served 11am-3pm & 5-8pm; sandwiches (from £2.45) are available throughout the day.

Five minutes north of the hotel is a lovely clearing on the loch shore beyond the boathouse where backpackers can **camp** for free. All that is asked is that you only stay one night and don't light a fire.

A small **boat** is operated (morning and evening) by Inversnaid Hotel to the viewpoint by Sloy Power Station at Inveruglas (£4) from where it is possible to flag down the **Citylink coaches** (Nos 914, 915 & 916) on the A82; the other option is to contact **Cruise Loch Lomond** (see p45) whose scheduled West Highland Way Rambler cruises include the walk from Rowardennan to Inversnaid.

❑ Rob Roy's Cave

The concealed entrance to Rob Roy's cave (see Map 19), supposedly a hideaway of the Highland hero, is thoughtfully marked with a large 'CAVE' in white graffiti by the entrance. It's quite a scramble to get there and there's not a lot to see.

If you want to explore take a torch with you so that you can investigate the nooks and crannies. Judging by the amount of droppings on the floor it's used more by errant sheep and goats than clandestine men.

Rob Roy MacGregor, the Robin Hood of the Highlands, was born in 1671, the third son of a clan chieftain. Like many Highlanders of the time he made a living by dealing cattle, both legally and illegally, and would occasionally set off for the Lowlands on cattle raids. Part of this 'business' was the taking of protection money. By the time he was 40 he had acquired a sizeable amount of land and was prospering as a dealer. He was well known throughout Scotland for being a fair businessman, fine swordsman and for his good looks and wild red hair earning him the Gaelic nickname 'Ruadh', meaning red, which became Anglicised to 'Roy'.

His infamous career as a bandit began when he made one deal too many. He had borrowed the large sum of £1000 from the Duke of Montrose to complete a transaction, but his trusted drover ran off with the money leaving Rob a wanted man. The duke seized his land and declared Rob an outlaw. Given refuge and encouragement by a distant relation, the Duke of Argyll, Rob set off on many rustling raids against their common enemy, Montrose.

He was on the run for over 10 years and was captured several times but always managed to escape in daring ways, boosting his image. In the end he turned himself in, was threatened with deportation but was eventually pardoned by the king. He lived out his final years in relative peace at home, with his wife, where he died aged 63.

Sir Walter Scott, the prolific 19th-century Scottish writer, did more for the reputation of Rob MacGregor than a lifetime of brigandry could ever achieve. In 1818 he published the highly romanticised novel, *Rob Roy*, which not only took the tale to a wider audience but also ensured that Loch Lomond became a key sight on any tour of the Highlands. By the time William Wordsworth's sister, Dorothy, came to see the cave in 1822 there was the full tourist set-up of lake steamer, Highland piper and boys selling trinkets. If anything, the cave is a quieter place today.

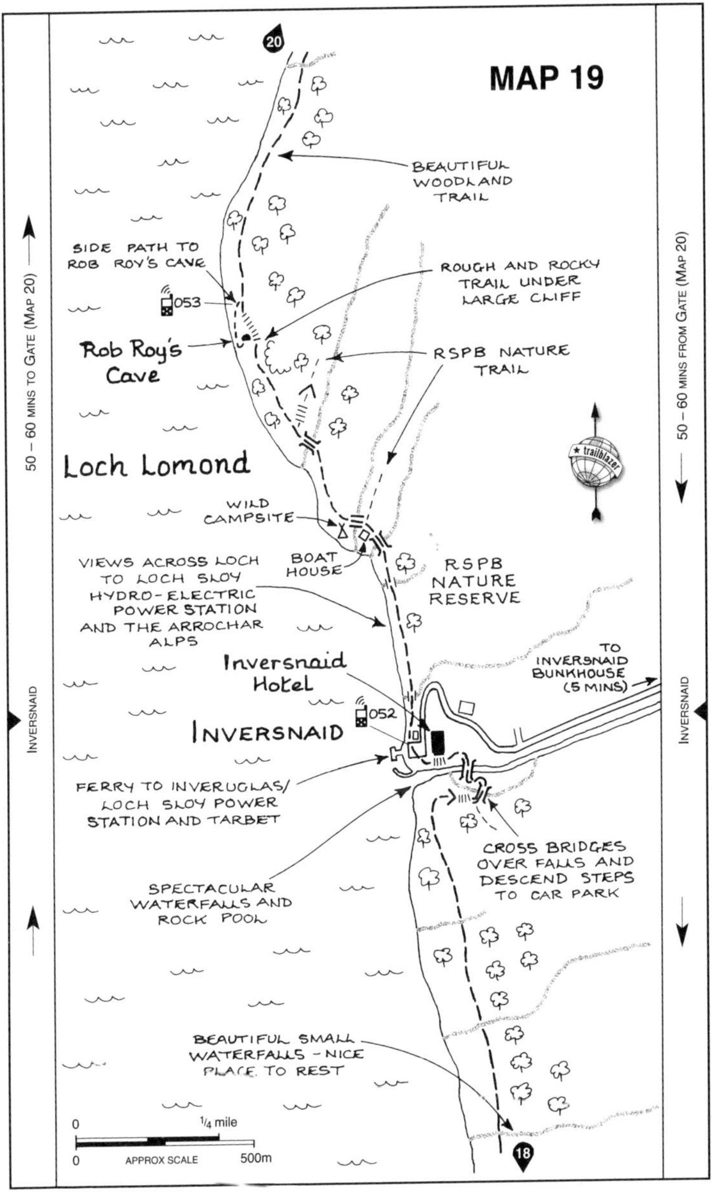

MAP 19

20

BEAUTIFUL WOODLAND TRAIL

SIDE PATH TO ROB ROY'S CAVE

ROUGH AND ROCKY TRAIL UNDER LARGE CLIFF

053

Rob Roy's Cave

RSPB NATURE TRAIL

Loch Lomond

WILD CAMPSITE

BOAT HOUSE

RSPB NATURE RESERVE

VIEWS ACROSS LOCH TO LOCH SLOY HYDRO-ELECTRIC POWER STATION AND THE ARROCHAR ALPS

Inversnaid Hotel

TO INVERSNAID BUNKHOUSE (5 MINS)

052

INVERSNAID

FERRY TO INVERUGLAS/ LOCH SLOY POWER STATION AND TARBET

SPECTACULAR WATERFALLS AND ROCK POOL

CROSS BRIDGES OVER FALLS AND DESCEND STEPS TO CAR PARK

BEAUTIFUL SMALL WATERFALLS – NICE PLACE TO REST

0 ¼ mile

0 APPROX SCALE 500m

18

50 – 60 MINS TO GATE (MAP 20)

INVERSNAID

50 – 60 MINS FROM GATE (MAP 20)

INVERSNAID

INVERSNAID TO INVERARNAN — MAPS 19-22

This **6½ miles (10km, 2½-3hrs)** provides some of the best walking so far. It has a reputation for being one of the hardest sections of the Way but recent path improvements have made it significantly easier.

The first three miles (5km) are on a rocky path winding through woodland across steep craggy slopes leading down to Loch Lomond. It is wild scenery marred only by the noise from the busy road on the western shore, now much closer as the loch narrows. Just north of Inversnaid is the **RSPB Inversnaid Nature Reserve** (💻 www.rspb.org.uk/reserves/guide/i/inversnaid), a beautiful ancient oakwood, home to redstarts, pied flycatchers and wood warblers. There is a short nature trail that starts and finishes by the Way. Another mile north from here is **Rob Roy's Cave** (see box p132) which lies a hop and a skip from the main trail amongst a craggy mess of rocks.

Near ***Doune Bothy*** (see Map 21; which provides very basic free shelter) the woodland opens out giving far-reaching southerly views. The trail then climbs away from Loch Lomond to a wide pass before descending into **Glen Falloch** (Map 22). Soft scenery dominated by water and woodland give way to the rocky fells and mountain views of the Highlands.

ARDLUI — Map 21, p136

Ardlui is on the opposite side of Loch Lomond to the trail and provides a useful start or finish for a walk along part of the Way. There are regular **buses** (Citylink Nos 914, 915 & 916) and **trains** to/from Glasgow and Fort William (for details see pp44-8). If you are simply looking for somewhere for the night you would be better off continuing to Inverarnan.

The **ferry** (Apr-Sep 9am-7pm, Oct only in the daylight hours) to Ardleish (run by Ardlui Hotel) costs £3 per person (minimum charge £5) and is summoned by raising the ball on the signal mast during hours of operation. If you are walking in winter you must arrange a ferry by telephone.

Ardlui Store (Mon-Fri 9am-2pm & 4-6pm, Sat-Sun 9am-6pm) is a newsagent with basic food supplies and fruit and veg.

The attractive ***Ardlui Hotel*** (☎ 01301-704243, 💻 www.ardlui.com; 1S/1T/7D/1F; ♥; WI-FI in reception; 🐕 £5; £47.50-55pp, sgl £45-55), at the head of the loch, has views south to Ben Lomond and gardens running down to a small anchorage and marina. There is a restaurant and bar with **food** (Easter to Oct daily 8am-9.15pm, Nov to Easter Mon-Fri noon-2pm & 6-8pm, Sat & Sun noon-9pm). There are also two **camping pods** (walkers' bothy; 1D or T, £30 per pod, £40 if for three people) but the rate doesn't include a sleeping bag. Reservations for the camping pods are recommended. The **campsite** (contact the hotel) by the very noisy road costs £7pp.

INVERARNAN — Map 22, p137

The Way goes right past the excellent ***Beinglas Farm*** (☎ 01301-704281, 💻 www.beinglascampsite.co.uk; Easter-Oct) where you can pitch your **tent** (£7.50pp; 🐕 £1). The immaculate showers are free, there's a washing machine and dryer (£3-4 for a wash, £1-2 to dry) and a sheltered area for cooking.

They also have four **camping cabins**, each sleeping up to four (£14.50pp for three or four, £17.50pp for two people, sgl occ £25); sleeping bags can be hired for £3.50. **B&B** is also available (2D/2T/4F; £37.50-42.50pp, sgl occ £60-70 and £105-120 for up to three in a family room).

The small **shop** (daily 7.30am-9.30pm) stocks all the food campers and walkers could need including essentials such as stove fuel, insect repellent and midge nets. Also on site is a **bar and restaurant**: they serve breakfast daily

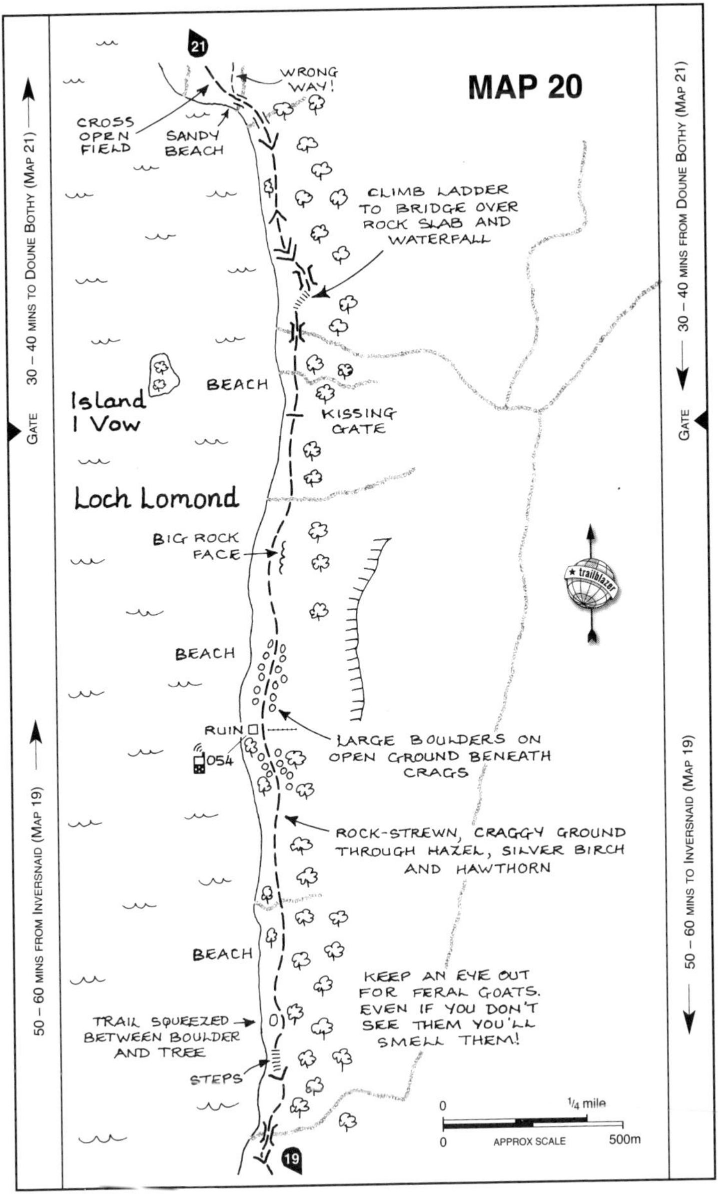

MAP 20

30 – 40 MINS TO DOUNE BOTHY (MAP 21)

GATE

50 – 60 MINS FROM INVERSNAID (MAP 19)

30 – 40 MINS FROM DOUNE BOTHY (MAP 21)

GATE

50 – 60 MINS TO INVERSNAID (MAP 19)

21

WRONG WAY!

CROSS OPEN FIELD

SANDY BEACH

CLIMB LADDER TO BRIDGE OVER ROCK SLAB AND WATERFALL

BEACH

Island I Vow

KISSING GATE

Loch Lomond

BIG ROCK FACE

BEACH

RUIN

054

LARGE BOULDERS ON OPEN GROUND BENEATH CRAGS

ROCK-STREWN, CRAGGY GROUND THROUGH HAZEL, SILVER BIRCH AND HAWTHORN

BEACH

KEEP AN EYE OUT FOR FERAL GOATS. EVEN IF YOU DON'T SEE THEM YOU'LL SMELL THEM!

TRAIL SQUEEZED BETWEEN BOULDER AND TREE

STEPS

19

trailblazer

0 1/4 mile

0 APPROX SCALE 500m

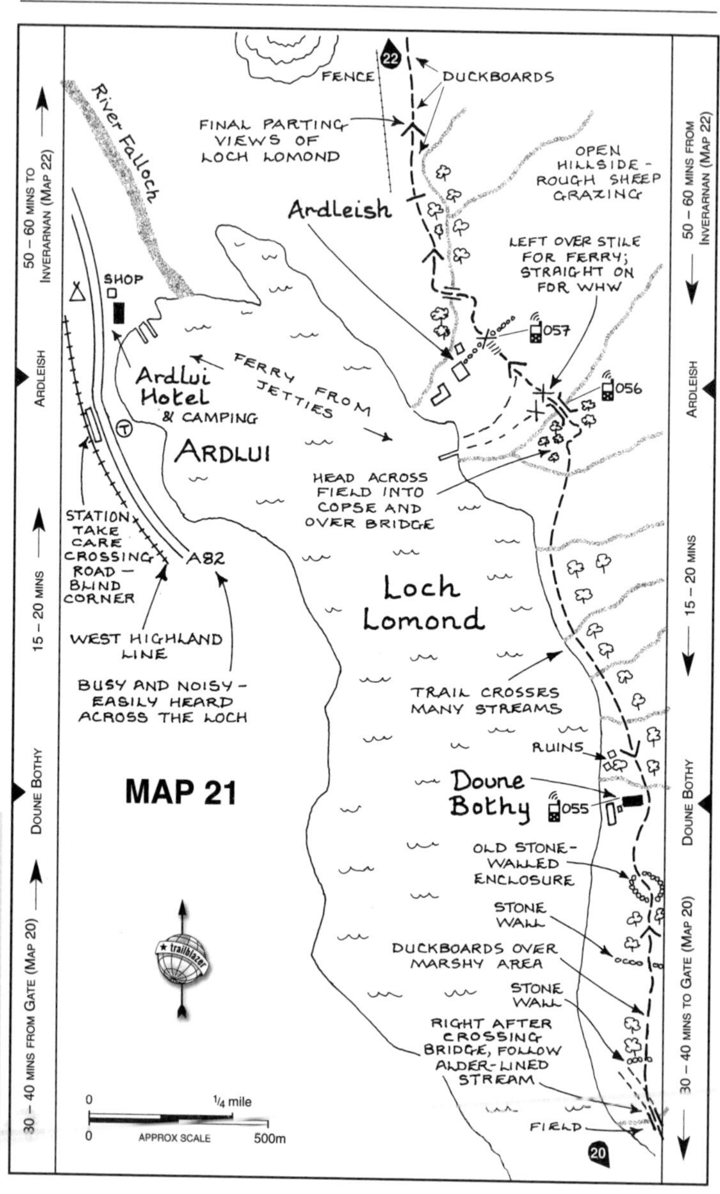

MAP 21
FENCE
DUCKBOARDS
FINAL PARTING VIEWS OF LOCH LOMOND
River Falloch
OPEN HILLSIDE - ROUGH SHEEP GRAZING
Ardleish
LEFT OVER STILE FOR FERRY; STRAIGHT ON FOR WHW
SHOP
057
056
055
Ardlui Hotel & CAMPING
FERRY FROM JETTIES
ARDLUI
HEAD ACROSS FIELD INTO COPSE AND OVER BRIDGE
STATION
TAKE CARE CROSSING ROAD - BLIND CORNER
A82
Loch Lomond
WEST HIGHLAND LINE
BUSY AND NOISY - EASILY HEARD ACROSS THE LOCH
TRAIL CROSSES MANY STREAMS
RUINS
Doune Bothy
OLD STONE-WALLED ENCLOSURE
STONE WALL
DUCKBOARDS OVER MARSHY AREA
STONE WALL
RIGHT AFTER CROSSING BRIDGE, FOLLOW ALDER-LINED STREAM
FIELD
22
20
trailblazer
0 1/4 mile
0 APPROX SCALE 500m
50 – 60 MINS TO INVERARNAN (MAP 22)
ARDLEISH
15 – 20 MINS
DOUNE BOTHY
30 – 40 MINS FROM GATE (MAP 20)
50 – 60 MINS FROM INVERARNAN (MAP 22)
30 – 40 MINS TO GATE (MAP 20)

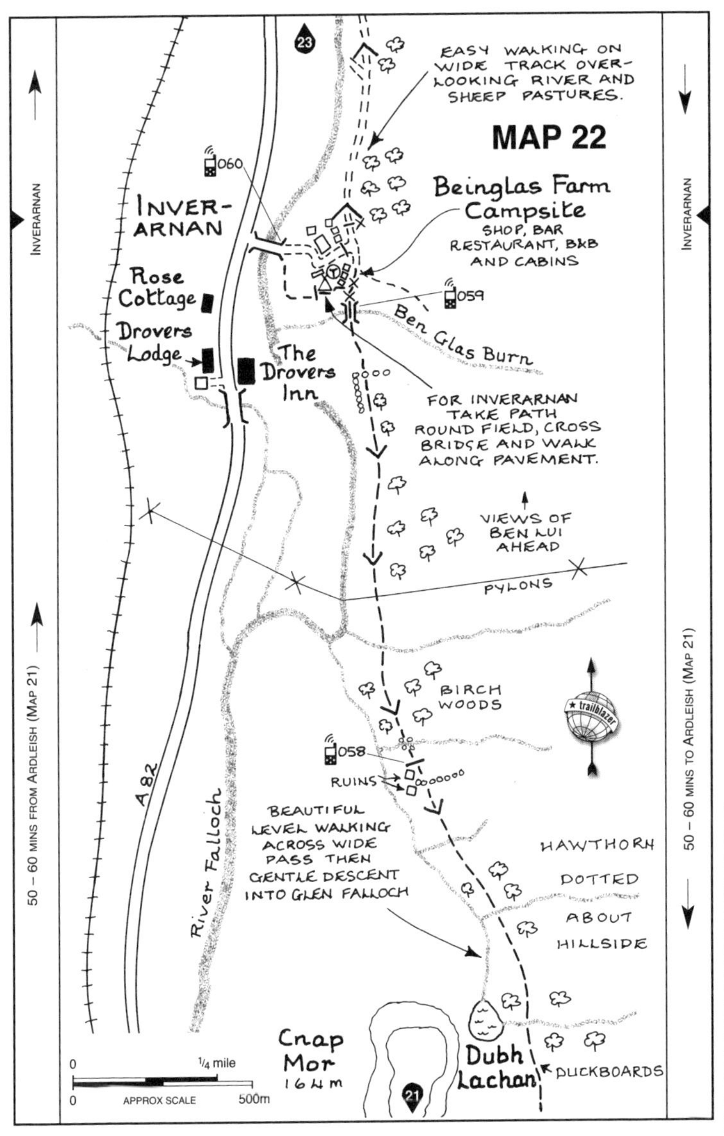
MAP 22
EASY WALKING ON WIDE TRACK OVER-LOOKING RIVER AND SHEEP PASTURES.
060
INVER-ARNAN
Beinglas Farm Campsite
SHOP, BAR RESTAURANT, B&B AND CABINS
059
Rose Cottage
Drovers Lodge
The Drovers Inn
Ben Glas Burn
FOR INVERARNAN TAKE PATH ROUND FIELD, CROSS BRIDGE AND WALK ALONG PAVEMENT.
VIEWS OF BEN LUI AHEAD
PYLONS
BIRCH WOODS
058
RUINS
BEAUTIFUL LEVEL WALKING ACROSS WIDE PASS THEN GENTLE DESCENT INTO GLEN FALLOCH
HAWTHORN DOTTED ABOUT HILLSIDE
A82
River Falloch
Cnap Mor 164m
Dubh Lochan
DUCKBOARDS
0 1/4 mile
0 APPROX SCALE 500m
23
21
INVERARNAN
50 – 60 MINS FROM ARDLEISH (MAP 21)
50 – 60 MINS TO ARDLEISH (MAP 21)
trailblazer

7.30-9.30am (a full Scottish breakfast is around £7.50); snacks (toasties for £3.50) and more filling meals, such as steak pie (£10-12), are served noon to 9.30pm.

It's a 10-minute walk to the main hamlet where B&B can be found at the pretty ***Rose Cottage*** (☎ 01301-704255, 💻 rosecottage58@yahoo.com; 1T/1D/1F; ☕; WI-FI; from £32.50pp, sgl occ £45-55).

A stone's throw away is the self-styled 'world famous' ***Drovers Inn*** (☎ 01301-704234, 💻 www.thedroversinn.co.uk; 2S/4T/5D/1D with Jacuzzi/2F, some share facilities; ☕; 🐕 £5; £25-50pp; sgl/sgl occ £30-35; family room £60-95) and, opposite, the more sober ***Drovers Lodge*** (6D/6T/4D with Jacuzzi; £25-45pp; sgl occ £30-35).

The Drovers Inn (above) is not to be missed whether for its original good-value **food** (summer Mon-Sat 7.30am-10pm, Sun noon-10pm, winter Mon-Sat 11.30am-9.30pm, Sun noon-9.30pm), excellent real ales, or its wide selection of whisky. It's an eccentric mix of smoke-blackened walls,

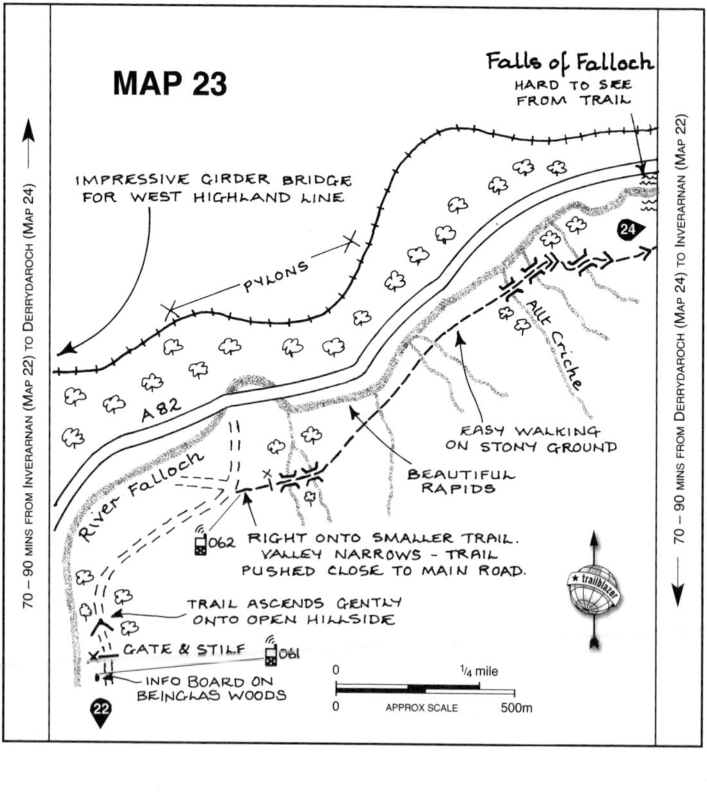

MAP 23

70 – 90 MINS FROM INVERARNAN (MAP 22) TO DERRYDAROCH (MAP 24)

70 – 90 MINS FROM DERRYDAROCH (MAP 24) TO INVERARNAN (MAP 22)

Falls of Falloch
HARD TO SEE FROM TRAIL

IMPRESSIVE GIRDER BRIDGE FOR WEST HIGHLAND LINE

PYLONS

A82

Allt Criche

River Falloch

EASY WALKING ON STONY GROUND

BEAUTIFUL RAPIDS

062 RIGHT ONTO SMALLER TRAIL. VALLEY NARROWS - TRAIL PUSHED CLOSE TO MAIN ROAD.

TRAIL ASCENDS GENTLY ONTO OPEN HILLSIDE

GATE & STILE

061

INFO BOARD ON BEINGLAS WOODS

22

24

trailblazer

0 ¼ mile

0 APPROX SCALE 500m

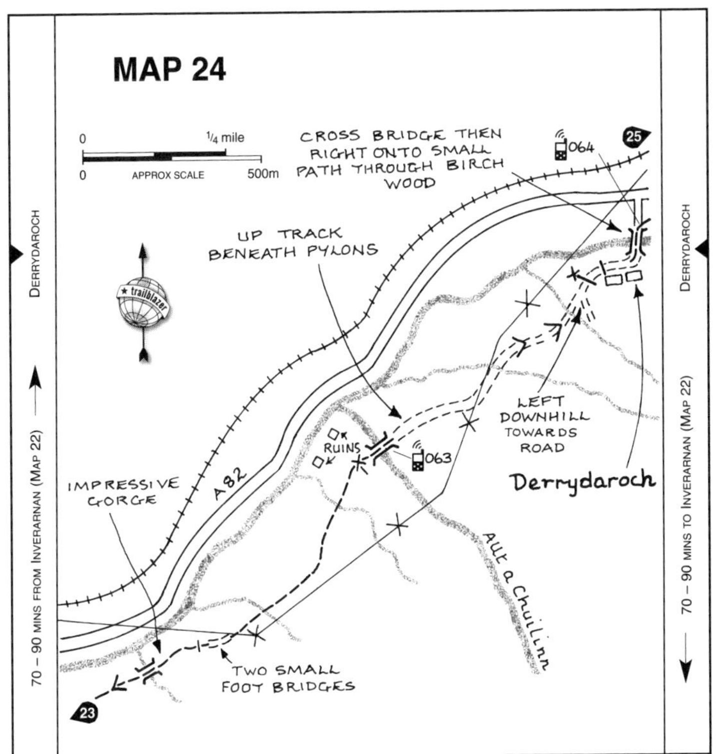

sagging velvet-covered chairs and moulting stuffed animals. There's even a stuffed haggis, said to be a real one, in the entrance hall and the place is reputed to be haunted.

Bar staff wear kilts and T-shirts. The menu varies but may include Drovers Steak Pie (£9.95); haggis, neeps and tatties (£8.95); and bangers and mash (£5.75 or £8.95). Packed lunches are available from £6.95.

Citylink **coaches** (Nos 914, 915 & 916) can make a request stop in the village (see public transport map and table pp44-48).

INVERARNAN TO CRIANLARICH — MAPS 22-26

The Way shares the next **6½ miles (10km, 2-2½hrs)** through **Glen Falloch** with a traffic-laden road, the Highland Line railway, and scores of electricity pylons. If you are able to ignore them the walking is pleasant and undemanding. Good tracks and a section of old military road follow the beautiful River Falloch and then climb easily over rough sheep pasture to the edge of a conifer plantation. The busy village of **Crianlarich**, the halfway point of the Way, is 15 minutes off the main trail.

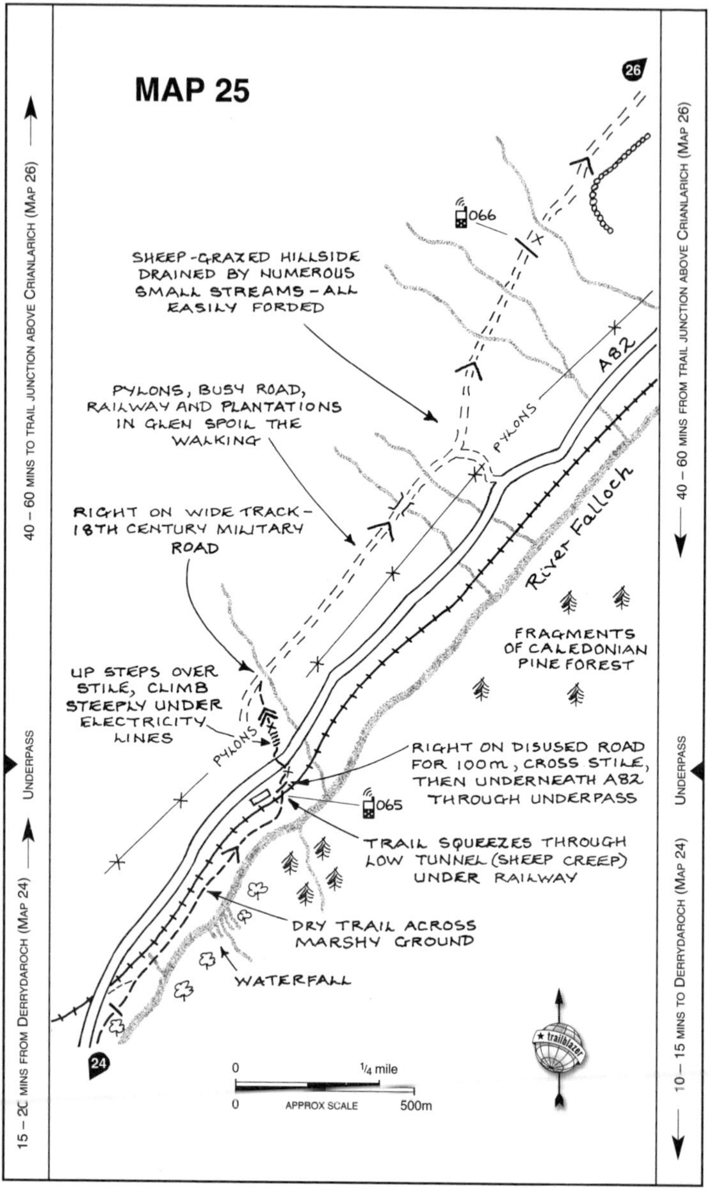

MAP 25

40 – 60 MINS TO TRAIL JUNCTION ABOVE CRIANLARICH (MAP 26) →

UNDERPASS

15 – 2C MINS FROM DERRYDAROCH (MAP 24) →

← 40 – 60 MINS FROM TRAIL JUNCTION ABOVE CRIANLARICH (MAP 26)

UNDERPASS

← 10 – 15 MINS TO DERRYDAROCH (MAP 24)

26

066

SHEEP-GRAZED HILLSIDE DRAINED BY NUMEROUS SMALL STREAMS – ALL EASILY FORDED

PYLONS, BUSY ROAD, RAILWAY AND PLANTATIONS IN GLEN SPOIL THE WALKING

A82

PYLONS

RIGHT ON WIDE TRACK – 18TH CENTURY MILITARY ROAD

River Falloch

FRAGMENTS OF CALEDONIAN PINE FOREST

UP STEPS OVER STILE, CLIMB STEEPLY UNDER ELECTRICITY LINES

PYLONS

RIGHT ON DISUSED ROAD FOR 100m, CROSS STILE, THEN UNDERNEATH A82 THROUGH UNDERPASS

065

TRAIL SQUEEZES THROUGH LOW TUNNEL (SHEEP CREEP) UNDER RAILWAY

DRY TRAIL ACROSS MARSHY GROUND

WATERFALL

24

0 1/4 mile

0 APPROX SCALE 500m

trailblazer

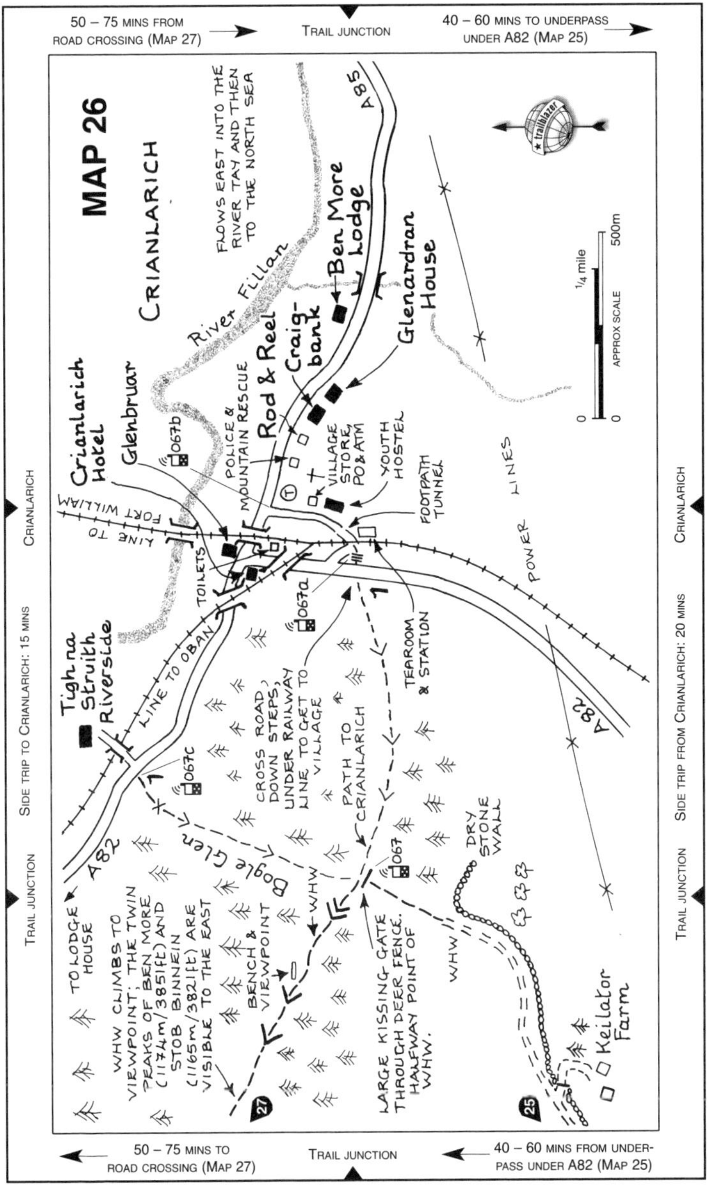

50 – 75 MINS FROM ROAD CROSSING (MAP 27) →

TRAIL JUNCTION

40 – 60 MINS TO UNDERPASS UNDER A82 (MAP 25) →

MAP 26

CRIANLARICH

FLOWS EAST INTO THE RIVER TAY AND THEN TO THE NORTH SEA

River Fillan

A85

Ben More Lodge

Craig-bank

Glenardran House

Rod & Reel

POLICE & MOUNTAIN RESCUE

Crianlarich Hotel

Glenbruar

067b

VILLAGE STORE, PO & ATM

YOUTH HOSTEL

FOOTPATH TUNNEL

POWER LINES

LINE TO FORT WILLIAM

TOILETS

067a

TEAROOM & STATION

Tigh na Struith Riverside

LINE TO OBAN

CROSS ROAD, DOWN STEPS, UNDER RAILWAY LINE TO GET TO VILLAGE

PATH TO CRIANLARICH

067c

A82

Dogle Glen

067

DRY STONE WALL

TO LODGE HOUSE

WHW CLIMBS TO VIEWPOINT; THE TWIN PEAKS OF BEN MORE (1174m/3851ft) AND STOB BINNEIN (1165m/3821ft) ARE VISIBLE TO THE EAST

BENCH & VIEWPOINT

WHW

LARGE KISSING GATE THROUGH DEER FENCE. HALFWAY POINT OF WHW.

WHW

Keilator Farm

27

25

APPROX SCALE 0 – 1/4 mile; 0 – 500m

CRIANLARICH

SIDE TRIP TO CRIANLARICH: 15 MINS

TRAIL JUNCTION

CRIANLARICH

SIDE TRIP FROM CRIANLARICH: 20 MINS

TRAIL JUNCTION

← 50 – 75 MINS TO ROAD CROSSING (MAP 27)

TRAIL JUNCTION

← 40 – 60 MINS FROM UNDER-PASS UNDER A82 (MAP 25)

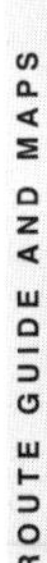

CRIANLARICH — Map 26, p141

Crianlarich is no beauty spot. Cars and lorries thunder through the heart of the pebble-dashed village along the A85 and A82 which join here. Don't let this put you off making the short detour to the village; there are some pleasant surprises and essential services.

Services

Londis **village store** (daily 8am-6pm) is well stocked with a wide range of food, including fruit and veg, basic medicines, maps and guides, footcare, socks and all stove fuels except Coleman Fuel. It's also an off-licence, newsagent and **post office** (Mon, Tue, Thur, Fri 9am-12.30pm & 1.30-5.30pm, Wed 9am-1pm, Sat 9am-12.30pm) and it has a Link **cash machine** inside.

The nearest **medical centre** is at Killin (☎ 01567-820213; Mon-Fri 8am-6pm) about 12 miles (19km) east of Crianlarich. Appointments are essential.

There are **buses** (Citylink No 913, 914, 915, 916 & 973) to and from Glasgow, Callander, Stirling, Edinburgh, Oban, Dundee and Fort William. In addition the railway station is served by **trains** from Glasgow, Fort William and Oban making it an ideal place to start or finish a walk. [See pp44-8].

The local **taxi** firm is 24/7 Cars (☎ 01838-300307, 🖳 www.247taxis.co.uk).

Where to stay

The best place to stay is ***Tigh na Struith Riverside Guest House*** (☎ 01838-300235, 🖳 www.riversideguesthouse.co.uk; 1S or D/2T shared facilities, 1D/2F en suite; WI-FI; 🐕 £3; £27.50-30pp, sgl £35-45; Mar-Oct), a quiet and friendly B&B on the outskirts of the village by the river and far from the noisy road. To get here from the Way come down the Bogle Glen path. Packed lunches (£5.50) are available.

Right in the village centre, by the main road junction and the railway bridge, is ***Glenbruar B&B*** (☎ 01838-300214, 🖳 www.bedandbreakfastcrianlarich.co.uk; 1D/1T/1D, T or F; WI-FI; 🐕; £30pp, sgl occ £39), a charming little cottage. A packed lunch costs £4.95 and a two-/three-course evening meal is £9.95/13.95; booking is preferred. They also have a hot tub.

Through the tunnel under the railway and down the hill is the modern ***Crianlarich Youth Hostel*** (☎ 01838-300260, 🖳 www.hostellingscotland.com; 64 beds, 2T, most rooms have six beds but some have 3/4/5; some rooms are en suite; £16.25-18.75pp). **Internet** access is £1 for 20 mins, the hostel is licensed, has a small shop and meals are available. It's open daily from mid March to late October but Fridays to Sundays only from November to February.

Further along, on the main road is ***Craigbank Guest House*** (☎ 01838-300279, 🖳 craigbankguesthouse.com; 2D/3D or T/1D, T or F; ☕; WI-FI; 🐕; £31pp, sgl occ £35-40; mid Mar to end Oct). They also have a small **bunkroom** (£25pp for two people sharing, for more the rate may vary) that sleeps up to four people.

Crianlarich Hotel (☎ 01838-300272; 🖳 crianlarich-hotel.co.uk; 4S/32D, T or F; ☕; WI-FI; 🐕 £5; £24-57.50pp, sgl/sgl occ £39.50-89.50) is a large attractive Victorian hotel in the heart of the village, with a friendly welcome (for humans and dogs). Rates vary with the seasons, what type of room you are booking and whether you are reserving for a weekday or weekend. They have a small selection of books for sale on the local area.

Nearby is the slightly more upmarket ***Glenardran House*** (☎ 01838-300236; 🖳 www.glenardran.co.uk; 1S/1T/1D/2F; ☕; WI-FI; £32pp, sgl from £37). Packed lunches (from £5) are available.

Quarter of a mile further east along the A85 is ***Ben More Lodge Hotel*** (☎ 01838-300210, 🖳 www.ben-more.co.uk; 8D or T/1T/2F; WI-FI in bar/restaurant; 🐕; £24.95-33pp, sgl occ £29-42) with B&B accommodation in cosy wooden chalets.

Where to eat and drink

Don't miss the chance to visit the ***Station Tearoom*** (☎ 01838-300204, 🖳 www.crianlarich-station-tearoom.co.uk; Mar-Nov Mon-Sat 7.30am-4pm, Sun 9am-3pm), a rare treat of a café in the old waiting rooms on the platform. There's hot and cold filling food, such as bacon rolls (£2.20), cheese and tomato rolls (£2) and fish & chips to eat in (£7) or take-away (£6).

The ***Rod and Reel*** (☎ 01838-300271, 💻 www.rodandreelpub.co.uk; Easter to end Oct Mon-Sat 11am-11pm, Sun 12.30pm-11pm, food served till 8.45pm, Nov to Easter Fri & Sat 11am-11pm, Sun 12.30-11pm) is a popular meeting place and a cheap place to eat with everything from toasties (£3.95) to haggis, neeps and tatties (£7.50).

Ben More Lodge Hotel (see Where to stay; food served summer daily 8-9am, noon-3pm & 6-9pm; weekends only winter) serves excellent pub food in generous portions. The menu includes steak pie for £9.95 and fish & chips for £8.95. Non residents are welcome and there's a nice peaceful patio at the back.

CRIANLARICH TO TYNDRUM — MAPS 26-29

The first 2½ miles (4km) of this **6-mile (10km)** section are through a large conifer plantation high on the valley side with views over the *strath*. The trail descends to the flat valley bottom, crosses the main road and River Fillan and makes a circuitous route through farmland.

It then goes past the ruined priory of St Fillan (see box below) before crossing the road again. The Way follows the river briefly and then heads across a compact moorland into the small but busy village of **Tyndrum (2-2½hrs)**.

STRATHFILLAN
Map 27, p144 & Map 28, p145

Two miles west of Crianlarich where the main trail crosses the A82 is ***Ewich House*** (☎ 01838-300300, 💻 www.ewich.co.uk; 2S/2T/2D; ☕; WI-FI; £37.50pp, sgl £40; Feb-Oct), a large rambling farmhouse which is nearly 200 years old. Packed lunches (from £3.50) are available.

Strathfillan Wigwams (Map 28; ☎ 01838-400251, 💻 www.wigwamholidays.com/Strathfillan_Wigwam_Village), at Auchtertyre Farm, just over half a mile after crossing the A82, has accommodation to suit all budgets. **Camping** costs £8pp. They also have 22 **wigwam bunkhouses** – the small ones cost £34 for two sharing (plus £10pp for up to four people); large wigwams cost £40 for two (plus £10pp for up to five people). All the wigwams have electric heating and lighting, power sockets and mattresses; the large ones also have a fridge. Wigwam occupants have access to a toilet, shower (£1) and kitchen block, the kitchen is fully equipped with washing machine and dryer (metered). Bedding can be hired for £5. In addition there are five **lodges** (£55-65 per lodge based on two sharing, £10 for each extra person, up to eight people per lodge). There's also a **yurt** (£65 per night based on two sharing, £10 for each extra person; up to five people).

❑ St Fillan

St Fillan was an Irish evangelist who, like many other missionaries, had come to Scotland to convert the Picts and the Scots to Christianity in the 7th century. He was active throughout the region of Breadalbane and it is possible that he had a chapel on the site of the priory remains on Kirkton Farm (Map 28). A 12th-century monastery on this site was made into a priory in 1318 by Robert the Bruce who was a strong believer in the cult of St Fillan, even taking a holy relic of the saint into battle at Bannockburn in 1314. Many miracles are associated with him and there is a nearby pool in the River Fillan, known as the Holy Pool, said to cure insanity.

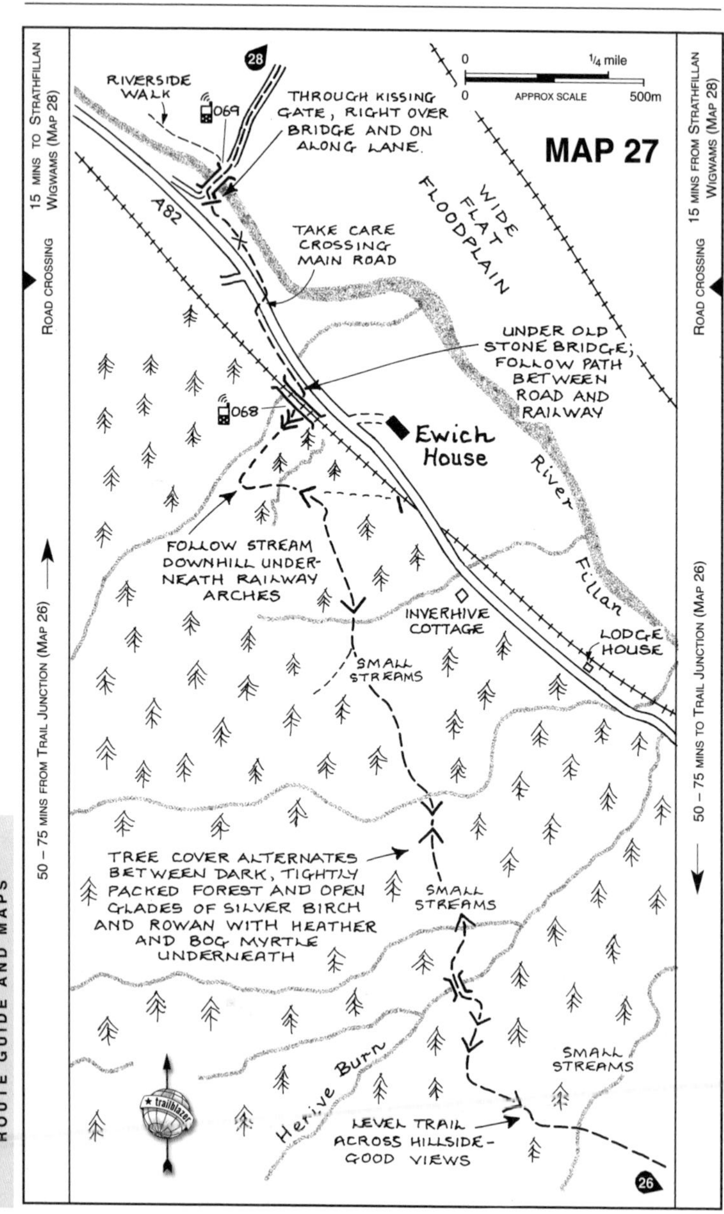
15 mins to Strathfillan Wigwams (Map 28)
Road crossing
50 – 75 mins from Trail Junction (Map 26)
15 mins from Strathfillan Wigwams (Map 28)
Road crossing
50 – 75 mins to Trail Junction (Map 26)
28
0
1/4 mile
0
APPROX SCALE
500m
MAP 27
RIVERSIDE WALK
069
THROUGH KISSING GATE, RIGHT OVER BRIDGE AND ON ALONG LANE.
A82
WIDE FLAT FLOODPLAIN
TAKE CARE CROSSING MAIN ROAD
UNDER OLD STONE BRIDGE; FOLLOW PATH BETWEEN ROAD AND RAILWAY
068
Ewich House
River Fillan
FOLLOW STREAM DOWNHILL UNDERNEATH RAILWAY ARCHES
INVERHIVE COTTAGE
LODGE HOUSE
SMALL STREAMS
TREE COVER ALTERNATES BETWEEN DARK, TIGHTLY PACKED FOREST AND OPEN GLADES OF SILVER BIRCH AND ROWAN WITH HEATHER AND BOG MYRTLE UNDERNEATH
SMALL STREAMS
SMALL STREAMS
Herive Burn
trailblazer
LEVEL TRAIL ACROSS HILLSIDE - GOOD VIEWS
26

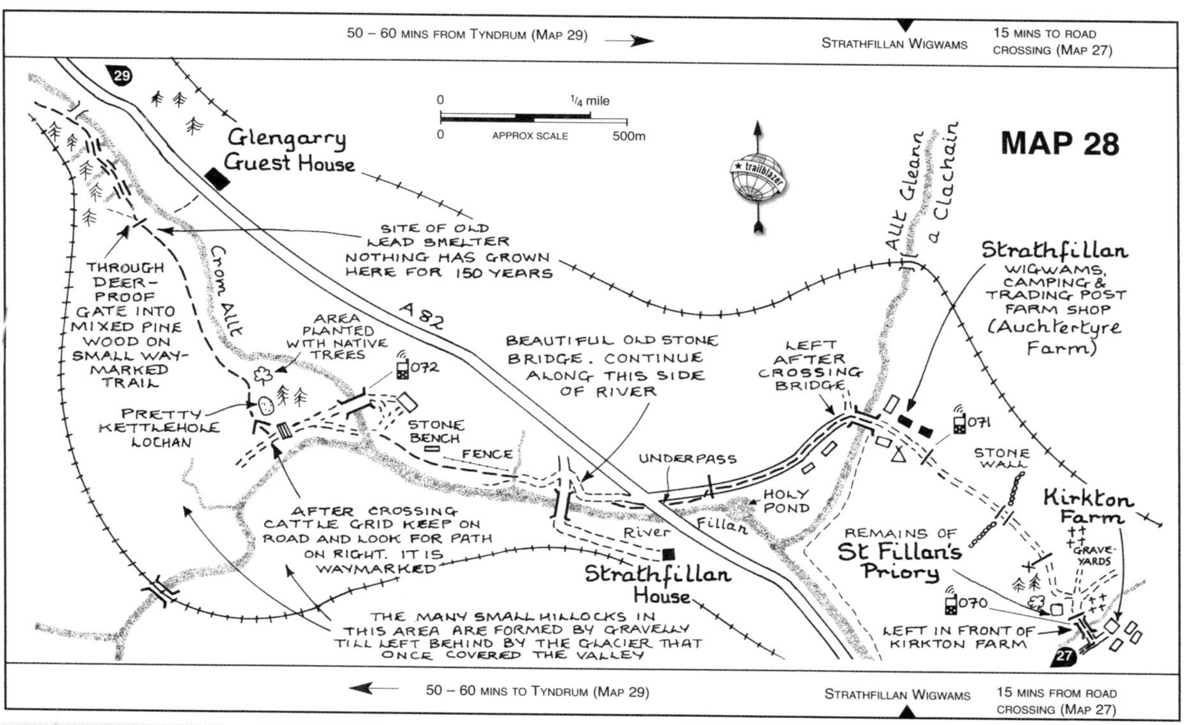
50 – 60 mins from Tyndrum (Map 29)
Strathfillan Wigwams
15 mins to road crossing (Map 27)
MAP 28
0
1/4 mile
0
APPROX SCALE
500m
trailblazer
29
Glengarry Guest House
SITE OF OLD LEAD SMELTER NOTHING HAS GROWN HERE FOR 150 YEARS
Allt Gleann a Clachain
Strathfillan
WIGWAMS, CAMPING & TRADING POST FARM SHOP (Auchtertyre Farm)
THROUGH DEER-PROOF GATE INTO MIXED PINE WOOD ON SMALL WAY-MARKED TRAIL
Crom Allt
A82
AREA PLANTED WITH NATIVE TREES
072
BEAUTIFUL OLD STONE BRIDGE. CONTINUE ALONG THIS SIDE OF RIVER
LEFT AFTER CROSSING BRIDGE
071
PRETTY KETTLEHOLE LOCHAN
STONE BENCH
FENCE
UNDERPASS
STONE WALL
HOLY POND
Kirkton Farm
AFTER CROSSING CATTLE GRID KEEP ON ROAD AND LOOK FOR PATH ON RIGHT. IT IS WAYMARKED
River Fillan
REMAINS OF St Fillan's Priory
GRAVE-YARDS
Strathfillan House
070
THE MANY SMALL HILLOCKS IN THIS AREA ARE FORMED BY GRAVELLY TILL LEFT BEHIND BY THE GLACIER THAT ONCE COVERED THE VALLEY
LEFT IN FRONT OF KIRKTON FARM
27
50 – 60 mins to Tyndrum (Map 29)
Strathfillan Wigwams
15 mins from road crossing (Map 27)

Their farm **shop** (daily Apr-Oct 9am-8pm; Nov-Mar to 6pm) sells the essentials for campers as well as a large variety of meats (buffalo, ostrich, kangaroo and the like) which can be cooked on a camp fire. **Internet** access costs £1 for 30 minutes.

Strathfillan House (Map 28; ☎ 01838-400228, 🖳 www.tyndrum.com; 1T/1D/1F; WI-FI; £30-35pp, sgl occ from £40; mid Mar to end Oct) is a converted manse with comfortable rooms. The double room is en suite; the other rooms share facilities. If they can the owners will provide lifts to the village for an evening meal.

The owners of the excellent ***Glengarry Guest House*** (Map 28; ☎ 01838-400224, 🖳 www.glengarryhouse.com; 2D or T/1F; WI-FI; £33pp, sgl occ £33-66) are most welcoming and friendly. A two-course evening meal costs £15; advance booking preferred. A packed lunch costs £5.

TYNDRUM Map 29

The tiny village of Tyndrum has grown so rapidly that it has come to resemble one vast car park. It has traditionally been a stopping-off point for travellers heading to or from Oban and Fort William and as such it has been subject to an array of developments attempting to lure sedentary holidaymakers to part with their money: two vast coach-tour hotels, a roadside restaurant, a tourist information centre and The Green Welly Stop shopping emporium have all brought acres of tarmac for parking. Thankfully people walking can by-pass most of this and still find somewhere to stay.

Services

Don't forget to stock up on supplies here. Apart from in Glencoe Village, there are no more shops until Kinlochleven. **Brodie's** (7am-6pm) is a family-run village **store** and **post office** (Mon-Fri 9.30am-1.30pm) open a staggering 364 days a year, with plenty of food for backpackers. There's another **mini grocery store** (Apr-Oct daily 7am-10pm, Nov-Mar daily 8am-9pm) in the Green Welly petrol station where you'll also find a Link **cash machine**. The **outdoor equipment store** in the Green Welly Stop (☎ 01301-702089; daily Apr-Oct 8.30am-5.30pm; Nov-Mar to 5pm) sells all the kit you could need including fuels; they operate a **currency exchange** service and there is a **cash machine** (£1.50; until 10pm) in the petrol station.

The plush **tourist information centre** (TIC; ☎ 01838-400246; daily late Mar to end Oct 10am-5pm) has a good bookshop on the local area, there's a public phone here and internet access (£1 for 20 mins).

Transport

[See pp44-8] Tyndrum is blessed with two railway stations, the lower one for the Glasgow–Oban line and the upper for Glasgow–Fort William **trains**. There are also **buses** (Citylink Nos 913, 914, 915, 916 & 973) to and from Glasgow, Callander, Stirling, Edinburgh, Oban, Dundee and Fort William.

Where to stay

On entering the village, next to the lower station, is the ***By The Way Hostel and Campsite*** (☎ 01838-400333, 🖳 www.tyndrumbytheway.com; WI-FI; hostel and hobbit houses open all year; camping, trekker huts and camping cabins Mar/Apr-Oct) which offers a variety of accommodation and a small **shop** (open daily in season, more limited hours at other times), selling

❑ Lead mining

Just before crossing the A82 in Tyndrum (Map 29) heading north, you pass a row of old miners' cottages known as Clifton village. It is named after Sir Robert Clifton who discovered a vein of lead nearby in the 1740s, the mining of which provided employment for the village for over a century.

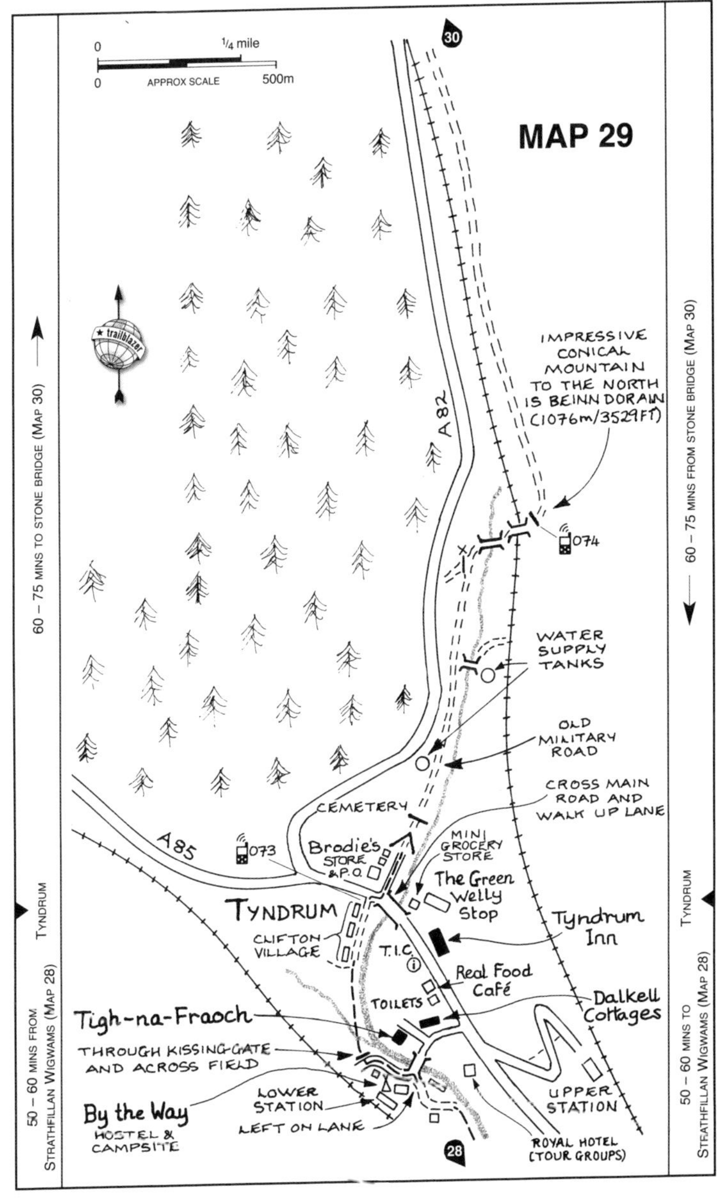

0
1/4 mile
0
APPROX SCALE
500m
MAP 29
30
trailblazer
60 – 75 MINS TO STONE BRIDGE (MAP 30)
60 – 75 MINS FROM STONE BRIDGE (MAP 30)
A82
IMPRESSIVE CONICAL MOUNTAIN TO THE NORTH IS BEINN DORAIN (1076m/3529FT)
074
WATER SUPPLY TANKS
OLD MILITARY ROAD
CROSS MAIN ROAD AND WALK UP LANE
CEMETERY
A85
073
Brodie's STORE & P.O.
MINI GROCERY STORE
The Green Welly Stop
TYNDRUM
Tyndrum Inn
CLIFTON VILLAGE
T.I.C.
Real Food Café
TOILETS
Dalkell Cottages
Tigh-na-Fraoch
THROUGH KISSING GATE AND ACROSS FIELD
By the Way HOSTEL & CAMPSITE
LOWER STATION
LEFT ON LANE
UPPER STATION
ROYAL HOTEL (TOUR GROUPS)
28
TYNDRUM
50 – 60 MINS FROM STRATHFILLAN WIGWAMS (MAP 28)
TYNDRUM
50 – 60 MINS TO STRATHFILLAN WIGWAMS (MAP 28)

❑ A Scottish gold rush

In addition to being a major transport crossroads, Tyndrum could also soon become the centre of a Scottish goldrush and you may see people panning in local streams. The town, of course, has long had an association with lead mining: you walk past some remnants of the industry just before entering the village, while the nearby hamlet of Clifton is made up of former mining cottages.

Panning for gold in Tyndrum

Now, however, there are plans to open a commercial gold- and silver-mine at Cononish, a couple of miles south-west of Tyndrum. The mining company Scotgold (which, despite the name, is largely Australian-owned) plans to extract around four and a half tonnes of gold after initial drilling in 2012 produced positive results.

The seam itself was actually discovered about twenty years ago, but has never been mined commercially due to the difficulty in extracting the gold from the quartz rock in which it is embedded. However, given the high price that the precious metal currently fetches on the commodity market, opening the mine is now seen as a viable – indeed profitable – proposition.

According to the surveys, a tonne of rock would yield up to ten grams of gold worth around £215 on the current market. This means that the mine could yield hundreds of millions of pounds. Given that they also think that there is an estimated 25 tonnes of silver in the mine, the time seems right to extract the minerals.

The village would also benefit, with the mine employing around 60 people for eight years. In addition the mine could also be a boon to tourism, with plans being mooted for a gold-mining visitor centre in the village, as well as opportunities for tourists to go on 'gold-panning experiences'. Jewellery shops selling items made from Tyndrum gold are also expected to open.

It is hoped that the mine will produce around 200kg of gold a year from 2014 – enough to produce 30,000 wedding rings per annum – with another 500kg being extracted each year by sending rocks for processing elsewhere.

Nor is this the end of the story, for Scotgold has licences to explore a 2200 sq km area of the southern Highlands for gold. Indeed, forecasters are predicting that there could be as much as five times more gold in the region than there is in Tyndrum. The recent discovery of a seam just 10km from Tyndrum suggests that it could contain more than three times the amount of gold present at Cononish.

The only possible cloud on the horizon could come from environmental concerns. Situated just inside the boundary of Loch Lomond and the Trossachs National Park, and in the catchment for the River Tay, the mine will have to achieve a high environmental standard if it is to get the green light from the authorities. The mine hopes to satisfy these demands by adopting chemical-free methods to extract the gold, using crushing machinery, water and gravity to separate the gold from the rock in vast drums. The estimated 500,000 tonnes of waste, or 'tailings', will then be stored in small lagoons, though these could in turn upset trekkers on surrounding mountains such as Ben Lui, from where the lagoons will be visible.

walkers' essentials, on site. **Camping** costs £8pp. They also have: **trekker huts** (22 beds; each hut costs about £38/45/50/55 for 2/3/4/5 people; 🐕); **camping cabins** (£30 for two sharing, sgl occ £20) and **hobbit houses** (2S/1D; £40/45/50 for 2/3/4 guests), the latter being the most luxurious. Occupants of the trekker huts, camping cabins and hobbit houses can use the shower/toilet block (Mar-Oct only) and other facilities provided for campers; however, they must provide their own bedding (sleeping-bag hire £4) and cooking utensils. The modern, functional **hostel** has rooms (3T/1D shared facilities; £21pp, sgl occ £28) and dormitories (18 beds; £16pp); there are also catering facilities and bedding is provided. By The Way is owned by walkers so they have all the facilities walkers need. Their website is also worth looking at as it contains lots of practical information for West Highland Way walkers.

On Lower Station Rd there are two quiet B&Bs in comfortable modern bungalows. ***Tigh-na-Fraoch*** (☎ 01838-400354, 🖳 www.tigh-na-fraoch.com; 1D or T/1D/1D, T or F; ●; WI-FI; from £33pp; Mar-Oct) is the first you reach. Therapies such as Indian head massage are sometimes available; contact them for further details. A packed lunch costs £5.

Next is ***Dalkell Cottages*** (☎ 01838-400285, 🖳 www.dalkell.com; 1S or T/2D/4D or T; some rooms share facilities; ●; WI-FI; £34-41pp, sgl £40, sgl occ £57-65). Three of the double rooms have king-sized beds. They also have a cottage (1D/1D or T; ●; WI-FI) which can be rented nightly on a B&B basis (£85 for two people, additional people £35pp).

On the busy A82 is ***The Tyndrum Inn*** (☎ 01838-400219, 🖳 www.thetyndruminn.co.uk; 5S/7T/6D/4F; WI-FI; from £40pp, sgl £30-40, sgl occ £50-75). Three of the single rooms share facilities but all the other rooms are en suite. The rate includes a buffet breakfast.

Where to eat and drink

There are burgers from £6.95 and a haddock supper for £7.60 at ***The Real Food Café*** (☎ 01838-400235, 🖳 www.therealfoodcafe.com; summer daily 11am-9pm, to 10pm on Fri, winter Mon-Thur 11am-7pm, Fri-Sun to 8pm). The name makes it sound like a health food café but they do at least use fresh ingredients and the prices are good. While you eat you can watch the birds flitting about on the numerous bird feeders outside.

The Green Welly Stop self-service restaurant (see also Services; 🖳 www.thegreenwellystop.co.uk; daily Apr-Oct 8.30am-5.30pm; to 5pm Nov-Mar) is a good place for a snack; main courses from £6.95, salads and pastries from £1.95. You can also buy sandwiches, fruit and cakes to take away. They have a Link **cash machine** (£1.50). Next door is the ***Snack Stop*** (Apr-Oct daily 7am-9pm, Nov-Mar daily 4-9pm), also part of the Green Welly complex, serving fast food such as pizzas (5-9pm only).

At the time of research ***The Tyndrum Inn*** had been taken over by new owners and food was available only in the bar (11am-9pm, 10pm in summer). The bar menu (standard pub food) is extensive and the new restaurant will focus on seafood and steaks.

TYNDRUM TO BRIDGE OF ORCHY — MAPS 29-32

Nearly **seven miles (11km, 1¾-2¼hrs)** of good, mostly level walking along the worn cobbled surface of the old military road surrounded by wonderful mountain scenery. There is little shelter along this open stretch so be prepared in poor weather. Once again the valley is shared with the main road and railway.

Fortunately the road soon parts company with the Way to run on the western side of the valley, while the trail follows the Glasgow to Fort William line along the east side. It is a little used railway and those trains that do pass are more of a curiosity than an annoyance.

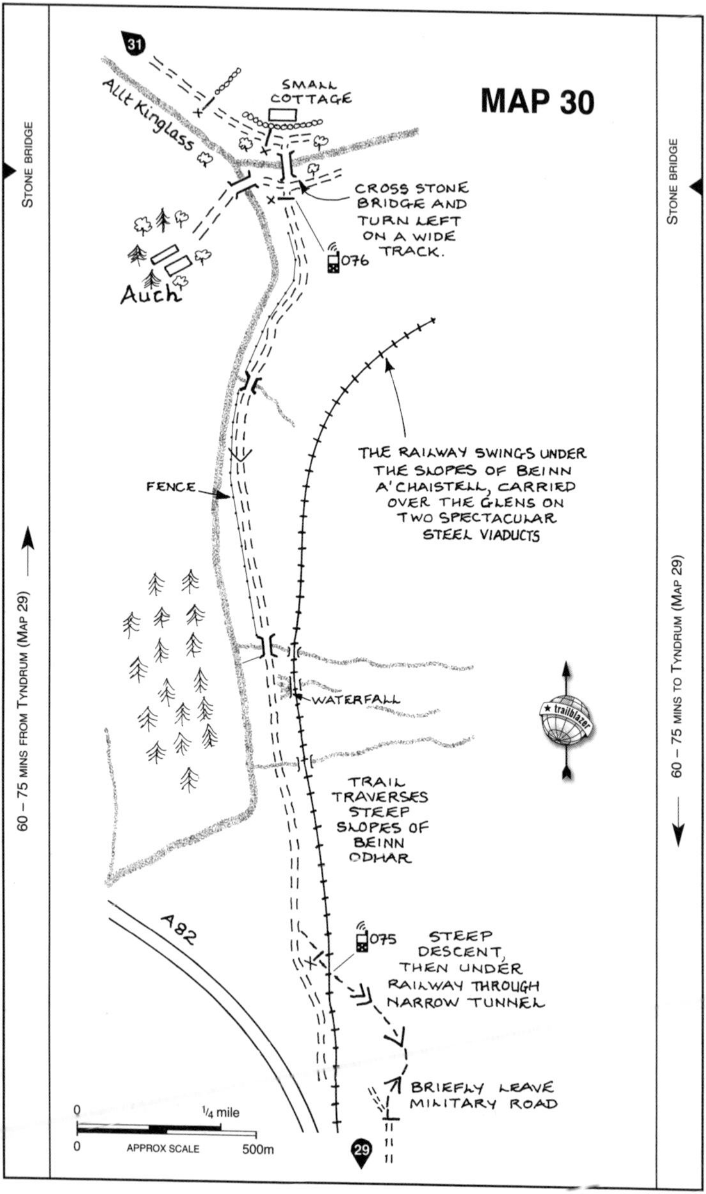

MAP 30

31

SMALL COTTAGE

Allt Kinglass

Auch

STONE BRIDGE

CROSS STONE BRIDGE AND TURN LEFT ON A WIDE TRACK.

076

THE RAILWAY SWINGS UNDER THE SLOPES OF BEINN A'CHAISTEIL, CARRIED OVER THE GLENS ON TWO SPECTACULAR STEEL VIADUCTS

FENCE

60 – 75 MINS FROM TYNDRUM (MAP 29)

60 – 75 MINS TO TYNDRUM (MAP 29)

WATERFALL

trailblazer

TRAIL TRAVERSES STEEP SLOPES OF BEINN ODHAR

A82

075

STEEP DESCENT, THEN UNDER RAILWAY THROUGH NARROW TUNNEL

BRIEFLY LEAVE MILITARY ROAD

0 ¼ mile

0 APPROX SCALE 500m

29

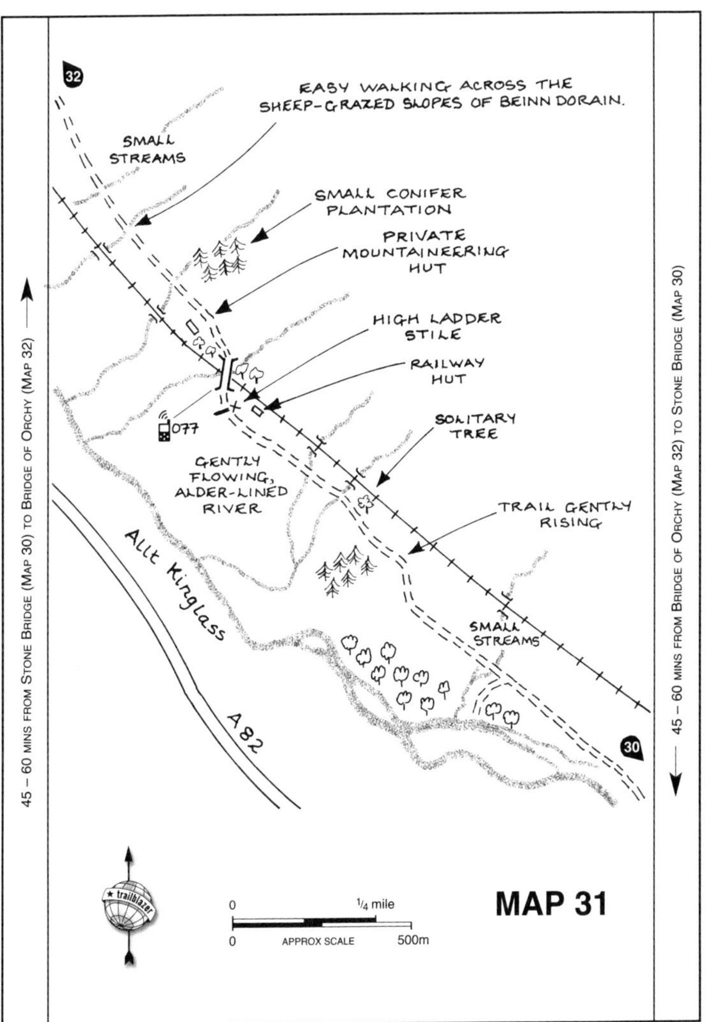

❑ Important note – walking times

Unless otherwise specified, **all times in this book refer only to the time spent walking**. You will need to add 20-30% to allow for rests, photography, checking the map, drinking water etc. When planning the day's hike count on 5-7 hours' actual walking.

❑ Drove roads, military roads and the railway

For much of its route the West Highland Way makes use of historical lines of communication, in particular drove roads and military roads. The growth of cattle rearing in the Highlands in the 17th and 18th century created a network of drove roads through the mountains. These stretched from as far north as Skye to the main markets at Falkirk and Crieff where the cattle would be sold on to Lowland and English cattle dealers. Many of the old inns along the Way sprang up at this time to provide accommodation for the drovers and grazing for the animals. Inverarnan, Tyndrum, Inveroran, Bridge of Orchy and Kingshouse all saw almost 100,000 sheep and 10,000 cattle moved past each year.

The metalled military roads that the West Highland Way follows for substantial distances from Inverarnan northwards were built in the 18th century after the uprisings in 1715 and 1745 by the Jacobites, as the supporters of the Stuart kings were known. Better roads were needed to move the English troops quickly through the mountains if they were to have any success in suppressing this rebellion. General Wade started the frenetic building in 1725 and gave his name to them but it was his successor, Major Caulfeild, who completed the most difficult roads through the Highlands which walkers now tread.

The West Highland Line from Glasgow to Fort William, which the Way also follows for much of its distance, was completed in stages from 1880 to 1901. The railway linked many of the isolated communities in the Highlands to the rest of Scotland and encouraged the farmers to specialise in sheep as they could be moved quickly to market. It also heralded the start of mountain tourism opening up the Highlands to walkers and climbers from the industrial towns and cities. There are fantastic mountain walks right from the train beginning at stations such as Crianlarich and Bridge of Orchy and the remote moorland stations such as Rannoch and Corrour give access to wild walking country far from civilisation.

BRIDGE OF ORCHY — Map 32

Little more than a hotel, two bunkhouses and a railway station, Bridge of Orchy is a tranquil hamlet under the spectacular slopes of Beinn an Dothaidh and Beinn Dorain (see p154). There aren't any shops in the village but there is a **post office** open one morning a week (Tue 9.30-11.30am), near the station but it may soon be moved into the old church.

Trains and **buses** (Citylink Nos 914, 915 & 916) run to Fort William and Glasgow (see public transport map and table pp44-8).

Where to stay and eat

Across the elegant 18th-century bridge over the River Orchy is a popular free **campsite**. However, there are no facilities and it can be midgy at times.

Some years ago the station building was converted into the ***West Highland Way Sleeper*** (☎ 01838-400548, 🖳 info@westhighlandwaysleeper.co.uk) a tiny but comfortable **bunkhouse**. However, they only accept group bookings. There are two rooms with 3-tiered bunk beds, one sleeps six (£100) and the other nine (£145). Meals can be arranged if booked in advance. Booking in advance is advised especially in the main season.

The other place to stay is at the imposing ***Bridge of Orchy Hotel*** (☎ 01838-400208, 🖳 www.bridgeoforchy.co.uk; 2T/7D/1D, T or F; ♥; WI-FI in public areas;

£45-60pp, sgl occ £75) where the rate includes breakfast. Their new **bunkhouse** was under construction at the time of research but should be open in May 2013.

The hotel's ***Caley Bar*** is the place to drink and eat with well-kept cask ales from the Belhaven and Harviestoun Brewery and delicious **food**; the menu changes regularly but food is available all day until about 9pm. In the bar there are dishes such as lamb's liver with creamy mash, roast potatoes, red wine and bacon sauce (£7.95); food in the restaurant is a little more expensive (eg roast pork for £12.95) but worth it. On chilly days they serve hot mulled wine (£5.25). Even if you're not staying here you can have breakfast (7.30-9.30am in summer, from 8am in winter) for £10.

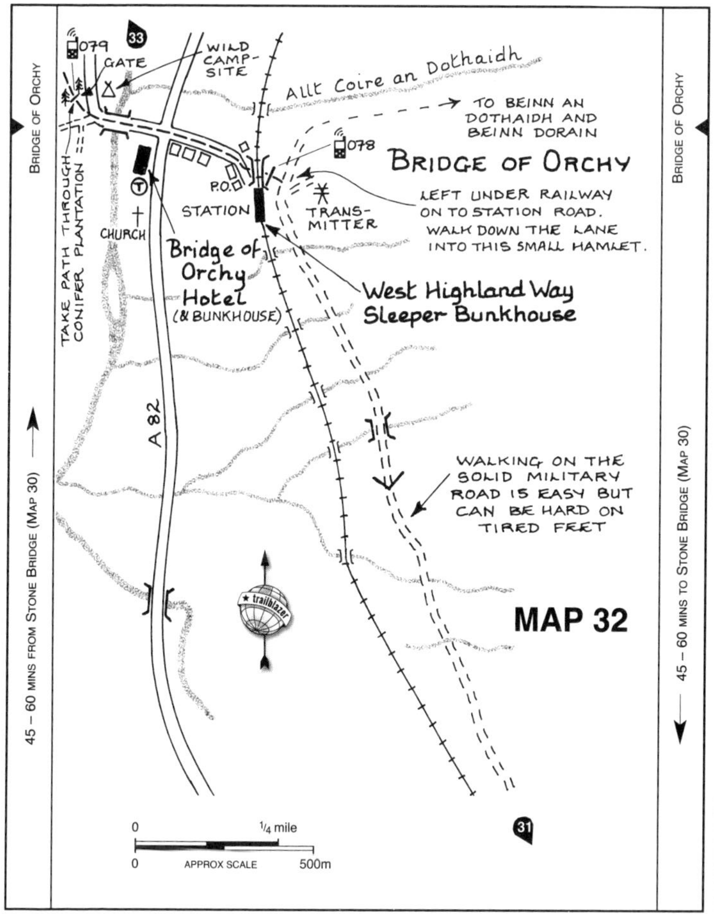

Ascent of Beinn Dorain and Beinn an Dothaidh

This is a moderately strenuous climb of two Munros above Bridge of Orchy with wonderful views over Rannoch Moor from Beinn an Dothaidh; 7½ miles (12km), 6-7 hours with short breaks.

You need to be an experienced hillwalker as navigation can be difficult in poor visibility (see p182). Take care not to wander onto the steep ground on the western side of the mountains. You will need one of the following maps: OS Explorer 377 (1:25,000) or OS Landranger sheet 50 (1:50,000).

From Bridge of Orchy station go through the underpass and head east into Coire an Dothaidh towards the obvious *bealach* (744m/2440ft). Turn right (south) along a path to climb the broad north ridge of Beinn Dorain to the summit (1076m/3529ft).

Beinn Dorain
(1076m/3529ft)

Note that the true summit is 200m beyond a false summit. Return to the bealach and climb north-north-east up the steep south ridge of Beinn an Dothaidh to its summit (1004m/3293ft). Retrace your steps to Bridge of Orchy.

For more information see Trailblazer's *Scottish Highlands – The Hillwalking Guide* by Jim Manthorpe.

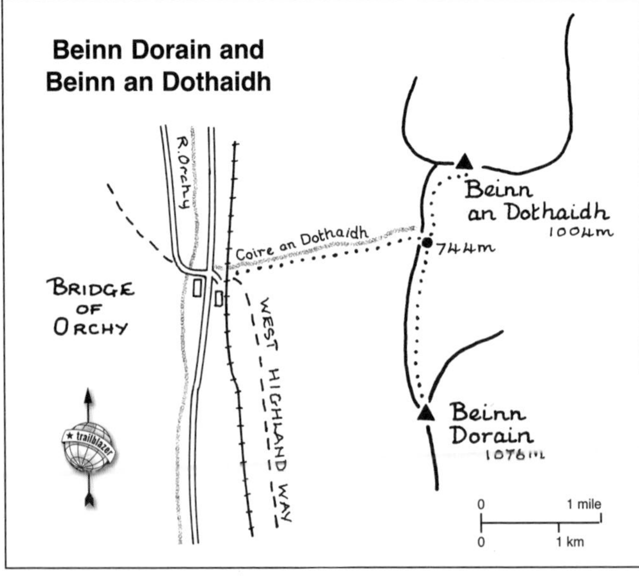

BRIDGE OF ORCHY TO KINGSHOUSE MAPS 32-38

This superb, challenging **13-mile (21km, 4-5hrs)** section starts easily with three miles (5km) of pleasant walking over a small ridge to the **Inveroran Hotel** and then round the head of **Loch Tulla** (Map 34).

Just beyond Victoria Bridge an old cobbled drove road (see box p152) slowly ascends on to **Black Mount**, a rising of high moorland between the large mountains surrounding Coire Bà (see box p156) west of the trail and the vast expanse of **Rannoch Moor** to the east. This track carries you direct and dry-shod across this desolate landscape. This is the remotest and wildest section of the whole Way; there are no escape routes, nor is there much shelter, for the next 10 miles (16km), so come prepared as the weather here is notoriously cruel. From the highest point of 445m (1460ft) the Way descends to the main road and the isolated **Kings House Hotel** with views to the stunning mountains of **Glen Coe**.

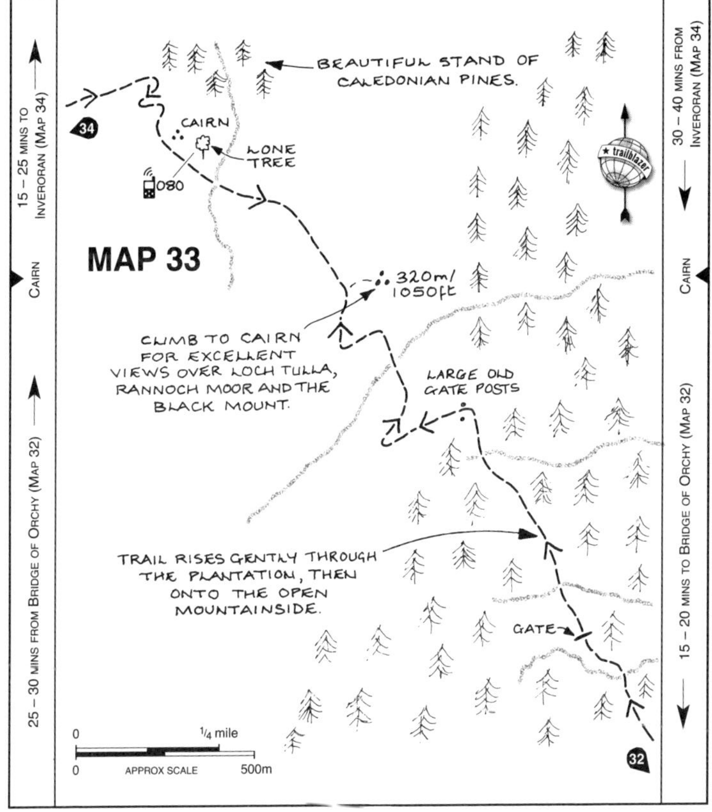

ROUTE GUIDE AND MAPS

❑ Traversing the Black Mount Hills – the Clachlet Ridge

For strong, experienced hillwalkers with good map-reading skills there is a magnificent high-ridge walk between Inveroran and Kingshouse which can be used as an alternative to the Way. It goes over the tops of Stob Ghabhar, Aonach Mor, Clach Leathad and Meall a' Bhuiridh to the west of the route taken by the Way. This is a long day's outing of between 11 and 15 miles (18-24km) depending on which route you take – make sure you are well prepared (see p56). You will need either OS Explorer Maps 377 and 384 (1:25,000) or OS Landranger sheets 41 and 50 (1:50,000).

INVERORAN — Map 34

If location is everything ***Inveroran Hotel*** (☎ 01838-400220, 🖳 www.inveroran.com; 1S/2T/3D/3F; ➡; WI-FI variable; £42-45pp, sgl £42, sgl occ £42-60; mid Mar to end Oct) has it all. Built in 1708 at the beautiful western end of Loch Tulla this is as secluded as you could wish. Dorothy Wordsworth visited in 1803 and was not impressed by the food ('the butter not eatable, the barley cakes fusty, the oat-bread so hard I could not chew it') but things have improved greatly since then.

Coffee, tea and snacks are available from 10am to 3pm; the ***Walkers' Bar*** (entrance around the back) is open 11am-11pm and evening meals are served daily. They offer a bar meal (£8) for walkers. Alternatively they have three sittings (6.30, 7 and 7.30pm) in the restaurant where a two-/three-course meal costs £16/20. A packed lunch costs £7.

The spectacular **camping** area 400 metres west of the hotel by the bridge is free; however, it is sometimes subject to flooding so camping may be less appealing in wet weather. Campers can order a full cooked breakfast (from £8) the night before. There's a **water tap** on the outside wall at the back if you need to fill up your bottles.

❑ Coire Bà

As you cross a part of the moor, aptly named **The Moss** (Map 36, p159), look west into Coire Bà, the largest mountain amphitheatre in Scotland, cradled by the stunning hills of the Black Mount Deer Forest, rising to a height of 1108m (3634ft) at the summit of Meall a' Bhuiridh on the northern rim. To the east the more modest cone of Meall Beag (476m/1561ft) rises beyond the shore of the lochan.

KINGSHOUSE — Map 38, p161

The West Highland Way does not descend into Glen Coe but skirts to the east of its mountain entrance passing close to **Glencoe Ski Centre/Mountain Resort** (☎ 01855-851226, 🖳 www.glencoemountain.co.uk), a particularly insensitive development in such immensely beautiful surroundings. The chairlift (Mar/Apr-Oct daily 9am-4.30pm, Dec-Mar/Apr daily 8.30am-4.30pm; closed Nov; £10 return) takes walkers, skiers and snowboarders up the slopes of Meall a'Bhuiridh; there is a viewpoint at 720m/2400ft.

A ***café*** (daily 9am-9pm) is situated above the enormous car park and serves a range of light meals including bacon rolls (£2.50). They also have a ***campsite*** with 20 pitches (£6pp) and six ***microlodges*** (£50) each sleeping up to four people. Showers (£1) are available for all.

The only other **accommodation** on the Way before Kinlochleven, 8 miles (13km) away, is the welcoming 18th-century drovers' stop, ***Kings House Hotel*** (☎ 01855-851259, 🖳 www.kingy.com; 5S/4T/9D/4F; some shared facilities; ➡; WI-FI; 🐕

cont'd on p162

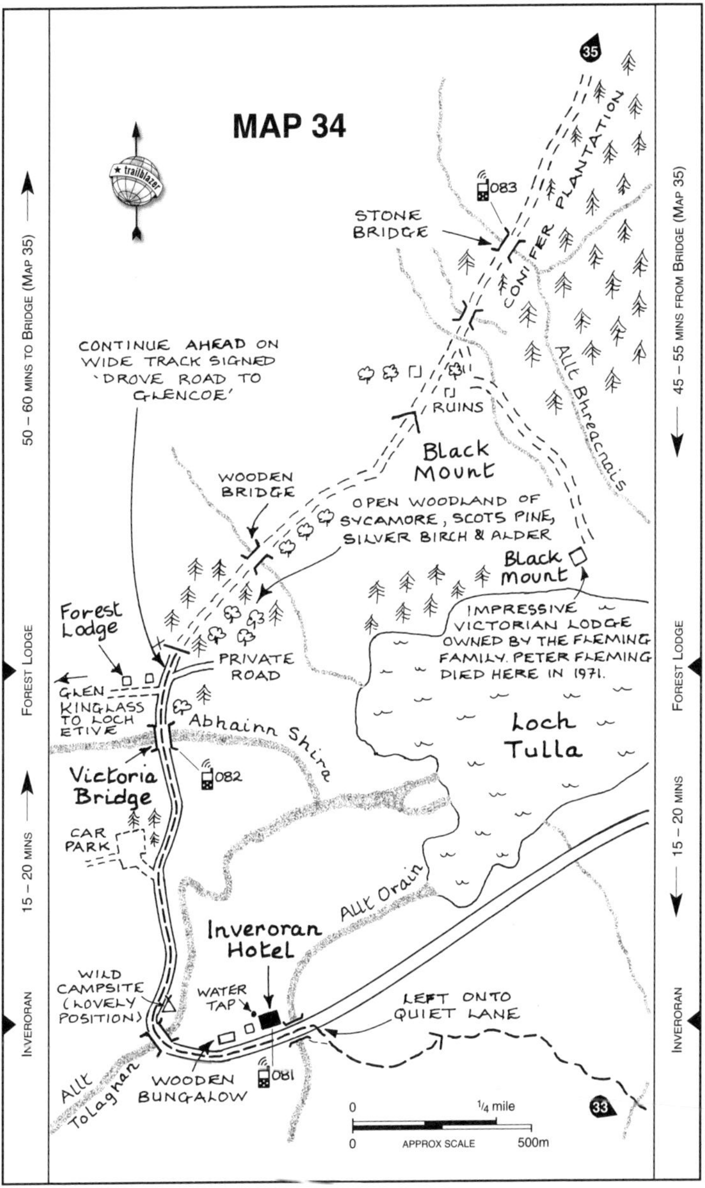

MAP 34

trailblazer

50 – 60 MINS TO BRIDGE (MAP 35) →

FOREST LODGE

15 – 20 MINS →

INVERORAN

← 45 – 55 MINS FROM BRIDGE (MAP 35)

FOREST LODGE

← 15 – 20 MINS

INVERORAN

35

083

STONE BRIDGE

CONIFER PLANTATION

Allt Bhreacnais

CONTINUE AHEAD ON WIDE TRACK SIGNED 'DROVE ROAD TO GLENCOE'

RUINS

Black Mount

WOODEN BRIDGE

OPEN WOODLAND OF SYCAMORE, SCOTS PINE, SILVER BIRCH & ALDER

Black Mount

IMPRESSIVE VICTORIAN LODGE OWNED BY THE FLEMING FAMILY. PETER FLEMING DIED HERE IN 1971.

Forest Lodge

PRIVATE ROAD

GLEN KINGLASS TO LOCH ETIVE

Abhainn Shira

Loch Tulla

Victoria Bridge

082

CAR PARK

Allt Orain

Inveroran Hotel

WILD CAMPSITE (LOVELY POSITION)

WATER TAP

LEFT ONTO QUIET LANE

Allt Tolaghan

WOODEN BUNGALOW

081

33

0 — 1/4 mile

0 — APPROX SCALE — 500m

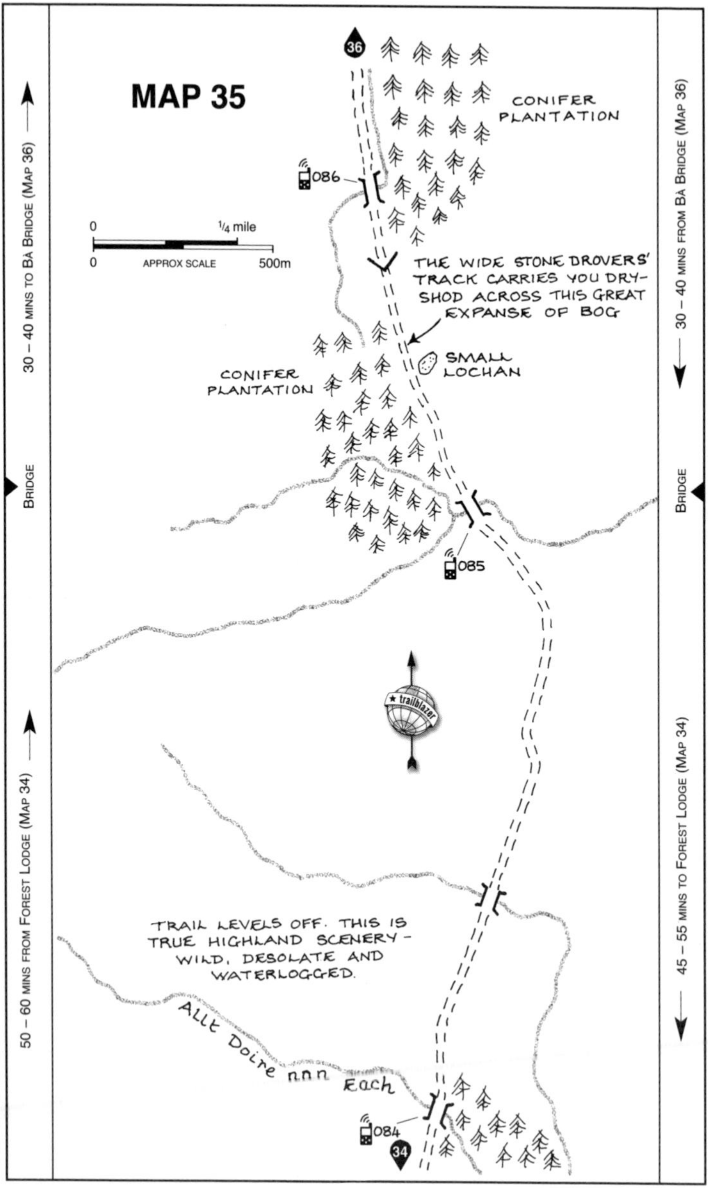

MAP 35

36

CONIFER PLANTATION

086

0 ¼ mile

0 APPROX SCALE 500m

THE WIDE STONE DROVERS' TRACK CARRIES YOU DRY-SHOD ACROSS THIS GREAT EXPANSE OF BOG

SMALL LOCHAN

CONIFER PLANTATION

085

trailblazer

TRAIL LEVELS OFF. THIS IS TRUE HIGHLAND SCENERY - WILD, DESOLATE AND WATERLOGGED.

Allt Doire nnn Each

084

34

30 – 40 MINS TO BÀ BRIDGE (MAP 36)

BRIDGE

50 – 60 MINS FROM FOREST LODGE (MAP 34)

30 – 40 MINS FROM BÀ BRIDGE (MAP 36)

BRIDGE

45 – 55 MINS TO FOREST LODGE (MAP 34)

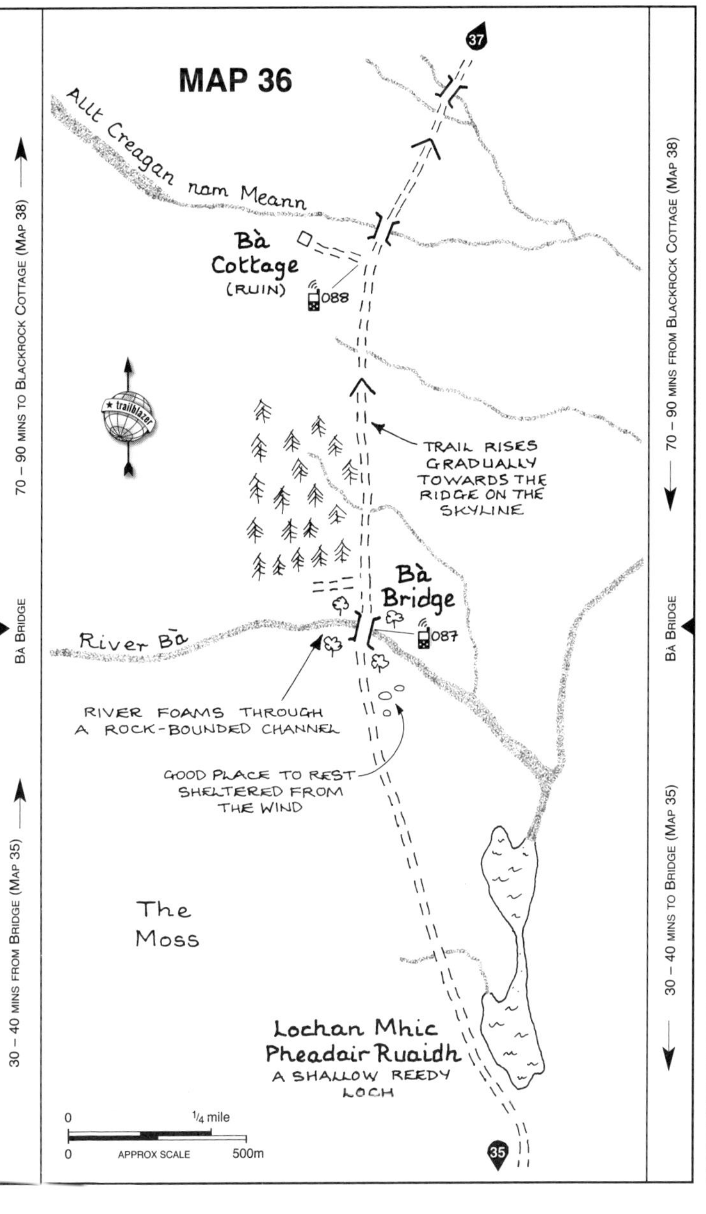
MAP 36
Allt Creagan nam Meann
Bà Cottage
(RUIN)
088
TRAIL RISES GRADUALLY TOWARDS THE RIDGE ON THE SKYLINE
Bà Bridge
087
River Bà
RIVER FOAMS THROUGH A ROCK-BOUNDED CHANNEL
GOOD PLACE TO REST SHELTERED FROM THE WIND
The Moss
Lochan Mhic Pheadair Ruaidh
A SHALLOW REEDY LOCH
0
1/4 mile
0
APPROX SCALE
500m
37
35
trailblazer
70 – 90 MINS TO BLACKROCK COTTAGE (MAP 38)
BÀ BRIDGE
30 – 40 MINS FROM BRIDGE (MAP 35)
70 – 90 MINS FROM BLACKROCK COTTAGE (MAP 38)
BÀ BRIDGE
30 – 40 MINS TO BRIDGE (MAP 35)

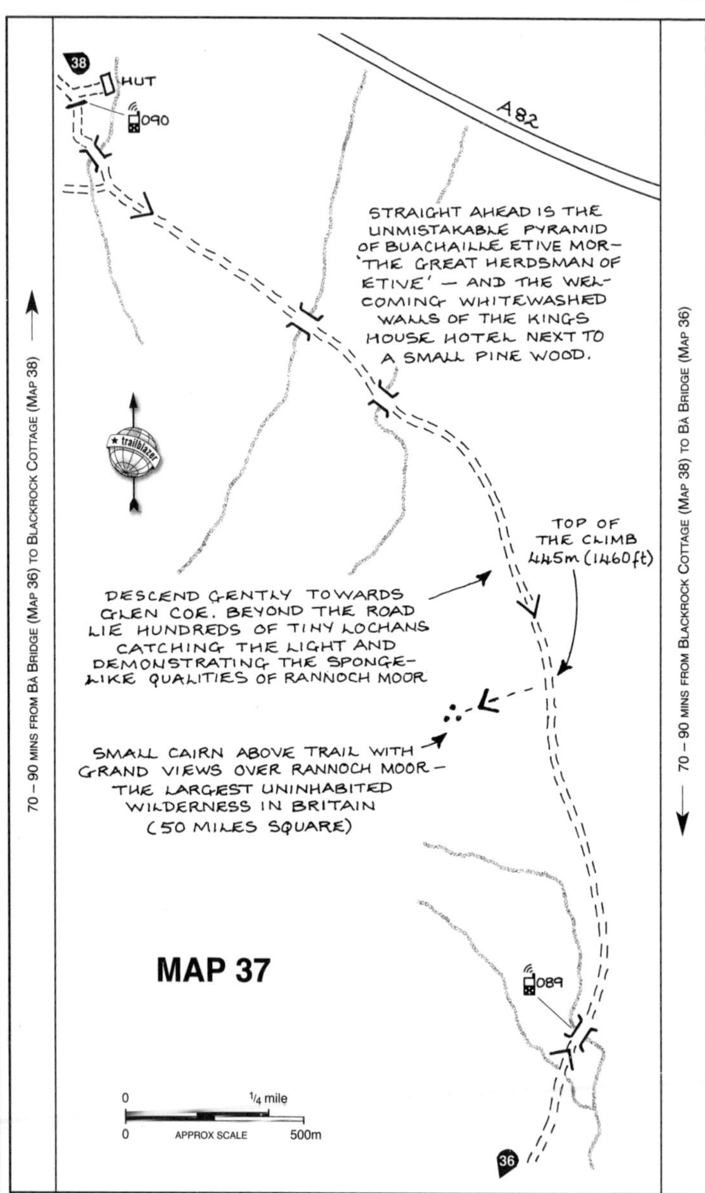
38
HUT
090
A82
STRAIGHT AHEAD IS THE UNMISTAKABLE PYRAMID OF BUACHAILLE ETIVE MOR – 'THE GREAT HERDSMAN OF ETIVE' – AND THE WELCOMING WHITEWASHED WALLS OF THE KINGS HOUSE HOTEL NEXT TO A SMALL PINE WOOD.
70 – 90 MINS FROM BÀ BRIDGE (MAP 36) TO BLACKROCK COTTAGE (MAP 38)
70 – 90 MINS FROM BLACKROCK COTTAGE (MAP 38) TO BÀ BRIDGE (MAP 36)
TOP OF THE CLIMB 445m (1460ft)
DESCEND GENTLY TOWARDS GLEN COE. BEYOND THE ROAD LIE HUNDREDS OF TINY LOCHANS CATCHING THE LIGHT AND DEMONSTRATING THE SPONGE-LIKE QUALITIES OF RANNOCH MOOR
SMALL CAIRN ABOVE TRAIL WITH GRAND VIEWS OVER RANNOCH MOOR – THE LARGEST UNINHABITED WILDERNESS IN BRITAIN (50 MILES SQUARE)
MAP 37
089
0
1/4 mile
0
APPROX SCALE
500m
36

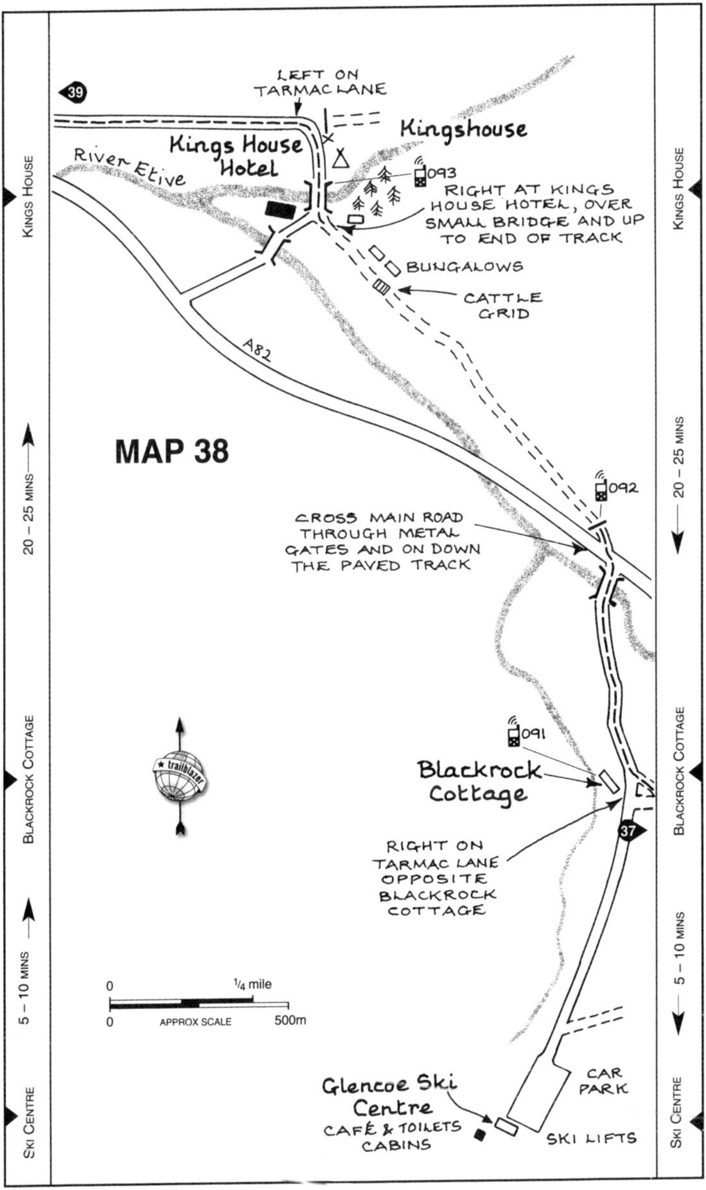

MAP 38

39

LEFT ON TARMAC LANE

Kingshouse

Kings House Hotel

River Etive

093

RIGHT AT KINGS HOUSE HOTEL, OVER SMALL BRIDGE AND UP TO END OF TRACK

BUNGALOWS

CATTLE GRID

A82

092

CROSS MAIN ROAD THROUGH METAL GATES AND ON DOWN THE PAVED TRACK

091

Blackrock Cottage

37

RIGHT ON TARMAC LANE OPPOSITE BLACKROCK COTTAGE

trailblazer

0 1/4 mile

0 APPROX SCALE 500m

CAR PARK

Glencoe Ski Centre

CAFÉ & TOILETS

CABINS

SKI LIFTS

KINGS HOUSE

20 – 25 MINS

BLACKROCK COTTAGE

5 – 10 MINS

SKI CENTRE

£4.50; £32-35pp, sgl £30-35, family room £75-96). They charge less for the rooms above the bar as they can be noisy. Breakfast (served 8-9.30am) is an extra £5.95pp for continental or £7.95 for a full Scottish. **Food** is also served daily from noon to 8.30pm. Filled paninis cost from £4.95 and there are delicious hot meals such as haddock & chips, or a scrumptious venison burger and chips (£8.50) and a gut-busting steak balmoral (rib-eye steak on a bed of haggis) for £14.95. The flagstone-floored climbers' bar is round the back; you won't feel out of place with muddy boots and a large pack. On the wall there are some inspiring photos of local climbing.

You can **camp** for free on the other side of the bridge. However, there are no facilities and the hotel doesn't open its toilets for campers in the morning. This would be fine were it not for a complete lack of natural cover to crouch behind. You have been warned! Campers can have breakfast in the hotel but hotel guests are given priority. There's a water tap outside the hotel.

At busy times of the year Kingshouse is a notorious bottle-neck on the West Highland Way. If you can't get a bed, catch a bus, from the stop on the A82, to Glencoe village (see below) where there is more choice. Several Citylink **coaches** pass daily (see public transport map pp44-8).

GLEN COE

Although the West Highland Way doesn't run through either the valley of Glen Coe, or Glencoe village it is well-worth making a side trip for a day if your schedule allows. There can be no finer introduction to the Scottish mountaineering scene than to tick off a Glen Coe Munro and finish the day in the Boots Bar of Clachaig Inn. If you're feeling the need for a day without walking there's plenty to do in the valley, or simply laze around in beautiful surroundings.

Getting to Glencoe Village

Walking from Kingshouse to Glencoe is only for masochists. It is 9 miles (14km) of walking on or very close to the busy A82. It's better to hitch or catch a Citylink **bus** (see public transport map and table pp44-8). To hitch from Kingshouse first walk half a mile towards Glencoe to the layby otherwise cars can't stop for you on this busy road. Places to stay and eat are spread along 3 miles (5km) of the bottom of the glen so decide where you want to be. For the centre of the village, where there are shops and B&Bs, get dropped at Glencoe Hotel. For Clachaig Inn, the campsite, hostel and bunkhouse get off the bus earlier, either at the western end of Loch Achtriochtan from where you can walk along the minor road to Clachaig Inn, or, if you miss that, at the next car park on the right from where you can cross the river on a footbridge and walk through the small forest to the lane.

Local **taxi companies** include Alistair's (☎ 01855-811136, 🖳 www.alistairstaxis.co.uk) and 24/7 (☎ 01838-300307).

Glencoe Village

Supplies can be bought at **Nisa General Store** (Mon-Sat 7.30am-7pm, Sun 8am-7pm) and there's also a useful **cash machine** inside. There is a **post office** (Mon, Tue, Thur, Fri 9am-1.30pm) nearby and a **medical centre** (☎ 01855-811226; Mon, Tue & Thur 8am-1pm & 2-6pm, Fri 8am-1pm & 2-4pm, Wed 8am-1pm) a mile west in Ballachulish.

The little **Glencoe and North Lorn Folk Museum** (☎ 01855-811664, 🖳 www.glencoemuseum.com; Easter-Oct Mon-Sat 10am-4.30pm; £3), in a heather-thatched cottage next to Nisa, has a quirky mixture of artefacts. The **National Trust for Scotland Visitor Centre** (☎ 01855-811307/729, 🖳

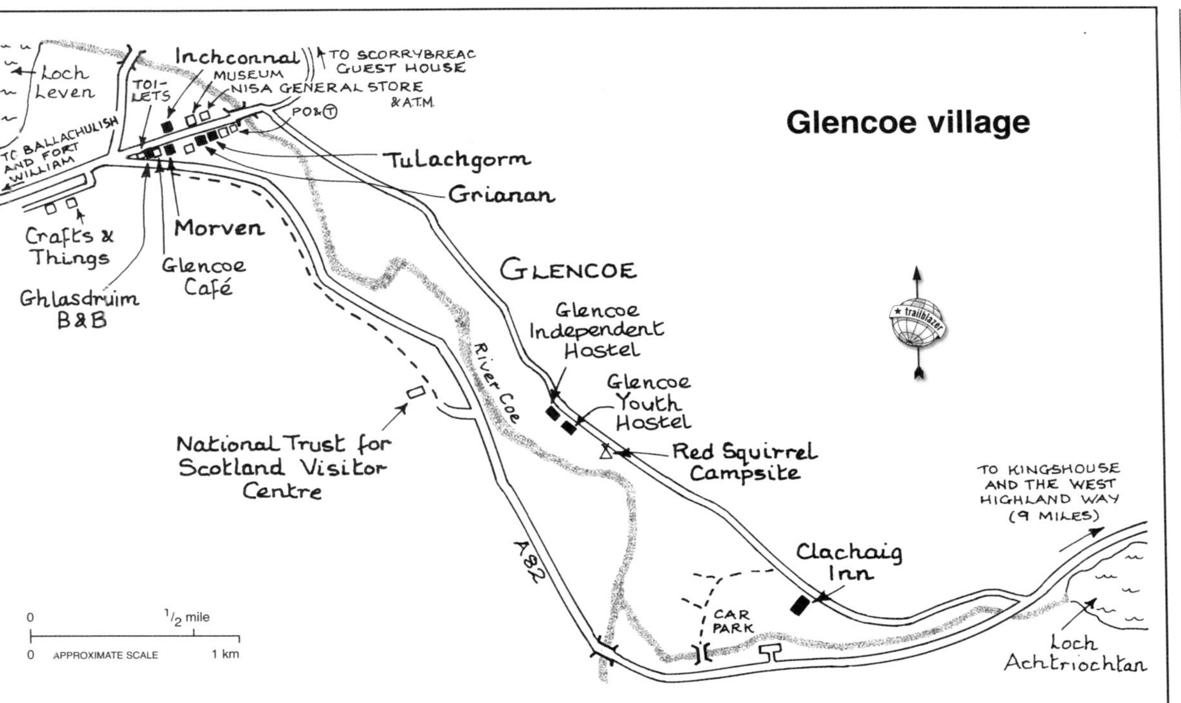
Glencoe village
Loch Leven
TO BALLACHULISH AND FORT WILLIAM
TOI-LETS
Inchconnal
MUSEUM
NISA GENERAL STORE & A.T.M.
TO SCORRYBREAC GUEST HOUSE
PO&T
Tulachgorm
Grianan
Crafts & Things
Morven
Glencoe Café
Ghlasdruim B&B
GLENCOE
Glencoe Independent Hostel
Glencoe Youth Hostel
Red Squirrel Campsite
River Coe
National Trust for Scotland Visitor Centre
A82
TO KINGSHOUSE AND THE WEST HIGHLAND WAY (9 MILES)
Clachaig Inn
CAR PARK
Loch Achtriochtan
0
1/2 mile
0
APPROXIMATE SCALE
1 km

www.glencoe-nts.org.uk; late Mar-Nov daily 9.30am-5.30pm, Nov-late Mar Thur-Sun 10am-4pm, closed late Dec and early Jan) has an exhibition (admission £6; NT members free) with an interesting short video on the massacre (see box opposite) as well as displays on mountaineering and natural history. There is also a ***café***, free WI-FI and an outlook station where it is possible to get weather reports and advice on walks in the area. The drawback is that it's difficult to get to on foot being 1½ miles south along the busy A82. There is a footpath all the way but it's not a great walk.

Places to stay and eat ***Clachaig Inn*** (☎ 01855-811252, 💻 www.clachaig.com; 1S/7T/10D/5F; ☕; WI-FI; 🐕 £7.50; £47-52pp, sgl £47-50, sgl occ £94-96) has been a meeting place for outdoor addicts for years and is deservedly popular. There's always a good range of independent ales and up to 300 malt whiskies which you can either sip in the Bidean Lounge or down one after the other in the Boots Bar where there's live music every Saturday night. Great **food** is available (snacks from 10am, bar menu noon-9pm) from haggis (£9.80) to boar burger (£12.95).

Walking west along the lane towards the main village, in 10 minutes you pass ***Red Squirrel Campsite*** (☎ 01855-811256, 💻 www.redsquirrelcampsite.co.uk; 🐕; £9.50pp; open all year). It is by a swimming hole in the river and is a pleasant farm site popular with walkers and climbers.

Five minutes further on is ***Glencoe Youth Hostel*** (☎ 01855-811219, 💻 www.hostellingscotland.com; 56 beds, 10 rooms most with 5-6 beds) where a dorm bed costs £16-22pp (£56 for the twin room) and it's open all year. Meals available. They have **internet** access (£1 for 20 mins) and WI-FI as well as a small shop, a washing machine (£2) and a drying room.

Accommodation is even better value at ***Glencoe Independent Hostel*** (☎ 01855-811906, 💻 www.glencoehostel.co.uk; open all year but check in advance Nov-Dec; WI-FI), but their Alpine **bunkhouses** (£12.50-14.50pp) are often booked up with groups, particularly at weekends and in the main season. The **hostel** (26 beds; £13.50-17.50pp) offers access to a kitchen, toilets and drying room, and there is also a self-contained **log cabin** for 2-3 people (£19-25pp). They also have self-contained **caravans** sleeping up to six people, which are mainly for weekly lets, but if there is availability they will let them for stays of two nights (from £16.50pp for four sharing). Bedding is provided everywhere but towels are not provided in the bunkhouses or hostel. There are no other facilities along the 1¼ miles of lane from here to the village.

Just before crossing the bridge into the village a road on the right goes to ***Scorrybreac Guest House*** (☎ 01855-811354, 💻 www.scorrybreac.co.uk; 1T/3D/1F; ☕; WI-FI £2.50 per stay; £28-33pp, sgl occ £56-66) which has comfortable accommodation. Packed lunches (£4.50) are available if requested the night before.

Over the bridge, strung out either side of the main street, are several B&Bs including: ***Tulachgorm*** (☎ 01855-811391; 1D/1T, share bathroom; ☕; £20pp, sgl occ £40; Easter-Oct); ***Grianan*** (☎ 01855-811322; 1D/1D, T or F, shared bathroom; ☕; 🐕; £22pp, sgl occ £44; Easter-Oct); and ***Morven*** (☎ 01855-811544, 💻 www.morvenbnb.com; 1D/1T or F; WI-FI; 🐕; £24pp, sgl occ £35; open all year), a comfortable and friendly B&B in an attractive traditional stone cottage. ***Ghlasdruim B&B*** (☎ 01855-811593, 💻 maureen@ken110.orangehome.co.uk; 1S/1T/1D/1F; WI-FI; £25-27.50pp, sgl £33; open all year);

❑ Mountains and massacre

Glen Coe is one of the most scenically impressive valleys in Scotland. Standing guard at its entrance is the spectacular arrowhead mountain Buachaille Etive Mor, 'the great herdsman of Etive.' As you descend into the glen towards Loch Achtriochtan the road is squeezed by the precipitous walls of the Bidean nam Bian massif to the south and the incredible line of the Aonach Eagach ridge to the north. It is a perfect playground for climbers and hill-walkers and arguably the home of Scottish mountaineering.

However, the notoriety of the valley has more to do with the events of 1692 than gymnastic exploits on the crags. The massacre of the MacDonalds by Highland troops is a bloody tale of deception. While Highland history is full of such awful events the Glencoe massacre is the one that everyone remembers. One reason for this infamy is the horrific nature of the premeditated plan to exterminate the MacDonald clan in cold blood after they had provided hospitality to their potential murderers for two weeks. This was sanctioned by men in high office, including the crown. The other reason is that the dreadful episode has been exploited by generations of writers and provides ample fuel for the tourist industry of today.

and ***Inchconnal*** (☎ 01855-811958, 🖳 www.inchconnal.com; 1D/1D, T or F; ❤; WI-FI; £25-26pp, sgl occ £50-52; Easter-Oct) are also in this area.

The Glencoe Café (☎ 01855-811168, 🖳 www.glencoecafe.co.uk) is open daily 9am-5pm (10am-4pm in winter). They serve a range of soups, cakes and light lunches to eat in or take away. The **coffee shop** at ***Crafts and Things*** (☎ 01855-811325, 🖳 www.craftsandthings.co.uk) is open daily 9.30am-5.30pm (Nov-Easter Mon-Fri 10am-5pm, Sat & Sun 9.30am-5pm).

DAY WALKS AROUND GLEN COE see map p167

Here are some suggestions with grid references to help those with hillwalking experience plan a walk (see also p56); the times given below are approximate and include essential short stops. You'll need one of the following maps, each of which covers the area: OS Explorer 384 (1:25,000), OS Landranger sheet 41 (1:50,000), Harvey's Superwalker 'Glencoe' (1:25,000), Harvey's Walker's Map 'Glencoe' (1:40,000). Further hill-walking ideas for Glen Coe and the rest of the Highlands can be found in Trailblazer's *Scottish Highlands – The Hillwalking Guide*.

Allt Coire Gabhail

(Grid square 1655) A beautiful and easy walk of 3 miles (5km, 2hrs) up to a hidden valley where the MacDonalds hid their stolen cattle. Start at the car park at GR171568 and return the same way.

Circuit of Buachaille Etive Beag

(9 miles/14km; 4½ to 6 hours) A long low walk round the 'little herdsman of Etive' via Lairig Eilde and Lairig Gartain. There are several stream crossings making the circuit difficult after heavy rain. Start/finish at GR187563 by the Scottish Rights of Way Society sign to Loch Etiveside.

Ascent of Buachaille Etive Beag

(5½ miles/9km; 5 to 6 hours) A straightforward, moderately strenuous climb taking in two Munros. Start at GR187563 by the Scottish Rights of Way

Society sign to Loch Etiveside and follow this path for about 500m. Leave it and head south up the side of the mountain to the pass at GR188545. From here climb steeply north-east to the summit of Stob Coire Raineach (925m/3034ft), then return to the pass and climb south-west to a minor summit (902m/2959ft) and continue along the narrow ridge to Stob Dubh (958m/3142ft). Return the same way.

Ascent of Buachaille Etive Mor

(9 miles/14km; 6½ to 8½ hours) A full, strenuous walk on one of Scotland's best-loved mountains. Start at Altnafeadh GR221563, cross the footbridge over the River Coupall and follow the path all the way to the back of Coire na Tulaich.

The route ascends up the steep scree-covered headwall of the corrie (take care) and onto a flat pass. Head east to the summit of Stob Dearg (1022m/3352ft), the first Munro. Most walkers then retrace their steps to the top of Coire na Tulaich and, rather than descending, continue west and then south-west along the wide ridge over Stob na Doire (1011m/3316ft) and Stob Coire Altruim (941m/3086ft) to the second Munro, Stob na Broige (956m/3136ft).

The usual descent is from the pass between Stob Coire Altruim and Stob na Doire down into Lairig Gartain and then back along the path to Altnafeadh.

❑ Flesh eating plants on the West Highland Way

In the large swathes of acid peat bog and damp moorland present on the West Highland Way live two of Britain's more unusual species of flora. Nutrients are limited in these saturated lands so the plants that do survive here have to find them from somewhere other than the ground on which they stand – with sometimes ingenious results.

Two, in particular – the **sundew** (*Drosera rotundifolia*, see photo opposite p64) and **butterwort** (also known as the **bog violet**; *Pinguicula vulgaris*) have resorted to snacking on the local fauna for their nutrition. Using sticky droplets of digestive enzymes on their leaf hairs, they trap and digest any small insects that should happen to land on them, including midges, thereby providing the plants with the essential nitrogen they need for heathy growth.

Butterworts are so-called as it was thought that the juices from the leaves, when rubbed onto cows' udders, would charm the milk from the cow. In fact, though the efficacy of these plants on milk production is unknown, what is true is that the bactericide that stops the insects from decomposing before they are digested would have helped to prevent udder infections. The other use of this bacteria on the leaves was to curdle the milk and to turn it into a type of yoghurt.

Sundews are useful to humans too. The plant contains plumbagin, a naturally occurring antibiotic, and is used by modern herbalists to treat a number of respiratory conditions. In Lancashire it was referred to as 'youth grass' and throughout Europe it was made into a liquor with spices and called Rosa Solis, which claimed not only to be an aphrodisiac but also a fortifying panacea. There are also some who still believe that it is a useful cure for lovesickness, with the plant's ability to lure and trap unsuspecting insects leading some to believe that it could work on humans too. People would thus place the plant secretly into the clothing of the object of their desire in the hope that they too would become similarly ensnared.

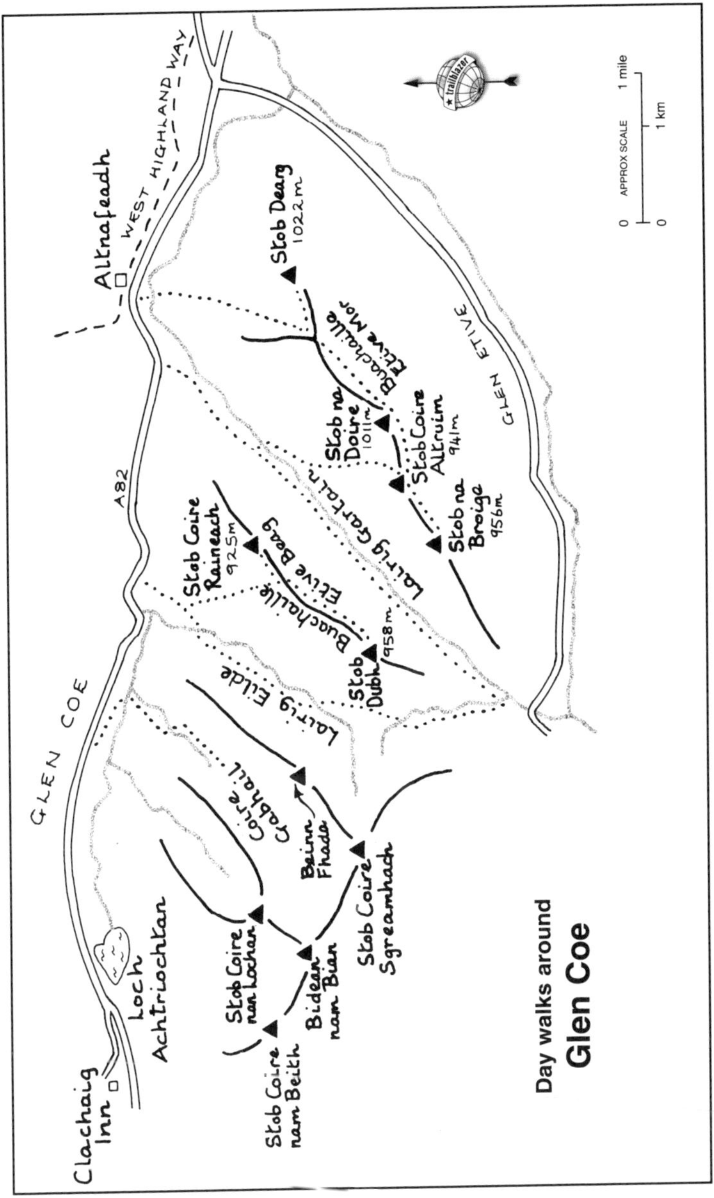

Day walks around Glen Coe

Clachaig Inn

Loch Achtriochtan

Glen Coe

A82

Altnafeadh

West Highland Way

Stob Dearg 1022m

Buachaille Etive Mor

Stob na Doire 1011m

Stob Coire Altruim 941m

Stob na Broige 956m

Glen Etive

Lairig Gartain

Stob Coire Raineach 925m

Buachaille Etive Beag

Stob Dubh 958m

Lairig Eilde

Coire Gabhail

Beinn Fhada

Stob Coire Sgreamhach

Stob Coire nan Lochan

Bidean nam Bian

Stob Coire nam Beith

trailblazer

APPROX SCALE 0 1 mile 0 1 km

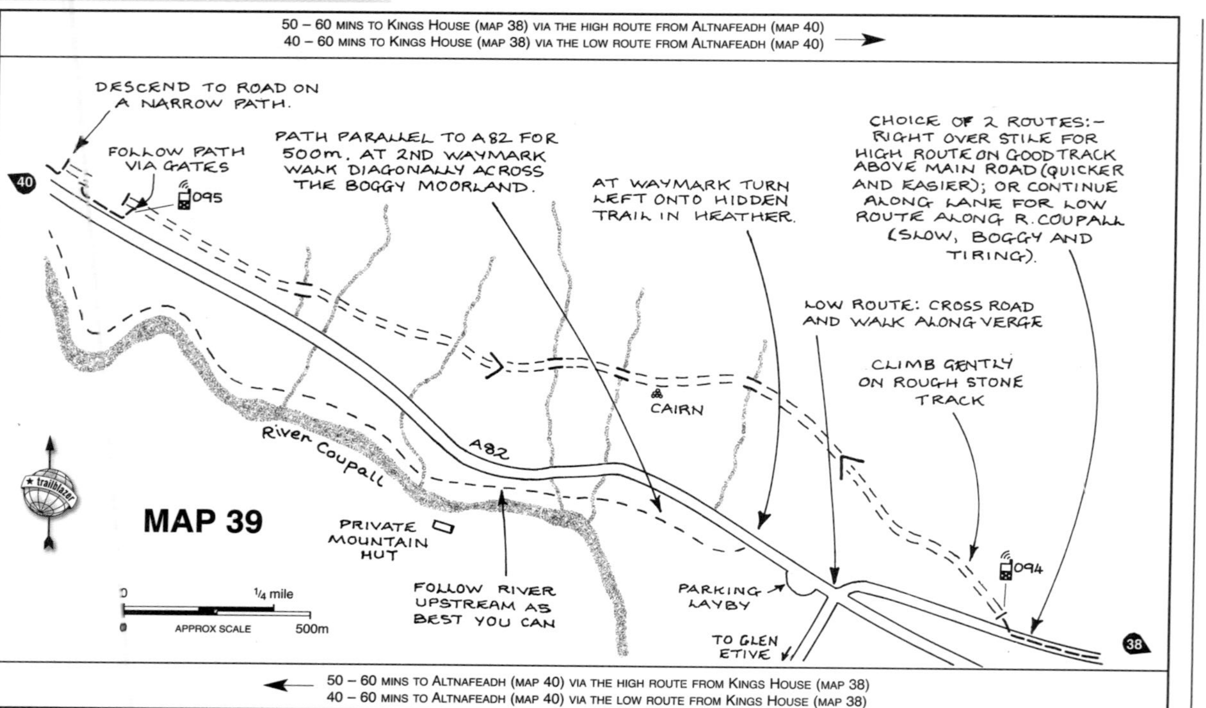
50 – 60 mins to Kings House (map 38) via the high route from Altnafeadh (map 40)
40 – 60 mins to Kings House (map 38) via the low route from Altnafeadh (map 40)
DESCEND TO ROAD ON A NARROW PATH.
FOLLOW PATH VIA GATES
095
PATH PARALLEL TO A82 FOR 500m. AT 2ND WAYMARK WALK DIAGONALLY ACROSS THE BOGGY MOORLAND.
AT WAYMARK TURN LEFT ONTO HIDDEN TRAIL IN HEATHER.
CHOICE OF 2 ROUTES:- RIGHT OVER STILE FOR HIGH ROUTE ON GOOD TRACK ABOVE MAIN ROAD (QUICKER AND EASIER); OR CONTINUE ALONG LANE FOR LOW ROUTE ALONG R. COUPALL (SLOW, BOGGY AND TIRING).
LOW ROUTE: CROSS ROAD AND WALK ALONG VERGE
CLIMB GENTLY ON ROUGH STONE TRACK
CAIRN
A82
River Coupall
094
MAP 39
PRIVATE MOUNTAIN HUT
FOLLOW RIVER UPSTREAM AS BEST YOU CAN
PARKING LAYBY
TO GLEN ETIVE
0
1/4 mile
APPROX SCALE
500m
trailblazer
40
38
50 – 60 mins to Altnafeadh (map 40) via the high route from Kings House (map 38)
40 – 60 mins to Altnafeadh (map 40) via the low route from Kings House (map 38)

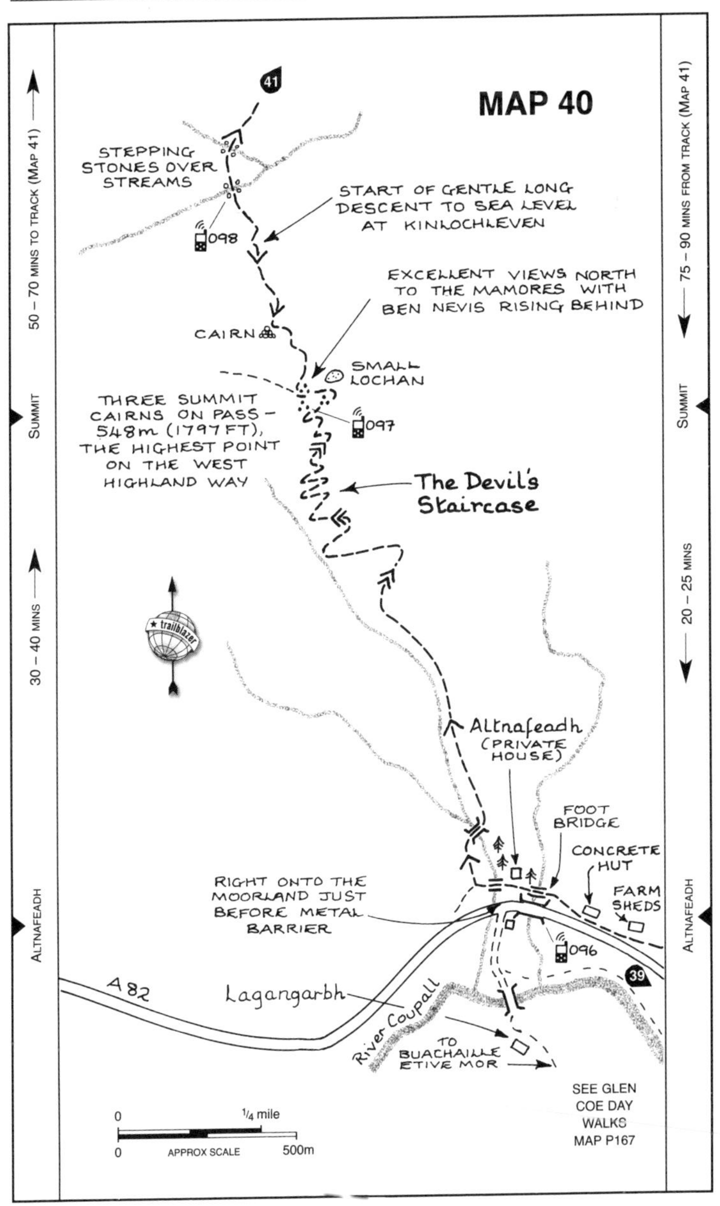

MAP 40
50 – 70 MINS TO TRACK (MAP 41)
SUMMIT
30 – 40 MINS
ALTNAFEADH
75 – 90 MINS FROM TRACK (MAP 41)
SUMMIT
20 – 25 MINS
ALTNAFEADH
41
STEPPING STONES OVER STREAMS
098
START OF GENTLE LONG DESCENT TO SEA LEVEL AT KINLOCHLEVEN
EXCELLENT VIEWS NORTH TO THE MAMORES WITH BEN NEVIS RISING BEHIND
CAIRN
SMALL LOCHAN
THREE SUMMIT CAIRNS ON PASS – 548m (1797 FT), THE HIGHEST POINT ON THE WEST HIGHLAND WAY
097
The Devil's Staircase
trailblazer
Altnafeadh (PRIVATE HOUSE)
FOOT BRIDGE
CONCRETE HUT
FARM SHEDS
RIGHT ONTO THE MOORLAND JUST BEFORE METAL BARRIER
096
39
A82
Lagangarbh
River Coupall
TO BUACHAILLE ETIVE MOR
SEE GLEN COE DAY WALKS MAP P167
0
1/4 mile
0
APPROX SCALE
500m

KINGSHOUSE TO KINLOCHLEVEN MAPS 38-42

This **8½ miles (14km, 2½-3¼hrs)** gives spectacular walking across inspiring mountainous terrain. The route is easy to follow but can be extremely exposed in wet, windy or snowy conditions as there is nowhere to shelter.

The unpleasant walk parallel to the A82 from Kingshouse to Altnafeadh is over quickly and the climb to the highest point on the West Highland Way begins: the **Devil's Staircase** (Map 40). This ascent of 259 metres (850ft) up the south side of the ridge between Kingshouse and Kinlochleven is feared by Way walkers but although it's a sustained climb, it's not nearly as hard as the name would suggest. In all likelihood it was christened by the soldiers who had to carve this sinuous military road up the bleak hillside in the 1750s. You follow the old road as it climbs to the pass (548m/1797ft) where there are views over the Glen Coe peaks and, in good weather, north over the Mamores to Ben Nevis.

From the top it's a long descent across rugged mountainside and then on a steep four-wheel-drive track down to **Kinlochleven**, an ugly, modern village set amidst dramatic Highland scenery.

KINLOCHLEVEN Map 42, p173

The planned factory village of Kinlochleven was called 'the ugliest on two thousand miles of Highland coast' by WH Murray in his 1968 guide to the West Highlands. Sadly it is no more picturesque today, even though the aluminium smelter (see box opposite) which necessitated its construction has closed. Despite this utilitarian feel, the village is a pleasant place to stay largely because of the magnificent surroundings and the friendliness of the people. The **Aluminium Story Visitor Centre** (☎ 01855-831021; Mon, Tue, Thur, Fri 9am-12.30pm & 1.30-5.30pm; Wed & Sat 9am-1pm) has displays telling the story of this part of the town's history.

Kinlochleven has reinvented itself as a major outdoor activity centre, which fits in well with the Lochaber region's unofficial status as the 'Outdoor Capital of the UK'. The location is certainly ideal for such an ambition and the transformation of the old smelter building into the biggest indoor articulated rock climbing wall and ice wall in Britain draws the outdoor fraternity to the village when the weather outside is too foul. **The Ice Factor** (☎ 01855-831100, 🖳 www.ice-factor.co.uk; daily 9am-7pm, Tue & Thur to 10pm) also incorporates a sauna and steam room (£5/3 non-climbers/climbers; bring a towel). Instructors are usually available between 10am and 6pm for novices but check in advance; booking for any of the facilities is particularly recommended in school holidays.

Another worthwhile sight is the impressive **Grey Mares Tail waterfall**, a short walk along the path that starts beside the Scottish Episcopal Church.

If you're walking over the first week in May you'll hear the **Scottish Six Day Motorcycle Trials**, based here, even before you see them. B&Bs will be booked out.

Services

Kinlochleven is isolated at the head of Loch Leven and gets little through traffic. Stagecoach No 44 **bus** goes to Fort William via Glencoe Junction (see public transport map and table pp44-8).

There's a **bank** but it's open only on Thursday. The **cash machine** is outside the Aluminium Story Visitor Centre which houses the **post office** (Mon, Tue, Thur, Fri 9am-12.30pm & 1.30-5.30pm; Wed & Sat 9am-1pm). The library (☎ 01855-832047; term time Mon, Wed & Fri 9am-5pm, Tue & Thur to 8pm, Sat to 1pm; school hols Mon-Sat 10am-1pm & 2-5pm, Tue & Thur also 6-8pm; **internet access** free) is in the High School and next to the Community Centre (☎ 01855-831119; Mon-Fri 9am-9pm, Sat

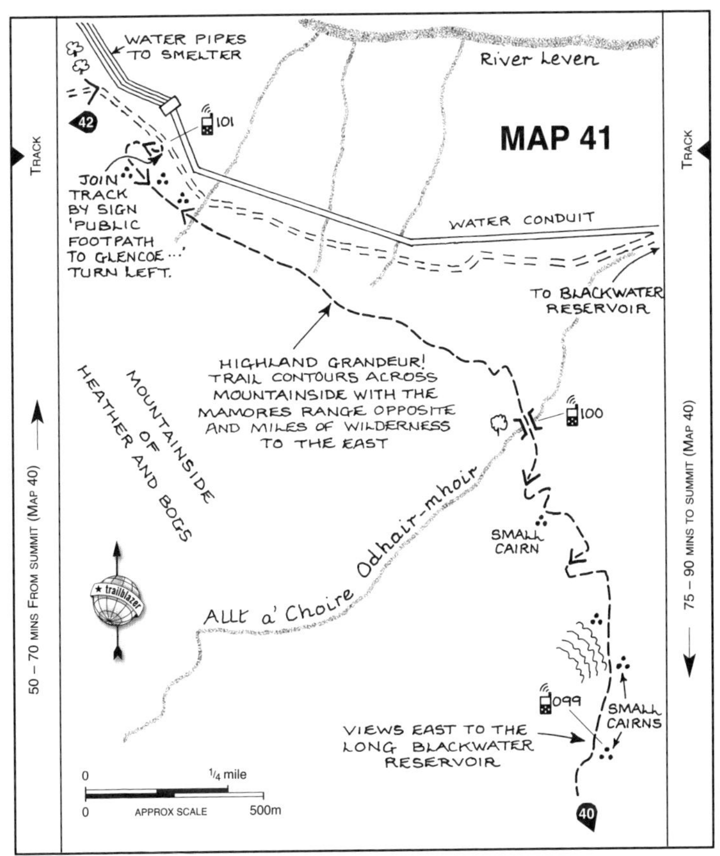

❑ Aluminium and Blackwater Reservoir

The eight-mile (13km) long Blackwater Reservoir (off Map 41) was created by the Blackwater dam, the largest in Europe at the time, which was built between 1905 and 1909. The muscle power came from unemployed migrants and 3000 skilled navvies, the itinerant labourers who constructed so much of industrial Britain. It was designed to supply the water to power the hydro-electric (HEP) plant at the new aluminium smelter in the purpose-built village of Kinlochleven.

At the time, the smelter was one of the largest in the world and the newly formed village thrived and steadily expanded as its prosperity grew. But by the end of the 20th century competition from more modern plants and newer methods of smelting meant that it was no longer viable.

9am-1pm) where internet access is also free.

For supplies try the **General Store** (Mon-Wed 7.30am-9pm, Thur-Sat 7.30am-10pm, Sun 9am-9pm) or the Co-op **supermarket** (daily 7am-10pm) opposite. The Ice Factor is home to a small **outdoor equipment store** (daily 10am-6pm).

Where to stay

Budget accommodation The best **campsite** (£6pp; 🐕) is behind ***MacDonald Hotel*** (Map 43; ☎ 01855-831539, 🖳 www.macdonaldhotel.co.uk), Fort William Rd, with beautiful views down the loch. They also have nine four-bed **cabins** (🐕); the nightly rate (£10-18pp) depends on how many are in each cabin. Bedding (£2) can be hired. There are also showers, toilets, a laundry and a drying room and, using natural deterrents, they are trying to make the area as midge-free as possible.

There is also **camping** (30 pitches; £7pp; Mar-Oct) at ***Blackwater Hostel*** (☎ 01855-831253, 🖳 www.blackwaterhostel.co.uk), and **bunkhouse** accommodation (39 beds; 1T/three 3-bed/five 4-bed/one 8-bed; all en suite) from £16.50pp inclusive of bedding and with full cooking facilities (£40 for two sharing a room and £66 for four). They also have **microlodge hobbits** (four 2-bed, £35; three with 1D/2S beds; £45 for two sharing, £50 for four). The bunkhouse and hobbits are open all year. However, crockery, cutlery and bedding aren't provided, though a sleeping bag (£5) can be hired if requested in advance.

They also have another bunkhouse, ***West Highland Lodge Bunkhouse*** (32 beds; eight 4-bed rooms; £15pp, £35pp for two sharing a room; shared facilities), high up on the hillside behind the old visitor centre, which they open when necessary. Both bunkhouses and the campsite have a drying room. Towels are not provided.

B&Bs There is no shortage of B&B accommodation here. As you enter the village the estate of houses on the right has several places. The first you get to is ***Forest View*** (☎ 01855-831302, 🖳 www.forestviewbnb.co.uk; 2T/1D/1F, one twin and the double share toilet; WI-FI; £30-35pp, sgl occ £45-50), at 24 Wades Rd. They also offer internet access. Next is ***Quiraing*** (☎ 01855-831580, 🖳 quiraing@aol.com, 43 Lovat Rd; 2D, shared bathroom/1F en suite; ▼; WI-FI; £30-35pp, sgl occ £35). Booking is required between October and March and is recommended at other times.

On round the crescent is ***Failte*** (☎ 01855-831394, 🖳 marion.sweeney10@yahoo.co.uk, 6 Lovat Rd; 2T, shared bathroom; ▼; WI-FI; 🐕; £28pp, sgl occ £36; Apr-Oct).

Hermon (☎ 01855-831383, 🖳 www.hermonkinlochleven.co.uk, 5 Rob Roy Rd; 2T/1D; ▼; WI-FI; £30pp, sgl occ £40) is a large bungalow and they can also provide packed lunches (£5) if booked in advance.

B&B is also on offer at ***Highland Getaway*** (☎ 01855-831258, 🖳 www.highlandgetaway.co.uk; 3D/3T/1F; ▼; WI-FI restaurant only; £38-42pp, sgl occ £55). They will pick up from Kings House Hotel (see p156), for £40 return trip, if walkers would like a two-night stay with them.

Nearby is ***Allt-na-Leven*** (☎ 01855-831366, 🖳 www.bedandbreakfastkinlochleven.co.uk; 23-24 Leven Rd; 1D or T/3F; WI-FI; £36pp, sgl occ £65), a popular place run by friendly, helpful people. A packed lunch costs £6 and they can provide an evening meal (£15/17 for 2/3 courses) if booked in advance. They will also do a load of washing for £7.50; use of the drying room for wet boots/clothes is free.

One of the plushest places is ***Tigh-na-Cheo Guest House*** (off Map 42; ☎ 01855-831434, 🖳 www.tigh-na-cheo.co.uk, Garbhein Rd; 1S/1S or D/3T/3D/1F; ▼; WI-FI; 🐕 £5; £30-37pp; sgl £40-48; mid Mar to end Oct) on a rise overlooking the loch and mountains. They also have a drying room and will pick up/drop off from both Kings House Hotel and Glencoe, though a charge (£30 per lift) is payable. A packed lunch costs £6.

Close by, on the same road and with similar views is ***Edencoille*** (☎ 01855-831358, 🖳 www.kinlochlevenbedandbreakfast.co.uk; 6D or T/2D, T or F; ▼; WI-FI; £36pp, sgl occ £65). A packed lunch (£6) is available if requested by the night before. They will also do a load of washing for you.

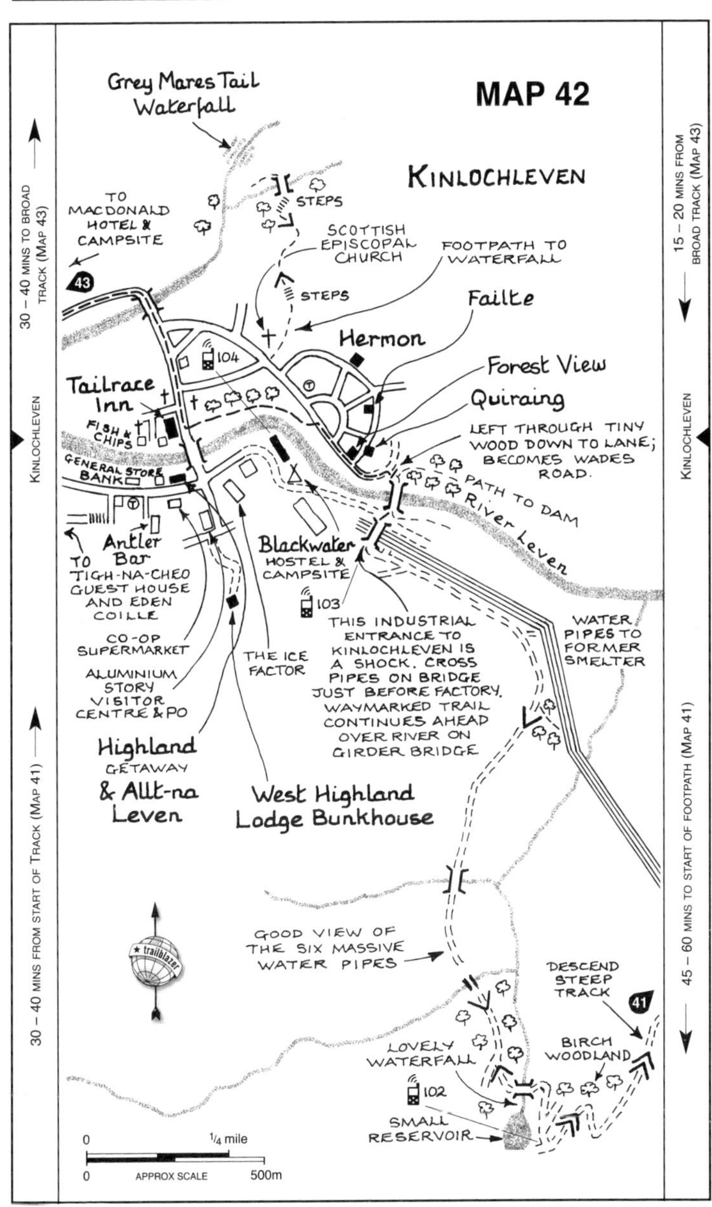
MAP 42
KINLOCHLEVEN
30 – 40 MINS TO BROAD TRACK (MAP 43)
15 – 20 MINS FROM BROAD TRACK (MAP 43)
KINLOCHLEVEN
KINLOCHLEVEN
30 – 40 MINS FROM START OF TRACK (MAP 41)
45 – 60 MINS TO START OF FOOTPATH (MAP 41)
Grey Mares Tail Waterfall
TO MACDONALD HOTEL & CAMPSITE
43
STEPS
SCOTTISH EPISCOPAL CHURCH
FOOTPATH TO WATERFALL
STEPS
Failte
Hermon
Forest View
Quiraing
104
Tailrace Inn
FISH & CHIPS
GENERAL STORE
BANK
LEFT THROUGH TINY WOOD DOWN TO LANE; BECOMES WADES ROAD.
PATH TO DAM
River Leven
TO TIGH-NA-CHEO GUEST HOUSE AND EDEN COILLE
Antler Bar
Blackwater HOSTEL & CAMPSITE
103
CO-OP SUPERMARKET
THE ICE FACTOR
THIS INDUSTRIAL ENTRANCE TO KINLOCHLEVEN IS A SHOCK. CROSS PIPES ON BRIDGE JUST BEFORE FACTORY. WAYMARKED TRAIL CONTINUES AHEAD OVER RIVER ON GIRDER BRIDGE
WATER PIPES TO FORMER SMELTER
ALUMINIUM STORY VISITOR CENTRE & PO
Highland GETAWAY & Allt-na Leven
West Highland Lodge Bunkhouse
GOOD VIEW OF THE SIX MASSIVE WATER PIPES
DESCEND STEEP TRACK
41
LOVELY WATERFALL
BIRCH WOODLAND
102
SMALL RESERVOIR
0
1/4 mile
0
APPROX SCALE
500m
trailblazer

Hotels ***Tailrace Inn*** (☎ 01855-831777, 🖳 www.tailraceinn.com; 3T/2D/1F; WI-FI; £30-37pp, sgl occ £40-50) is in the centre of the village on Riverside Rd.

MacDonald Hotel (Map 43; see Campsite; 5T/4D/1F; ☕; WI-FI; 🐕 £5; £32-42pp, sgl occ £40-55; family room £79-114) is beautifully located on the outskirts of town. Free **internet access** is also available.

Where to eat and drink

In the main part of the village ***Tailrace Inn*** (see Hotels) serves food all day until 11pm starting with breakfast from 8am. For non-residents a cooked/veggie breakfast costs £6.95 and a 'light' breakfast £4.25. They also do packed lunches for £5 (order the night before). In the restaurant and bar there's filling mince and tatties for £6.95 and steak and ale pie for £9.25.

Near the inn is the ***Riverside Chippy*** (☎ 01855-831349; Tue-Sat 5-9pm) with some seats but they are basically a take-away serving fish and chips from £4.15. ***Highland Getaway Restaurant*** (see B&Bs; daily 9am-4pm & 6-8.30pm) offers the likes of Glencoe-style chicken with haggis for £11.50 and steak for £14.95. During the day the café serves both hot and cold snacks.

There's a decent ***café*** (daily 9am-5pm) inside The Ice Factor, where you can watch the climbers whilst munching on a sandwich or slice of pizza, as well as a ***bar*** (bar meals served 6-9pm).

For drinking, the ***Antler Bar*** is the locals' place. The ***Bothy Bar*** is a dedicated walkers' watering hole at the ***MacDonald Hotel*** (see Campsite & Hotels). It has wonderful views down the length of Loch Leven and good pub grub is served daily 8am-9pm. Campers' breakfasts (booking recommended) are served in the restaurant each morning (£6 for a full Scottish). Packed lunches cost £5.

KINLOCHLEVEN TO FORT WILLIAM — MAPS 42-49

The final tough but rewarding **15 miles (24km, 4¾-6½hrs)** crosses a beautiful high pass and then undulates through repetitive forests to the end of the West Highland Way, now right in the centre of Fort William.

It's a long sustained 250m (820ft) climb out of Kinlochleven on a steep winding trail through birch trees. At the top you continue on a wide track, the old military road, which traverses the mountain side with glorious views over **Loch Leven** to the mountains of Glencoe. From here the trail rises gently through a wide U-shaped valley to a broad pass, the **Lairigmor** (Map 45) at 330m/1082ft. This can be exposed in bad weather. The Way descends and then climbs again through a series of dense conifer plantations with occasional views of **Ben Nevis**, Britain's highest mountain. A final descent on forest tracks takes you into **Glen Nevis** from where it's only a short walk along the road to **Fort William**.

GLEN NEVIS

Map 48 p181 & Map 49 p185

Pastoral Glen Nevis is surrounded by some of the finest mountains in Britain and as a result the valley has an excited buzz of activity throughout the year.

For those who would prefer to end their walk in the open countryside rather than on the streets of Fort William there's a B&B, a youth hostel, a couple of bunkhouses and one large campsite, the only one in the area. These are all perfectly situated for an ascent of Ben Nevis.

Services

Ioned Nibheis, the Glen Nevis **visitor centre** (Map 49; ☎ 01397-705922; daily Easter to May 9am-5pm, Jun-Aug 8.30am-6pm, Sep-Oct 9am-5pm, Nov-Easter 9am-3pm) is well worth a look in if only to get an accurate **weather forecast** and **avalanche**

(cont'd on p179)

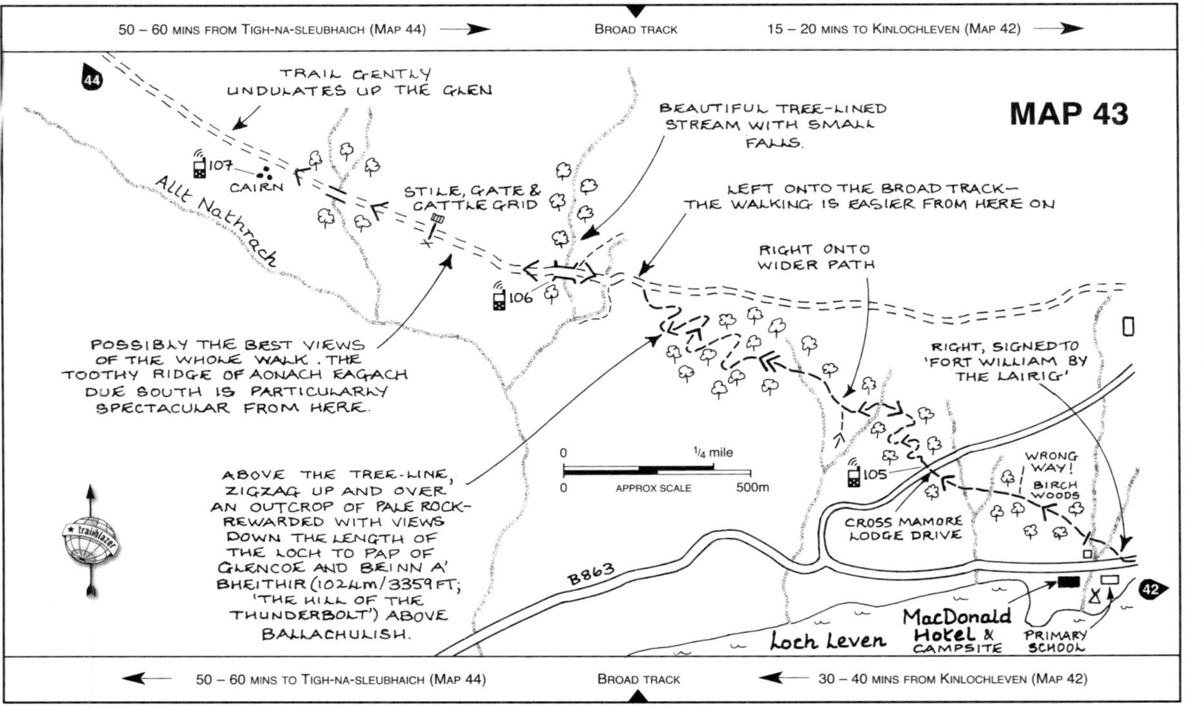
50 – 60 MINS FROM TIGH-NA-SLEUBHAICH (MAP 44)
BROAD TRACK
15 – 20 MINS TO KINLOCHLEVEN (MAP 42)
44
TRAIL GENTLY UNDULATES UP THE GLEN
MAP 43
BEAUTIFUL TREE-LINED STREAM WITH SMALL FALLS.
107
CAIRN
Allt Nathrach
STILE, GATE & CATTLE GRID
LEFT ONTO THE BROAD TRACK– THE WALKING IS EASIER FROM HERE ON
RIGHT ONTO WIDER PATH
106
POSSIBLY THE BEST VIEWS OF THE WHOLE WALK. THE TOOTHY RIDGE OF AONACH EAGACH DUE SOUTH IS PARTICULARLY SPECTACULAR FROM HERE.
RIGHT, SIGNED TO 'FORT WILLIAM BY THE LAIRIG'
0 1/4 mile
0 APPROX SCALE 500m
105
WRONG WAY!
BIRCH WOODS
ABOVE THE TREE-LINE, ZIGZAG UP AND OVER AN OUTCROP OF PALE ROCK– REWARDED WITH VIEWS DOWN THE LENGTH OF THE LOCH TO PAP OF GLENCOE AND BEINN A' BHEITHIR (1024m/3359FT; 'THE HILL OF THE THUNDERBOLT') ABOVE BALLACHULISH.
trailblazer
CROSS MAMORE LODGE DRIVE
B863
42
Loch Leven
MacDonald Hotel & CAMPSITE
PRIMARY SCHOOL
50 – 60 MINS TO TIGH-NA-SLEUBHAICH (MAP 44)
BROAD TRACK
30 – 40 MINS FROM KINLOCHLEVEN (MAP 42)

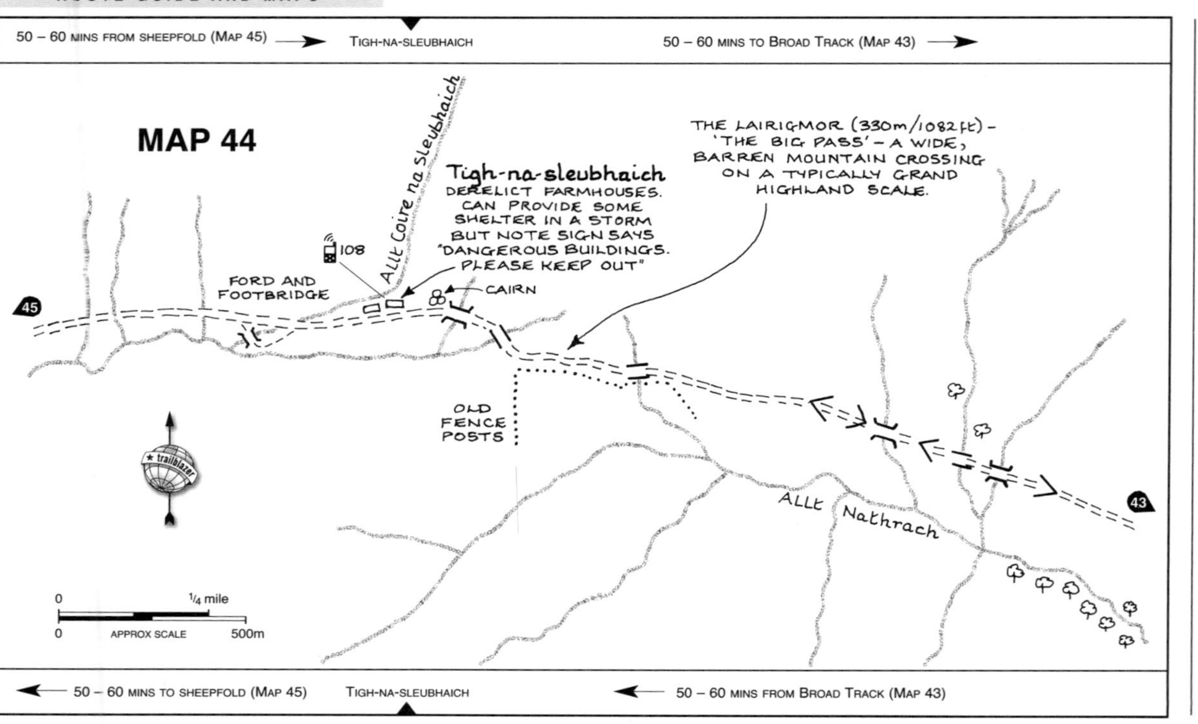
ROUTE GUIDE AND MAPS
50 – 60 MINS FROM SHEEPFOLD (MAP 45) → TIGH-NA-SLEUBHAICH
50 – 60 MINS TO BROAD TRACK (MAP 43) →
MAP 44
Allt Coire na Sleubhaich
Tigh-na-sleubhaich
DERELICT FARMHOUSES. CAN PROVIDE SOME SHELTER IN A STORM BUT NOTE SIGN SAYS "DANGEROUS BUILDINGS. PLEASE KEEP OUT"
THE LAIRIGMOR (330m/1082ft) - 'THE BIG PASS' - A WIDE, BARREN MOUNTAIN CROSSING ON A TYPICALLY GRAND HIGHLAND SCALE.
108
FORD AND FOOTBRIDGE
CAIRN
45
OLD FENCE POSTS
trailblazer
Allt Nathrach
43
0
1/4 mile
0
APPROX SCALE
500m
← 50 – 60 MINS TO SHEEPFOLD (MAP 45) TIGH-NA-SLEUBHAICH
← 50 – 60 MINS FROM BROAD TRACK (MAP 43)

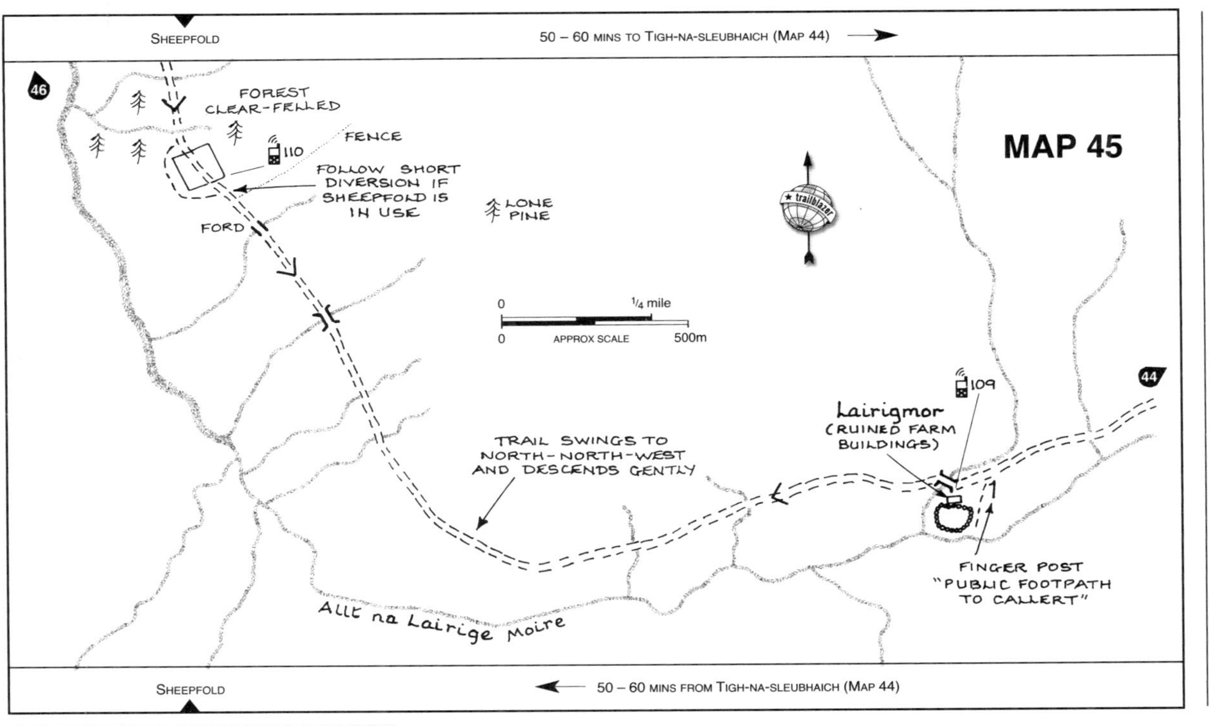
SHEEPFOLD
50 – 60 MINS TO TIGH-NA-SLEUBHAICH (MAP 44)
46
FOREST CLEAR-FELLED
FENCE
110
FOLLOW SHORT DIVERSION IF SHEEPFOLD IS IN USE
FORD
LONE PINE
MAP 45
trailblazer
0
1/4 mile
0
APPROX SCALE
500m
44
109
Lairigmor
(RUINED FARM BUILDINGS)
TRAIL SWINGS TO NORTH-NORTH-WEST AND DESCENDS GENTLY
FINGER POST "PUBLIC FOOTPATH TO CALLERT"
Allt na Lairige Moire
SHEEPFOLD
50 – 60 MINS FROM TIGH-NA-SLEUBHAICH (MAP 44)

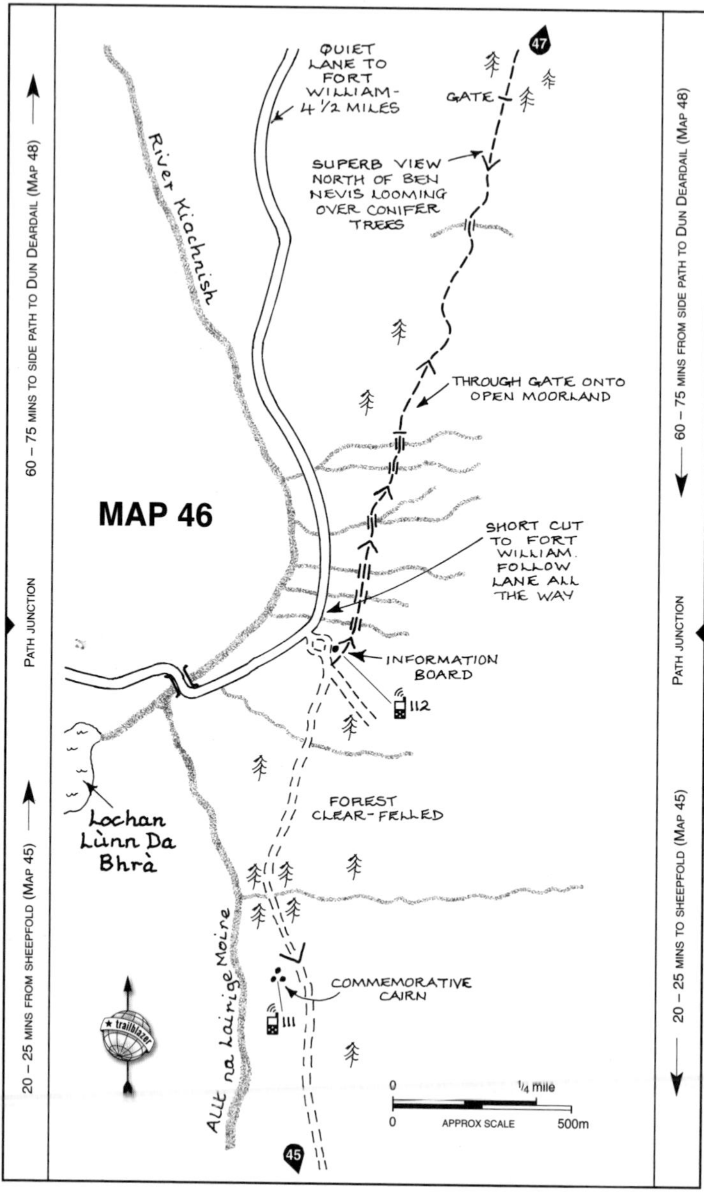

MAP 46

60 – 75 MINS TO SIDE PATH TO DUN DEARDAIL (MAP 48)

PATH JUNCTION

20 – 25 MINS FROM SHEEPFOLD (MAP 45)

60 – 75 MINS FROM SIDE PATH TO DUN DEARDAIL (MAP 48)

PATH JUNCTION

20 – 25 MINS TO SHEEPFOLD (MAP 45)

47

QUIET LANE TO FORT WILLIAM- 4 1/2 MILES

GATE

River Kiachnish

SUPERB VIEW NORTH OF BEN NEVIS LOOMING OVER CONIFER TREES

THROUGH GATE ONTO OPEN MOORLAND

SHORT CUT TO FORT WILLIAM. FOLLOW LANE ALL THE WAY

INFORMATION BOARD

112

Lochan Lùnn Da Bhrà

FOREST CLEAR-FELLED

Allt na Lairige Moire

COMMEMORATIVE CAIRN

trailblazer

0 1/4 mile

0 APPROX SCALE 500m

45

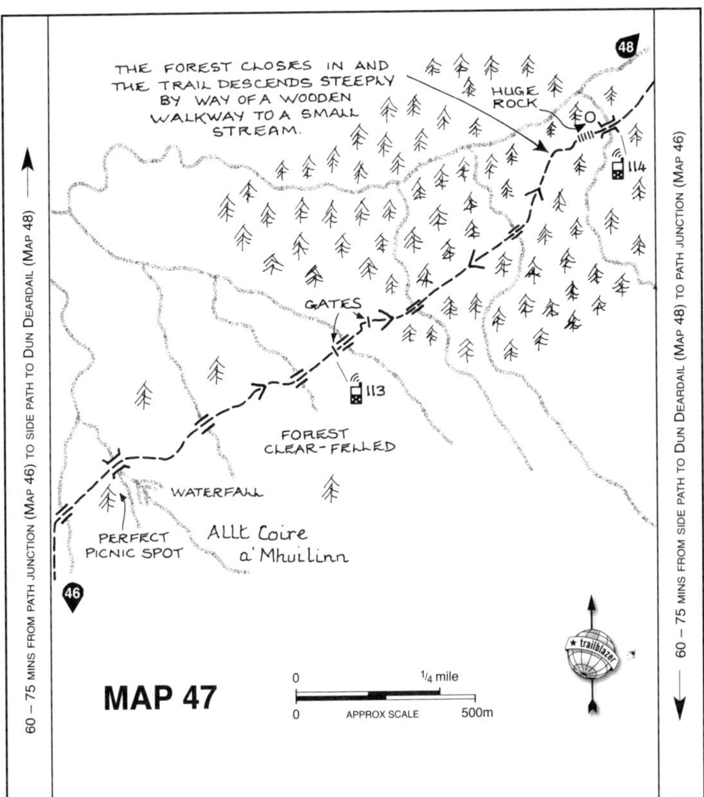

reports. There is an excellent exhibition on the natural history and environment of the area, a bookshop) and they stock outdoor gear; the staff also have a wealth of local knowledge.

Stagecoach's No 41 **bus** service runs up and down the glen and can be flagged down if it is safe to stop (see pp44-8).

Where to stay

Glen Nevis Caravan and Camping Park (Map 48; ☎ 01397-702191, 💻 www.glen-nevis.co.uk; £6.80-10.40 for one person in a backpack tent, £10.60-13.60 for two people; mid Mar to end Oct) is a vast acreage of neatly cut grass and conifers sprawling over the bottom of the glen. It has a laundry (£2 wash) and a well-stocked **shop** (mid Mar to end Oct daily 8am-5.30pm, till 10pm in the main season).

Just up the glen from here is the popular ***Glen Nevis Youth Hostel*** (Map 48; ☎ 01397-702336, 💻 www.glennevishostel.co.uk; 91 beds; two 2-/3-bed, one 4-bed, one 5-bed, four 7-bed, one 8-/9-/10-/11-bed; some rooms are en suite; WI-FI; £18-22pp, twin/triple/quad room £50/75/90) which is open all year. Meals are available and the hostel is licensed; it has laundry facilities (£2 per wash) as well as a drying room and offers **internet access** (£1 for 20 mins).

Another good place to stay in a beautiful position at the start of the Ben Nevis path is ***Ben Nevis Inn*** (Map 49; ☎ 01397-701227, 🖳 www.ben-nevis-inn.co.uk; £15.50pp), a carefully renovated barn, which has a basic **bunkhouse** (24 beds) with kitchen facilities and a drying room; bedding is provided. Booking is recommended particularly in the summer months.

Next door, ***Achintee Farm*** (Map 49; ☎ 01397-702240, 🖳 www.achinteefarm.com) has a range of accommodation including a **hostel** with a dormitory (five beds) for £17pp, a room with two beds, and one with three single beds (£19pp). Each unit has its own shower, toilet and cooking facilities; bed linen is included. There is **B&B** (1D/2D or T; ☛; WI-FI; £38-45pp, sgl occ £65; Mar to end Oct) accommodation in the farmhouse. Packed lunches are available for B&B guests and everyone can use their drying rooms. Two-night bookings preferred.

Where to eat and drink

Between Glen Nevis Caravan & Camping Park and the youth hostel are two places: ***Café Beag*** (Map 48; ☎ 01397-705443; daily 8am-6pm, to 10pm at weekends), in a wooden building, serves breakfasts, lunches and traditional Sunday roast lunches as well as dinners at the weekend. ***Glen Nevis Restaurant and Lounge Bar*** (☎ 01397-705459; Mar/Apr to end Oct, restaurant daily 6-9.30pm) is a modern building with the air of a motorway service station.

At ***Ben Nevis Inn*** (see Where to stay); excellent food is available daily noon-9pm (Thur-Sun only in winter); the menu changes regularly but during the day may include filled ciabatta (from £5.55) and in the evening haddock & chips (£10.50) and chicken and haggis rumbledethumps (£11.95). Light snacks are served till closing time at 11pm. It's the kind of place you could spend all day listening to (the occasional) live acoustic music, warming yourself by the woodburner and luxuriating in the glorious views up the glen.

BEN NEVIS

See map p183

You remember your first mountain in much the same way you remember having your first sexual experience, except that climbing doesn't make as much mess and you don't cry for a week if Ben Nevis forgets to phone next morning.

Muriel Gray *The First Fifty – Munro-bagging without a beard*

It is impossible to say who first climbed the highest mountain in Britain. Locals have been walking these hills since the beginning of time and would have been guides to the visitors who first left a record of their ascents in the 18th century. Although nowhere near the first to ascend the mountain, some credit must go to Clement Wragge who climbed the peak every day without fail for two years to take weather readings. Happy to set out in all conditions, he soon became known as 'inclement Wragge'. He was no-doubt glad when a weather observatory was built on the summit in 1883 and a substantial path made to service it; now the 'tourist route'. The observatory was abandoned in 1904.

Today 75,000 walkers a year attempt to reach the summit so don't think you'll get the place to yourself. Mass tourism has been a part of the Ben's life since the railway reached Fort William in 1894. Thankfully the tackiness of a summit hotel and pony rides to the top were abandoned soon after the ideas were conceived.

Climbing Ben Nevis

Climbing the highest mountain in Britain at the very end of having walked the West Highland Way makes a superb ending to your Highland adventure. However, do not underestimate those 1344 metres (4406ft) to the summit. It may not sound that high in comparison with the highest peaks in other coun-

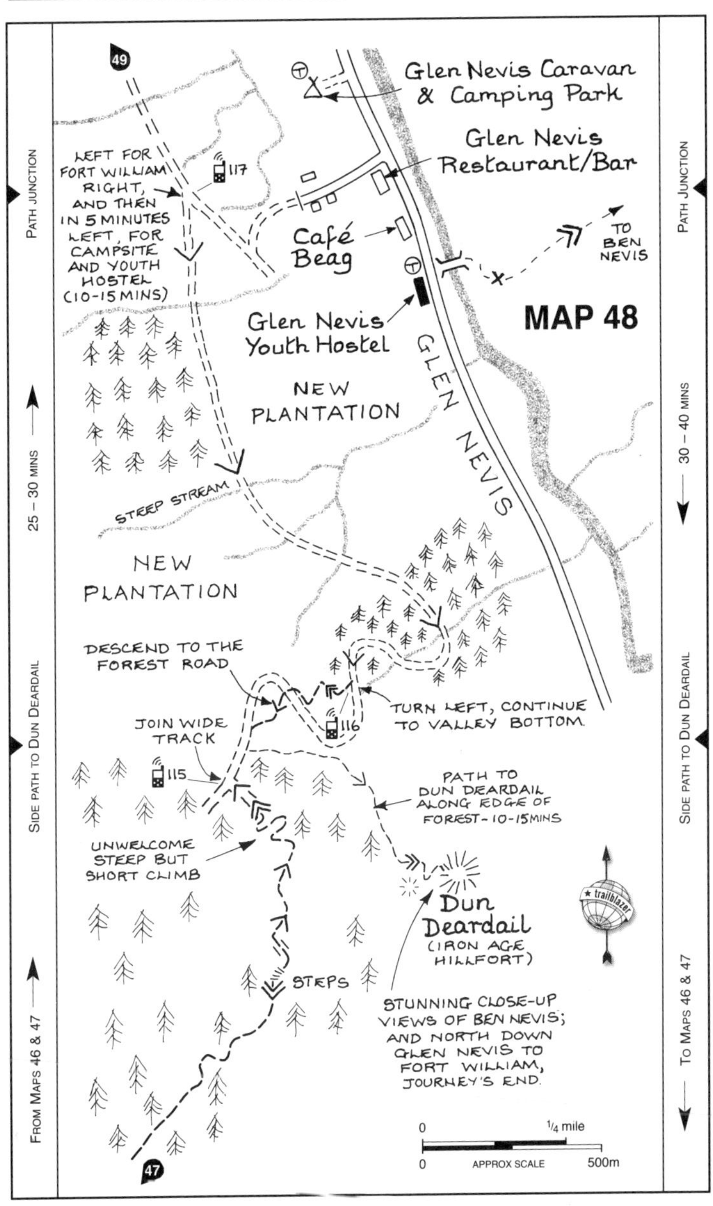
49
Glen Nevis Caravan & Camping Park
Glen Nevis Restaurant/Bar
LEFT FOR FORT WILLIAM RIGHT, AND THEN IN 5 MINUTES LEFT, FOR CAMPSITE AND YOUTH HOSTEL (10-15 MINS)
117
Café Beag
TO BEN NEVIS
Glen Nevis Youth Hostel
MAP 48
GLEN NEVIS
NEW PLANTATION
STEEP STREAM
NEW PLANTATION
DESCEND TO THE FOREST ROAD
TURN LEFT, CONTINUE TO VALLEY BOTTOM
JOIN WIDE TRACK
116
115
PATH TO DUN DEARDAIL ALONG EDGE OF FOREST - 10-15MINS
UNWELCOME STEEP BUT SHORT CLIMB
Dun Deardail (IRON AGE HILLFORT)
trailblazer
STEPS
STUNNING CLOSE-UP VIEWS OF BEN NEVIS; AND NORTH DOWN GLEN NEVIS TO FORT WILLIAM, JOURNEY'S END.
0
1/4 mile
0
APPROX SCALE
500m
47
PATH JUNCTION
25 – 30 MINS
SIDE PATH TO DUN DEARDAIL
FROM MAPS 46 & 47
PATH JUNCTION
30 – 40 MINS
SIDE PATH TO DUN DEARDAIL
TO MAPS 46 & 47

tries but it has a fearsome reputation for accidents and as with all mountains in the Highlands, you should not contemplate climbing it unless you are suitably equipped and knowledgeable (see p56).

There are several routes to the top. By far the most popular is the badly named **Tourist Route** (significantly harder than its belittling name would suggest) ascending from Glen Nevis along the well-trodden line of the former pony track all the way to the summit. This route (see p184) takes about 5½ to 6½ hours in total. Some find it a relentless slog, particularly on the upper reaches of the mountain and especially when accompanied by scores of other walkers, as you will be on most days in summer. It is, however, the only option for those who would not class themselves experienced hillwalkers.

For the latter category there is a superb route that provides a tough, long, but grand day out, befitting of Britain's highest mountain. The **Carn Mor Dearg Arête Route** (see p184) follows the normal route initially and then detours under the spectacular north face to climb Carn Mor Dearg (CMD), a significant mountain in its own right. From here it follows the narrow, rocky, crescent line of the Carn Mor Dearg Arête and then up the Ben's boulder-covered south-eastern slopes to the summit plateau. Descent is down the normal route. The whole trip takes about 8½ to 9½ hours.

Safety

The normal route is along a well-graded trail, easy to follow in good visibility, but a mountain path none the less. Expect loose rock and scree underfoot, patches of snow even late in the year and some steep sections. The alternative CMD route is largely on steep, rough ground with a fair bit of exposure in places. It is a long route, requiring stamina with some sections of easy scrambling. Neither route is suitable in snow or ice unless you are an accomplished winter mountaineer.

The main difficulties on Ben Nevis occur on the summit plateau in poor visibility. The plateau is broad, relatively featureless and fringed to the north by a wall of crags which drop precipitously into Coire Leis below. The gullies that cut into this rock wall have too frequently ensnared lost walkers and climbers wandering round the plateau in white-out conditions. The other real danger is that in an effort to avoid these gullies the walker aims too far south, missing the descent path and straying onto the dangerous ground at the top of the notorious Five Finger Gully on the west side of the plateau. In poor visibility, a frequent occurrence as the summit is in cloud an average of 300 days a year, your navigation must be spot on. Snow and cloud together can create a lethal formula. See the box below about poor visibility navigation.

For either route you must take one of the following maps: OS Landranger Sheet 41 (1:50,000), OS Explorer 392 (1:25,000), Harvey's Walker's Map 'Ben Nevis' (1:40,000) or Harvey's Superwalker 'Ben Nevis' (1:25,000). If

❑ Poor visibility navigation notes

To get safely off the summit in severe conditions you must walk from the summit trig point on a **grid** bearing of 231° for 150 metres. Then follow a **grid** bearing of 281° to get off the plateau and onto the Tourist Route. **Remember** to add the number of degrees of magnetic variation to your compass to obtain the magnetic bearing you should follow.

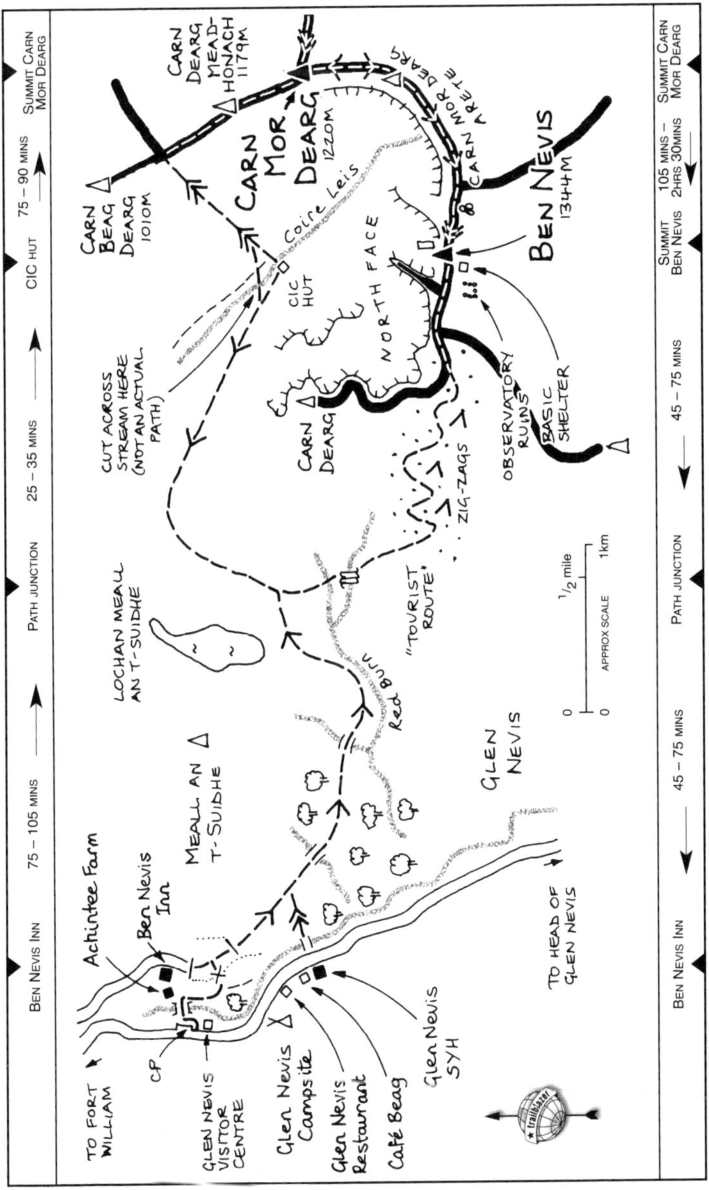

Ben Nevis Inn — 75 – 105 mins → — Path junction — 25 – 35 mins → — CIC hut — 75 – 90 mins → — Summit Carn Mor Dearg

Ben Nevis Inn — ← 45 – 75 mins — Path junction — ← 45 – 75 mins — Summit Ben Nevis — ← 105 mins – 2hrs 30mins — Summit Carn Mor Dearg

To Fort William
CP
Glen Nevis Visitor Centre
Achintee Farm
Ben Nevis Inn
Glen Nevis Campsite
Glen Nevis Restaurant
Café Beag
Glen Nevis SYH
To head of Glen Nevis
Meall an t-Suidhe
Lochan Meall an t-Suidhe
Glen Nevis
Red Burn
"Tourist route"
Zig-zags
Cut across stream here (not an actual path)
Carn Dearg
North Face
CIC hut
Coire Leis
Carn Beag Dearg 1010m
Carn Dearg Meadhonach 1179m
Carn Mor Dearg 1220m
Carn Mor Dearg Arete
Observatory ruins
Basic shelter
Ben Nevis 1344m
0 — ½ mile
0 — 1km
Approx scale
trailblazer

you have a choice, the latter is the best with its enlarged map of the summit of Ben Nevis; a real help in getting off the mountain in poor visibility.

Tourist route

From the youth hostel in Glen Nevis, cross the footbridge over River Nevis and turn left over a ladder-stile. Take heed of any pertinent safety or weather information on the notice board here. The path climbs steeply to join the main trail from the visitor centre and Achintee Farm.

The trail climbs gently across the side of Meall an t-Suidhe, up two zigzags and over three small bridges. Follow it into the ravine created by the Allt na h-Urchaire (Red Burn) which falls off the western flanks of the Ben and then up onto a broad grassy pass on which **Lochan Meall an t-Suidhe** (Halfway Lochan) sits. Don't be tempted to cut across the zigzags as this causes further erosion on this intensively used path. South-east of the lochan the trail divides by a short, low stone wall. This junction is about 1½ hours' walking from the start including one or two essential stops. It's at least another 2 to 2½ hours from here to the summit. An indistinct trail continues straight ahead across the col above Lochan Meall an t-Suidhe. This is the start of the route via CMD (see below). The main trail doubles back on itself and climbs easily across the western slopes of Carn Dearg. Cross the **Red Burn** below a waterfall (fill up with water) and begin ascending the interminable zigzags up the severely eroded flank of the mountain. There are lots of short cuts but they do not make the going easier or quicker either on the ascent or coming back down. They are steep, extremely slippery and best avoided.

As you ascend, the huge shoulder of Carn Dearg (1221m/4005ft) spreads out to your left. You may be able to make out the orange emergency shelter just west of its summit. Eventually the route crosses a rock band and at last you climb more gently onto the vast **summit plateau** (3½ to 4 hours from the start). Among the boulder-strewn landscape are all manner of man-made structures: an emergency shelter, cairns, memorial plaques, the ruins of an observatory and the trig point. The summit is no place for quiet reflection. On most days you will be surrounded by the trappings of the modern world, crackling crisp packets, chirping mobile phones, the pervading smell of cigarette smoke, yet if the cloud is high the views are superb. The descent is back the way you came and takes about 2 to 2½ hours.

Emergency shelter at the summit

Carn Mor Dearg Arête Route

Follow the Tourist Route to Lochan Meall an t-Suidhe. Where the paths divide, continue straight on across the col. After five minutes there's a large cairn where a faint trail branches left towards the outflow of the lake. Ignore this, keeping straight on along the main trail which climbs gently to another large cairn on the horizon. The trail begins to descend and turns sharply east (right) into Coire Leis under the impressive northern crags of Ben Nevis. Leave the path after a few hundred metres picking your way down over the rough heather- and bilberry-covered slopes to the **Allt a' Mhuilinn**. This is the last reliable place for water until you descend off the Ben.

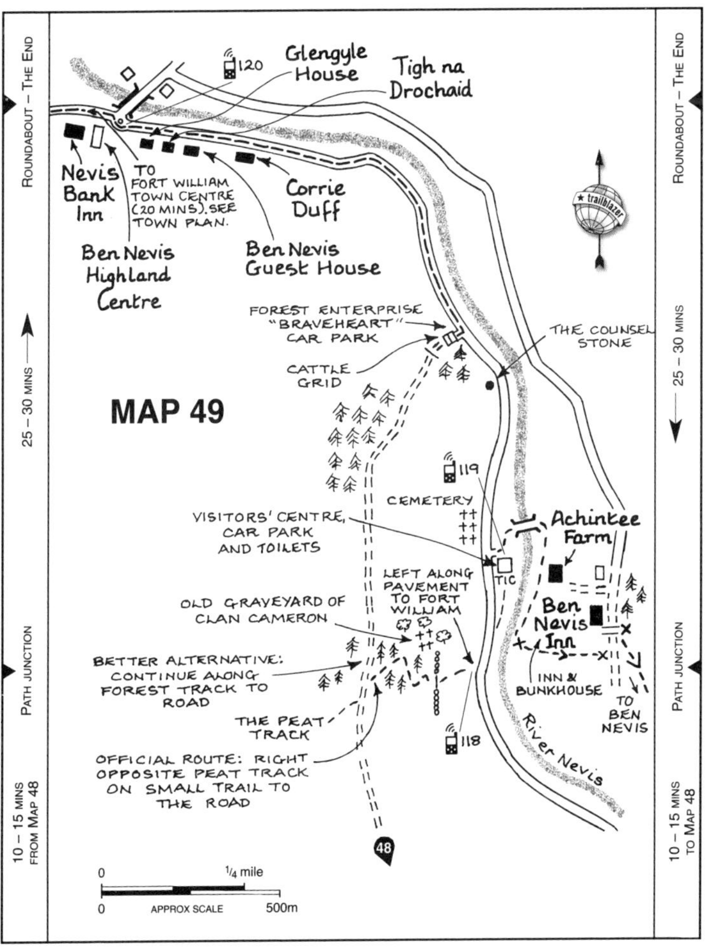

❑ The Counsel Stone (*Clach Chomhairle*) Map 49

Also called Samuel's stone (*Clach MicShomhairle*), this erratic boulder at the side of the Glen Nevis road is said to have been placed here to commemorate the victory of a Highland chieftain. A much more alluring legend, however, says that it has the power to give advice or counsel and at certain times of the year can be found revolving. If you catch it in the act you will discover the answers to three questions asked before it comes to rest.

Choose a safe crossing point and head directly up the grassy, boulder-covered slopes ahead of you, climbing steeply to the ridge between Carn Beag Dearg and Carn Dearg Meadhonach. Continue climbing, more gently now, to the pink granite summit of **Carn Dearg Meadhonach** where there's a cairn and small stone windbreak. The views of the fearsome northern cliffs of Ben Nevis are awe-inspiring from here with snow lingering all year in shaded pockets. To the east the Nevis Range chairlift transports summer tourists and winter skiers up the northern slopes of Aonach Mor.

Descend south to a small col, then up and over the summit of **Carn Mor Dearg** (1220m/4002ft) and onto the spine of the arête. This sweeps round to the south-west dropping to a col and then ascends to some aluminium abseil posts. From here there are wonderful views south over the Mamores. Climb steeply up the grey south-east slopes of Ben Nevis on broken rock and boulders. The paths are indistinct. Take care in poor visibility not to stray too close to the corrie edge. Rejoin the mass of humanity on the summit. The trip time so far including a few short stops is about six to seven hours. The descent is down the Tourist Route (see p184).

If the ascent of Ben Nevis inspires you to discover more of Scotland's hills take a look at Trailblazer's *Scottish Highlands – The Hillwalking Guide*.

❑ The End!

Long-distance paths have a tendency to peter out in unspectacular fashion rather than with a grand flourish and the West Highland Way is no exception, ending its winding course with a pavement trudge along the traffic-laden A82 into Fort William, an anticlimax to say the least. The official end used to be by the roundabout at the start of the Glen Nevis road but it's now been moved to the town square, closer to the pubs for a celebratory drink.

The obligatory pose with the **walker statue** marking the end of the West Highland Way in Fort William

For most walkers the West Highland Way really comes to an end when they drop down into Glen Nevis and start walking along the road. The tarmac underfoot signals the return to society and the end of living every day among the hills and woods. Why not savour the moment and pause a little longer in the open, rather than rushing into the busy streets of Fort William. If the occasion calls for a few drinks or a good meal, take a short detour and walk up to the Ben Nevis Inn (see p180), a dedicated walkers' pub, to celebrate among more fitting surroundings.

The adventure, the challenges, the freedom and the joys of living in nature are suddenly no more... How does someone who has just come out of the woods adjust back to the 'real' world? My answer is: only superficially. When we return to our daily work, home and family routines, we need to keep a firm grip on those valuable lessons and discoveries about ourselves learned in nature... The challenge now before us is to incorporate nature's lessons into our daily lives.

Ray Jardine *Beyond Backpacking*

FORT WILLIAM see map p189

Spoilt by thoughtless modern development and a busy ring road, few would make a special journey to visit Fort William were it not for the magnificent natural treasures that surround it. Its stunning location near the foot of the highest mountain in Britain, overlooking Loch Linnhe and at the western end of the Great Glen, manages to overpower the concrete and industrial sprawl. The original c1650 fort was demolished in the 19th century to make way for the railway, heralding the start of mass tourism which still plays an important role in the local economy.

The pedestrian-only High St now panders to the eclectic taste of the Highland tourist, from tartan and tweeds to the latest petroleum-derived high fashion for the mountains and plenty of West Highland Way memorabilia. Now that the official end of the West Highland Way has been moved into the centre of Fort William you'll need to walk past all these anyway – rather like having to walk through the gift shop as you leave any tourist attraction today. There are, however, pubs and restaurants in which to celebrate the completion of your walk, countless B&Bs for resting your weary legs and convenient transport connections to the rest of Scotland for the journey home.

Services

The **tourist information centre** (☎ 01397-701801, 🖳 www.visit-fortwilliam.co.uk; Easter-July & Sep-Oct Mon-Sat 9am-5pm, Sun 10am-4pm, July & Aug daily 9am-6pm Oct-Easter Mon-Sat 9am-5pm, Sun 10am-3pm) is at 15 High St.

At the northern end of the High St there's a **Tesco Metro** (Mon-Sat 7am-9pm, Sun 9am-5pm) and over by the station **Morrison's** (Mon, Tue, Wed & Sat 8am-8pm; Thur & Fri 8am-9pm; Sun 9am-6pm).

There are several **banks** along the High St, three **chemists**, a **post office** (Mon-Sat 9am-5.30pm) in WH Smith's and a **library** (Mon & Thur 10am-8pm, Tue & Fri 10am-6pm, Wed & Sat 10am-1pm) – a good place to wile away the hours or surf the **internet** on a miserable day. Nevisport also has WI-FI. On Belford Rd there's a **hospital** (☎ 01397-702481) with a casualty department.

Another popular activity in the rain is gear shopping. Fort William has several large **outdoor equipment shops** all open daily, including Mountain Warehouse on the High St, Nevisport which also has a café and bar (see Where to eat) and Ellis Brigham Mountain Sports near the station. Up-to-date **weather forecasts** are posted at all of them.

Campers, or anyone feeling sweaty after their exertions, might appreciate the shower (£2) at the **Nevis Centre** (☎ 01397-700707; 🖳 www.neviscentre.co.uk; daily 9am-10pm), behind Morrison's. It also houses a concert hall and a 10-pin bowling alley and plays host to a number of annual events, including Fort William Mountain Festival (see p14) in February.

Transport

[See also pp44-8] The bus station and railway station are at the northern end of town. There are **coaches** (Citylink and Shiel) to and from Glasgow, Edinburgh, Inverness, the Isle of Skye and Mallaig and **trains** to and from Mallaig and Glasgow.

Local **buses** (Stagecoach Highlands and Citylink) go to Glen Nevis, Kinlochleven and Glencoe.

For a **taxi** there's **Greyhound** (☎ 01397-705050) and Full Moon (☎ 01397-703670), or you could **hire a car** (from £32 a day) for the day from Easydrive (☎ 01397-701616, 🖳 www.easydrivescotland.co.uk).

What to see and do

In town The **West Highland Museum** (☎ 01397-702169, 🖳 www.westhighlandmuseum.org.uk; Cameron Sq; Apr-Oct Mon-Sat 10am-5pm, Mar & Nov-Dec to 4pm; free) is a treasure trove of fascinating artefacts on the Highlands, well worth a visit. There's a secret portrait of Bonnie Prince Charlie, displays about the crofting life and lots of information on Ben Nevis, including the story of Henry Alexander who drove his Model T Ford to the summit in 1911.

By the roundabout on Achintore Rd is the **Lime Tree Gallery** (see also Where to stay). Entrance is free and the gallery is open daily 10am-10pm except November.

If you want something more active, **Alpine Bikes** (☎ 01397-704008, 💻 www.alpinebikes.com; Easter to Oct daily 9am-5.30pm, Nov to Easter Mon-Sat only), on the High St, has quality mountain bikes for hire (£22/day, £20/day if booked in advance).

There's an indoor swimming pool and gym at **Lochaber Leisure Centre** (☎ 01397-704359; Mon-Fri 7.15am-9.30pm, Sat 7.15am-4.30pm, Sun 9.15am-4.30pm).

Out of town Also available are: a 90-minute **cruise** (☎ 01397-700714, 💻 www.crannog.net/cruises.asp; Mar-Oct daily 10am, noon, 2pm and 4pm; £12.50) down Loch Linnhe on Crannog's (see Where to eat and drink) boat, *Souter's Lass*; a tour of **Ben Nevis Distillery** (☎ 01397-700200, 💻 www.bennevisdistillery.com; July & Aug Mon-Fri 9am-6pm, Sat 10am-4pm, Sun noon-4pm, rest of year Mon-Fri 9am-5pm, Easter to Sep Sat 10am-4pm; £4) with a chance to sip a whisky at the end; **canoeing** on the Caledonian Canal (☎ 01463-725500; 💻 www.scottishcanals.co.uk); **Caledonian Canal Visitor Centre** ☎ 01320-366493; daily Easter-Oct 10am-1pm & 2-5.30pm); or riding the *Jacobite* **steam train** to Mallaig (☎ 0845-128 4681, 💻 www.westcoastrailways.co.uk; late June to late Sep daily, mid May to late June & late Sep to end Oct Mon-Fri); visit the TIC for more information on these and other possible day trips in the area.

Where to stay

Bunkhouses and hostels There's a good selection of bunkhouses and hostels in Fort William for those on a tight budget. Right in the centre is ***Bank Street Lodge Bunkhouse*** (☎ 01397-700070, 💻 www.bankstreetlodge.co.uk; 43 bunk beds; WI-FI; £17pp) with beds in varying-sized rooms (3-7 beds). Bedding is provided and there are full cooking facilities. Bank Street Lodge also offers B&B-style accommodation (see B&Bs).

On Alma Rd there's the busy ***Fort William Backpackers*** (☎ 01397-700711, 💻 scotlandstophostels.com/fort-william; 38 beds; WI-FI; dorm bed £17-18pp, £45-47 for a private twin room), a colourful independent hostel. Continental breakfast is £2, or you can just have a few slices of toast for 40p. The rate includes bedding and guests can use the kitchen and sitting room during the day; **internet** access (80p for 30 mins) is available.

South of town ***Calluna Bunkhouse*** (☎ 01397-700451, 💻 www.fortwilliamholiday.co.uk; ☕; WI-FI; 🐕) has four apartments, one sleeping four, two sleeping eight and another up to six. Usually it can only be booked on a weekly basis with rates around £370-550 per week but it is sometimes available for overnight stays (dorm bed £16-18pp; sole occupancy £64-136 per night) and for a dorm room it is not necessary to be part of a group; bedding is provided and there are cooking facilities. Phone to see if they've got space before making the long trek there.

B&Bs The difference in price between hostels/bunkhouses and some of the cheaper bed and breakfasts is negligible when you take the cost of breakfast into account. Some of the nicest places are conveniently located at the top of the Glen Nevis road. ***Corrie Duff Guest House*** (☎ 01397-701412, 💻 www.corrieduff.co.uk; 2T/4D, T or F; ☕; WI-FI; 🐕 £5; £34pp, sgl occ £34-42), the first you get to, is one of the best-value places in Fort William. All the rooms are clean and comfortable. New owners take over in early 2013.

Just on from here is the smart ***Ben Nevis Guest House*** (☎ 01397-708817, 💻 www.bennevisguesthouse.co.uk; 2D/1T/3T or F; ☕; WI-FI; small 🐕 £10 per stay; £30-40pp, family rooms £75-130).

Next is tidy, comfortable ***Tigh na Drochaid*** (☎ 01397-704177, 💻 www.glennevisbb.co.uk; 1D/1T; WI-FI; £25-32.50pp, sgl occ from £35). Also here and also very good is ***Glengyle House*** (☎ 01397-708622, 💻 www.glengylehouse.com; 2D/2T; WI-FI; £30-35pp, sgl occ £60).

On Belford Rd there are several good B&Bs but since this is the main road it could be a little noisy. ***Berkeley House*** (☎ 01397-701185, 💻 berkeleyhouse67@hot

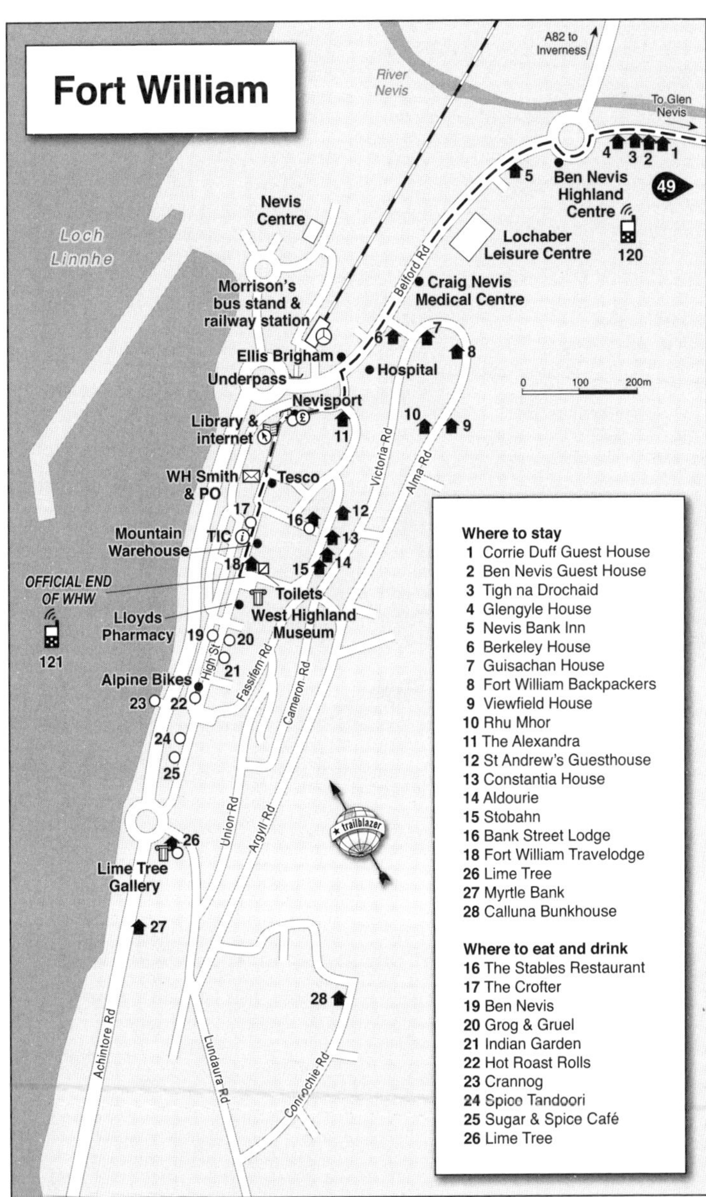

Fort William
A82 to Inverness
River Nevis
To Glen Nevis
Loch Linnhe
Nevis Centre
Ben Nevis Highland Centre
49
Lochaber Leisure Centre
120
Belford Rd
Craig Nevis Medical Centre
Morrison's bus stand & railway station
Ellis Brigham
Hospital
Underpass
Nevisport
Library & internet
WH Smith & PO
Tesco
Victoria Rd
Alma Rd
Mountain Warehouse
TIC
OFFICIAL END OF WHW
Toilets
West Highland Museum
Lloyds Pharmacy
121
High St
Fassifern Rd
Cameron Rd
Alpine Bikes
Union Rd
Argyll Rd
trailblazer
Lime Tree Gallery
Achintore Rd
Lundaura Rd
Connochie Rd
0 100 200m
Where to stay
1 Corrie Duff Guest House
2 Ben Nevis Guest House
3 Tigh na Drochaid
4 Glengyle House
5 Nevis Bank Inn
6 Berkeley House
7 Guisachan House
8 Fort William Backpackers
9 Viewfield House
10 Rhu Mhor
11 The Alexandra
12 St Andrew's Guesthouse
13 Constantia House
14 Aldourie
15 Stobahn
16 Bank Street Lodge
18 Fort William Travelodge
26 Lime Tree
27 Myrtle Bank
28 Calluna Bunkhouse
Where to eat and drink
16 The Stables Restaurant
17 The Crofter
19 Ben Nevis
20 Grog & Gruel
21 Indian Garden
22 Hot Roast Rolls
23 Crannog
24 Spice Tandoori
25 Sugar & Spice Café
26 Lime Tree

mail.com; Belford Rd; 1T/6D/2F; WI-FI in some rooms; £30-40pp, sgl occ £50-70) has tidy rooms.

Alma Rd is a good area as it's quiet, centrally located and has views overlooking the town. There's smart ***Guisachan House*** (☎ 01397-703797, 💻 www.fortwilliamholidays.co.uk; 2S/5T/7D/3F; ♥; WI-FI; £27-35pp, sgl £35); homely and friendly ***Viewfield House*** (☎ 01397-704763, 💻 sandra@todd9064.freeserve.co.uk; 1S/1T/2D, T or F; WI-FI; 🐕; £22-28pp, sgl £27; Apr-Oct) and ***Rhu Mhor*** (☎ 01397-702213, 💻 www.rhumhor.co.uk; 1T/1D/5D, T or F; some rooms share facilities; WI-FI; £21-34pp; sgl occ £31-61; Easter to Oct) which is set in wild secluded gardens. They can provide both vegetarian and vegan breakfasts if requested in advance. Pedestrian access is from Victoria Rd.

Fassifern Rd is packed with B&Bs, a selection of which follows. Starting at the northern end is one of the most interesting buildings in town, ***St Andrew's Guesthouse*** (☎ 01397-703038, 💻 www.fortwilliam-accommodation.co.uk; 2T/3D/1D, T or F; 1D/1T share facilities; WI-FI; £28-34pp, sgl occ £55; Mar-Oct), a beautifully turreted stone house dating back to 1880.

Constantia House (☎ 01397-702893, 💻 www.constantiahouse.co.uk; 2S/1T/2D, T or F; some share facilities; WI-FI; £20-28pp) has nice clean rooms, and ***Aldourie*** (☎ 01397-704809; 2T shared facilities/1D en suite; £25-27pp, sgl occ £25-54) provides a friendly welcome for walkers; there are good views over the loch from some of the rooms.

Just up from here is ***Stobahn*** (☎ 01397-702790, 💻 boggi@supanet.com; 1T/2D/1D, T or F en suite, 1D with private facilities; WI-FI; small 🐕; £28-32pp, sgl occ £30-32) with comfortable rooms.

Below here on Bank St is ***Bank Street Lodge*** (see Bunkhouses and hostels; (1S/2T/6D/5F; WI-FI; £26pp, sgl £26, sgl occ £35, £63-114 for family room); note that the rate does not include breakfast but guests can make their own in the kitchen or go to the Stables Restaurant (see Where to eat) nearby.

Guest houses and hotels Right beside the new official end of the West Highland Way is the equally new ***Fort William Travelodge*** (Fort William ☎ 0871 984 6419, booking line ☎ 0871 984 8484; 💻 www.travelodge.co.uk; 30D/30F; ♥; WI-FI £5/hr; 🐕 £20) on the High St. Rates depend on demand; if you book early (online) you can get a room for £19 but if not expect to pay up to £50 (sgl occ full room rate). The breakfast buffet costs an extra £7.65 (£6.65 if booked online) but if you want to get an early start you may prefer to get a breakfast bag (£4.50).

Further back along the Way, just as it enters the town but by the noisy A82, there's ***Nevis Bank Inn*** (☎ 01397-705721, 💻 www.nevisbankinn.co.uk, Belford Rd; 4S/14D or T/2F; ♥; WI-FI; from £69-92.50pp, sgl £110).

The Alexandra Hotel (☎ 01397-702241, 💻 www.strathmorehotels.com; 7S/86 D, T or F; ♥; WI-FI; 🐕 £5; £45pp, sgl £65) is a large old hotel in the centre. They sometimes have special packages, so it's always worth contacting them.

If you're unlucky and everywhere is booked try looking on Achintore Rd, the A82 south to Glencoe and Glasgow. This is wall-to-wall guest houses overlooking Loch Linnhe, but it's an unnecessarily long way to walk if you don't have to. At the start of Achintore Rd, by the roundabout, is ***Lime Tree*** (☎ 01397-701806, 💻 www.limetreefortwilliam.co.uk; 1T/4D/4D, T or F; ♥; WI-FI; 🐕 £10; £40-60pp, sgl occ £50-120) which has luxurious rooms and also incorporates a restaurant (see Where to eat) and an art gallery (see p187). They have a map room (with historical maps) and a mountaineering library but perhaps of more practical use to walkers is their drying room.

A cheaper option is ***Myrtle Bank*** (☎ 01397-702034, 💻 www.myrtlebankguesthouse.co.uk; 3S/21D or T/2F, some share facilities; WI-FI; £25-40pp, sgl £25-40). In addition to the rooms in the main house they have a modern block with a number of rooms, some adjoining, which are more suitable for groups or families.

Where to eat and drink

All along the High St there is a good selection of **take-away places** including Indian, Chinese, fish and chips, and burger bars as well as several pubs.

Cobbs (🖳 cobbs-at-nevisport.co.uk; Mon-Sat 9am-5pm, Sun to 4.30pm), the alpine-style café upstairs at **Nevisport**, is popular during the day with dishes such as soup and roll or fish & chips (£7.50). There's a bar (noon-11pm) downstairs.

The Stables Restaurant (☎ 01397-700730) below Bank Street Lodge (see Where to stay) is open all day (Apr-Oct 8am-'late') in the main season but evenings only (Tue-Sat 5-9pm) the rest of the year.

There are two good Indian restaurants. Operating for nearly 30 years, ***The Indian Garden*** (☎ 01397-705011; daily noon-2pm & 5.30-11.30pm) is at 88 High St. It serves all the usual subcontinental favourites including baltis from £7.95. Open similar hours, glitzy ***Spice Tandoori*** (☎ 01397-705192) is further south but has great views over Loch Linnhe.

If you're after imaginative pub grub, including Mexican, Cajun, steaks, burgers, and an excellent range of Scottish independent ales, go to ***Grog & Gruel*** (☎ 01397-705078, 🖳 www.grogandgruel.co.uk) halfway along the High St. Food is served in **The Alehouse** (Mon-Sat noon-9pm, Feb-Nov Sun 5-9pm, from 12.30pm in the peak season) and in the **restaurant** (evenings 5-9pm). Dishes include quesadillas from £6.95 in the bar and boar burgers (£12.95). There's live music about four times a month in summer, usually on Thursday nights.

Almost opposite is the ***Ben Nevis*** (☎ 01397-702295; food served daily in the bar noon-5pm and in the restaurant Easter to Oct noon to 9 or 10pm), with a wide selection of quality pub grub from £5.95; the menu is the same in the bar and the restaurant. Another good pub for bar meals is ***The Crofter*** which has main dishes from £6.55.

Further south along the High St is ***Hot Roast Rolls*** (Mon-Sat 9.30am-3.30pm), serving their eponymous signature dish – tasty and filling rolls such as beef and horseradish or ham and mustard, all at £2.95 – from 11am. The breakfast rolls are served from 9.30am.

At the southern end of the High St ***Sugar and Spice Café*** (☎ 01397-705005; Feb-Nov Mon-Sat 10am-5pm, Dec-Jan to 4pm) has taken over the Fired Art Pottery Café. During the day it is a café (summer daily 10am-4pm, winter from 11am) and in the evening a Thai restaurant (daily 6-9pm).

If you're looking for somewhere to celebrate in style one of the best places for local food is ***Crannog Seafood Restaurant*** (☎ 01397-705589, 🖳 www.crannog.net; daily noon-2.30pm & 6-9.30pm, to 9pm in winter). Freshly caught seafood such as salmon (£16.95) is superbly cooked and very reasonably priced. There is always one meat dish (such as lamb, venison or beef) on the menu. They also do a two-course £12.95 lunch menu.

Some of the finest dining in Fort William can be found at ***Lime Tree*** (see Where to stay; daily 6-9pm); they have a set menu costing £27.95/29.95 for two/three courses.

❑ The Great Glen Way

Just getting into your stride? Now that you've completed the West Highland Way why not continue your journey along the Great Glen Way, the natural extension to the West Highland Way. From Fort William on the west coast it picks a low-level route for 73 miles (117km) through the Great Glen Fault all the way to the City of Inverness on the east coast. It closely follows the line of the Caledonian Canal passing three great lochs along the way: Loch Lochy, Loch Oich and the highlight, Loch Ness. After the rigours of the West Highland Way the gentler canal towpaths, old drove roads and forest tracks used by the Great Glen Way will feel like a breeze.

For more information see 🖳 www.greatglenway.com.

APPENDIX A – MAP KEYS

Trail map key

West Highland Way	Plank bridge	Boulders
Other path	Bridge	Crags or cliffs
4 x 4 track	Cattle grid	Building or ruin
Tarmac road	Water	Accommodation
Steps	River	Campsite
Slope	Stream	PO Post Office
Steep slope	Waterfall	Church
Gate	Stone wall	Public telephone
Stile	Conifer trees	Water point
Stile and gate	Deciduous trees	8 Map continuation

Town plan key

Where to stay	Tourist information	Bus stop/station
Where to eat & drink	Library/bookstore	Rail line & station
Campsite	Internet	Park
Post office	Museum/gallery	CP Car park
Bank/ATM	Church/cathedral	Other
Building	Public toilet	

APPENDIX B – GAELIC

Gaelic was once spoken all over Scotland but there are now only about 80,000 Gaelic speakers mainly in the north-west of Scotland. Gaelic names of geographical features are found all along the West Highland Way; some of the most common words are listed below.

abhainn river
acarsaid anchorage
achadh/achaidh field
adhar/adhair sky
àite/àiteachan place/places
Alba Scotland
Albannach/Albannaich Scot
allt/uillt stream/burn
aonach ridge/moor
àrd/àird high

bàgh/bàigh bay
baile town
bàn white/fair
bàthach byre
beag small
bealach mountain pass/col
beinn/beinne/bheinn mountain
bidean pinnacle
bó/bà cow
bodach/bodaich old man
bruthach slope
buachaille herdsmen
buidhe/bhuidhe yellow

cailleach old woman
caisteal castle
cala harbour
calman/calmain dove
caol narrows/strait
caora sheep
càrn cairn or rounded rocky hill
cas steep
cath battle
cathair chair
ceann end/at the head of (often anglicised to kin)
cearc hen
ceum step
cìobair shepherd
ciste chest
clach/clachan stone/hamlet
cnap lump/knob/small hill
cnoc hill
coille/choille wood/forest
coire/coireachan/choire corry/corries (cirque)
craobh tree
creag rock/cliff/crag
crom crooked
cruach stack
cumain bucket

dearg red
diallaid saddle
dobhran/dorain otter
dorcha dark
dorus door
drochaid bridge
druim back/ridge
dubh black
duinne brown
dun fortress/mound

each horse
eag notch
eaglais church
earb roe deer
eilean island
eòin bird

fada long
fasgadh shelter
feòla flesh
feur grass
fiacaill tooth
fiadh deer
fionn white/holy
fithich raven
fraoch heather
fuar cold

gabhar goat
Gaidheal Highlander
Gaidhealtach Highlands
gaoth wind
garbh rough
geal white
glas grey/green

gleann	glen/valley
gorm	blue
innis	meadow
iolair	eagle
lach	duck
lairig	pass/col
leathann	broad
liath	grey
linne	pool
loch	lake
lochan	small lake
machair	field
mam	hill
meal/meall	round hill
monadh	moor
mor/mhor	big
mullach	top
neul	cloud
nid	nest
odhar	dun-coloured
òigh	maiden
or	gold
poca	sack
ràmh	oar
rathad	road
ruadh	red
sàil	heel
sgor/sgorr/sgurr	peak
sionnach	fox
slat	rod
sneachda	snow
spidean	pinnacle
sròn	nose
stac	peak/point
stob	peak/point
strath	a long, wide valley
tigh/taigh	house
tioram	dry
toll	hole
tom	hillock
tràigh	beach
uaine	green
uamh	cave
uiseag	lark
uisge	water

APPENDIX C – WAYPOINTS

Each GPS waypoint below was taken on the route at the reference number marked on the map as below. This list of GPS waypoints is also available to download from the Trailblazer website – 💻 www.trailblazer-guides.com.

Map	No	GPS Waypoint	Description
A	001	N55° 52.203' W04° 16.866'	Entrance to Kelvingrove Park
A	002	N55° 52.767' W04° 17.119'	Queen Margaret Bridge
A	003	N55° 53.544' W04° 18.047'	Kelvin Aqueduct
B	004	N55° 53.924' W04° 18.359'	Bridge across River Kelvin
B	005	N55° 54.540' W04° 17.877'	Join River Kelvin
C	006	N55° 55.099' W04° 16.464'	Bridge across River Kelvin
C	007	N55° 55.670' W04° 16.890'	Path goes under A879 Balmore Rd
D	008	N55° 55.657' W04° 17.122'	Bridge over Allander Water to north
D	009	N55° 56.474' W04° 18.849'	Milngavie Railway station
1	010	N55° 56.503' W04° 19.069'	Official start of WHW
1	011	N55° 57.125' W04° 19.252'	Path to car park and Milngavie
1	012	N55° 57.630' W04° 20.105'	Second path off east to Mugdock CP
2	013	N55° 57.825' W04° 20.557'	Gate onto road
2	014	N55° 58.381' W04° 20.989'	Boat shed
2	015	N55° 59.090' W04° 20.817'	Path over stream
3	016	N55° 59.245' W04° 21.180'	Turn right off road; go through stile
3	017	N55° 59.719' W04° 21.425'	Stream
4	018	N56° 00.207' W04° 21.483'	Left off path onto route of old Blane Valley Railway; over stile
4	019	N56° 01.239' W04° 22.256'	Gate before Beech Tree Inn
4	020	N56° 01.375' W04° 22.330'	Double gates
5	021	N56° 01.711' W04° 22.806'	Single gate
5	021a	N56° 01.740' W04° 22.853'	Junction in Killearn
5	022	N56° 02.722' W04° 22.315'	Under road bridge
6	023	N56° 02.767' W04° 23.974'	Path crosses A81
6	024	N56° 03.118' W04° 24.245'	Gartness
7	025	N56° 02.966' W04° 25.477'	Bridge across stream
7	026	N56° 03.217' W04° 25.945'	Easter Drumquhassle Farm
8	027	N56° 03.922' W04° 26.341'	Turn off road
8	027a	N56° 03.951' W04° 27.155'	Drymen Green
8	028	N56° 04.162' W04° 25.973'	Left through gate; turn away from road
8	029	N56° 05.056' W04° 26.619'	Join road
9	030	N56° 05.369' W04° 28.973'	Gate
10	031	N56° 05.736' W04° 29.477'	Through gate onto open moorland
10	032	N56° 05.970' W04° 30.132'	Bridge
10	033	N56° 05.825' W04° 31.492'	Top of Conic Hill
11	034	N56° 05.406' W04° 31.989'	Kissing gate
11	035	N56° 05.071' W04° 32.650'	Steps off road
11	036	N56° 05.765' W04° 33.352'	Bridge over stream
12	037	N56° 06.003' W04° 33.610'	Path off road
12	038	N56° 06.342' W04° 34.135'	Path crosses track
12	039	N56° 06.634' W04° 34.678'	Path meets road

Map	No	GPS Waypoint	Description
13	040	N56° 06.766' W04° 34.860'	Bridge over stream
13	041	N56° 07.119' W04° 35.355'	Bridge over Tigh an Laoigh
13	042	N56° 07.259' W04° 35.528'	Path leaves road
13	043	N56° 07.617' W04° 36.429'	Car park
14	044	N56° 07.697' W04° 36.813'	Beachside hut
14	045	N56° 08.128' W04° 37.623'	Stone building
14	046	N56° 08.300' W04° 37.768'	Bridge across stream
15	047	N56° 08.966' W04° 38.494'	Rowardennan Hotel
15	048	N56° 09.472' W04° 38.596'	Rowardennan Lodge Youth Hostel
16	049	N56° 10.169' W04° 39.037'	Track to Ptarmigan Lodge
17	050	N56° 11.803' W04° 40.723'	Path divides; go straight ahead
18	051	N56° 13.179' W04° 40.544'	Bridge by Cailness
19	052	N56° 14.578' W04° 41.100'	Inversnaid
19	053	N56° 15.219' W04° 41.648'	Path to Rob Roy's Cave
20	054	N56° 16.137' W04° 41.524'	Ruin
21	055	N56° 17.557' W04° 41.745'	Doune Bothy
21	056	N56° 18.082' W04° 42.175'	Bridge over stream
21	057	N56° 18.203' W04° 42.248'	Go through wall
22	058	N56° 19.167' W04° 42.742'	Gate
22	059	N56° 19.780' W04° 43.004'	Cross Ben Glas Burn
22	060	N56° 19.902' W04° 43.217'	Bridge over River Falloch
23	061	N56° 20.368' W04° 42.941'	Information board
23	062	N56° 20.602' W04° 42.693'	Junction of paths; turn right
24	063	N56° 21.356' W04° 40.822'	Cross Allt a Chuilinn
24	064	N56° 21.647' W04° 40.185'	Path leaves road (after crossing bridge)
25	065	N56° 22.131' W04° 39.493'	Tunnel under railway line
25	066	N56° 22.797' W04° 38.988'	Gate and stile
26	067	N56° 23.377' W04° 37.956'	Kissing gate before junction
26	067a	N56° 23.450' W04° 37.117'	Steps by A82
26	067b	N56° 23.553' W04° 37.036'	Join A85
26	067c	N56° 23.720' W04° 37.679'	Path off A85 towards WHW
27	068	N56° 24.715' W04° 39.581'	Cross railway
27	069	N56° 24.966' W04° 39.802'	Bridge over River Fillan
28	070	N56° 25.127' W04° 39.635'	Bridge by St Fillan's Priory
28	071	N56° 25.407' W04° 40.099'	Gate
28	072	N56° 25.501' W04° 41.601'	Cross Crom Allt
29	073	N56° 26.296' W04° 42.803'	Path meets A85
29	074	N56° 26.968' W04° 42.528'	Gate after bridge over railway
30	075	N56° 27.826' W04° 42.936'	Narrow tunnel under railway bridge
30	076	N56° 29.013' W04° 43.097'	Gate before junction
31	077	N56° 29.778' W04° 44.631'	Bridge across railway
32	078	N56° 31.005' W04° 45.837'	Gate before railway
32	079	N56° 31.091' W04° 46.277'	Gate into conifer plantation
33	080	N56° 31.913' W04° 47.636'	Lone tree
34	081	N56° 31.968' W04° 48.446'	Inveroran Hotel
34	082	N56° 32.376' W04° 48.820'	Victoria Bridge
34	083	N56° 33.111' W04° 47.917'	Bridge over Allt Bhreacnaig
35	084	N56° 33.514' W04° 47.669'	Cross Allt Doire nan Each
35	085	N56° 34.385' W04° 47.640'	Bridge over stream
35	086	N56° 34.889' W04° 47.916'	Bridge over stream

Map	No	GPS Waypoint	Description
36	087	N56° 35.743' W04° 48.453'	Bà Bridge
36	088	N56° 36.289' W04° 48.458'	Track to Bà Cottage
37	089	N56° 36.817' W04° 48.016'	Bridge over stream
37	090	N56° 38.190' W04° 49.444'	Gate
38	091	N56° 38.240' W04° 49.543'	Blackrock Cottage
38	092	N56° 38.590' W04° 49.647'	Gate after crossing road
38	093	N56° 39.068' W04° 50.435'	Bridge by Kings House Hotel
39	094	N56° 39.239' W04° 51.323'	Gate off road
39	095	N56° 39.638' W04° 53.270'	Follow path via gates
40	096	N56° 39.879' W04° 54.190'	Bridge over stream
40	097	N56° 40.554' W04° 54.853'	Highest point of WHW
40	098	N56° 40.852' W04° 55.078'	Stepping stones over stream
41	099	N56° 41.173' W04° 55.001'	First small cairn
41	100	N56° 41.629' W04° 55.209'	Bridge over Allt a'Choire Odhair-mhoir
41	101	N56° 42.042' W04° 56.308'	Junction of path and track
42	102	N56° 41.880' W04° 56.801'	Small reservoir
42	103	N56° 42.729' W04° 57.349'	Cross pipes
42	104	N56° 42.867' W04° 57.625'	Blackwater Hostel
43	105	N56° 43.139' W04° 58.671'	Path crosses lane
43	106	N56° 43.414' W04° 59.661'	Bridge across stream
43	107	N56° 43.570' W05° 00.519'	Cairn
44	108	N56° 43.974' W05° 02.911'	Derelict farmhouses
45	109	N56° 43.803' W05° 04.281'	Lairigmor
45	110	N56° 44.195' W05° 06.313'	Sheepfold
46	111	N56° 44.693' W05° 06.583'	Commemorative cairn
46	112	N56° 45.081' W05° 06.507'	Information board
47	113	N56° 46.240' W05° 05.524'	Gate
47	114	N56° 46.574' W05° 04.835'	Bridge across stream
48	115	N56° 47.176' W05° 04.396'	Join wide track
48	116	N56° 47.411' W05° 04.316'	Turn left onto forest track
48	117	N56° 48.180' W05° 04.781'	Join main track
49	118	N56° 48.492' W05° 04.669'	Join road
49	119	N56° 48.559' W05° 04.641'	Tourist information centre, Glen Nevis
49	120	N56° 49.279' W05° 05.640'	Roundabout Glen Nevis road/A82
Ft Wlm	121	N56° 49.077' W05° 06.661'	End of WHW

APPENDIX D – TAKING A DOG

TAKING DOGS ALONG THE WAY

Many are the rewards that await those prepared to make the extra effort required to bring their best friend along the trail. You shouldn't underestimate the amount of work involved, though. Indeed, just about every decision you make will be influenced by the fact that you've got a dog: how you plan to travel to the start of the trail, where you're going to stay, how far you're going to walk each day, where you're going to rest and where you're going to eat in the evening etc.

If you're also sure your dog can cope with (and will enjoy) walking 10 miles or more a day for several days in a row, you need to start preparing accordingly. Extra thought also needs to go into your itinerary. The best starting point is to study the village and town facilities table on p31 (and the advice below), and plan where to stop and where to buy food.

Looking after your dog

To begin with, you need to make sure that your own dog is fully **inoculated** against the usual doggy illnesses, and also up to date with regard to **worm pills** (eg Drontal) and **flea preventatives** such as Frontline – they are, after all, following in the pawprints of many a dog before them, some of whom may well have left fleas or other parasites on the trail that now lie in wait for their next meal to arrive. **Pet insurance** is also a very good idea; if you've already got insurance, do check that it will cover a trip such as this.

On the subject of looking after your dog's health, perhaps the most important implement you can take with you is the **plastic tick remover**, available from vets for a couple of quid. These removers, while fiddly, help you to remove the tick safely (ie without leaving its head behind buried under the dog's skin).

Being in unfamiliar territory also makes it more likely that you and your dog could become separated. For this reason, make sure your dog has a **tag with your contact details on it** (a mobile phone number would be best if you are carrying one with you); you could also consider having it **microchipped** for further security.

When to keep your dog on a lead

• **On mountain tops** It's a sad fact that, every year, a few dogs lose their lives falling over the edge of steep slopes.

• **When crossing farmland**, particularly in the lambing season (around May) when your dog can scare the sheep, causing them to lose their young. Farmers are allowed by law to shoot at and kill any dogs that they consider are worrying their sheep. During lambing, most farmers would prefer it if you didn't bring your dog at all. The exception is if your dog is being attacked by cows. A couple of years ago there were three deaths in the UK caused by walkers being trampled as they tried to rescue their dogs from the attentions of cattle. The advice in this instance is to let go of the lead, head speedily to a position of safety (usually the other side of the field gate or stile) and call your dog to you.

• **Around ground-nesting birds** It's important to keep your dog under control when crossing an area where certain species of birds nest on the ground. Most dogs love foraging around in the woods but make sure you have permission to do so; some woods are used as 'nurseries' for game birds and dogs are only allowed through them if they are on a lead.

What to pack

You've probably already got a good idea of what to bring to keep your dog alive and happy, but the following is a checklist:

- **Food/water bowl** Foldable cloth bowls are popular with walkers, being light and take up little room in the rucksack. You can get also get a water-bottle-and-bowl combination, where the bottle folds into a 'trough' from which the dog can drink.
- **Lead and collar** An extendable one is probably preferable for this sort of trip. Make sure both lead and collar are in good condition – you don't want either to snap on the trail, or you may end up carrying your dog through sheep fields until a replacement can be found.
- **Medication** You'll know if you need to bring any lotions or potions.
- **Tick remover** See above
- **Bedding** A simple blanket may suffice, or you can opt for something more elaborate if you aren't carrying your own luggage.
- **Poo bags** Essential.
- **Hygiene wipes** For cleaning your dog after it's rolled in stuff.
- **A favourite toy** Helps prevent your dog from pining for the entire walk.
- **Food/water** Remember to bring treats as well as regular food to keep up the mutt's morale. That said, if your dog is anything like mine the chances are they'll spend most of the walk dining on rabbit droppings and sheep poo anyway.
- **Corkscrew stake** Available from camping or pet shops, this will help you to keep your dog secure in one place while you set up camp/doze.
- **Raingear** It can rain!
- **Old towels** For drying your dog.

What to pack

When it comes to packing, I always leave an exterior pocket of my rucksack empty so I can put used poo bags in there (for deposit at the first bin we come to). I always like to keep all the dog's kit together and separate from the other luggage (usually inside a plastic bag inside my rucksack). I have also seen several dogs sporting their own 'doggy rucksack', so they can carry their own food, water, poo etc – which certainly reduces the burden on their owner!

Cleaning up after your dog

It is extremely important that dog owners behave in a responsible way when walking the path. Dog excrement should be cleaned up. In towns, villages and fields where animals graze or which will be cut for silage, hay etc, you need to pick up and bag the excrement.

Staying with your dog

In this guide we have used the symbol 🐕 to denote where a hotel, pub or B&B welcomes dogs. However, this always needs to be arranged in advance and some places may charge extra. Hostels (both SYHA and independent) do not permit them unless they are an assistance (guide) dog; smaller campsites tend to accept them, but some of the larger holiday parks do not. Before you turn up always double check whether the place you would like to stay accepts dogs and whether there is space for them; many places have only one or two rooms suitable for people with dogs.

When it comes to eating, most landlords allow dogs in at least a section of their pubs, though few restaurants do. Make sure you always ask first and ensure your dog doesn't run around the pub but is secured to your table or a radiator.

Henry Stedman

APPENDIX E – DISTANCE CHART

	Glasgow	MILNGAVIE	Dumgoyne	Gartness	Easter Drumquhassle	Drymen	Balmaha	Cashel	Rowardennan	Inversnaid
Milngavie	10									
	16									
Dumgoyne	17	**7**								
	27	***11***								
Gartness	20	**10**	3							
	32	***16***	*5*							
Easter Drumquhassle	21	**11**	4	1						
	33.5	***17.5***	*6.5*	*1.5*						
Drymen	22	**12**	5	2	1					
	35	***19***	*8*	*3*	*1.5*					
Balmaha	29	**19**	12	9	8	7				
	46	***30***	*19*	*14*	*12.5*	*11*				
Cashel	32	**22**	15	12	11	10	3			
	51	***35***	*24*	*19*	*17.5*	*16*	*5*			
Rowardennan	36	**26**	19	16	15	14	7	4		
	57.5	***41.5***	*30.5*	*25.5*	*24*	*22.5*	*11.5*	*6.5*		
Inversnaid	43	**33**	26	23	22	21	14	11	7	
	68.5	***52.5***	*41.5*	*36.5*	*35*	*33.5*	*22.5*	*17.5*	*11*	
Inverarnan	49.5	**39.5**	32.5	29.5	28.5	27.5	20.5	17.5	13.5	6.5
	78.5	***62.5***	*51.5*	*46.5*	*44*	*43.5*	*32.5*	*27.5*	*21*	*10*
Crianlarich	56	**46**	39	36	35	34	27	24	20	13
	88.5	***72.5***	*61.5*	*56.5*	*55*	*53.5*	*42.5*	*37.5*	*31*	*20*
Strathfillan	59.5	**49.5**	42.5	39.5	38.5	37.5	30.5	27.5	23.5	16.5
	94.5	***78.5***	*67.5*	*62.5*	*61*	*59.5*	*48.5*	*43.5*	*37*	*26*
Tyndrum	62	**52**	45	42	41	40	33	30	26	19
	98.5	***82.5***	*81.5*	*66.5*	*65*	*63.5*	*52.5*	*47.5*	*42*	*30*
Bridge of Orchy	69	**59**	52	49	48	47	40	37	33	25
	109.5	***93.5***	*82.5*	*77.5*	*76*	*74.5*	*63.5*	*58.5*	*52*	*41*
Inveroran	72	**62**	55	52	51	50	43	40	36	29
	114.5	***98.5***	*87.5*	*82.5*	*81*	*79.5*	*68.5*	*63.5*	*57*	*46*
Kingshouse	82	**72**	65	62	61	60	53	50	46	39
	130.5	***114.5***	*103.5*	*98.5*	*97*	*95.5*	*84.5*	*79.5*	*73*	*62*
Kinlochleven	90.5	**80.5**	73.5	70.5	69.5	68.5	61.5	58.5	54.5	47.5
	144.5	***128.5***	*117.5*	*112.5*	*111*	*109.5*	*98.5*	*93.5*	*87*	*76*
Glen Nevis	103	**93**	86	83	82	81	74	71	67	60
	164.5	***148.5***	*137.5*	*132.5*	*131*	*129.5*	*118.5*	*113.5*	*107*	*96*
FORT WILLIAM	106	**96**	89	86	85	84	77	74	70	63
	169.5	***154***	*142.5*	*137.5*	*136*	*134.5*	*123.5*	*118.5*	*112*	*101*

West Highland Way
DISTANCE CHART
(including Glasgow to Milngavie walking route)

miles/*kilometres* (approx)

Inverarnan	Crianlarich	Strathfillan	Tyndrum	Bridge of Orchy	Inveroran	Kingshouse	Kinlochleven	Glen Nevis
6.5								
10								
10	3.5							
16	*6*							
12.5	6	2.5						
20	*10*	*4*						
19.5	13	9.5	7					
31	*21*	*15*	*11*					
22.5	16	12.5	10	3				
36	*26*	*20*	*16*	*5*				
32.5	26	22.5	20	13	10			
52	*42*	*36*	*32*	*21*	*16*			
41	34.5	31	28.5	21.5	18.5	8.5		
66	*56*	*50*	*46*	*35*	*30*	*14*		
53.5	47	43.5	41	34	31	21	12.5	
86	*76*	*70*	*66*	*55*	*50*	*34*	*20*	
56.5	50	46.5	44	37	34	24	15.5	3
91	*81*	*75*	*71*	*60*	*55*	*39*	*25*	*5*

INDEX

Page references in bold type refer to maps

TRAILBLAZER TREKKING GUIDES

Europe
Corsica Trekking – GR20
Dolomites Trekking – AV1 & AV2
Scottish Highlands – The Hillwalking Guide
Tour du Mont Blanc
Walker's Haute Route: Mt Blanc to the Matterhorn

South America
Inca Trail, Cusco & Machu Picchu

Africa
Kilimanjaro
Moroccan Atlas – The Trekking Guide

Australasia
New Zealand – The Great Walks

Asia
Nepal Trekking & The Great Himalaya Trail
Sinai – the trekking guide
Trekking in the Everest Region
Trekking in Ladakh

Inca Trail, Cusco & Machu Picchu
Alexander Stewart, 5th edn, £13.99
ISBN 978-1-905864-55-3, 320pp, 65 maps, 35 photos
The Inca Trail from Cusco to Machu Picchu is South America's most popular trek. Practical guide with detailed trail maps, plans of Inca sites, guides to Lima, Cusco and Machu Picchu. Now includes the Santa Teresa Trek, the Choquequirao Trail and the Vilcabamba Trail. Two challenging new treks included linking the above treks. With a history of the Incas by Hugh Thomson.

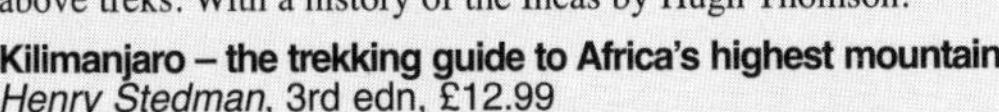

Kilimanjaro – the trekking guide to Africa's highest mountain
Henry Stedman, 3rd edn, £12.99
ISBN 978-1-905864-24-9, 368pp, 40 maps, 30 photos
At 19,340ft the world's tallest freestanding mountain, Kilimanjaro is one of the most popular destinations for hikers visiting Africa. It's possible to walk up to the summit: no technical skills are necessary. Includes town guides to Nairobi and Dar-Es-Salaam, and a colour guide to flora and fauna. Includes Mount Meru.

Sinai – the trekking guide *Ben Hoffler,* 1st edn, £14.99
ISBN 978-1-905864-41-6, 288pp, 74 maps, 30 colour photos
Trek with the Bedouin and their camels and discover one of the most exciting new trekking destinations. The best routes in the High Mountain Region (St. Katherine), Wadi Feiran and the Muzeina deserts. Once you finish on trail there are the nearby coastal resorts of Sharm el Sheikh, Dahab and Nuweiba to enjoy. **Due April 2013.**

The Walker's Haute Route – Mt Blanc to the Matterhorn
Alexander Stewart, 1st edn, £12.99
ISBN 978-1-905864-08-9, 256pp, 60 maps, 30 colour photos
From Mont Blanc to the Matterhorn, Chamonix to Zermatt, the 180km (113-mile) Walker's Haute Route traverses one of the finest stretches of the Pennine Alps – the range between Valais in Switzerland and Piedmont and Aosta Valley in Italy. Includes Chamonix and Zermatt guides.

Moroccan Atlas – the trekking guide
Alan Palmer, 1st edn, £12.99
ISBN 978-1-873756-77-5, 268pp, 54 maps, 40 colour photos
The High Atlas in central Morocco is the most dramatic and beautiful section of the entire Atlas range. Towering peaks, deep gorges and huddled Berber villages enchant all who visit. With 44 detailed trekking maps, 10 town and village guides including Marrakech.

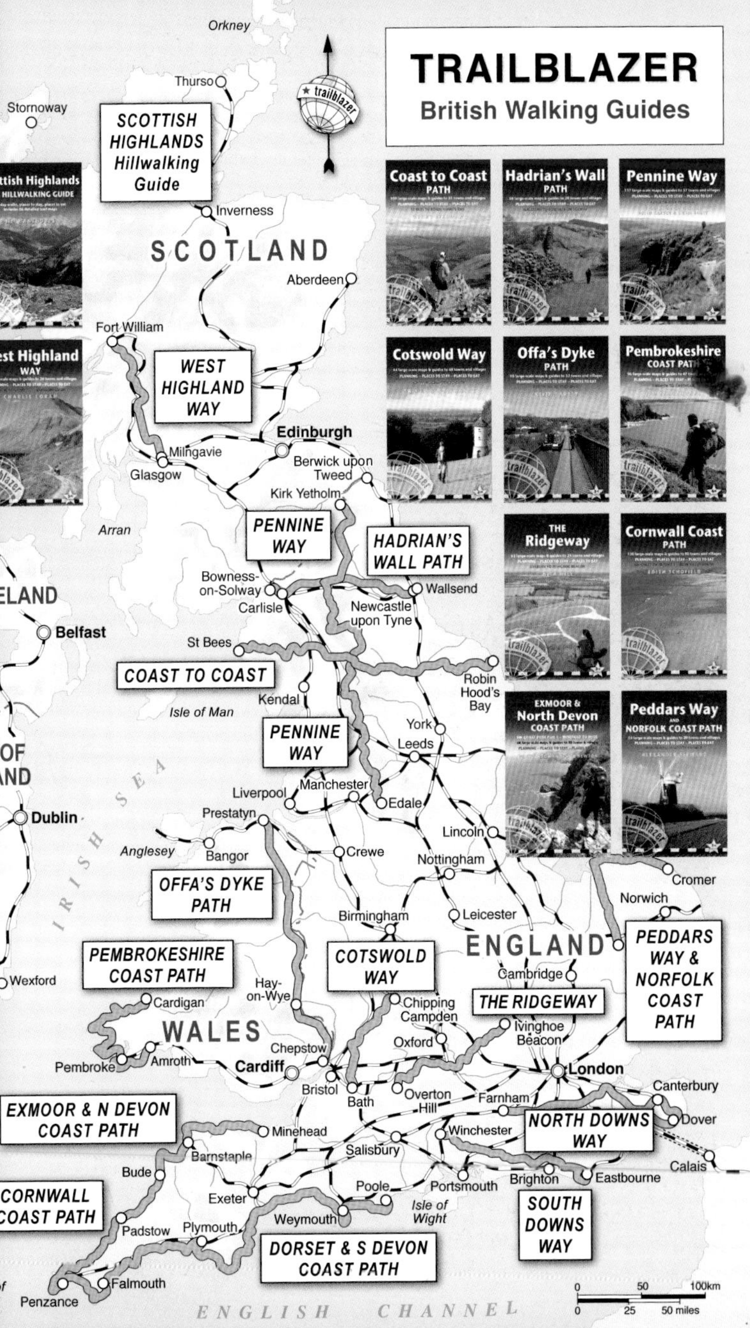

TRAILBLAZER
British Walking Guides
SCOTTISH HIGHLANDS Hillwalking Guide
WEST HIGHLAND WAY
PENNINE WAY
HADRIAN'S WALL PATH
COAST TO COAST
PENNINE WAY
OFFA'S DYKE PATH
PEMBROKESHIRE COAST PATH
COTSWOLD WAY
THE RIDGEWAY
PEDDARS WAY & NORFOLK COAST PATH
EXMOOR & N DEVON COAST PATH
NORTH DOWNS WAY
CORNWALL COAST PATH
SOUTH DOWNS WAY
DORSET & S DEVON COAST PATH
Coast to Coast PATH
Hadrian's Wall PATH
Pennine Way
Cotswold Way
Offa's Dyke PATH
Pembrokeshire COAST PATH
THE Ridgeway
Cornwall Coast PATH
EXMOOR & North Devon COAST PATH
Peddars Way AND NORFOLK COAST PATH
SCOTLAND
WALES
ENGLAND
IRISH SEA
ENGLISH CHANNEL
Orkney
Thurso
Stornoway
Inverness
Aberdeen
Fort William
Edinburgh
Milngavie
Glasgow
Berwick upon Tweed
Kirk Yetholm
Arran
Bowness-on-Solway
Carlisle
Wallsend
Newcastle upon Tyne
Belfast
St Bees
Robin Hood's Bay
Kendal
Isle of Man
York
Leeds
Liverpool
Manchester
Edale
Dublin
Prestatyn
Lincoln
Anglesey
Bangor
Crewe
Nottingham
Cromer
Norwich
Birmingham
Leicester
Wexford
Cambridge
Hay-on-Wye
Cardigan
Chipping Campden
Ivinghoe Beacon
Oxford
Chepstow
Pembroke
Amroth
Cardiff
London
Bristol
Bath
Overton Hill
Farnham
Canterbury
Dover
Minehead
Winchester
Salisbury
Barnstaple
Calais
Bude
Exeter
Poole
Portsmouth
Brighton
Eastbourne
Isle of Wight
Weymouth
Padstow
Plymouth
Falmouth
Penzance
0 50 100km
0 25 50 miles

TRAILBLAZER TITLE LIST

Adventure Cycle-Touring Handbook
Adventure Motorcycling Handbook
Australia by Rail
Australia's Great Ocean Road
Azerbaijan
Coast to Coast (British Walking Guide)
Cornwall Coast Path (British Walking Guide)
Corsica Trekking – GR20
Cotswold Way (British Walking Guide)

Dolomites Trekking – AV1 & AV2
Dorset & Sth Devon Coast Path (British Walking Gde)
Exmoor & Nth Devon Coast Path (British Walking Gde)
Hadrian's Wall Path (British Walking Guide)
Himalaya by Bike – a route and planning guide
Inca Trail, Cusco & Machu Picchu
Indian Rail Handbook
Japan by Rail

Kilimanjaro – The Trekking Guide (includes Mt Meru)
Mediterranean Handbook
Morocco Overland (4WD/motorcycle/mountainbike)
Moroccan Atlas – The Trekking Guide
Nepal Trekking & The Great Himalaya Trail
New Zealand – The Great Walks
North Downs Way (British Walking Guide)
Norway's Arctic Highway

Offa's Dyke Path (British Walking Guide)
Overlanders' Handbook – worldwide driving guide
Peddars Way & Norfolk Coast Path (British Walking Gde)
Pembrokeshire Coast Path (British Walking Guide)
Pennine Way (British Walking Guide)
The Ridgeway (British Walking Guide)
Siberian BAM Guide – rail, rivers & road
The Silk Roads – a route and planning guide
Sahara Overland – a route and planning guide

Scottish Highlands – The Hillwalking Guide
Sinai – The Trekking Guide
South Downs Way (British Walking Guide)
Tour du Mont Blanc
Trans-Canada Rail Guide
Trans-Siberian Handbook
Trekking in the Annapurna Region
Trekking in the Everest Region
Trekking in Ladakh
Trekking in the Pyrenees
The Walker's Haute Route – Mont Blanc to Matterhorn
West Highland Way (British Walking Guide)

For more information about Trailblazer and our expanding range of guides, for guidebook updates or for credit card mail order sales visit our website:

www.trailblazer-guides.com

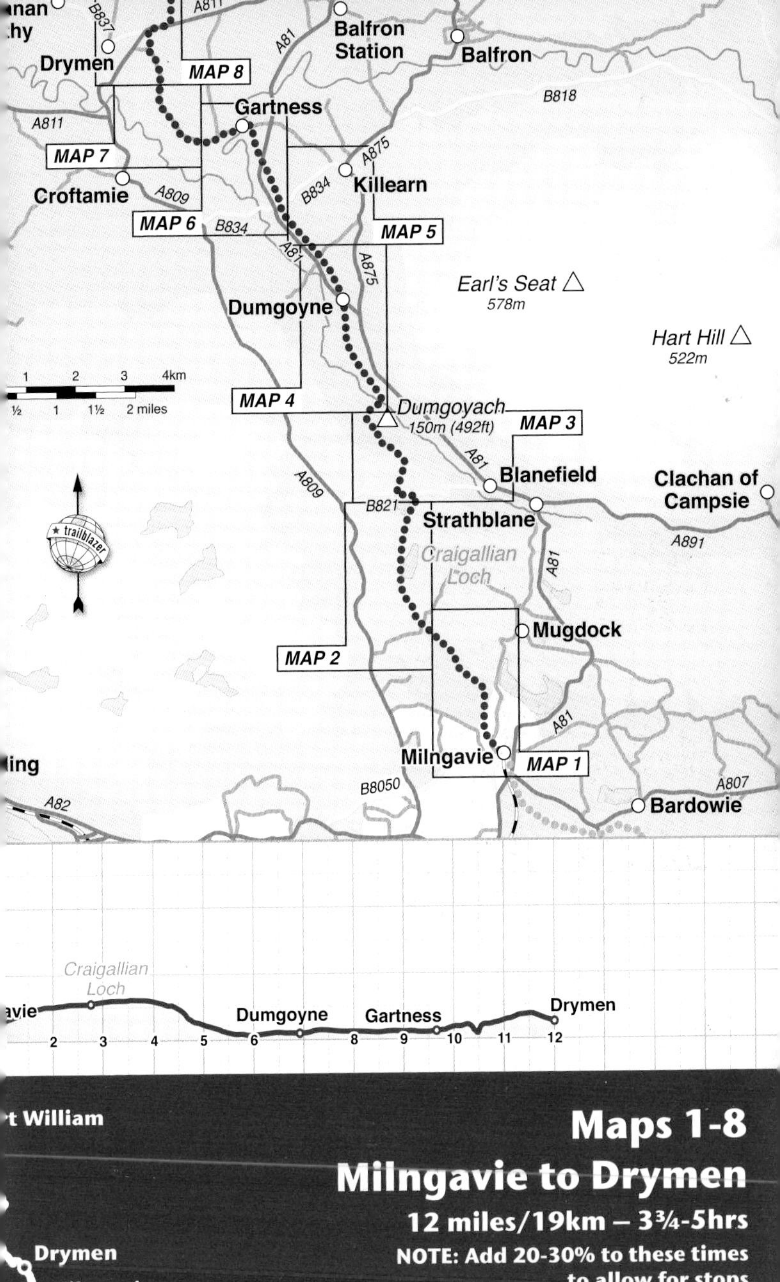

Maps 1-8
Milngavie to Drymen

12 miles/19km – 3¾-5hrs

NOTE: Add 20-30% to these times to allow for stops

Drymen

Milngavie

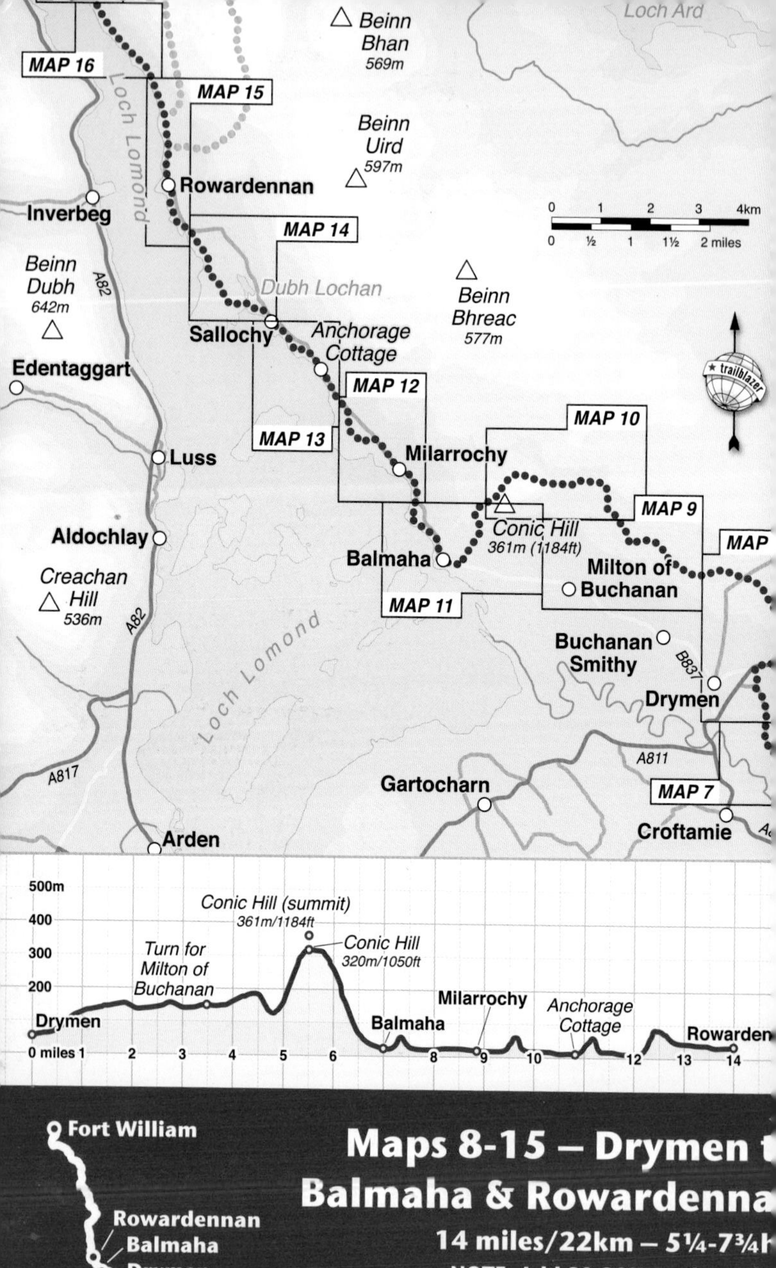

Maps 8-15 – Drymen t
Balmaha & Rowardenna

14 miles/22km – 5¼-7¾h

NOTE: Add 20-30% to these tim
to allow for sto

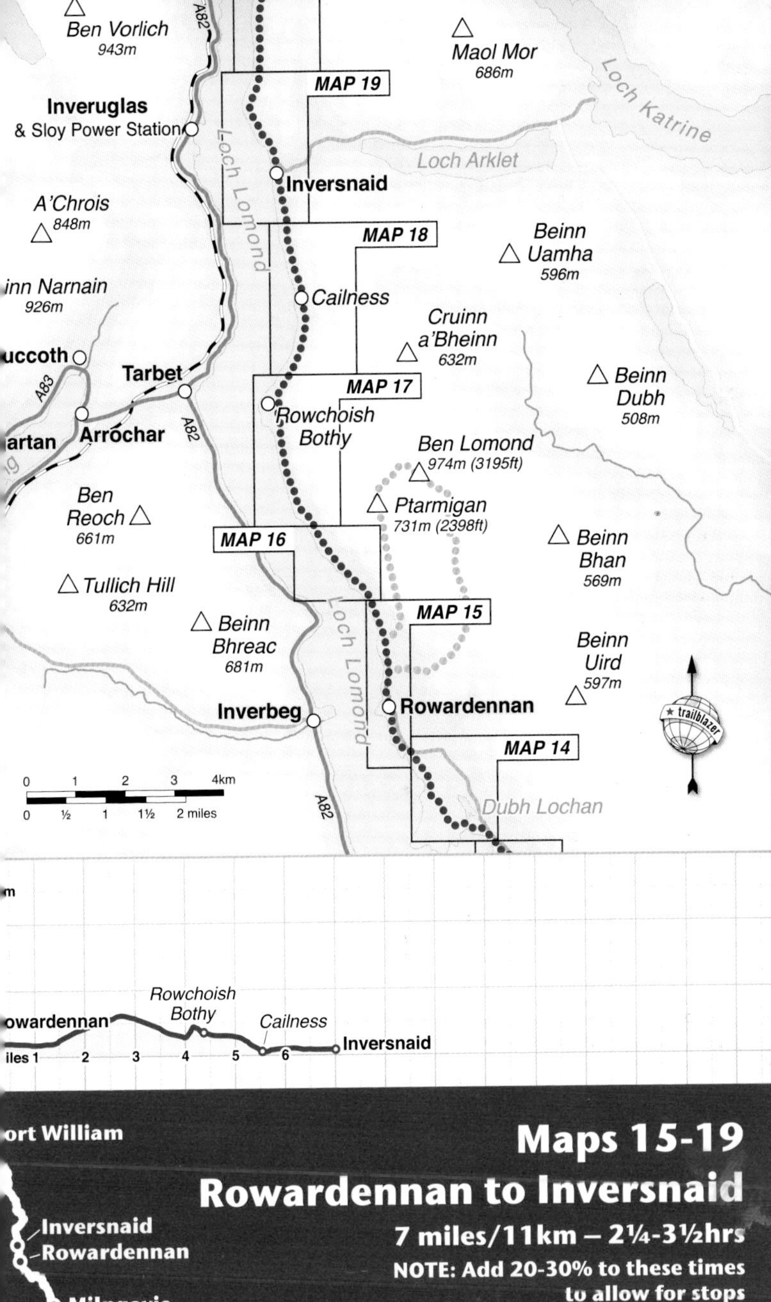

Ben Vorlich
943m
A82
MAP 19
Maol Mor
686m
Loch Katrine
Inveruglas
& Sloy Power Station
Loch Lomond
Loch Arklet
Inversnaid
A'Chrois
848m
MAP 18
Beinn
Uamha
596m
926m
Cailness
Cruinn
a'Bheinn
632m
Tarbet
A83
MAP 17
Beinn
Dubh
508m
Rowchoish
Bothy
Arrochar
A82
Ben Lomond
974m (3195ft)
Ben
Reoch
661m
Ptarmigan
731m (2398ft)
MAP 16
Beinn
Bhan
569m
Tullich Hill
632m
MAP 15
Beinn
Bhreac
681m
Loch Lomond
Beinn
Uird
597m
Inverbeg
Rowardennan
trailblazer
MAP 14
0 1 2 3 4km
0 ½ 1 1½ 2 miles
A82
Dubh Lochan
Rowchoish
Bothy
Cailness
Inversnaid
1 2 3 4 5 6
Inversnaid
Rowardennan
Milngavie
Maps 15-19
Rowardennan to Inversnaid
7 miles/11km – 2¼-3½hrs
NOTE: Add 20-30% to these times
to allow for stops

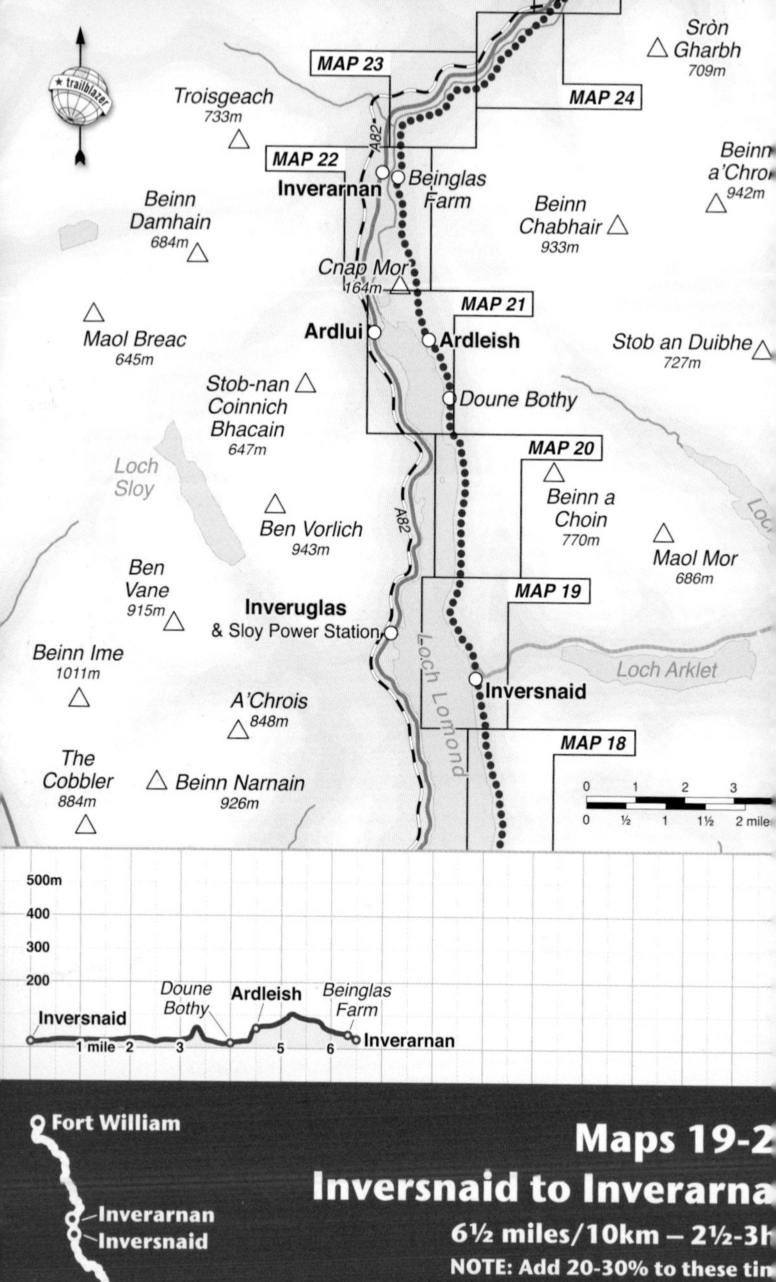

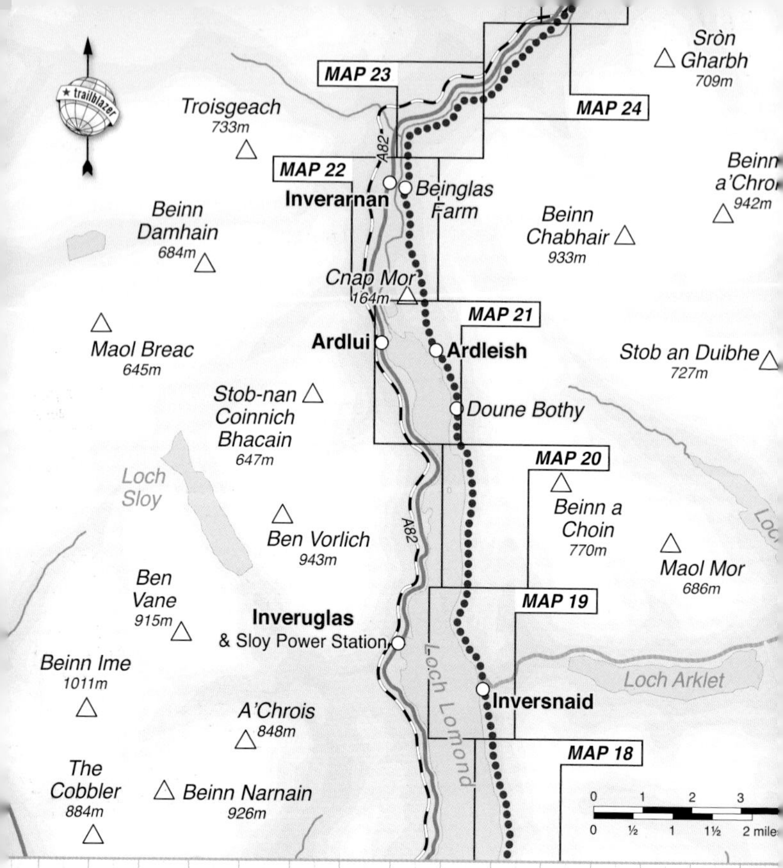
trailblazer
MAP 23
MAP 24
MAP 22
MAP 21
MAP 20
MAP 19
MAP 18
Sròn Gharbh
709m
Troisgeach
733m
A82
Inverarnan
Beinglas Farm
Beinn a'Chro
942m
Beinn Damhain
684m
Beinn Chabhair
933m
Cnap Mor
164m
Maol Breac
645m
Ardlui
Ardleish
Stob an Duibhe
727m
Stob-nan Coinnich Bhacain
647m
Doune Bothy
Loch Sloy
Beinn a Choin
770m
Ben Vorlich
943m
Maol Mor
686m
Ben Vane
915m
Inveruglas
& Sloy Power Station
Loch Lomond
Loch Arklet
Inversnaid
Beinn Ime
1011m
A'Chrois
848m
The Cobbler
884m
Beinn Narnain
926m
0 1 2 3
0 ½ 1 1½ 2 mile

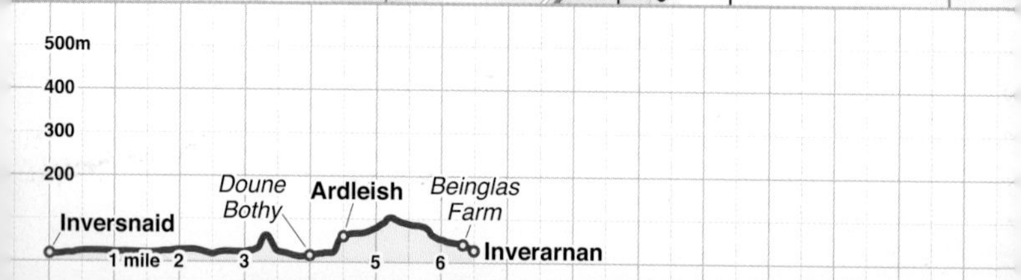
500m
400
300
200
Inversnaid
Doune Bothy
Ardleish
Beinglas Farm
Inverarnan
1 mile
2
3
5
6

Fort William
Inverarnan
Inversnaid
Milngavie

Maps 19-2
Inversnaid to Inverarna

6½ miles/10km – 2½-3h

NOTE: Add 20-30% to these tin to allow for sto

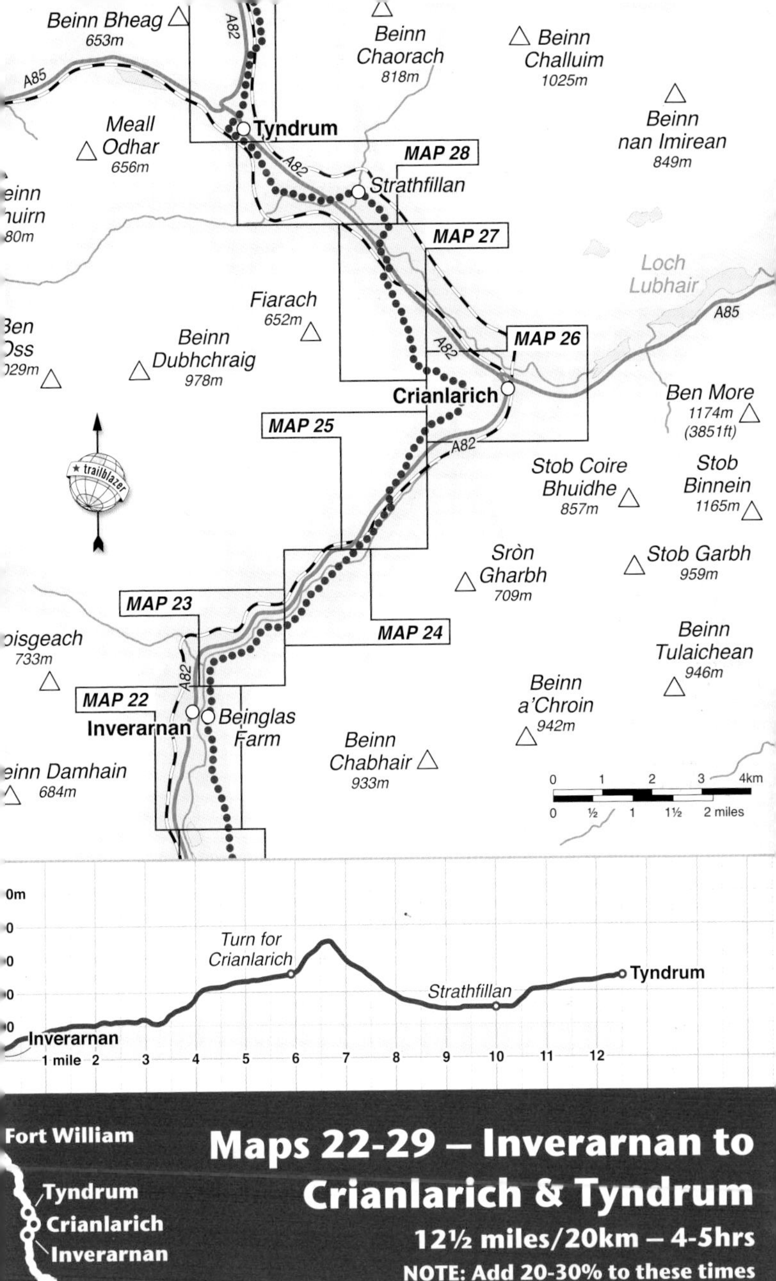

Maps 22-29 – Inverarnan to Crianlarich & Tyndrum

12½ miles/20km – 4-5hrs

NOTE: Add 20-30% to these times to allow for stops

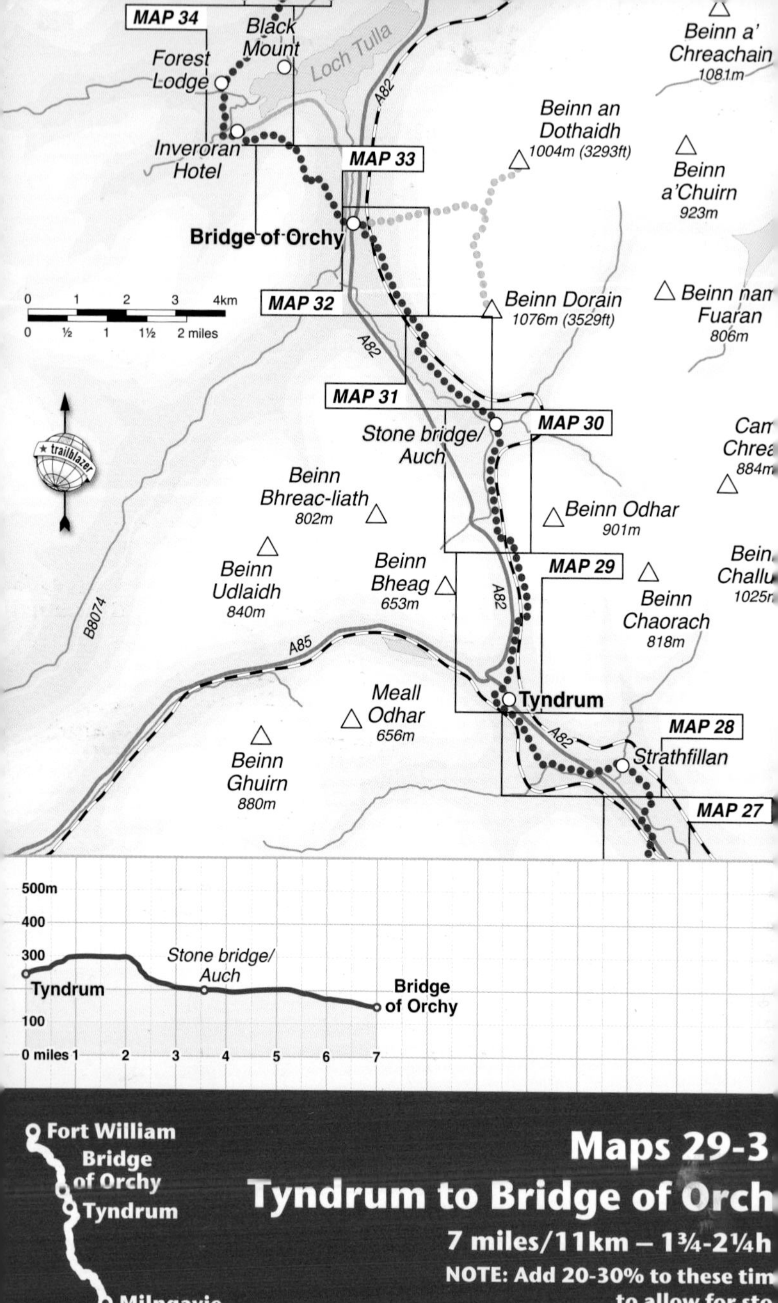

Maps 29-3

Tyndrum to Bridge of Orch

7 miles/11km – 1¾-2¼h

NOTE: Add 20-30% to these tim to allow for sto

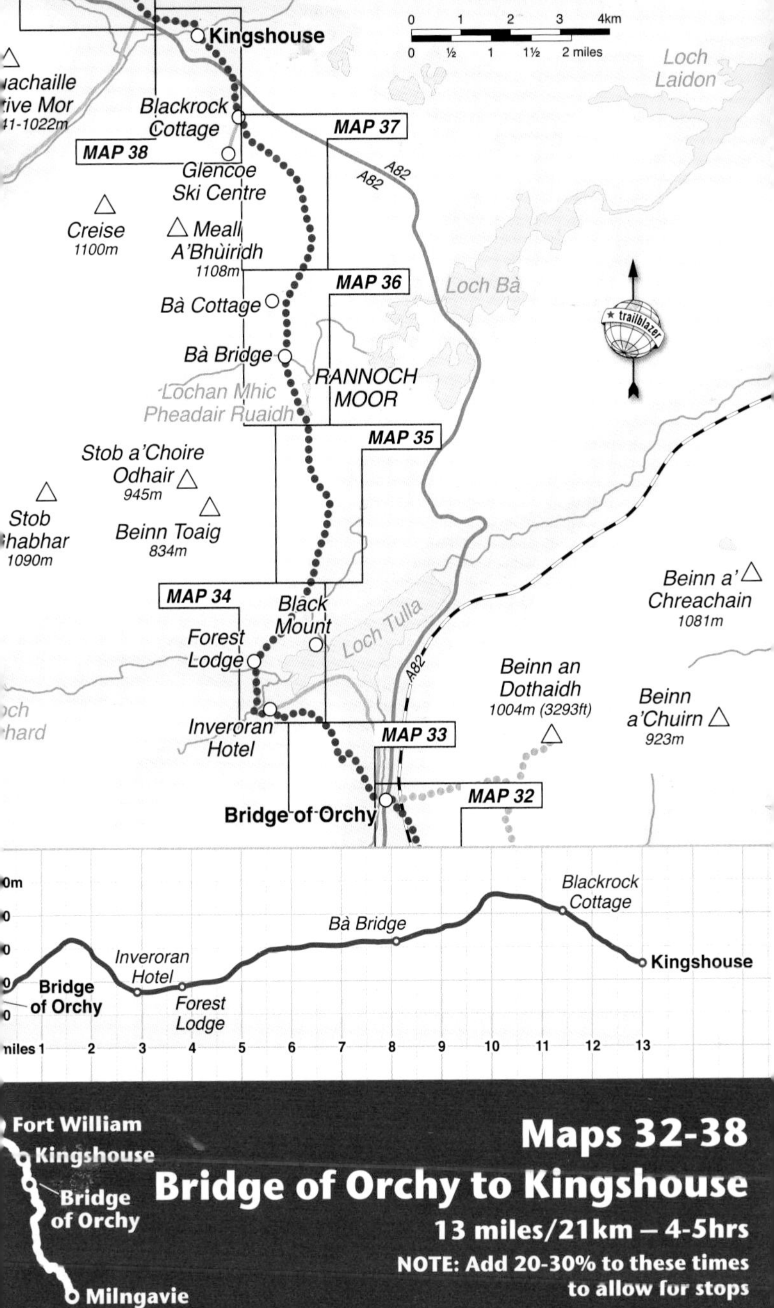

Kingshouse
0 1 2 3 4km
0 ½ 1 1½ 2 miles
Loch Laidon
Blackrock Cottage
MAP 37
MAP 38
Glencoe Ski Centre
A82
Creise 1100m
Meall A'Bhùiridh 1108m
MAP 36
Loch Bà
Bà Cottage
Bà Bridge
RANNOCH MOOR
Lochan Mhic Pheadair Ruaidh
MAP 35
Stob a'Choire Odhair 945m
Beinn Toaig 834m
1090m
trailblazer
Beinn a' Chreachain 1081m
MAP 34
Black Mount
Loch Tulla
Forest Lodge
Beinn an Dothaidh 1004m (3293ft)
Beinn a'Chuirn 923m
Inveroran Hotel
MAP 33
MAP 32
Bridge of Orchy
Blackrock Cottage
Bà Bridge
Inveroran Hotel
Kingshouse
Bridge of Orchy
Forest Lodge
1 2 3 4 5 6 7 8 9 10 11 12 13
Fort William
Kingshouse
Bridge of Orchy
Milngavie
Maps 32-38
Bridge of Orchy to Kingshouse
13 miles/21km – 4-5hrs
NOTE: Add 20-30% to these times to allow for stops

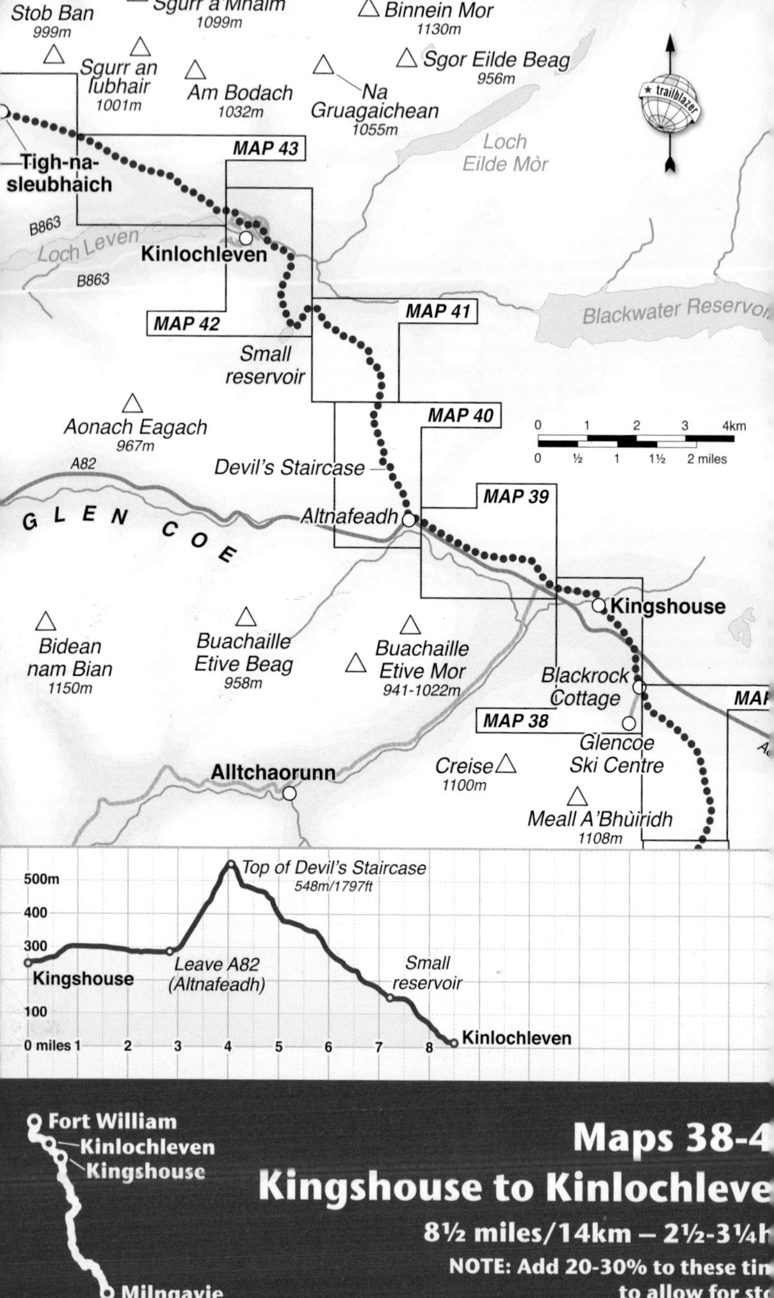
Stob Ban
999m
Sgurr a'Mhaim
1099m
Binnein Mor
1130m
Sgurr an Iubhair
1001m
Am Bodach
1032m
Na Gruagaichean
1055m
Sgor Eilde Beag
956m
trailblazer
Loch Eilde Mòr
Tigh-na-sleubhaich
MAP 43
B863
Loch Leven
Kinlochleven
B863
MAP 42
MAP 41
Blackwater Reservoi
Small reservoir
Aonach Eagach
967m
MAP 40
0 1 2 3 4km
0 ½ 1 1½ 2 miles
A82
Devil's Staircase
GLEN COE
Altnafeadh
MAP 39
Kingshouse
Bidean nam Bian
1150m
Buachaille Etive Beag
958m
Buachaille Etive Mor
941-1022m
Blackrock Cottage
MAP 38
Glencoe Ski Centre
Creise
1100m
Alltchaorunn
Meall A'Bhùiridh
1108m
Top of Devil's Staircase
548m/1797ft
500m
400
300
100
Kingshouse
Leave A82 (Altnafeadh)
Small reservoir
Kinlochleven
0 miles 1 2 3 4 5 6 7 8
Fort William
Kinlochleven
Kingshouse
Milngavie
Maps 38-4
Kingshouse to Kinlochleve
8½ miles/14km – 2½-3¼h
NOTE: Add 20-30% to these tin
to allow for st

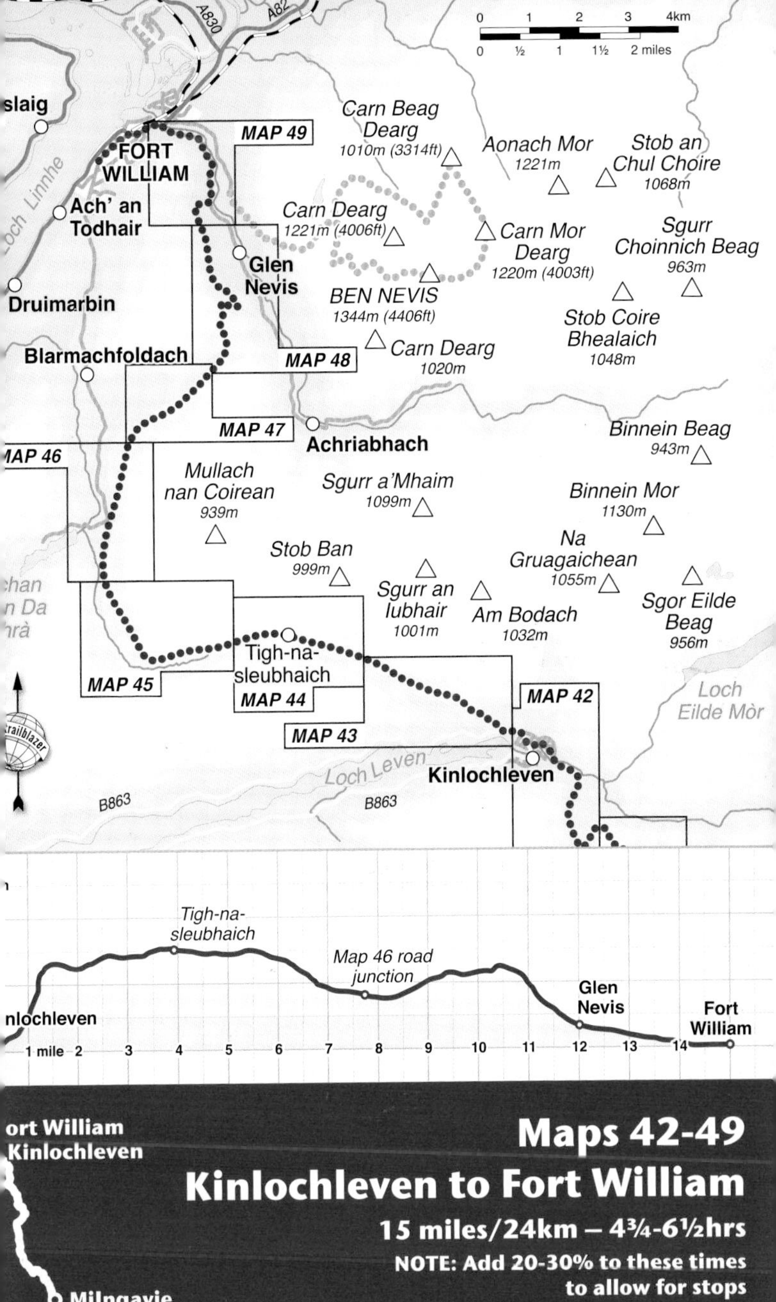

ort William
Kinlochleven
Milngavie

Maps 42-49
Kinlochleven to Fort William

15 miles/24km – 4¾-6½hrs

NOTE: Add 20-30% to these times to allow for stops

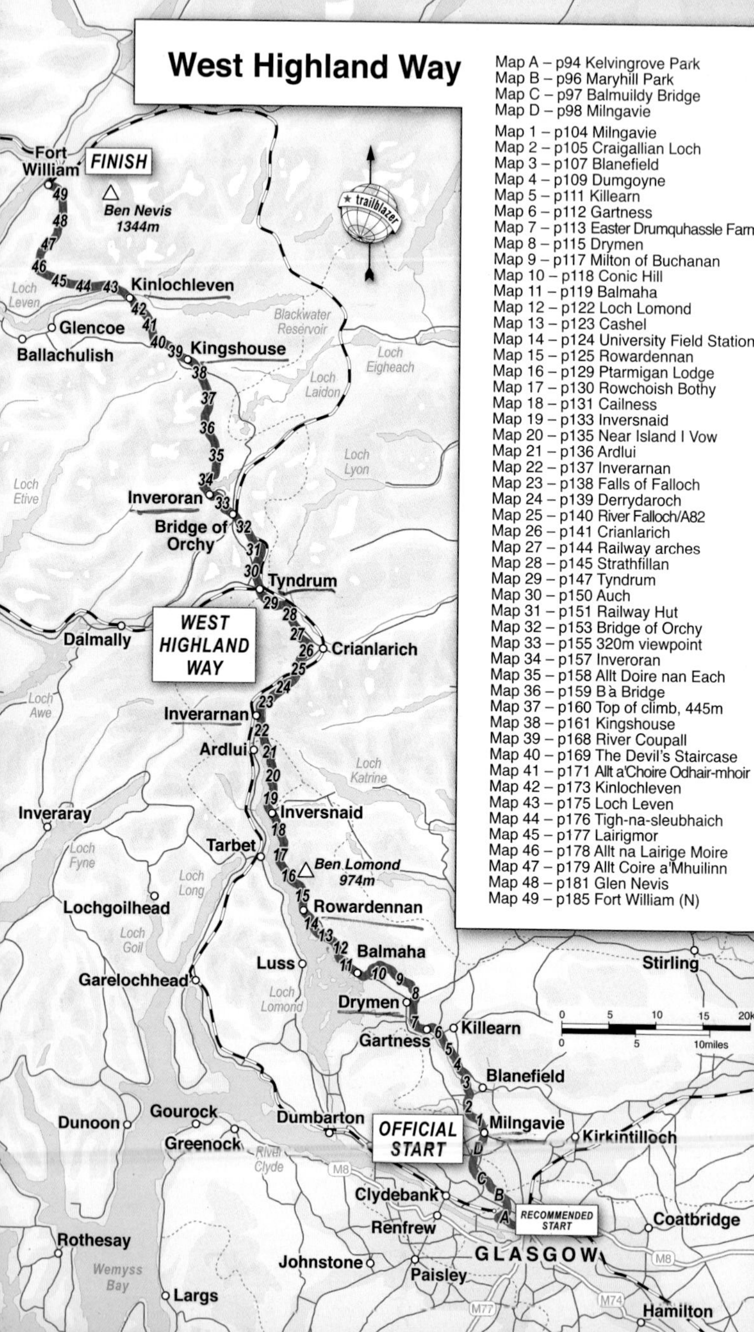
West Highland Way
Map A – p94 Kelvingrove Park
Map B – p96 Maryhill Park
Map C – p97 Balmuildy Bridge
Map D – p98 Milngavie
Map 1 – p104 Milngavie
Map 2 – p105 Craigallian Loch
Map 3 – p107 Blanefield
Map 4 – p109 Dumgoyne
Map 5 – p111 Killearn
Map 6 – p112 Gartness
Map 7 – p113 Easter Drumquhassle Farm
Map 8 – p115 Drymen
Map 9 – p117 Milton of Buchanan
Map 10 – p118 Conic Hill
Map 11 – p119 Balmaha
Map 12 – p122 Loch Lomond
Map 13 – p123 Cashel
Map 14 – p124 University Field Station
Map 15 – p125 Rowardennan
Map 16 – p129 Ptarmigan Lodge
Map 17 – p130 Rowchoish Bothy
Map 18 – p131 Cailness
Map 19 – p133 Inversnaid
Map 20 – p135 Near Island I Vow
Map 21 – p136 Ardlui
Map 22 – p137 Inverarnan
Map 23 – p138 Falls of Falloch
Map 24 – p139 Derrydaroch
Map 25 – p140 River Falloch/A82
Map 26 – p141 Crianlarich
Map 27 – p144 Railway arches
Map 28 – p145 Strathfillan
Map 29 – p147 Tyndrum
Map 30 – p150 Auch
Map 31 – p151 Railway Hut
Map 32 – p153 Bridge of Orchy
Map 33 – p155 320m viewpoint
Map 34 – p157 Inveroran
Map 35 – p158 Allt Doire nan Each
Map 36 – p159 B'à Bridge
Map 37 – p160 Top of climb, 445m
Map 38 – p161 Kingshouse
Map 39 – p168 River Coupall
Map 40 – p169 The Devil's Staircase
Map 41 – p171 Allt a'Choire Odhair-mhoir
Map 42 – p173 Kinlochleven
Map 43 – p175 Loch Leven
Map 44 – p176 Tigh-na-sleubhaich
Map 45 – p177 Lairigmor
Map 46 – p178 Allt na Lairige Moire
Map 47 – p179 Allt Coire a'Mhuilinn
Map 48 – p181 Glen Nevis
Map 49 – p185 Fort William (N)
Fort William
FINISH
Ben Nevis
1344m
trailblazer
Kinlochleven
Loch Leven
Glencoe
Ballachulish
Blackwater Reservoir
Kingshouse
Loch Eigheach
Loch Laidon
Loch Lyon
Loch Etive
Inveroran
Bridge of Orchy
Tyndrum
Dalmally
WEST HIGHLAND WAY
Crianlarich
Loch Awe
Inverarnan
Ardlui
Loch Katrine
Inveraray
Inversnaid
Tarbet
Loch Fyne
Ben Lomond
974m
Loch Long
Lochgoilhead
Rowardennan
Loch Goil
Balmaha
Luss
Stirling
Garelochhead
Loch Lomond
Drymen
Killearn
Gartness
Blanefield
Dunoon
Gourock
Dumbarton
OFFICIAL START
Milngavie
Kirkintilloch
Greenock
River Clyde
M8
Clydebank
RECOMMENDED START
Coatbridge
Renfrew
Rothesay
GLASGOW
M8
Johnstone
Paisley
Wemyss Bay
Largs
M77
M74
Hamilton
0 5 10 15 20km
0 5 10miles